Letters from Tove

TOVE JANSSON
Letters from Tove

Edited by

Boel Westin and Helen Svensson

Translated by

Sarah Death

University of Minnesota Press

Minneapolis

First published in 2014 as *Brev från Tove Jansson* by Schildts &
Söderströms, Helsinki, Finland

Copyright Tove Jansson, Moomin Characters™

Selection, Introduction, and commentaries copyright Boel Westin and
Helen Svensson

English translation copyright 2019 Sarah Death and Sort of Books

First University of Minnesota Press edition, 2020

Published by the University of Minnesota Press
111 Third Avenue South, Suite 290
Minneapolis, MN 55401-2520
http://www.upress.umn.edu

A Cataloging-in-Publication record for this book is available from the
Library of Congress.

ISBN 978-1-5179-0957-4 (hc) | ISBN 978-1-5179-1010-5 (pb)

Printed in the United States of America on acid-free paper

The University of Minnesota is an equal-opportunity educator and
employer.

25 24 23 22 21 20   10 9 8 7 6 5 4 3 2 1

CONTENTS

Tove Jansson in the mid-1950s, in her Helsinki studio.

INTRODUCTION

"THE LETTER" IS THE TITLE OF ONE OF TOVE JANSSON'S EARLY SHORT stories. The last chapter in her 1989 novella *Rent spel* (*Fair Play*) has the same title. Both of them centre on the significance of a letter. This was something about which Tove Jansson knew a lot. She was a great correspondent, writing frequently and at length to her family, friends and lovers. Her works teem with letters in a variety of forms, from bobbing messages in bottles to notes and epistolary novels. Letters are written, sent and read in many different places. And lying on the bureau in the Moomin House are Snufkin's spring letters.

In *Letters from Tove* we have gathered the letters to those to whom she felt closest, those who were her companions in life, work and love. Our selection is drawn from various extended correspondences that have been preserved. They span six decades, between 1932 and 1988, offering a variety of perspectives on the ways in which Tove Jansson describes her life and work over the years. The first letters are written to her family, her parents Signe Hammarsten Jansson and Viktor Jansson plus her younger brothers, Per Olov and Lars. They were written during Tove Jansson's time studying in Stockholm and on two extended trips abroad in the 1930s. These are followed by three sequences of letters, all begun in the 1940s: to photographer Eva Konikoff, author Atos Wirtanen and director Vivica Bandler. The long correspondences with graphic artist Tuulikki Pietilä and translator Maya Vanni begin in the 1950s and continue into the following decades. Publisher Åke Runnquist and Tove Jansson start writing to each other in the 1960s and their correspondence extends into the late 1980s. There is also a section of letters from Tove Jansson to her mother Signe Hammarsten Jansson, written after Viktor Jansson's death in 1958.

All these addressees were of significance to Tove Jansson as a human being, writer and artist, and close to her over an extended period – all her life, in the case of her family, of course. Her letters to them present varying pictures of Tove Jansson the letter writer, depending on whether she is writing as a daughter, lover or friend. Events and individuals can be described in different ways to suit particular recipients, and be seen in different lights. The recipient is often a co-writer, too. But, for Tove Jansson, letter writing is also a way of getting close to others, as in a conversation: "while I am writing, I have you here", she says in a 1946 letter to Vivica Bandler. Similar phrases crop up elsewhere. "Tuulikki, I am longing to read more of the book that is all about you", she writes to Tuulikki Pietilä in summer 1956.

Tove Jansson always wrote by hand, never on a typewriter, and her letters are sometimes illustrated, often with pictures of herself in a variety of situations. In her younger days she would write in both pencil and ink, varying her writing paper from occasion to occasion, but later on she usually wrote on unlined white paper in black felt-tipped pen. Writing letters to her closest contacts was a long-felt need for her, but her growing fame drastically altered the conditions of her correspondence. Tove Jansson received an average of two thousand letters a year and she answered almost all of them. This meant that from 1954, when she achieved her major international breakthrough with the Moomin cartoon strip, to the years preceding her death in 2001, she had 92,000 letters to answer. And yet this does not include many of her letter-writing years. "I have lost my enthusiasm for writing letters after all the years of Moomin business, an overwhelming daily task of writing to people I didn't know and didn't like," writes Tove Jansson to her friend Eva Konikoff at Christmas 1961. But there is still a little margin left for "privacy and free will".

The correspondence reproduced in *Letters from Tove* falls into the latter category. There is an extensive amount of material, and we have selected 160 of the hundreds of letters after reading through them all. The letters to these recipients were first used in Boel Westin's 2007 biography *Tove Jansson. Ord, bild, liv* (English edition, *Tove Jansson: Life, Art, Words*, 2014), in which a number of the quotations and longer extracts are reproduced. But they have not previously been published in an edition with commentaries.

This volume of letters is divided into chapters, one for each addressee, with the letters arranged in chronological order. There is an introduction at the start of each chapter to the addressee and his or her relationship with Tove Jansson. The letters have been reproduced orthographically from Tove Jansson's writing. This includes punctuation and speech marks. She occasionally misspells names, places and words or uses personal spellings such as "galloppera" (set off at a gallop), but these have been left unchanged. Those dates and the places given in square brackets [ ] are based on postmarks and/or information contained in the letters. In the few cases in which letters have been abbreviated to cut out digressions of a peripheral nature, this is indicated by [...]. Some of the letters extend to ten or twelve pages and we wanted to include as many letters as possible to show the breadth of Tove Jansson's repertoire as a correspondent. The list of 'Sources' (p.488) gives details of where the letters are kept. The majority of them are in private ownership, but some are in archives.

The commentaries that precede a number of the letters describe events and circumstances that are crucial to contextual understanding. Tove Jansson sometimes writes letters in swift succession, but sometimes quite a long time elapses between them. Explanatory notes about people and places are to be found at the end of each letter. Individuals normally only appear the first time they are mentioned. In order to keep the commentaries relatively concise, more marginal individuals are omitted. The notes also include some translations, and clarifications of words and expressions. This applies particularly to Finland-Swedish expressions and "Finlandisms", but there is also clarification of the language mixing found particularly in the letters written from France and Italy.

In the commentaries, Tove Jansson is abbreviated to 'TJ'. The diaries and notes referred to in the introductions are to be found in Boel Westin's biography. The many parallels to Tove Jansson's literary texts are discussed in several places, but this book's readers are generally left to see and discover them for themselves.

Tove Jansson's letters tell us about herself. They encompass descriptions of her life and work, of people and landscapes, and shift between hope and despair, yearning and happiness. They deal with love and friendship, loneliness and solidarity, and also with politics, art, literature and society. But a letter also documents a juncture in time, stops the clock and tells us about things that otherwise get forgotten or sink into the depths of memory. Tove Jansson's letters describe their period in time through expressions, thoughts and events, and can be read as a blend of biographical and cultural history. They can be literary and lyrical, observant and analytical; they can be cheery, sad, exhilarated, melancholy and sometimes entirely workaday. But they rarely leave us unmoved.

Boel Westin and Helen Svensson

Translator's note: English words and local place names
Tove Jansson's letters are written in Swedish but quite often include words or phrases in English; these have been set in *italics* and their original spelling has been left unchanged. Underlinings have been retained from the original letters.

Local place names appear as written in the letters, for example, FIRENZE rather than FLORENCE. Tove Jansson commonly refers to Helsinki by its old Swedish name of HELSINGFORS (or H:FORS) and abbreviates Stockholm as STHLM.

"How I do wonder about the future?"

LETTERS TO THE FAMILY
1932–1933

Signe Hammarsten Jansson at her desk. In the background is Viktor
Jansson's marble head of a six-year-old Tove, and to the right of it a
photograph of her that was used on some of the first Moomin books.

Per Olov Jansson and Viktor Jansson in Helsinki in the 1940s. Per
Olov was called up in March 1940.

Tove Jansson's letters to the Hammarsten Jansson family in Helsinki are divided into two periods. The first includes letters from Stockholm 1932–33 and two long sequences of letters from Tove Jansson's travels before the war, to Paris (1938) and Italy (1939). The second comprises letters from Tove Jansson to her mother, Signe Hammarsten Jansson, written after the death of her father Viktor Jansson in 1958.

When Tove Jansson is sixteen, she goes to Stockholm to study at Tekniska skolan, the Technical School, now the University College of Arts, Crafts and Design. There she attends a three-year course in drawing for advertising and design, lasting from 1930 to 1933. While she is studying in the city, she lives with her maternal uncle Einar Hammarsten and his family, his wife Anna-Lisa and his daughter Ulla. Their address is Norr Mälarstrand 26, within walking distance of the school in Mäster Samuelsgatan.

Tove Jansson writes her first letters to her family in Helsinki during her time in Stockholm. They are interiors from her final year as a student at "Teknis" and from daily life in her uncle's family. There are stylistic parallels with the diaries Tove Jansson kept at the same time – the rather nonchalant, impromptu attitude she adopts for reporting on herself and her projects – yet at the same time her letters express the respect for work that characterises her life and all her activities. The importance of her close family and wider circle of relations is striking, both in the affection with which, in the letters, she addresses her close family in Helsinki and in her accounts of the Hammarsten branch of the family in Stockholm. In the small number of letters that have survived (all from 1932–33), the sense of responsibility she feels towards her family is palpable. One senses friction between her fascination with fine art and the necessity of training for a profession. Tove Jansson is thrown into helping provide for her family at an early age. "I have to become an artist for the family's sake," she writes in her diary in 1931, her first year in Stockholm. In the very first letter in this volume (4.12.1932), Tove Jansson writes to her "Beloved Papa and Mama" to tell them about the hectic weeks at the school just before Christmas and how much she looks forward to coming home to Helsinki.

Her parents had met each other in 1910 in Paris, where they were both studying art. They married in 1913 – on Blidö in the Stockholm archipelago, where Signe Hammarsten's parents had a summer house –

and moved into 4B Lotsgatan in Helsinki/Helsingfors. Their daughter Tove Marika was born on 9 August 1914 and she had two brothers, Per Olov, born in 1920, and Lars, born in 1926. In 1933, the family moved to the Lallukka artists' house, which had just been built at 13 Apollogatan. For the summer they rented a house in the Pellinge archipelago, just outside Borgå.

Viktor Jansson (1886–1958) was born and raised in Helsinki. His father, Julius Victor Jansson, had been employed at the Stockmann department store and later owned a haberdashery shop. His mother's name was Johanna Karlsson. They had four children, but only Viktor and his brother Julius (known as Jullan), survived. Viktor's father died when Viktor was six, leaving the family in straitened circumstances. But Johanna Karlsson – who received a full secondary education and continued her studies at a school of commerce – ran the shop and made sure her boys were educated, too. The shop later went bankrupt, but by then Viktor had trained at the Finnish Art Association's school of drawing in Helsinki and been to Paris on an art scholarship. Since his youth, Viktor Jansson had been known as "Faffan", a name that was also used within the family.

Signe Hammarsten (1882–1970) was born in Hannäs in Sweden and was the daughter of a clergyman. The family moved to Stockholm when she was in her early teenage years. Her father, Fredrik Hammarsten, was later appointed vicar at the Jakob church in the centre of Stockholm. Signe Hammarsten was the second of six children, having an older sister and four younger brothers. She dreamt of becoming a sculptor, but the family's economy would only stretch to a full education for the sons. Instead she had to make do with an art course at the Advanced School of Applied Arts (which she financed herself by working), a section of the Technical School that trained teachers of drawing. She later took up a teaching post at the Wallin school in Stockholm and was known for setting up a Scouting group for girls with two colleagues, before the official founding of the Girl Scout movement in 1911. After her marriage to Viktor Jansson, Signe Hammarsten Jansson, who worked under the name "Ham", became well known in Finland for her drawings and caricatures and her designs for postage stamps. She was also known as Ham within the family.

In this volume, Signe Hammarsten's siblings and their families feature in Tove Jansson's letters to the family and also those to other addressees. The eldest of the children was Elsa Hammarsten. She married a German clergyman, Hugo Flemming, and left Sweden. Tove went to visit her and her family when she was on a trip to Germany in the summer of 1934. The Hammarsten brothers – Torsten, Olov, Einar and Harald (known as H2) – all went into branches of the sciences. One became a mining engineer, the others a biologist, a chemist and a mathematician. They had an aura of adventure and excitement about them, especially Torsten, Einar and Harald, whose frequently explosive natures made quite an impression on their niece. They are vividly described in the short story "Mina älskade morbröder" (My Beloved Uncles) in the 1998 collection *Meddelanden* (Messages). The letters tell us about Ängsmarn, the house on Blidö in the northern Stockholm archipelago where the Hammarsten family spent its summers. The uncles built assorted houses there, while their sister Elsa would take up residence in the one their parents Fredrik and Elin Hammarsten had built when they bought the plot in 1905. The Jansson family would come to visit over the summer and, in her time as a student in Stockholm, Tove Jansson was often on Ängsmarn. In the first chapter of *Bildhuggarens dotter* (1968, *The Sculptor's Daughter*) – which opens with the words "Grandfather was a clergyman and used to preach to the King" – the setting unfolds as if in a creation myth.

Viktor Jansson's family did not get to see the young Tove Jansson quite so often and visits to the Jansson clan are not described at any length in her diaries. But Viktor's brother and his family feature in the letters, and Tove Jansson the adult writer slips a canny paternal grandmother with a button shop into *The Sculptor's Daughter*.

The letters to the family are often directed to her mother – addressed as "Beloved Mama" or "Beloved" – but a number are written to both parents and some to "Beloved everybody". Reading the letters reveals clearly that they were intended for the whole family. Tove Jansson writes, for instance, to her "own beloved papa" on 27.3.1938: "Correspondence usually goes via Mama, of course, but I know you all speak to me through her letters and I often take them as being 'from the family', just as my answers are intended for all of you." She often signed the letters "Noppe", a pet name she had within the family.

* * *

Beloved Papa and Mama!

Seeing as it is Sunday evening, and about two weeks until I leave and a week since I last wrote, I think I can let myself tell you all the bits of silly nonsense that have been going on here. It's always so busy anyway as Christmas approaches and I don't really know whether I like the way time starts speeding by. Apart from the snow, which is stubbornly late, all the signs of Christmas have arrived. Drottning-gatan and Regeringsgatan are swathed in garlands and lights as usual, and every last little tobacconist's has its share of cotton wool and tinsel in the window.

I wonder if the snow has already settled where you are? If people are buying Christmas presents as wildly as they are here? I think the most sensible thing would be for me to buy whatever presents I need when I get home, since you write that things aren't so awfully expensive there. But even so, I've come to an agreement with various friends to scrap the exchange of goods. The family here being an exception, of course. I'm giving Uncle Harald a lovely bowl I bought a month or so ago – Ulla some extra bits and bobs for the train set her doting parents gave her for her 3rd birthday. I'm giving Uncle Einar and Anna-Lisa *Tales of the North*, which I've bound in dark-green leather, with claret-coloured endpapers, and taken a lot of time over. It looks pretty splendid, with lots of stitching and gold on the spine, inlays and oriental gold tooling on the front. I wanted to keep it for all of you ... but.

Teknis is a real rush. The women's-teacher training course is due to wind up with a flourish before Christmas – in printing we're a bit better off, though they're working us hard, too. By some stroke of genius, we've got croquis 4 days a week from 5 to 7. In the lunch breaks there's a lot of folk dancing, and the keen types stay on until 9. This evening, as it happens, I feel incredibly lazy, and can't fathom how I shall bring myself to care about plaster painting on both Monday and Tuesday. Today Uncle Harald, KF (Svenberg senior) and I were over at the boatyard where he keeps *Thalatta*, looking into the possibility of finding space for a reserve motor and assorted other innovations incl. stainless steel sink. Harald is intending to take her up to the North Cape this summer and then he, plus boat, will take the train to the Gulf of Bothnia and relaunch *Thalatta*. Isn't it a glorious programme, just think, the entire west coast of Norway, the fjords and mountains – it's enough to make one's face fall with longing to get away – somewhere.

Uncle Einar and Anna-Lisa are always dreaming of the tropics. They recall their times in the Canaries and say if ... if! This Christmas at any rate they're getting away to Grövelsjön for some skiing on a special kind of short ski to improve their technique. Admittedly that's hardly tropical – but still! I shall be leaving at about the same time.

But before that, there's the Teknis Christmas party (may it sink without trace!). A committee was set up ages ago, responsible both for the refreshments and the mental sustenance. It proceeded (as regards the latter) to squabble for weeks over the programme – then lapsed into apathy. Big meeting. At which I proposed dissolving the committee and sharing the responsibility equally between individual class members. All fine and good. But they immediately elected a <u>new one</u>. Nobody wanted to write anything. So in desperation I dreamt up some student-revue nonsense in the bath over 3 evenings and read it for them yesterday. The whole lot is in verse, by the way. So now I've an almighty task on my hands to get the wretched thing up to scratch. – Our number 2 is <u>useless</u>. None of us have any of the skills for this sort of entertainment. – the December sketch has been cancelled, instead we had to go to Nordiska Museet on Saturday, choose something from our subject area there and complete a study. It's to be a kind of competition. I found a beautiful wooden saint in a murky corner, but after two hours it was deepest twilight there. The colours impossible to make out, and I'd made a right old mess of it by the time I handed it in. It was cold and raw there, too – I only just escaped a terrible cold. [...]

I've rearranged the furniture in my room. I shifted the bed, with its sawn-off legs, away from the rheumatism-inducing outside wall, put the desk in pride of place and got rid of the atmospheric lighting. The walls are relatively bare, because just at the moment I feel in need of spartan simplicity and calm around me. – I lit my first Advent candle. And while it was burning I opened the parcel from all of you. Thank you my beloved dears! The little pigs were received with great satisfaction and gratitude when I distributed them. – I'd forgotten that Little Christmas came so early this year!

I've tried to get various drawings and place cards accepted here, but it's absolutely impossible to get anybody to take any notice. Instead I think I shall be receiving a small sum from above for my contribution to one of the H:fors daily papers, my interesting article on the surrealists! Imagine my surprise! But the whole thing is rather amusing, I must say. I hope by all the stars in the Zodiac that dear Elisabeth won't show all my letters to editors and close relations. I suppose I shall have to be really careful what I write then. The titles of the surrealists' paintings, for instance, were plucked out of thin air. Haha! – The young man from the College hasn't deigned to ask me out dancing yet. If he does it now, I won't have the time. And anyway, I shall never learn to dance properly – it is a strange gift and a manic art which not all have the privilege of mastering.

Over Christmas it would be so nice if you could teach me a bit about etching, Mama. Then we could go to croquis together. Go skiing with Poloni. Head for Bronkan. So many possibilities, anything we like. Oh, I can hardly wait! I shall try to get my Christmas break extended – into January this time. Wouldn't that be a good idea?

Do you know if Aava plans to spend Christmas with us? Is Jenny still there? Has Polon had his grades yet? There are so many things I want to know. Here, it's all much the same as ever, but everyone's so tired, wherever you look. It seems to me that the world ought to stop for a while, and everything in it – and just breathe, in and out, for a long time. I'm sure nobody would have time for that, though. – One thing is worrying me. It's possible that Carin Cleve won't have the money to stay on at Teknis this spring. That would make me really unhappy, because there's nobody else I care about. – She sends you her best wishes. Everybody here does, lots of best wishes. I might not write to you any more now except 1 telegram about when I arrive. Just think, 1 Sunday to go! It makes me want to start packing right away!

With lots of love and hugs from your Noppe.
Kisses to the boys!

Croquis: Life drawing in which the models change position after only a few minutes.
Thalatta: Uncle Harald's boat.
my interesting article: The notice "Impressions from the Surrealist Exhibition in Stockholm" (art review section of the Helsinki

periodical *Svenska Pressen*, 27.11.1932) includes a quotation from
letter written by TJ to Elisabeth Wolff in November 1932. TJ
is not named; the letter is said to be from "a young art novice in
Stockholm".

dear Elisabeth: TJ's friend Elisabeth Wolff.

Poloni: Per Olov Jansson. He is also referred to as Polon and later as
Peo and Prolle.

Bronkan: Better known as Bronda, a popular café (and restaurant) in
Helsinki, very popular with artists in the 1920s and 1930s.

Carin Cleve: A fellow student on the course at Teknis (the Technical
School). She became a good friend of TJ and later spent several
periods living in Finland, while she was keeping company with Wolle
Weiner. See Letters to Eva Konikoff.

SATURDAY [*Postmark 7.3.1933*]

Beloved Mama!

Thank you, dearest, for your last letter! I was in raptures as I took it
with me to Teknis and Carin was delighted, as you can imagine! We've
been planning that trip to Pellinge for her for so long. Goodness, how
nice that could be! With her love of solitude, and being a swimmer and
in the same line of work, yet still not the troublesome kind of guest:
Maud-Smedberg-entertainment-please-ooh-how-dull-it-is-here! I'm
not in the least worried about anything like that, you see. After all, the
walking tour is not really going to work – it seems pointless for you
to have to travel over to Sweden and back like that, just for fun. But
even so, don't you think it could be difficult finding room for her, food
and so on? Answer truthfully, please, because nothing could be more
hateful to me than causing you unnecessary financial worries. – Next
week Carin and I plan to start a month's course at the Welamson
private school for half price (15kr.) I've thought the matter over and
it seems a wise move. So two evenings a week we'll have teaching
and figure drawing – clothed models, from various parts of town
and, I hope, a lot of fun. Last time I did Carin in pastels in her green
ballet skirt. We've also decided to set aside one day a week, Thursday,
for Croquis, because otherwise we'll never get away in the evenings.

In your little green letter (I love getting pale green letters from you)
I'm just reading your question about my grant. That's funny, didn't I
write and say it was 300 kr? A goodly little sum. Now don't you go

sending anything back – it would really upset me, and besides, I'd only lose some of it when I changed the money! – I see you're also concerned about Einar. Blood clot gone, just like that – didn't I tell you? As for what they did – took out his gastric ulcer, about 10cm of intestine and sewed him up again. He's not going to behave himself at all – so he claims, full of optimism. No more nasty surprises as a result of the operation. Reading on, I find Papa's work, Polon's planned skiing trip, Jenny handing in her notice, the big party, and all that.

I hope Papa had a good birthday and that my letter and parcel got there in time. This letter probably won't be as long – I mainly just wanted to say thank you for letting Carin come. She'll probably write, too – I think.

The plan of Lalukka is up on my wall. I can sit and look at it and imagine us strolling in and out of the rooms like little dots. Just think how dependent we are on our surroundings, and how much they can influence us. I do so wonder about the future. Well anyway, wondering is about all I'm fit for this Saturday evening. I haven't anything particularly amusing to tell you – so it's probably best if I have a bath now – and go to bed. Perhaps something of note will happen tomorrow. Goodnight – dearest.

Sunday evening. The something of note was a long skate on Erstaviken Bay. I was able to borrow an ice prod and spikes from Harald, Maria's gloves – and with Torsten's skates and Uncle Einar's lunch bag off I went, all the way out to Kalvholmen. It was gorgeous, I can tell you! Now I feel horribly tired, yet somehow thoroughly rested. Knutte's here, and the Wollins. We've just had a cup of tea and everyone's very animated. Harald's just pulled off the trick of spiking Knutte's "Three Stars" with mosquito repellent while K. was out in the kitchen pinching jam. Einar's playing Beethoven and Aunt Anna-Lisa's worked the conversation round to the servant problem. The baby's asleep. The yard outside my window is in full moonlight. Very beautiful. I shall paint it in pastels some time. I think I'll go and do a bit of washing up, Maria will like that. She's in a pretty grumpy mood with the whole household at present. Harald finds it almost impossible to calm her down. Then I shall wash some gloves – and go back to join the conversation. Farewell beloved, and write to me soon!

your Tove.

PS Uncle Einar sends best regards and says Professor Henchel would very much like to have a plaster statuette like the one he, Einar, has got. He wonders how much it would cost. Do write and let us know! That little one with the babe in arms.

Maud Smedberg: one of Tove Jansson's classmates at Broberg School.
Lalukka: misspelling of Lalluka, the new artists' house in Tölö, to which the Jansson family moved in 1933.

UNDATED [*Postmark 8.5.1933*]

My beloved Mama!

It's Sunday, I just got your letter. Baby Ulla's got a cold and a bit of a temperature; that's keeping her parents busy. Harald's out at the boatyard putting the final touches to the boat. It's pouring with rain outside, yesterday a blue spring rain, but now grey and sometimes sleety. I'm painting a little thing for Cleve, it's her birthday tomorrow, and I've got plenty of time to think and have complete peace and quiet.

You've sent me a lot of money, but have said nothing about coming over. You wish me all the best, and are trying to make sure Elisabeth has as much to fill her stay here as possible, while you're fed up with Helsingfors and having a totally hellish time. – You tell me to enjoy myself and that it's important to dress nicely – but what about you?

I am a part of you, more so than the boys – regardless of <u>how</u> I turn out later, your distress is mine – how can I care one jot about Sweden when you're not here? I'm coming home, and soon. I'm coming home, just the way I was when I left, as soon as I sort some things out, a bit of work, a few friends, a few relations, and come to terms with myself. But it may well be that I can now understand you better, help you better, and painstakingly start to appreciate how lucky I am to have you and the rest.

Do write and thank them, Einar et al. Write to Olov and family – and Torsten and family. I've been to pay my respects to them all, though the final solemn leave-taking is still to come. Torsten & co. will be moving from 18 Kvarngatan at Whitsun. Einar says their house looks like a farm labourer's hovel. I can believe it. They're growing ever more bitter, and by constantly harping on the same theme they're going to find themselves sinking into the isolation they currently pretend their indifferent family has consigned them to. Also at Whitsun Olov is due to have an operation for gastric ulcers. Einar and family will be moving at about that time, out to Ängsmarn, which they don't like any more, to work. Harald will be setting off on his sailing trip. He's on his own and leads, at least as far as outsiders can see, the ideal bachelor life, independent and in a position to indulge his own hobbies to a large extent. And yet it's all just a cover for what is basically loneliness. *Thalatta*, his skiing expeditions, planned months in advance, are they enough? His friends are getting married and separating again, going their different ways, and perhaps he can't yet see, or won't, how solitary he is growing.

No, enough – they all have their own lives to get on with.

So do write and thank them.

This is a time of great difficulty and doubt, but I believe, though I've no grounds for my conviction, that everything will be so much better, very soon. I'm looking forward to coming home. Why shouldn't I? It isn't hard to leave a temporary environment, and people with whom one is such good friends that one sheds a parting tear but six months later recalls them only hazily, as if they weren't real. But one can take up one's profession again at any time, that's the main thing, and all the little people one has met, be and been helped or annoyed by, ultimately amount to no more than a couple of blurred pencil lines in an old, old sketchbook. Berga has become one of those. Sometimes I think about it, sometimes I miss it, but mostly that Easter feels as unreal as a dream.

You are always close to me. One night, I knew you were weeping about something. Even if at times a lot of things seem to be what I want, and have always longed for, they are drawn backwards through time and I grow indifferent to them, while you, and all of you at home, stand out even more clearly.

Write and tell me, just once, whether you will come over if I send money. I'm going to make a withdrawal, on Manne's advice. Give Papa and the boys a big hug.

Your Noppe, always.

"I think about you all the time"

LETTERS TO THE FAMILY
1938–1939

Tove Jansson painting at the Ateneum, Stockholm.

France 1938

TOVE JANSSON SPENDS THE SPRING OF 1938 IN PARIS. She had been awarded a scholarship and travelled to Paris in mid-January via Denmark and Germany, arriving there on the 27th. She writes many letters home, giving her account of assorted milieux, art schools and "compatriots". She commences her art studies at the Académie de la Grande Chaumière, where both her parents once studied, but applies to transfer to Atelier d'Adrien Holy, which has fewer students. Adrien Holy is a Swiss artist who had established himself in Paris in the 1920s. Tove Jansson is later accepted at the eminent École des Beaux-Arts, which she attends for two weeks. But she dislikes the atmosphere at the school and returns to Holy's studio at the end of March. It is to remain her favourite among all the art schools in Paris. In May her father comes to visit, and stays for three weeks. In June she goes to Brittany, where she paints, and travels from village to village on foot. Tove Jansson's journey home took her via Germany, Stockholm and the Hammarstens' summer house, Ängsmarn. She reaches Helsinki on 12 July after almost exactly six months abroad.

* * *

SATURDAY 12 FEB. –38 [*Paris*]

Beloved Mama!

Tomorrow is Sunday – these days I appreciate as much as you do the chance to sleep in on a Sunday! I have had a shower and washed my mop of hair and feel nice and warm. Carlstedt (who is petrified of germs by the way) claims it is lethal to use the bathtub here. This evening I "cooked" for the first time, i.e. a salad with lots of herbs and spices, and enjoyed a dinner for one with vin blanc, cheese and pancake. And violets on the table. Irina has been down here a couple of times – during the day I secretly abducted her and we went to Le Dôme and took a couple of turns on Montparnasse. The girl was in a quiver of delight. But I am starting to have my suspicions, there are strange goings-on here and there in this Nordic hotel. I have never known such intrigue on all fronts, I think I shall try my hardest to get out of this hornet's nest. They come to me one and all with their lamentations about each other, pledges of secrecy, accusations, explanations. Ouf! – Oh well. Ça va, as long as I just listen with a stupid, sympathetic look.

– I so enjoyed getting your letter. Whenever I am passing through the hotel lobby, even if it isn't post time, my eyes are irresistibly drawn to pigeonhole 13. And I feel an absurd rush of joy if I see a flash of white in the gloom. Just imagine your following me on the map! Hôtel des Terrasses is right on the corner of Boul. St. Jacques which I go along every morning as far as the beautiful lion sculpture and then carry on to Chaumière along Raspail. I generally walk home via Port Royal because there's sometimes such a lively and colourful market there. That way takes twenty minutes, if I walk briskly enough. Opposite my window there is a property with a tall, empty façade. When the wind blows, a broken gutter keeps knocking against the wall, and in the evenings I can see the Métro trains with their lights go thundering by. This is a quiet district, with no real noise in the streets. The hotel itself is ideal – the room too, though I'd like to move the whole lot a bit closer to the centre – preferably leaving the Finnish colony behind! You needn't worry about me being lonely – that's the last thing I am! One evening Carlstedt dragged me out for a Dubonnet, and then we had dinner, followed by coffee at Dôme, a lecture on astrology, a stroll along the Seine, and I got to bed at 1 o'clock. Another day Ragnar wanted me to come to some exhibitions, Vlaminck, Vuillard, Bonnard, Dufy, Brayer (my professeur). We encountered one Gert Markus from the Ateneum who dragged me to the Rotonde to listen to Helsingfors gossip while Ragnar went off to hunt for a "proper" Baltic herring bake. And Marcus is threatening to ring, soon. One tends to run into Hageli all over the place, at least if one frequents that dive Boudet on Raspail. He's promised to show me some Negro dancing. Irina pops in now and then, glowing with conspiratorial fervour, and I gather Bäckens have asked why they never see me? Tyra Lundgren has written (I had no idea she was still in London!) to ask me to keep her clay damp and get in touch to tell her how things are going, and I would certainly be made welcome at Champions. And then there's Chataïn who I haven't found time to see! And the Rumanian from Pontoise and

Gabriel Berthout who doesn't want to dine alone. So you see, gentle Pausanias, I am far from lonely! Almost wish – well ...! – I'm still going round in my fur – sometimes a raincoat with a warm dress underneath, but there's absolutely no need for muff and galoshes. The ladies are wearing leather and thin spring coats; people wear pretty much what they like, and I am glad of my Russian cat. The temperature shoots up and down like crazy and it's always windy here, and damp.

14 FEB. –38 [*written on Le Dôme's notepaper*]
Beloved! letter contd.

One always somehow ends up here after one's wanderings round town, and it is in these environs or somewhere around Boul. Mich. or behind the Luxembourg Gardens that I shall look for a new hotel. I've been running around looking all day – 6 hours. I reckon they're all more or less the same, concierges, stairs and wallpaper, and French hotels under 400 fr. are <u>utterly depressing</u>. Washbasin and enclosed courtyards and damp patches. I'd stay on at Glacière for March, too, but it's so out of the way and the Finnish colony drives me up the wall. But enough of that, let's talk about something more pleasant! Now is the holy hour of the apéritif. I can see Carlstedt out on the terrace, reminding me of yesterday's festivities at Boul. Blanche's negro dancing. I happened to be passing the Rotunda and caught sight of Birger, Hageli and Kræmers, some really nice Swedes. It was 11 o'clock at the time and the whole bunch seemed extremely lively after their Pernods, which created a fine effect with their milky green colour against the emerald green plates and the red table top. Hageli was making a racket you could hear from right out on the boulevard. They called me in and in no time we were all strolling along to Boul. Blanche to "take a look at Fernanda, rose of Martinique". This wasn't "proper" negro dancing, because you can only go to that in the company of a coloured person. But they were beautiful, putting body and soul into their dancing, laughing out loud with delight and completely caught up in what they were doing. Birger taught me what you have to do – it consisted mainly of shaking yourself in a wholly improvised way, stiff little steps, "like walking on loose desert sand", and you really have to concentrate on the music, and follow it, to make anything of it at all. I only had one Fils gin but it cost 25 fr! So it was certainly a costly pleasure to behold Fernanda! But great fun – like nothing I have ever experienced before. And then there was art chat, of course, someone said something thoughtless and then they were all at each other's throats. It's always like that – just when one wants to get immersed in an atmosphere, something new and lovely – all the old Helsingfors intrigues come tumbling in again. If they could just leave painting alone for a change!

Today I went to find out about my carte d'identité – it costs 200 fr. and they want 6 photographs, all the same. I had a couple of sheets of polyphotos done and I shall send you one in due course, with violets, earrings and "the whole works". Oh, and I got a letter of recommendation from the Finnish legation, took it to the Louvre and got a carte à demi tarif to the state art gallery.

Today from half 9 to half 12 I painted for the first time at Olie, rue Broca. I like it there – just the right number of novices taking an interest in the model's pose and forever squabbling about bits of coloured cloth, mirrors and reflected light. The studio is in a nice inner courtyard and you get up to it by climbing a steep spiral staircase, painted blue. No need to worry here about people making off with your equipment while your back is turned, like at Chaumière, and the whole atmosphere makes me feel much more like working. I've more energy left for croquis in the evenings, too. But it's incredible how quickly the days go, I don't feel as if I'm getting anything done. I haven't been able to write to you anywhere near as often as I've wanted now everybody in the world wants "illustrated letters from my travels". Isn't that silly. I've sent off at least 35 letters and cards, and then those beloved dopes go and write back straight away! But I really mustn't grumble – it's so nice when there's a letter waiting in the hall. It's 7 o'clock now and I can start to think about going to Boudet for something to eat – I want something practical and filling today because I had no breakfast and was up until 4 o'clock this morning. Ouch. (and what's more, the cleaner was impertinent this morning.) I forgot, you see, that even the banks take a siesta between midi and 2, hadn't a sous left from my first "withdrawal" (which I'd calculated would get me to the last of the month!), and after 2 there's no food to be had anywhere. Let me tell you – Paris is definitely the right place to deal a blow to the final vestiges of one's inferiority complex! One simply <u>has</u> to get over it to survive. If you are the least bit shy, compliant, apologetic or anxious, you end up feeling like a doormat before the day is over. All the concierges, constant little faux pas in matters of etiquette and French custom, the women with their devastating self-confidence, beauty and refinement of dress, haughty garçons, cheeky gamines, sales assistants who try to cheat you as much as possible and almost despise you if you don't haggle, a blasé restaurant clientele always eager to find fault etc. Eugéne Sommer has taught me lots of little details that are tremendously important here, and helped me in every way. He has even written an extremely "correct" letter to Chataïn, which I shall send off this evening to request a rendezvous. But with every passing day I feel safer, happier, calmer. And I know I've got to become free myself if I'm to be free in my painting. You'll understand better why I want to shake off my "compatriots" if you bear in mind that I <u>have</u> to be rid of all the old detritus clinging to me, everything that reminds me of the years of my "bondage". That's why I sometimes go out with Eugéne, his unfettered calm. – M. Champion came up for a few minutes' chat just now. Everyone who comes here takes a quick tour of the restaurant to see if anyone they know is here. Now I'm off to eat, à bientôt!

The hotel. At Boudet I collided with Birger again and after dinner we went to find Hageli and see how he was doing after yesterday. Then we took a walk to a funfair beyond Glacière, where the broad boulevard was packed with gypsy caravans along its whole length. I would rather have liked a ride on the bumper cars and the flying chairs but they claimed we were "too smartly dressed" for that. This is quite a "red" area, I understand, and one has to be careful. On that subject, I've had a very sweet, moving letter from Tapsa, written in Swedish. It made me really happy; it was full of his concern for me and his wish (albeit a melancholy one) that I should be well and enjoy myself. I've also heard from Torsten, a jolly long letter that I had to read in four or five stages. It's rather unfortunate that I'm finding it so hard to focus on any kind of proper, polished "correspondence", it's just the most unliterary scribble of memories and thoughts as they flutter by, repetitions and childish drivel. All I'm doing is "talking". But there are so many new things going on around me that I'm simply boulversé. If only you were here with me now! Then perhaps I could really bring it all alive for you. You know what, the flowers are so gorgeous here. It's terribly hard to resist buying them from the stalls with their piles of tight little bouquets, flaming with colour. Especially after the sudden violent showers that leave the wet boulevards shimmering yellowy-white or clear violet, that's when the flowers look loveliest!

I think your evening coat with all the little gold dots is awfully pretty. But you know what, Papa turns out to be quite right that I've no use for my poshest frock here. I thought I might go to an artists' dance or masked ball but I've heard such disreputable things about them that I've decided not to. If you're wearing "too much" they tear it off you on the way in, so most people wear nothing at all but smear paint on their bodies in a variety of extreme shades. And if the weather's warm they turn up at Dôme the next morning all streaky after a quick dip in some fountain. Good grief, can that be true! And there are "goings on" there that so embarrassed Carlstedt he went home before 11! That was a weird Stockholm story you told me. But if we always went around thinking horrible things like that might happen, we'd scarcely dare move a muscle. We'd be as wretched as Birger with his horror of germs.

Of course I think you'll cope with gold leather even though I'm not there! The bits of leather, gold and tools are in the medicine cupboard on my sleeping platform in a yellow wooden box Polon gave me, the oils in the old dolls' house in the studio or in Papa's or my wardrobe. You'll find the preparation in a square brown book with loose-leaf pages and a white label on the spine. – that's definitely in my bookshelf.

I've written a card and a "travel letter" to the Topsøes and also given them your thanks; I think that will do for now. But I'm sure they'd love to hear from you, as well. I'm glad your arm's getting better, I could tell from your handwriting how bad it must have been. Dearest, sometimes – well, often, I feel quite heartbroken that I can't be with you. I miss you all. Do you really think there's a chance Papa won't come? Tell him he absolutely must – to keep an eye on me, if nothing else! It would be such great fun to take my papa Faffan out for walks here – so many people have said he's got to come. Give my love to him and the boys! Good night beloved! Tomorrow I shall really splash the paint about. A big big big KISS from

your own Noppe.

Carlstedt: The artist Birger Carlstedt.
Irina: The artist Irina Bäcksbacka, daughter of art dealer Leonard Bäcksbacka.
Ragnar: The artist Ragnar Relander.
Hageli: The artist Hjalmar Hagelstam.
Bäckens: The Bäcks; that is, artist Yngve Bäck and his wife Märta Bäck.
Tyra Lundgren: Artist from Sweden.
Chataïn: Gilbert Chataïn. He and his wife are referred to in TJ's letter of 2 April 1938, for example.
Boul. Blanche: The Boule Blanche nightclub. The singer Moune de Rivel whom TJ got to know through Vivica Bandler after the war was one of its artistes. The club advertised a "Bal Negré".
Olie, rue Broca: A misspelling of Holy, Atelier d'Adrien Holy.
Tapsa: The artist Tapio Tapiovaara, a fellow student at the Ateneum. See further Letters to Eva Konikoff.
boulversé: misspelling of *bouleversée* – overwhelmed.
the Topsøes: On her way to Paris, TJ stayed with the Topsøe family in Copenhagen.

PARIS. SATURDAY 12 MARCH –38

Dearest Per-Olov!

On a bright day of sun and wind like this, I wish I could be at home with all of you to see in the spring. She needs no "help" here because there are no streams to clear the melting snow and ice from, only water pumped up into the gutters every day so the old women can wash their rags and lettuces. One day there was a thin layer of snow covering the city in the morning – Paris Soir devoted half a column to the phenomenon. Mama's told me about your skiing holiday and your floodlit slalom runs. How strange and far away that sounds! Today I went for a mooch along the Seine, wearing my fur for maybe the last time. "Ça va, little wolf," said the madame who sold me an old copy of Musset on the boquinistes quai. So I sat in the Luxembourg Gardens reading about the marriage of the muse and the poet because I was so tired of looking at art. I'd spent nearly three hours walking round the Salon des Independents being surprised at what an astonishing number of people fill their days daubing paint onto a stretched canvas. Because there was little more to it than that – most of the exhibitors clearly hadn't the faintest idea of the concept and point of all painting. A mural exhibition, on the other hand, huge works commissioned by the state from the best modern painters over the past year, made me feel very small and full of admiration. Rue de la Seine is where all the little art salons cluster, with perpetual openings of new exhibition, shops selling paints, antique dealers, here and there a greengrocer's stall, a bistro. Here's a map I've drawn of the streets I normally frequent – I've become almost like one of those genuine Parisians who have never been on the other side of the Seine. Rive droit – why bother to go there when one has everything in one's own district! [...]

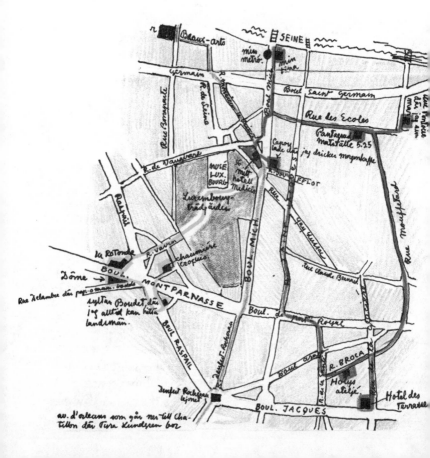

Other than that I'm really splashing the paint about. Regards to the whole family from me and give them a really hard hug!

And a big kiss for you from sister Noppe.

WEDNESDAY 16 MARCH –38. PARIS.

Beloved Mama!

Thanks for your letter, I felt absolutely sure it would be lying here waiting for me today! So now I've been accepted at Beaux Arts for the rest of the spring – I shall spend the next three weeks running between there and Holy's, and then I shall choose the one where I'm learning most. But my one lesson down at "the fine arts" certainly put me in a wickedly happy frame of mind and really gave me the urge to work. Yesterday I drew croquis 2 – 7 so I'd have something to show them. In the last two hours I really did manage to produce a some drawings that were fresher than anything I've done up to now, and I also took along a couple of head studies and presented myself at 10 o'clock this morning at d'Espagnan's studio. They have four professors of painting there and this was the only one the Bäcks knew anything about. Outside the door, someone had written in charcoal "Appartement des dames". I peered in cautiously and yes, it was true – about 50 young ladies, gesturing and chirruping in a major key. One came rushing over and started showering me in reproaches – and with this lot, you know, every fifth word rises to pianissimo: "Quoi! On n'entre comme ça dans une atelier! Qui etez vous, helas, alors! Eh bien!" I extracted myself from this horde of agitated females and took a look in Sabatte's studio next door. Then a caretaker came flapping over, scolded me and put me up against the wall, "attendez lá, oh mon Dieu ces anglaises!" Fine, I thought, I suppose I'll wait for this d'Espagnan, then, but I don't care for the way they run this establishment.

After I'd spent an hour cooling my heels waiting, a bearded novice came along and asked me to show him what I had done. Eh bien, I thought, it's better than standing here like a lump of wood while all these little red-haired beauties shrug at me en passant. He leafed through them, took me by the arm, "Vite, vite, venez!' Out onto the staircase: "It's Guérin you want, not here, be careful for goodness sake! Then he dragged me off to another studio where I was unceremoniously yanked in and put on a chair in the middle of the room, interrogated about my name, nationality, age, character, ideals, whether my hair was real, if I was in love, an optimist, and so on. The novices in a dense wall around me, my work spread out on the floor. "I like this better," I thought, but I was terribly embarrassed. Then another timid applicant arrived and endured the same treatment with poorly concealed mortification. Suddenly someone cried: "Voilá le Dieu!" And in came Guerin. Oh well, I thought, I suppose I shall have to show all my work again. But no. A bearded student adorned with a monocle approached this god and bowed. 'We have approved one of them, this one." "Good," said Guerin. "You will start on Monday." He cast the briefest of glances at the croqui on the top of my pile and then vanished. The first bearded gentleman came forward: "Now you are one of us. Don't look so stupid, you will be fine. I invite you to dejeuner, c'est l'abitude." No sooner said than done. I found the whole thing so ridiculous and charming that I went along, to a cheap Hungarian place. Coming out, I ran into Ester Helenius who instantly abducted me and gave me a lecture on art, then pressed my hand and thanked me for not consorting with Finns. Beamed and left me.

Now I am going to dress up smartly and go to the ambassadeur (that sounds impressive), where I will meet my compatriots quand même. First I shall pin some of my croquis up on my wall, because today, illogically enough, for perhaps the first time here, I really feel I can achieve something. The atmosphere over there was so youthfully encouraging and mischievous. So long!

Later, evening. Liberated from the fear of bacteria Carlstadt managed to instil in me, I have now had a bath, which was pretty lukewarm but nice anyway, darned my socks and done some cleaning. Ever since he, Skralstedt, went off to Africa things have calmed down on all troubling fronts. Bäcks got totally silly about him, particularly when he started talking about forms of social intercourse in sophisticated diplomatic circles, riding habits and underwear. I thought he was basically a terribly nice boy. He genuinely regretted everybody thinking such horrible things about him: "If I go with a girl – then I'm a seducer. If I'm out with a boy – homosexual. If I stay at home – then they all know what illness I've caught." It's true that his wife died but that was because she took too much morphine, she'd been using it for a long time. I'm saying all this to exonerate him a little, because I came to rather like him. He is quite feminine and talks far too unguardedly, but there's nothing bad in him.

Anyway, at the ministerial tea party I tried to remember everything he'd taught me about etiquette and went there with a whole gang of compatriots. Terribly elegant drawing rooms and piles of sandwiches and sweet things – but none of them bigger than a postage stamp. There were lots of Swedes and Finns, among them Bade and Helenius. One was expected to spend 2 hours teetering around on high heels making polite conversation about that day's on dit. (I'd rather have gone to Pontoise for a swim.) Before I went I dropped in on Irina with the secret ration of cigarettes and nail polish. She had translated my finely honed and poetic love letter to her Spaniard and bashfully asked if she might make the ending a little more affectionate. No, I said, don't give him false hopes. But in the end we decided to leave her a bit of room for manoeuvre after all, in case she can't hold to her "no", and added a couple of hopeful adjectives. As I was leaving she hugged me and gave me a Spanish brooch that I'd always admired. She is a delight, that girl, I can't fathom how anyone could treat her badly. I so wish I could have a frank little exchange of views with that gentleman, her father. To think, for instance, that the Spanish beloved went all the way to Reval and still had his ticket for Helsingfors, wrote to Bäxbacka and asked if he could come over and see her but got a point-blank refusal and went back to Salamanca. – Yes, you see, I write about all manner of things that I probably ought to keep to myself – but I do so enjoy talking to you like this before I turn in – and of course I know I can trust you to keep quiet. I've never met anyone other than you who can do that – I certainly can't! When I talk to you, at any rate, I find everything just comes spilling out of me! [...]

Yes, I know about the state stipendium next month. I wondered if you would kindly send in that still life with the red book and white pot of flowers against an open window, and the self-portrait with the Indian cloth in the background. And I'll send the third canvas from here. For the exhibition this month you can submit the two works I've mentioned. I need a bit of time to produce something decent. A landscape, for example. Don't know if I want to burden Irina with any extra luggage. She'd take it, of course, she so much wants to "give" me something for those miserable cigarettes. But F.Å.A. will organise it just as well. Do you think 130 fr. is too much? It's a fair amount, of course, but at least I'll get rid of all my winter stuff.

It's getting late, good night dearest! This letter is just meandering drivel I'm afraid, but it's only two days since I last wrote and not awfully much has happened in the meantime! But it's such fun sitting down for a chat with you – it's almost as if you were here. Bye for now! Love from

Noppe.

Friday, it's almost 6 p.m. now, I just came from Holy where I asked permission to carry on painting after midi. Phew! First I scratched out the whole model I've been doing all this week, turned her to face the opposite way and gave her a dress and a new head. Three hours later I was going crazy and turned her again, and in the end I turned her to the wall and did a little sketch of the "Apache cellar" where I went yesterday. It was fresh, but just one of those bluffs, a colour-composition-scrape of a picture, you know, the kind of thing you can't take any further, but maybe use to impress people who've never painted themselves. I started to feel hopeful and when the afternoon sun sent its gleaming streaks in among the easels and made the place into one big jumble of shadows, I did another sketch. Might carry on with it tomorrow, my last day at Holy's. I've been there five weeks now and still have three owing to me; I shall take those later in the spring, as I'm starting at Beaux Arts on Monday. It was dearer there than I expected so it's not worth registering just for the sake of the identity card. I'd just as soon take the plunge, it looks nice there. Incidentally, I've found out the name of that student with the beard who came and rescued me from the Appartement des Dames and took me to that Hungarian eating-house. Féri Gall, and a fine painter, it seems; he's won Grand Prix in Rome, and at Beaux Arts too. Paints in Rembrandt style, huge compositions. The reproductions he showed me made me feel quite faint. Yesterday he came dashing up when I was having coffee at Dupont and asked whether he ought to shave his beard off or not. I was absolutely sure he ought to keep it, for a week at least. Then we took a stroll around the Seine and he proved a very earnest and poetic gentleman. He doesn't approve of our century's rush and craving for entertainment, and expressed his pleasure at having found "a young lady equally serious and, he hoped, equally romantic", and what was more, with a Hungarian name, Marika. He was terribly kind and funny, but when he got too carried away with contemplation of the moon and talk of platonic friendship, I took him off to the Cave Apache at Boul. Mich. It's cheap and good fun, with non-stop singing, and sometimes when the "vamp" is to perform something particularly racy they put the lights out and just leave a little stump of candle burning in their mouldy old vaults. Féri almost took fright, but in the end he had a really good time and forgot he was a solitary being. Next week we might go and paint by the Seine.

Papa's box of sugared cranberries has arrived, though unfortunately I wasn't at home when Uhra Simberg brought it round. I might go and find her at rue de la Santé tomorrow. Give my love to Papa and a big thank you, it's so nice to have treats like that to enjoy in the evenings. All the "eating" here takes on such significance, it gets raised to the status of an event, almost a ritual. Me, just think!

Saturday. Oh yes, I forgot to tell you – last Sunday I saw my first butterfly and he was a brownish yellow. There he was on the asphalt, quivering, and since I had a flower in my buttonhole I let him crawl up onto it and come with me all the way down the boulevarde. Today I saw my second one, he was whitish-yellow. – Do you remember I had three art books for Christmas, I think they were on Cézanne, Matisse and Gauguin (or Manet?). Can you write and tell me what they were and how much they cost, because I've seen the same series here and I'd like to add to my set if they're cheaper here. – And I'll be immensely grateful for as many shoe, shirt, glove and stocking sizes as possible whenever you feel like letting me have them. I often see things of that kind I'd like to buy for you all, as gifts if nothing else. (Damn! There goes another of Sivén's fillings, a huge one. He won't get any discount on his painting if this carries on!). Today I went to Holy an hour early and popped in on madame Krok on the way with flowers for Uhra, who still wasn't up. She'd be out in town later, I knew that. She was glad I'd come but didn't think we ought to make any particular arrangements to meet. (And I'm not all that keen on playing cicerone, either – she's not the only one who's busy.) I gave her lots of tips on the subjects of art – sights worth seeing –

food and places of entertainment. She'll probably be at Boudet like the others, if one feels like meeting up with her. Gunvor Grönvik is in Italy and will be coming later in the spring, - Féri told me that in April we have to paint a naked model for a week with no critique, and if it's no good they chuck you out of Beaux Arts straight away. That sounds ghastly. My hand is going to shake so much I shall produce nothing but pointillism. Irina's gloomy because I won't be at Holy's the last week she's here – but que faire? I've already given her poetry, cigarettes and encouragement to last her for the next few days. She's scared of going home, that father of hers must be quite a ... Now I shall go on with an interior while the light lasts. Lots of love to everybody – and a particular hug for Papa for his parcel.

A big

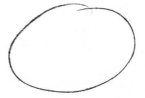

your own Noppe.

P.S. Had a letter from Karin F. who is keeping very busy with children's homes again. The work there is too much for her, her stomach doesn't like it. Elsa went down to Switzerland after her nervous breakdown, and stayed with Ingmar's Emy, but caught influenza there and was confined to bed for 10 days. But now, writes Karin, we've forgotten all those tedious things, we're so overjoyed about Austria. (!)

Sunday evening P.S. Another kiss just before this goes to press! Today I was at the Louvre and slept terribly late this morning. NOW I really feel it's Sunday! Just think, Beaux Arts starts at 8! I'm awfully nervous – they apparently like to play some kind of trick on newcomers. We'll have to see! Goodnight dearest!

Ester Helenius: Artist.
Skralstedt: TJ's nickname for Carlstedt.
Reval: the old name for Tallinn, capital of Estonia.

F.Å.A.: The shipping firm Finska Ångfartygs Ab (The Finnish Steamboat Company).

Féri Gall: This Hungarian artist colleague was the inspiration for the protagonist in TJ's short story 'Skägget' (The Beard).

Marika: TJ's middle name.

Cave Apache: A variety of nightclub featuring 'apache artistes' and 'apache dancing'.

Uhra Simberg: A textile artist.

Sivén: TJ's dentist in Helsinki.

Karin F.: Karin Flemming, TJ's cousin.

Ingmar: Ingmar Flemming, TJ's cousin.

Emy: Ingmar Flemming's wife, also known as Emmely.

WHEN TOVE JANSSON STARTED AT ÉCOLE DES BEAUX-ARTS in March, she describes what she was forced to undergo in the initiation tests and her first days as a student there. She leaves the school after about two weeks, giving an account of her exit in the short story "Quatz' Arts", which also depicts the carnivalesque throng at the art school. The story was published in *Svenska Pressen* on 30 July 1938. She wrote a number of short stories during her Parisian stay in 1938.

SUNDAY 27 MARCH 38. PARIS.

My own beloved Papa!

Your letter is in my bag, it made me feel all warm and happy. I <u>most definitely</u> realise that you care about me and are thinking of me even though you don't write very often. – Correspondence generally comes via Mama, of course, but I know you all speak through her letters and I often treat them as "from the family", just as most of my letters are intended for all of you.

When I went into the hotel bureau on Annunciation Day, Madame looked very important and curious and the entire staff stood there watching as I took the bundle of letters out of my pigeonhole. "Tout ça, c'est pour moi?" "Oui-oui-oui-oui", said Madame generously. "Just take them, you can have them all." (We always have to thank her when letters arrive for us!) Just imagine, you'd all remembered me!

I felt twice as happy as usual as I set off to walk to Hotel Lutetia to dance that evening, it was as if I had you all with me. – Of course I shall send something in for the state competition. It's turned pretty warm now; I can do a landscape painting, for instance. But I don't want to send anything in until I can see for sure that it's better than anything I've produced before. And now let me tell you a bit about Beaux Arts, which is currently hogging all my interest.

My first days there were quite trying. The main problem was that I happened to come in on a male model week, and that's the worst thing I know (presumably because it's the hardest), painting a mustachioed muscle man sturdily planted on both feet. And matters weren't helped by my dreading every repos, in case the students decided it was time to make me pay my "boir" in the restaurant next door. In a moment of weakness one of them, a certain Hungarian called Gáll who I've already mentioned, let slip the secret of boir. The victim, the new arrival, buys everyone (about 40 in all) a drink and then you have to get up on a table and sings songs from your homeland, then two youths grab your skirt and yank it over your head. That's the very least you can expect. Most people have to pose "au poils", tout a fait nue. That's what happened to Féri Gáll two years ago, for example. Alors – if they demand that, I shall give up on Beaux Arts altogether. I've been going around all week in my best black silk stockings and the yellow pants Mama made me just before I came away, with stomach ache from sheer nerves. It isn't easy being new. On se moque tout le temps, par example – coming over and giving my poor model study green hair and a Hitler leg band, pouring turpentine in my shoes, sending me running off for essence, expecting me to supply them with painters' rags and cigarettes, and one's expected to be as meek as a lamb, smiling indulgently and appreciatively at it all, c'est l'habitude. Young men can expect to get their tie or their fringe chopped off. It's le petit Patron, keeper of the "corbeille", and mediator of all "le Dieu's" orders (le Patron, our professeur), who leads this traditional initiation of the newcomers. In the old days you undressed "au poils" to be branded, it was considered a very great and fine thing to be accepted as a student at Beaux Arts. That's stopped now, but the stripping persists. Le Dieu, C. Guérin, is a Great Painter (in both senses). Whenever he comes in, they all stop shouting, "singing", throwing water at each other and charging round among the easels, and start quaking instead. (I'm quaking constantly, of course, because a notice on the wall in letters ½ a metre high says: "Le nouveaux ne parlent pas qu'a leur tour, et leur tour ne vient JAMAIS" – written a metre high.) And then the thunderclaps start.

Because he's strict; Holy is like a mild westerly breeze compared to Guerin. He bellows and scolds and gets sarcastic "– – – C'est Beaux Arts, ça, pas un Bal de nuit! De quel age avez Vous? Eh bien? Vous voulez devenir peintre, eh? Vraimaent – c'est formidable ça. Alors, il faut travailler, travailler, travailler, tous les jours, les nuits, toujours! Compris?" Guerin's a naturalist, or at any rate demands strict academic studies from us. So your terrible dream about my surrealist meta-morphosis was entirely unfounded! Each week we get 2 sujets pour choisir, this time for instance it's "Moses strikes the rock" and "People waiting for a bus". We have four days to get it done, so it's a rather more pressured sommittelu than at the Ateneum. I've chosen Moses but I haven't a clue how I'm going to fit him in. I expect things will go better once I start getting into the work and don't feel so nervous and awkward any more. The big Rome prize was awarded two days ago and everybody made straight for the restaurant to celebrate the event. What we drink on such occasions is covered by the 200 fr. we have to pay the Petit Patron when we join. In the bureau we have to pay 100 fr., so the whole affair turned out 3 times dearer than I'd counted on. At least the Carte d'identité was reduced to 60, but of course they made me pay 65 fr. extra for a stamp. It's so French, all these little supplements and additions. E.g. I once went to a cheap eatery with a sign in the window boldly advertising "5 fr. 75"! Inside, it turned out the cover charge was 1.50 and the bread 1.75, plus 75 for oil with the salad. Wine 2 fr. Voilà! Oh well. Before I knew it, one of the students started shouting Bois! and my cook was goosed. They promised me this was just a "preparatory" boir and I would "only" have to sing. So I plucked up my courage and sang "There was a Little Young Man", 'The Crow Song" and "Cuckoo, cuckoo, faraway cuckoo.' The last of these drew more attention that our Arab's surprising solo turn. – Today the weather's grey and cold. I've been to Irina's with a parcel for you, a few little things I hope she'll be able to take with her in her muff. She's supposed to be leaving on Wednesday morning, Mrs Bäck is taking her as far as Antwerp and putting her on the boat going directly to

Helsingfors. If she comes to see us, be careful not to talk too much about her stay in Paris. She's had quite a tricky time of it, poor little thing, with her father leaving her no freedom of movement and Bäck misunderstanding – and mistrusting – her. She's immensely kind, and a good friend to me. A big big kiss to you, dearest!

your own Noppe.

"Tout ça, c'est pour moi?": "Is all this for me?"

repos: Rest break.

"boir": Drink.

"au poils", tout à fait nue: Completely naked.

On se moque tout le temps: They are always teasing.

C'est l'habitude: That's usual.

corbeille: (Wastepaper) basket.

C. Guérin: Presumably the painter Charles Guérin.

Le nouveaux ne parlent pas qu'a leur tour, et leur tour ne vient JAMAIS: New students do not speak until it is their turn, and their turn NEVER comes.

C'est Beaux Arts, ça, pas un Bal de nuit! De quel age avez Vous? Eh bien? Vous voulez devenir peintre, eh? Vraimaent – c'est formidable ça. Alors, il faut travailler, travailler, travailler, tous les jours, les nuits, toujours! Compris?: This is Beaux Arts, not a dancing party! How old are you? Well, so you want to be a painter? That's wonderful. In that case you must work, work, work, all day and all night, always! Understood?

sujets pour choisir: Subjects to choose between.

sommittelu: Composition.

TOVE JANSSON RETURNS TO ATELIER D'ADRIEN HOLY AT the end of March. In a letter dated 24.4, she describes Holy's approach to teaching and his critiquing of her pictures.

SAT. 2 APRIL –38. PARIS.

Beloved Mama!

I've stretched and pinned about ten decent-sized new canvases, scraped my palettes clean, written a letter to Torsten, washed my gloves, eaten a pain blanc with haricot and am now sitting here feeling I've been a good and clever girl all round. Phew, what a lively time I've had! I just found another little cry for help from Féri down with the concierge, que faire. He's bound to be frantic when he doesn't find me at Beaux Arts on Monday and I expect Guerin will bring the roof down. I wonder if one can have the grippe for three weeks? Anyway, that's going to be my excuse when I go back after using up all the sessions I paid Adrien Holy for at the beginning of March. It will be nice and quiet working there with the six young ladies who wait until the breaks to shyly relate that week's experiences for the only young man, who makes little speeches about the meaning of art in return. Holy flits between the easels and calls us "his children", the Armenian girl's pug is asleep by the stove, it's all a perfect idyll, and at the foot of the winding blue stairs a little studio alley full of daffodils and fragments of sculpture. It might be a bit more –tedious, but I shall be able to work in peace. In three weeks I shall know whether I want to stay here or move back to Beaux Arts.

I won't lose more than a fortnight with Guerin, in any case, because they take a holiday over Easter, which Holy doesn't bother with. Yesterday I was sitting at home feeling gloomy and dull and dashing off an angry, glowering self-portrait. Then there was a knock, and in came Madame and Monsieur Chataïn, bearing a box of pastries. They had sought me out because they "had a feeling" I was all alone. That was kind of them, wasn't it? So they invited me back home for diner and then to a theatre, "l'atelier" in Montmartre, and a performance of a play from classical antiquity, but modernised. The scenery was fantastically well done, and the costume colours were beautiful. Pluto, who spoke argot by the way, came down to Earth and gave discontented humans all the money they wanted, then everything went to pot and they wanted their poverty back. That was the main thread. Tomorrow I've been invited to dejeuner with Madame, who'll be on her own with the kids; Gilbert's off to Belgium in his car for a few days. The Bäcks have been very kind, too. Things were a bit dismal at first after they found out about my cigarette smuggling, but now they've finally got Irina home to her father they've calmed down and are trying to unwind after the whole wretched episode. There were complications to the very last, they got to Antwerp an hour late for the boat, and only caught up with it in a motor launch after much telephoning, telegraphing and running about, and Irina had to climb aboard via a rope ladder, out at sea. Bad luck really does seem to pursue that girl! Everything's gone wrong for her, and the last thing she did was to pour some greasy stuff on her floor that drove the concierge wild, and set fire to her painter's smock. At any rate, she's made considerable artistic strides here without, as her papa feared, losing any of her "personality". It's true, though, that life would be impossible for her as a Spaniard's wife. There would be no painting, anyway. He didn't answer that farewell letter I devised with such effort and diplomacy, and Irina was depressed about that. I do hope she won't later reproach me for that "service", which was surely the most sensible thing to do, but not what she wanted deep inside.

So that's that. This evening it's the Grande Bal, the annual one, at Beaux Arts. I was to have gone with Féri attired in gold and to the sound of cymbals, but with things as they are, I really can't be off enjoying myself while he sits brooding up in his poky little studio. Wherever I go, this sort of mess ensues. I'm enclosing two photos of him in case you're interested in how he looks. Is he like your Hungarian? Didn't he also once say, "I don't want to see you for a week"? That's what Féri did, he wasn't going to jump straight into the Seine, but he wondered if I would plant flowers on his grave. Well, I hope you don't think I'm taking this as lightly as I make it sound. It's immensely sad to know one's ruined at least two or three months for another person, as that's how long these wretched things usually take. Perhaps longer in this case, since he wanted to marry me. Mais, parlons nous d'autres choses. I do wonder how to set about finding a hotel for Papa. He'd certainly be very comfortable at Hotel des Terrasses, but it is a little out of things. What I'd like best would be for him to take a room here at Medicis – but it's rather seedy and I don't know if the other rooms are as pleasant as mine. Maybe he'd like to share a room with me? It would be cheaper, after all. Will you ask him about all that, and whether there's a particular district he'd prefer, such as Montparnasse? It's going to be so much fun having him here – hope he can stay a bit longer. And also – is there any particular item of clothing I could give Per-Olov for a present on the 23rd.

Monday. Now all the canvases are glued, and the concierge has softened so much that she even lets me boil the water for my glue in her kitchen. Holy received his lost sheep with open arms today and veritably pounced on what I'd produced at Beaux Arts. He was beside himself over Moses and the muscle man. I really did escape from the dreadful Guerin in the nick of time – Beaux Arts was a place for having fun or hoping for the Prix de Rome, and possibly one gleaned some superficial technique to use in disguising one's mediocre talents. He danced around the studio and went quite pale at the thought of the terrible danger I'd escaped from. – Now I can have a little laugh to myself about it all. What an odd time it's been!

But I'm now extremely curious to see how I get on with my latest ploy, to stop smoking. So far I can officially claim 24 hrs. If I last more than a week I'll feel proud of myself, if I do two I get a new hat. The silly thing is that when I don't smoke I get this wild craving for patisserie, or chewing gum. – Yesterday at Madame Chataïn's was exceedingly tranquil. After dejeuner I devoted myself to drawing with the kiddies, ball games with them in the garden, playing with building bricks etc. We presented the drawings to Madame. When she finally let me go it was nearly evening and I went to Pontoise for a swim, and then to a colourised South Seas film. At the piscine I saw a gentleman in leopard-skin swimming trunks and a red cap with a bow at the back loudly hail each young man he met with a: Vous aimer ces femmes? There are some very strange fish here. In the bistro next to Beaux Arts I spent 10 minutes listening with growing astonishment to a boy I took for a particularly precocious and cynical thirteen-year-old – when he got up he proved to be a young lady, somewhat over 20. – I wonder whether I can be bothered to go back to that establishment at all. I can't understand, for instance, why you have to use the dirtiest colour you can come up with for the background, which happens to be an indeterminate beery shade, a beige-ish mauve made up of all the palette scrapings smeared there by students over the years. It's fair enough to "follow nature", but not to "paint it as it is" too much, you have to see the value of accentuating and intensifying the essentials and playing down anything that's superfluous to the picture.

This evening I'm off to rive droit for a stroll around the big boulevards. One eventually tires of the Quartier Latin. Lots of love to you and the others! Irina might come round tonight, with my muff. Take great care of yourself!

Tove.

grippe: Influenza.
argot: Slang.
Mais, parlons nous d'autres choses: Let's talk about something else.
Vous aimer ces femmes? Do you love these women?
That establishment: Beaux Arts.

PARIS. THURS. 14 APRIL −38

My beloved Mama!

Today it's thoroughly grey and cold – it's bound to rain on Good Friday again this year. I stayed home from Holy today to get my canvases ready for the State competition. I just went down for a 4 fr. breakfast, pain blanc, butter, cheese, boiled beans. And in spite of it being a "short day" and me not knowing what to do with my hands and fangs (as Samu says) because I'm so nervous about my tableaux drying, I can't stop myself answering your two lovely letters at slightly greater length. Or perhaps it's even three? I do so enjoy sitting down to chat to you about whatever occurs to me; it scarcely counts as a letter any more – no need to bother rounding it off properly, it's as if you're simply here with me for a bit, while I smoke my post-breakfast cigarette. My abstinence only lasted a week, so no hat for me. Or maybe a very small hat. You're right that I go round without one even though it isn't really chic, but foreigners are allowed to do that. Still, now I don't smoke until after breakfast, and a lot less than before – and what's more I know now that I <u>can</u> stop if I want.

Now just imagine, I shall be as fair as a flower in bloom before long, having been so carried away by my "success" at the Kunsthalle that I've gone and ordered myself a grey skirt suit! Sheer madness, isn't it? But I got the material terribly cheap at a gentleman's wholesaler's in rue du Temple. I went in and said I was buying for a tailor (which was partly true.) You grow very bold here – you have to, or helplessness and loneliness come washing over you. Imagine it, with black gloves, hat and stockings and the shoes you'll perhaps send with Papa and a little touch of blue or pink at the neck! I've already been for one fitting and it's going to be beautiful! Like this *[see illustration right]*. And I've had a permanent wave. I had to do all that because I was getting depressed about my painting and Féri and myself. As you well know, such things can help – it's funny, but true. These past few days I've been throwing oil paint around me like a lunatic. Holy's gone

to the country to paint trees before everything gets bunged up with "spinach", and what's more they've got a model I really don't like, because she looks like a woman I was scared of when I was a child, so my working from home for a week is fine. Next time they're going to paint a rather jolly still life with shells.

No, I'm not going back to Beaux Arts. But as I said, the experience was definitely worth the 300. And when I get home I shall make some money out of the whole thing by writing about it. For now I just want to paint and, in any time I have over, to look around and just "be". It's only now I feel I can start working calmly and in earnest. Expect I'll stay at Holy's until at least 15 May, then I very much want to go to Brittany. Somewhere with sea and flat, windswept beaches with all sorts of exciting bristly plants, and the indigenous population in attractive costumes and lots of boats with coloured sails. You know how we sometimes conjure up such an idyllic picture of a region we've never seen and are utterly convinced that it matches reality. I shall go on my own because I'm happiest that way. Everybody here makes promises and plans and talks about so much that they never actually do. And I'm starting to learn to enjoy myself all on my own. Carlstedt's given me an address where he says I'll find all the things I'm looking for. He's just back from Africa where he got through 50 litres of eau de cologne warding off the typhus epidemic, did 400 sketches and bought an alarming amount of brocade and jewellery. Now he's wondering whether to take some peacocks with him to Finland – and any day now we're off to the flea market to look for leopard skin!

Tomorrow, or even this evening if they dry in time (I paint almost exclusively with Mastic these days) I shall send my canvases by registered post, weighing exactly 2 kg. Because it's going to be so expensive I've had to make a selection so I'm sending: 1. "The woman at the mirror" (the one Irina is showing), 4 the still life with the doll, 2 the still life with the wine bottle, 8 the anemones, 3 the river at Jainville, 5 the apaché cellar, 7 Holy's studio, 6 my hotel room and a canvas of a 9 girl with lilies that I dashed off in two days in the most frantic exhibition rush. It might be more sensible after all to submit the things that are already on show, since they've already found some kind of favour with the powers that be. You'll have to see, you and Papa. But I'm convinced that the self-portrait and the studio window are both better than the things I've just done. The Muse knows. It did me good to hear that Irina thinks I've made progress – but despite her undoubted talent, she's no foolproof authority. Don't be embarrassed to write and tell me you don't like my pictures. I'd planned to send them with my winter clothes but when I rang FÅA they said it would take at least 15 days to send the suitcase home. So that's coming later, with the other paintings and drawings in it. [...]

You know what, it's done me some good to hear that people like my stuff. I was so depressed for a while because I could see my swift descent into a second-rater who would shame her forefathers. Now I believe in myself again.

– Now that I won't be going away any time in the next four weeks, at least – it doesn't matter when Papa comes. I know how much he dislikes deciding in advance. Just write a few days beforehand and tell me if I need to find a room for him.

Irina certainly set her prices rather on the high side. (Or her father did.) I'm happy with mine, don't want them any higher, not yet. It's stupid, anyway – there isn't a living soul who'd pay over 2500 for a canvas, unless he's a Serlachius. He's been here, incidentally, buying up French art like mad. As a result, Finland's risen considerably in French artists' estimation. A rich country that cares about supporting culture!

Wouldn't it be a better idea to take all my things with me to Brittany and then come straight home from there? But I'll have to see later on. And yes, I have considered allowing myself a week just to "fool about" somewhere. There's plenty to be learnt from one of those, too. Féri had planned "en ce temps là" a week in Fontainebleau for us to live and paint together, and it's largely because I got cold feet and refused that relations went downhill as they did. I'm very suspicious of young men who want to take you "to a quiet little place where we can stay at an idyllic inn together, undisturbed – and paint." Maybe if they varied their turn of phrase a bit – but I've heard it three times in a row already.

Well, the streets are quiet now. I think a lot gets exaggerated in the Finnish newspapers. – How nice that the party was so animated! It's made me sad that you so often feel you're the outsider somehow. And it's great that you sang at the Society of Illustrators! They can really do with it, they're complete spiritual sclerotics, the lot of them. Irina's right when she says our artists are gloomy and take no pleasure in their work. Here, the pleasure sometimes gets rather out of hand. I'm thinking of Beaux Arts (as a parallel to the Atenaeum). Yes, I could have studied there "to have a good time" but my pictures would undoubtedly have been less fun, everything brown-on-brown.

What a shame about Grandmother. I hope there isn't anything seriously wrong with her leg, but she always gets in such a state when she's ill. Of course I shall write. As soon as I get these canvases sent off. – Yes, I thought you'd like Irina. So her papa's already shut her up with her easel. She's abnormally docile, that girl.

Torsten wrote to me, too, a sort of distress call because I'd gone quiet for a couple of weeks. He asked if he was meant to "vanish from my landscape in shame". How daft it is to imagine oneself forgotten and out of favour if the other person doesn't write for a while! I only had my first letter from Carin Cleve yesterday. But we haven't fallen out, for all that. She's had a hard time, poor thing, and is finishing at Sköld's now, to try for the Academy. She's not coming here in the spring. – Now I must get back to my canvas. This letter looks rather untidy but I'm up to my neck in paint at the moment. Take great care of yourself and hugs to Papa and the boys.

Lots of love, your Noppe.

P.S. I shall sit here waiting for the Mastic to dry until 7 o'clock when the post office closes. If there are any patches of red or green that are too bright, say, there's nothing to stop you toning them down with a bit of oil paint. I honestly don't know myself any more what's good and what's useless – I'm glad to see the back of the whole bag of tricks! You can keep the photos of Féri. I might pack Sommers into my suitcase too, so you can see what <u>he</u> looked like. Thank you for the hepaticas. It's all violets here. KISSES!

Tove.

Samu: The artist Sam Vanni, sometimes called Samuli. See Letters to Maya Vanni.

"success" at the Kunsthalle: In the Annual Artists' Exhibition in April, TJ was awarded the Finnish Art Society's so-called "Ducat" prize of 3000 Marks.

Serlachius: Industrialist and art collector Gösta Serlachius.

Sköld: Otte Sköld, Swedish artist and professor of painting, ran his own art school in Stockholm.

hepaticas: A plant; a herbaceous perennial of the butttercup family, usually violet in colour.

SUNDAY 24 APRIL −38. PARIS.

Beloved Mama!

True, it is only three days since my last letter, but the long Sunday and good news from Holy lead me to substitute a rather longer epistle for the traditional card. You may remember me talking about a still life with shells, the first piece of work this spring I was pleased with.

Holy returned from his séjour in the country yesterday (he only gives his critiques once a week these days, but in great detail) and really liked the painting – said it was my best work. Sadly it's too late to send it in for the State Competition. He just wanted one corner of the background a bit warmer to intensify the light, and the outline of one of the shells accentuated. He also delivered his verdict on the woman with the lilies. He was pleased with me for tackling such a tricky problem. He very much liked the lilies and her face, but claimed (as Papa so often has!) that the canvas was disjointed because of the different manières, and would benefit from being cut in two. I don't intend doing that, however, and will try to solve the problem instead, even if I end up spoiling the whole thing. He also looked at a small study of a boy's head in which I had tried to clarify a pure cadmium purple background with elements of blue and brown against the boy's pale brown face and a light green blouse. I think Holy feels I'm making progress. Since getting the canvases sent off to Finland I've worked much better. That's partly because I no longer have the pressure of putting things on show or painting for exhibitions, partly because my interest isn't torn between work and emotional relationships with other people, and partly because I've decided to devote my remaining time here entirely to painting. You know that if we feel our work is going in a positive direction, if we're inspired by the urge to reproduce something beautiful we've seen and our thoughts are absorbed only in that, we are happy in our work even if we don't leave our room for a week. I have now succeeded (I think) in liberating myself from the influence of the

Sketch of the criticised picture of the woman with the lilies.

Beaux Arts, those over-admired idols and the urge to paint loud pictures, just to impress. Today I was at the Musée de Luxembourg and noted with a certain satisfaction that I no longer got stuck in front of every canvas, confusing myself with the diversity of manières and styles of perception, but calmly walked past things that did not fit with my way of seeing, and knew for sure <u>what</u> I liked and what I could learn from.

What I like now are the stylised paintings with their emphasis on planes (e.g. Matisse, Valadon), their clean, almost brazen colours. If one can neutralise their harshness with subtle light and air effects, I think it's possible to achieve a really beautiful result.

The other evening, despite my intentions, I went to Boudet for a chat. Calrstedt was there, Relander and a girl who was at Broban (Hageli's mother-in-law is in town so he's entirely tied up with her). We went to the Apache Cellar on the Boul. Mich., which was not a great success, however – Relu and his lady sulked non-stop because they had wanted to go to the music hall and then dancing afterwards. Carlstedt and I both thought that sort of programme would be far too expensive, for which of course the president's boy and the girl (who was invited) had no sympathy. The only real bit of fun (apart from a stain on my coat and an even bigger one, blue, on my behind) was that as I made my entrée, I slipped on the mouldy stone steps and went crashing right down into the cellar, where the tourists took it as an ingredient of the entertainment and applauded enthusiastically. Afterwards, Carlstedt and I tried to liven up our whingeing companions by taking them to a cheap bar on r. de la Gaité. (We went briefly into a cheap snail eatery, too, but when I tried to tell them all what a first-rate place I thought it, they started up their tasteless banter again and spoilt the whole thing.) They were still miserable, though, because the wine seemed the same as the beer at Bronkan. (whose homely atmosphere they were longing for, by the way.) Carlstedt and I decided to enjoy ourselves in spite of them and danced the cancan along the street, which met with silent and disapproving scorn. In desperation we proposed an onion soup at the Dôme. And there, things got really heated. Politics was what had been simmering under the surface all along. The Finnishness and Swedishness question flared up, and Relu and his consort both turned out to be aitosuomalaiset. Just imagine them, a sour and angry little circle in the heart of Paris, quivering with excitement as they hunt out the most hurtful comments, dig their way down into the most small-minded drivel, quote newspapers, shower each other with phrases and insults taken from the linguistic hatred one had left behind in a country one would prefer to remember with warmth – as "home". I didn't say a word for an hour and a half, but then I couldn't hold it in any longer and told them it was the curse of the world, these restrictive boundaries, this racial hatred, this linguistic baiting, this petty "you-can't-play-in-our-yard", this ludicrous labelling, and next time they showed any tendency to start hacking on about politics, I would just get up and leave. We paid for our onion soup in silence and parted without a goodnight. Fellow countrymen abroad! As the Germans say: "Gott behüte mich für Sturm und Wind/ und alle Deutschen die im Ausland sind."

I shall definitely be keeping away from Boudet from now on. Although there was one day when I had a very nice time with a couple of those dreadful fellow countrymen. We haven't rubbed shoulders enough yet, that was probably why. Collianders had found out my address and wandered by to invite me out to breakfast. Afterwards, Tito and I went to Place de la Nation, where a gigantic fairground has gone up. Despite the drizzle we had a lot of fun, went on the bumper cars and the merry-go-round, and saw the naked dancing in pink and mauve lighting, the calf with two heads and the consequences of immorality in wax, and ate candy floss with chestnuts.

I've promised to look after their little girl Maria one evening, so they can go out and enjoy themselves together. Ina has done some painting, mainly in the parks – and the one I was particularly taken with was a window with pink carnations against a grey courtyard. They are incredibly nice, both of them. I've had to revise my old opinion of Tito entirely. Can it be because he's a Believer nowadays?

One morning I paid a visit to the Chataïns, taking bonbons for the children, but it was all very subdued and flat. Perhaps the parents had quarrelled. Next week they are heading south, so "obligations" on both sides will spontaneously lapse, thank goodness. – It has been perishing and thoroughly grey here. A cold has been nipped in the bud with a remedy I bought for 20 fr. If any of you start getting a sore, tickly throat and feeling cold and hot at the same time etc, go out and buy Gonacrine tablets and suck those – they're very good. The nights are shockingly cold, but even during the day I wear my fur coat indoors. The first sunny day, I plan to go back to Nation and draw all the life at the fair. There should also be enough material there to give me the option of an illustrated article. Time for some painting now. A big hug to you all! I think about you all the time.

KISSES
your Tove.

PTO!

Monday. Holy's studio. The model, an amusing little lady in a blue hat against a bright blue, red and yellow background, is just taking a rest. Your letter with the critics' verdicts came this morning, I read them all the way here. Imagine Sigrittan writing so well about me – with a reproduction and everything. You bet I was happy! The thing now is to make sure I don't go and get worse – but I'm not afraid of that any more. I think my palette could get even brighter. Here in

Paris, you can't be afraid of colour, it sparkles everywhere; every little tobacconist's is painted in its own cheery shade and the air makes everything even more brilliant and alive. If I raise my whole palette here, there will still be plenty of time for me to tone it down and refine it back home.

Thanks for your letter! I'm over my cold today, just feeling a bit weak, that's all. I spent Sunday evening round at the Collianders', writing and looking after Maria while they went for a walk round town. They treated me to tea and eggs, coloured the Russian way.

It's hardly to be wondered at, you know, that Irina's mirror model shows the transition from the old era to something new. It was the first thing she painted at Holy's! The model is posing again now.

Lots of love – your own Noppe.

Broban: Brobergska samskolan, a mixed school in Helsinki, attended by TJ 1923–30.

the president's boy: The artist Ragnar Relander (Relu) was the son of Lauri Relander, president of Finland 1925–31.

aitosuomalaiset: True Finns.

Gott behüte mich für Sturm und Wind/ und alle Deutschen die im Ausland sind: God preserve me from storm and wind/ and all the Germans who are in a foreign land.

Collianders: Tito Colliander, artist and author, and his wife, the artist Ina Colliander. They converted to the Greek Orthodox faith in 1937.

Sigrittan: Art critic Sigrid Schauman, a frequent guest of the Jansson family.

VIKTOR JANSSON COMES TO PARIS ON 12 MAY. TOGETHER he and Tove visit his old Parisian haunts, many galleries and spend a lot of time socialising at bars and restaurants. But the surfeit of art takes its toll. "There were too many sculptures", writes the sculptor after visiting the Rodin museum, "but the park was wonderful". In his letters to Signe Hammarsten Jansson, Viktor Jansson writes of the pride he takes in his daughter and the affinity between them. And his love for his wife comes alive through their daughter: "Tove is my companion, but I often get the sense that it is you, beloved, I have at my side."

Beloved!

Here we sit, Papa and I, in my hotel room, drinking Cinzano and eating langouste, with my suitcases for a table. "It reminds me of a time in Italy with Signe," says Papa. He is so happy to be here in Paris that it is a pleasure to hear and see him. Together we search out places he remembers from the old days, your studios, Cawan's and his. Bistros, streets and extra-special corners and parks, and everywhere he tells me just what had happened on that spot, usually finding the setting unchanged. The first day was lovely. He arrived on the train you had said he would take, beaming, but tired after the hardships of Antwerp, which he's probably already written to you about. We took a taxi to the hotel, and its appearance initially rather put him off – it isn't exactly palatial! However, he liked his room, which I'd tried to make as nice as possible – it's on the floor below mine and in the mornings we can call to each other from our windows. After a quick bit of unpacking we looked at my paintings, which he found much better than those I'd sent home, and at my sketches and assorted other things I've acquired here. Then we ventured out, walked along Boulevard Saint Michel down to the Seine and dined chez les Cosmopolites, drank good wine and made quite an impression on the garçon, who is used to less reckless meals. Then we mooched through the little alleyways along the Seine from Notre Dame, where we turned and gradually made our way up to Montparnasse. Papa found it all very changed and exceedingly touristy with all its neon lights, new places of entertainment and its whole cosmopolitan air. We took a table at Dôme's pavement café and sat there watching the stream of people flowing by, complete with all those fantastical figures only Paris can produce. It was warm and a clear, moonlit night, Papa bought me a rose and we drank café noir and Benedictine.

I briefly ran up to Hageli, who lies very close by, and left a note with our greetings when I didn't find him in. After that we took a walk up towards rue de la Gaité, went into a bar or two that Papa knew, got to r. de Moulin de Beurre and then wrote the postcard to you. We mooched around like that until 3 o'clock and finally ended up at Dupont on Boul. Mich where we had choucroute. The hotel staff are terribly interested in Papa and especially, I think, in the fact that we always go out and come in together – it isn't very common here for a father and daughter to so obviously enjoy each other's company! On Friday morning (and I do believe it was the 13th, as well) we took a noir at Capoulade and walked all the way down r. St Jacques together, then I went to Holy and Papa to the Musée du Luxembourg. Then we met up a Boudet at ½ past 12 for a decent French dejeuner, took the métro to Strasbourg St Denis and worked our way slowly along the boulevarde to Place de l'Opera. We bought a few little things on the way, looked in the shop windows, went into a "1 hour's" and generally devoted ourselves to "just being" in the sunshine. On the way home we went along the quai where there are birds, kittens and tortoises for sale, you know, and sat for a while in Parc d'Ile de la Cité which Papa had never been to before! Back at the hotel we found a message from Hageli saying he'd meet us at Boudet, and set off for Montparnasse right away. – Well now – I see this letter of mine has turned into rather a "list" – but I expect Papa, who's sitting opposite me and writing more, will cover "general impressions," feelings, the personal side of things! And anyway, I imagine it's the small details that will be of particular interest to you? Alors – as Hageli still hadn't arrived we had an apéritif in a bistro opposite Boudet. As we were sitting there, Bäcken and wife came by and joined us at our table. We immediately got into a lively debate about art and clean forgot Hageli and dinner. Suddenly Märta said: "Don't turn round – but there he is, and he's got another new one." And he came up, a bit embarrassed and preoccupied, with a very pretty girl in rather a lot of make-up (which instantly put Papa off her!) on his arm. After the dinner, at which Hageli and his lady ate nothing but cheese and stared deep into each other's eyes, we went to Dôme, and afterwards to that Scandinavian place "Nordland". Hageli was completely lost to us and all at once he vanished, along with his young girl. Papa was a bit disappointed at not being able to talk to him as he'd hoped but consoled himself with the Bäcks and the Kræmers who happened to turn up later par hasard. Paris is a small world! (Especially in Montparnasse!) I was very aware that Papa was eager for it to be his treat, really needed it to be, and was feeling so free and happy that he wanted to take the whole world in his arms. So when everyone else insisted it was time to go home, we two went to Boul. Mich. and continued on our own, getting to bed at 3 o'clock again! The hotel is decidedly unsympathetic to the phenomenon!

– On Saturday I worked at Holy's for the last time while Papa was at the Louvre, and then we met for something to eat at Pantagruel (my cheap etudiant place, you know) and then took the métro to the flea market. Poor Papa was tired after his journey and everything, I could tell. But he livened up considerably when I found a beautiful African knife, which he bought for Lasse (and was awfully embarrassed when I started haggling!), and a nice bowl that he immediately wanted to give to me because he found it so attractive. We looked for a necklace for you, but couldn't find anything lovely enough, and as it got hotter we went into a little bar for a beer. And who should turn up but the Collianders! We've already run into all our Compatriots, it transpires, except Relander! Once we'd parted company with them we took the métro to Bäckens where we were plied with apéritifs and cakes and looked at Yngve's paintings. He's done a huge, colouristically magnificent piece for an exhibition here. On the subject of painting – I'm genuinely pleased that Sam got the prize He needed it. I can wait, and in fact I even think it more sensible. I found a droll card with fake lily-of-the-valley appliquéd to a sequin-studded pink bowl and a real blue ribbon round it, and sent it to him with my congratulations. We and the Bäcks dined at r. de Gaité in the evening, and then it was Dôme again! An extremely lively and fabulous night. Around 3 Märta dragged Yngve off home, and Papa and I went over to the bar side. Good grief, what oddities turn up there at night! We talked to an old woman in rags, barefoot and dirtier than anyone I've ever seen before, to Germans, Bolsheviks, Armenians, Swedes, Norwegians, a sailor in a ripped shirt that left his back bare, who later took his trousers off in the street outside to the amusement of the entire Dôme. I stood in a corner taking a spoonful of cough syrup de temps en temps, while Papa made the acquaintance of tout le monde. I could see that that gang of Scandinavians was more than unreliable, but thought Papa would discover that for himself, and that Dôme is something one always has to go through! Around six a brawl became an absolute necessity, among other things a Frenchman came in with a little dog that he hurled to the floor, and was almost lynched for it on the spot. I kept a careful eye on my beloved countrymen who kept trying to sneak away from their drinks and cause a fight. We finally escaped them at sunrise, with me diplomatically deflecting all their proposals of a future rendezvous. We took a taxi back to the hotel and crept up to our rooms like criminals, and slept until 2 o'clock today! Then I came down to Papa and said, "Well, how are you?" "Bloody hell," said Papa. "That's the last time. We've wasted a day – but now it's over!" That made me awfully glad and we kissed each other and went out into the rain and drank beer. Then we decided not to bother with the galleries, bought wine and some tinned food to bring back with us, and now we're sitting here in my room chatting to you. We'll be going out directly to eat and then to the market at Place de la Nation. We're so happy, so close, and perpetually talk about you. Papa tells me about the two of you in your early time here, and how he loves you, all of us. We talk about it all, everything that was left unresolved and has been festering away, and tell each other we had to meet so far away to get close to each other. May God grant it's the same back home as well. – Mama, it's adorable to hear how much he loves you! We write a few lines and then we talk about you. He says you and I should take a trip to Italy together. Shall we do that! – Papa's finishing off his letter now – it's already late and we're going out into town. You're always with us.

Your own happy Tove.

Cawan's and his: The artist Alvar Cawén (d.1935) and Viktor Jansson studied in Paris at the same time and were close friends.
a "1 hour's": A ticket for an hour at the cinema.

SUN 5 JUNE. –38. PARIS.

Beloved Mama!

We're having our morning coffee on the terrace at Capolades, while all around us people are already having their apéritifs. I slept for 12 hours at a stretch last night because Papa didn't want to be woken! We were sitting with Hageli in the Whitsun bustle at Dôme, but I went home earlier. It's cloudy today, rather nice after the past week's sudden heat, heavy and intense with thunderstorms in the air. I expect you are out at Pellinge now, you and Lasse – and Per-Olov is off on his sailing trip. I was supposed to write to him, to you too, long since, but I've been too tired in the evenings. Papa wrote yesterday while I went to a piscine "en plein air" (contd. at home) in Auteuil. I ought not to have left him alone, of course. When I got back he started to cry, he'd been scouring the district for a postbox and a shirt for Lasse and hadn't found either, and was jumpy and upset and sick of everything. I understand him. He's really missing you now. Some bother over his ticket home, little vexations, fatigue, they've all piled up in these final days – not helped, I sense, by his worrying that he ought to be cheerful and keen to arrange our itinerary. Anyway – this is an entirely natural reaction – and I now know for certain that the relationship between Papa and me has changed. I've often felt that we were both so nervy we might burst into tears if anyone provoked us even slightly, but quand même we've stayed good friends throughout – never annoyed or brusque. So I'm not too upset that these last days aren't exactly the happiest and, for Papa, dominated by homesickness – for me our time here has been a lovely, rounded experience in which even sources of irritation and the Dôme have played particular, even important, roles. I do so love Papa. – Just now he came dashing up from his room, where he's busy packing, for a drop of the vermouth we've parked with me and to offload a Stefan Zweig book it would be risky to take to Germany. (He's told you about the revised route for his journey, I assume?). While he was here he sheepishly handed over your present – the earrings and the little heart he'd overlooked in a corner of his suitcase. So sweet of you! Thank you so much. They're just the earrings I've been looking for here, to go with my red necklace. And I've got a few little presents for all of you – I wanted to hunt out lots, lots more – like at the flea market – but our browsing in the big stores has mainly, as you'll appreciate, consisted of finding presents for Papa to buy, and I didn't want to take up any time for myself – you know he doesn't like going round the shops. (I realise I'm writing this terribly sloppily, but I'm a bit stupid after a whole spring, tired.) He wants to take half of Paris home to you and the family! – And, well, I'm a bit sad and disappointed myself at the moment, too – on a private level. Among the Swedes here, you see, there was a certain Birger – awfully nice, attractive, and he made me fall in love with him. Everybody would spend all night at Dôme and when I was hanging about in the bar there, we used to talk – he wasn't drunk like the others and could talk sense and be fun. Now I've found out he's married – his family is arriving today. I can't help feeling it's a low trick to take off your wedding ring when you're abroad. I don't have much luck, do I? I'm starting to see the humorous side to it all, though. And I'm not angry with him. We had a lovely couple of days (at Dôme, that is). Alors. Now what did I want to say? Oh yes. When Papa's gone I shall shut myself away for two days and sew. More fool me, I've decided quand même to go, well-masked, to Beaux Arts' big masquerade on the 10th. Everybody's dressing up á là epoque François I and I'll be able to make a really lovely costume if I have a bit of time. I've already bought the fabrics, at the flea market – the dress itself is to be a stiff, shimmering satin, a lovely bright blue with pale yellow roses (20 fr.!). Gold tulle, floral (2 fr. m), white glass beads and golden net in my hair, woven with curtain tassels. I couldn't help deciding to go – wanted to leave Paris "dans la gloire" – not exhausted and tepid, but with a bang the morning after a happy evening with other young people. Don't worry that I'll very likely see Féri there, after spending time with the Swedes I find his beard, his romanticism, his jalousie and southern exaggeration positively disagreeable. – Today we met Hageli in the street, went for dinner with him, and later we sat talking at Dôme. Then we went to the Pantheon and looked at the great men's graves. That will, I'm sure, be our last "sightseeing", there was some talk of going to the cathedral in Chartres with a Swedish Jelin (who knows Segerstråle very well) but now we've decided to take our last days very easily. And that's for the best. Yesterday we were at Bobino again, the variety theatre on rue de la Gaité. It's a street Papa always makes for. And then I know he's missing you more than ever. We bought him a suit and a smart hat – in green. I think it bucked him up enormously, though he was a bundle of nerves until we finally found something he liked. One day we took a walk in brilliant sunshine all the way along the Champs Elysées to the Arc de Triomphe, looked at the grave of the unknown soldier and then spent the evening at the Comedie Français – "Ruy Blas", a dreadfully overblown verse piece with lots of falling on one knee and vibrating voices. Nothing much new has happened otherwise. One especially lovely memory for me is a morning after Dôme when Birger and I went to Les Halles and revelled in the barbaric profusion and all the colours, along the Seine, into Notre Dame and then to an indoor swimming pool. There's so much more I can tell you, and much better when we see each other. For now, I kiss you in spirit. Say hello to Lasse. It's <u>splendid</u> that he's going to have a friend. And those grades were <u>good</u>. Take the greatest care of yourself.

your Tove.

piscine "en plein air": Outdoor swimming pool.
a Swedish Jelin: The artist Hugo Gehlin from Sweden. TJ also had contact with him later on.
Segerstråle: Probably the artist Lennart Segerstråle.
"Ruy Blas": Play by Victor Hugo.

In June, Tove Jansson travels to Brittany, where she paints, sketches and goes on foot from village to village. One of her best-known Brittany paintings is *The Seaweed Burners*. There are in fact two paintings of that title, both dated 1938.

The Seaweed Burners, 1938.

Beloved Papa and Mama!

Midsummer is approaching, the second one I will be marking without you. I have never felt as far away from you as here on Ile de Sein, an island that seems isolated from the whole world, all of civilisation. And yet there's a lot here to remind me of Pellinge. The seaweed bobs along the bases of the rocks, but with ten times more force – like strong, gleaming octopus tentacles, the surf sprays high over the ground even when the sea is calm, rough marram grass grows on the dunes, where big shells and dead crabs lie in heaps, and around the lighthouses, built into the excavated tops of high rocks. Yesterday I went on a bus to St. Tugen from Pointe de Raz to see a "pardon", a religious procession. It advanced towards a big stone cross which was facing the sea, and the women and men took turns in singing a monotonous song. It was overcast and the dunes stretched as far as the eye could see, with not a single house or bush, just the occasional figure dressed in black. Beyond the ebb-tide beach a streak of green sea and from up in the village the sound of bells and music from the market fair swirled together strangely as the wind began to gust. It was beautiful but tremendously melancholy. – On the way home on the bus I met a woman from Ile de Sein who invited me to go out to the island with her on a fishing boat. I accepted, partly because it saved me having to get to Audierne, where I wasn't even sure I could get hold of a boat (they run at very irregular times because of the ebb tide), partly because the tourist hordes and guides at the point detracted so much from the unspoilt natural beauty of that wild headland. So you might be sitting in a rocky cleft somewhere, looking out over the seething, eddying water or the broom-covered hills – and there would be a sudden bawl of "Anschluss" or something like that, right beside you, and a bunch of young ladies in shorts and sunglasses would scramble by, followed by gentlemen decked out in plus-fours with bulky tele-scopes and photographic equipment, leaving in their wake sweet wrappers, cigarette ends and the echo of over-exercised adjectives – sometimes even a potent waft of perfume. C'est ça. So without a second thought I joined the little rowing boat, packing my things in just a couple of minutes. We went down to the boat, which lay in a deep, narrow little harbour to which we descended by some almost vertical steps, and set our course straight out to sea. On the way we passed a number of lighthouses in which the keepers live for several months at a time – two of them were so glad to see people that they danced and blew us kisses. It was dusk by the time we got there and I found myself a place to stay. A little restaurant, Raz du Sein, a whitewashed, two-storey building with green shutters in a courtyard full of hens and scruffy cats – its windows looking out over the harbour: a jumble of breakwaters and boats. My room is one of the most charming I've ever seen, bright blue with a mountain of a bed, piled with huge bolsters and draped with lace curtains, a Baroque gilt mirror, and nothing else. This morning the sun came out again and lent an intense glow to the golden-brown beaches. I went out to hunt for a present for my female companion from Pointe du Raz. It proved harder than I thought. There are two shops here, one selling fishing tackle, the other groceries. The entire population of the island amounts to 1200 residents. The women all wear black, and are dark-haired – not beautiful exactly, but with purebred, serious faces. At first I thought I kept on meeting the same woman; they all have weathered brown skin, the 20-year-olds look as if they were 30, and they all have middle partings, clogs and those curious black veils that look roughly like this *[see illustration right].*

The menfolk here don't wear those cheerful red trousers, and their boats have brown sails. – Then I finally found two jolly china bowls, which I popped through the window of my lodgings – like all the other women, my landlady was out burning seaweed for the production of iodine. I made a tour of the village – it didn't take many minutes. The houses are solidly built of light-coloured stone and enclosed by lots of walls winding unpredictably this way and that. The streets, if those crooked, metre-wide passages can be termed as such, barely run straight for more than ten steps – and all the doors are turned out towards the sea. Then I came to the dunes beyond the village, where thick, billowing smoke from vast numbers of fires was carried on the wind. I went up to one of the fires, watched them working for a while and then asked if I could help. They let me, but I could see they were thinking: "crazy tourist! She'll tire of the novelty within half an hour". (I'm the only "etrange" here.) But I proved them wrong, because I kept at it right up to midi, and carried on after dejeuner until 3 o'clock when it was all done. And I shall go there tomorrow, too, because I've seldom had such fun. – The seaweed's piled up in huge rectangular heaps where it's been stewing all winter, taking on a leathery consistency that the Bretons call "teil". I stood up there in my swimming togs in the brilliant sunshine, throwing down the seaweed, which was sometimes so compacted you could scarcely prize off a single alga, and then the whole lot is carried to the fire, which is laid over six square compartments in a row, penned in by flat stones. It has to be tended non-stop – i.e. anywhere you see the red of the fire you have to cover it over with the algae. Once the burning is done, you're left with a sticky black mass that cools and hardens – the stuff one used to find on the beach as a child and call coke. This is the most important industry here apart from crab fishing, which I'm going to try tomorrow afternoon – the solid iodine is expensive, costs about 60 fr. a kilo. I enjoyed running around in the smoke and "covering", and it was a beautiful sight: the women in black, the piles of gleaming seaweed against the intensely blue sea with the sailing boats constantly whooshing past. I shall do a painting of it later – I've so many subjects for pictures in mind, for when I get home! We were soon good friends and ate bread and crabs together. When it got too hot I waded into the sea and floated on my back, to their extreme amazement. The algae were so long (just the stems) that I could wind them round me several times and tie a nice bow on my front. There are some nasty little plants here that grab onto your toes if they get within reach, loads of strange algae, molluscs and other damn things lurking in the water, and I have great respect for them all. The jellyfish, on the other hand, are only where there's sand, and the octopuses only turn up in winter.

Oh, and I climbed up onto the warm boulders that are strewn around the eastern end of the island. There was one exactly like my image of the rock Victor Hugo calls "L'homme" in his "Toilers of the Sea," with a hollow at the top where you can lie curled up and scan the sky. The whole morning was one of the loveliest things I've experienced, not least because I got to use my muscles for once. It was so nice to feel one was "doing" something – I'm sure you know what I mean? – But then it was the end of the school day, all the island children came swarming out, and the pleasure was over. They'd never seen a woman in a bathing suit, and the bellowing horde of them pursued me eagerly pelting me with stones, to a chorus of barking mutts. In the end I was so furious that I produced an even louder bellow and chased after them. Panic broke out. Now they see me as some primeval wild woman, likely to gobble them up at the very least. If they only knew I was more scared of them than they of me. I've placated half a dozen of them in various ways, but they're like little dogs that yap at anything they don't know and can sense when you don't like them. Eh bien, I shall keep away from the horde after four and work at home. And there was another episode that did nothing to cheer me up. Someone had caught an albatross, tied up its beak and given it to the kids to play with. The wretched creature could barely walk, the children dragged it along with them by its mighty wings and of course found the bird's clumsy attempts to save itself hilarious. Rien à faire. My attempt to intervene was dismissed as completely idiotic. In the end I walked away, feeling sad. – It's getting dark now, the wind is rising. The light from the lighthouse flickers over my roof and there's a constant roar of surf. I miss you all this evening, though I know a wonderful new day lies ahead of me. I dream terrible things about you all at nights and have already started making enquiries about the availability of boats to Brest. Maybe there I'll be able to get some news of everyone. The postal service out here seems pretty primitive but perhaps this letter will reach you anyway, eventually. For midsummer I shall burn "teil" and think of you all. "Kina vo!" (au revoir). Hugs to Lasse. Best wishes to Impi! Grandmother's already in Åbo, I expect?

A kiss from your own Noppe.

Impi: Impi Hahl. She joined the Janssons as their housekeeper at about the time they moved to Lallukka and lived with them for several decades.

26/6 –38. BREST. [*Postcard*]

Beloved Mama.

It is evening, I am just back from Ile d'Ouessant, a brilliant, warm sea crossing, on which I saw flying fish for the first time. And tomorrow I'm off to Mont Michel, the little island rising directly out of the sea, a vast single rock with a castle on top. I still have a bit of time, and after a brief spell of fatigue and dejection I've regained my wanderlust, my longing to see as many things of beauty as possible. I had two delightful days on Ouessant – bathed in crystal green water and took walks across endless desolate stretches of land with grazing sheep, old ruins and immense, weirdly shaped boulders. There were four great lighthouses there, the Ile being "la clef entre l'Ocean et la Manche". It's an island without men, as they are all away at sea. It was wonderful at night, with the beams from the four lighthouses sweeping over the island. A feeling of boundless solitude. Greetings to Papa & Lasse! Love,

your own Noppe.

Italy 1939

IN THE SPRING OF 1939, TOVE JANSSON LEAVES FOR HER second extended visit abroad, this time to Italy. She feels the lure of Rome and masterpieces of Renaissance art. War is on its way, so there is no time to lose. In mid-April she makes the ferry crossing to Tallinn and travels on via Berlin and Munich to Verona, where she arrives on 18 April. She makes a brief detour to Lake Garda, and from there her itinerary is as follows: Venice – Padua – Florence – Assisi – Rome – Naples – Pompeii – Naples – Pestum – Amalfi – Positano – Capri – Naples – Rome (to which she takes a flight) – Orvieto – Siena – San Gimignano – Pisa – Forte dei Marmi. She spends over three weeks in Rome (5 May–1 June), but is otherwise constantly on the move. At the end of June, Tove Jansson travels on to Paris, where she stays for about a fortnight. On 17 July she sets off for home, travelling via Cologne, Berlin and Stettin, and rejoins her family at their summer place in Pellinge.

As previously, Tove Jansson writes to her family frequently and at length. She documents her travels by means of descriptions of settings and scenery, people and art. She addresses her letters alternately to "Sculptor Viktor Jansson" or "Artist Signe Hammarsten Jansson", but with only a few exceptions they are intended for the whole family. They are written in an easy, natural style with typical curiosity and frankness, the young woman wielding the pen never fighting shy of a challenge. She is indignant about the limits on freedom of movement for a woman on her own, but what matters to her most is following her own travel plans and travelling light.

26. APRIL –39. FIRENZE

Dearest everybody,

My letters seem to be coming thick and fast, but it's as if I want you with me all the time, moving from place to place. And I'm not writing to lots of other people at the same time, as I used to. I don't know how to adequately describe the sensation of happy liberation that's come over me down in Italy, liberation from the self-scrutiny, the sense of guilt, and I don't know what. Another trip and perhaps I shall entirely break free from the persistent "Baedecker frenzy". Travelling in the right way is a real art, and I am going to master it. You mustn't rush round to everything you "have to see" until you turn into a sopping sponge that very quickly feels "wrung out", sated and exhausted – and you experience nothing but aversion and emptiness. What I mean is – in a church, say, don't go systematically round the walls, casting an eye on every relief, madonna or crucifix and then, back in the open air, find you remember none of them, don't just cross off yet another "chiesa seen", but just stand where it's at its most beautiful and drink in the atmosphere, the character and feeling of the church – or in an art gallery, don't pause for a certain number of seconds in front of every picture but, ignoring the travel guide's star rating and the nameplates under the paintings, spend longer in front of what instantly and instinctively appeals to you, and pass swiftly by the others. One simply doesn't have the stamina for too much! Backberg – for example, came back here today after taking an express-train tour of Rome and Naples and was just tired and jaded. The Enckells gave me her telephone number and I arranged to meet her at Piazza Signoria. Then we went up to Fiesole with a Swedish textile designer, Miss Geijer, and walked around there as the urge took us, in a leisurely way without a map. Backberg declared it to be the best day of her whole trip – and why? WE completely unwound, dispensed with any kind of "programme" and were barely tourists any more. We found a trattoria high up on the hill where we could see out over the whole valley and Florence was spread before us, shimmering in the heat haze. Around us the orange trees (yes, finally!), heavy, luxuriant clusters of violet-coloured flowers, irises and little yellow roses growing like trees.

There we drank Chianti and merrily indulged in idle chatter about anything that occurred to us, without a care for yesterday or tomorrow. Then we went into the little monastery up there, where the monk spoke Swedish ("pretty little cells, please to look").

The Schaumans have left now, and send you greetings galore. It was nice to meet them, they were cheery and kind to me. Yesterday I went for a long night-time walk through the town with Elisabeth and we had such a good time together. Sigrid seemed very tired after the journey. Some well-meaning but misguided acquaintance had sent them prophesies of war when they were in Rome, so to Elisabeth's great disappointment they didn't dare go to Naples. To judge what we hear being passed round by word of mouth, things are likely to be calm for a while. The Thesleffs seemed in very low spirits last time I saw them and said very little. Now they've crept away to be by themselves and are already getting ready for the journey home. The Enckells are staying until Friday. – This morning I got myself a tessera for 5 days and went round some of the Uffizi galleries. Then I got carried away at the shops. I've bought a straw hat, a sort of "Viva Villa" sombrero, for 10 lira and a new and bigger bag, plus some gloves for 20. It's simply fatal, getting too absorbed in the shops – they have such wickedly gorgeous stuff. In Naples I'm going to buy white corals for Mama and me – they're cheaper there. If anyone's got any special requests, do write and tell me! The bits and pieces Sigrittan's bringing with her are just a little hello from me. For tonight I've got a new room, which looks out over the Arno. It costs 3 l. day more but is ten times nicer than the other one, which had a wall outside, 1½ m from the window and was bare and dreary. In here, the high ceiling has goddesses and flowers painted all over it, the tiled stove is lavishly ornamented and the bed the same only more so. The whole casa used to be a palace and parts of it are still reminiscent of one.

I've taken a bath and hidden those shoes that pinch behind the closet and darned some stockings. Everything's fine apart from a rash on one hand that the others say comes from eating dodgy seafood. All I had was one crab at Colomba, but maybe it was off. Goodnight everybody, and a big hug! Write and tell me in detail how you all are, especially Mama. Remember me to Gordin, and Ragni and Lauréns. How's the Society of Illustrators' exhibition going? Is Prolle going to lots of parties and did he get through his art history? Has Samu come home yet? And so on!

your own Noppe.

P.S. 26 April. –39.

It's drizzly today. Viktor Emanuel is gracing the Florentines with a visit, so everything is blockato, streets and piazzas and museums. I saw him drive past after a lot of men went rushing around in advance, telling the populace to clap. There are flags everywhere, and colourful banners hanging out of windows. Having found two or three churches that weren't blocked off and elbowed my way along at a rate of about twenty metres an hour, I escaped up to San Miniato and from there tried to make my way to Giardino Boboli. After a couple of hours' mountaineering I found it, but it was closed because the principessa was visiting Pitti. Casa Buonarotti too. I propped my legs up against a wall and bought some anemones, double, 15 different colours and 6x bigger than ours, for 1 l. 50 and now I'm drinking the vermouth Sigrittan and co. left for me. It's pouring down outside.

Elisabeth's bought a genuine fascist cap and is going to wear it for té dansante and so on in Helsingfors. Bellissimo! The compatriots are thinning out. But a few of us are going to grande Opera tonight, at any rate, it's going to be great fun – but expensive. – I'm assuming you won't send letters to the Ferma here, but direct to Rome? I'll go there one more time before I leave anyway, just to check.

P.S. Rash gone. – If you could find a dozen visiting cards, or even fewer would do, in Papa's wardrobe and send them to me, I'd be grateful. – (just pop a couple in your letter)

2 o'clock in the morning. For the first time in my life I've heard an opera that doesn't seem to me like a pointless combination of music and theatre. Il trovatore. Madonna mia, how they could sing! It was utterly beautiful. I got the ticket through our friendly Danish landlady at the guesthouse, and the whole crowd of us went by car, then when we got back she plied us with Chianti and cheese sandwiches. It's so heart-warming when people abroad are kind, slightly embarrassing somehow. The king was also at the opera, it being the opening night of a festival series featuring Italy's leading performers, and the flower of Florentine beauty and elegance was occupying every seat in the stalls. Such beautiful women, such dresses! The rest of us, the plebs, sat in the huge, banked amphitheatre of a gallery, just a set of stone steps really, with little cushions for hire, and so cramped that the whole row had to leave their seats if anyone wanted to go out to the toilet. Now I must sleep and nothing can stop me. Lots of love,

your own Noppe.

P.S. on the way home in the car, I almost fell out on a bend when the door flew open.

"*Baedecker frenzy*": refers to the German publisher Baedeker's travel guides.

Backberg: Regina Backberg, whom TJ met on the first leg of her trip, on the crossing from Helsinki to Tallinn.

The Enckells: Artist and writer Rabbe Enckell and his then wife Heidi.

The Thesleffs: the artist Ellen Thesleff and her sister Gerda Thesleff.

tessera: Ticket.

Gordin: Rafael Gordin, the Jansson family's doctor. See also letters to Eva Konikoff.

Ragni: The artist Ragni Cawén, Alvar Cawén's wife.

the Ferma: Ferma is used as a synonym of "post office". TJ often gives her address as "Ferma in posta", i.e. poste restante.

29 APRIL. –39 [*Florence*]

I read about "Adolt's" speech in an Italian newspaper, but it came across as just evasive, cautious and friendly. You didn't get a clear impression for or against. Here it's more or less exclusively German tourists and not a single English one.

Beloved!

It's still bucketing down on Firenze, and what with that and my head being so full of the art of various periods that I can barely digest it all, I'm staying at home for a few hours. I feel as if I'm working hard – let me tell you what I've achieved in a day and a half. Yesterday I went early to S. Croce, which I think is the loveliest church I've seen here, and stood in front of Robbia's blue and white madonnas, which I liked unreservedly. Then I went round Casa Buonarotti with Backberg, and it was a disappointment to me, you got no sense of the master ever having lived in those impersonal rooms. But museo Archiologico, which we found after a look at Perugino's frescos in S. Madd. del Pazzi, was simply splendid. I had never looked at (or walked past) the Etruscan sculptures and vases before, and their lines and palette – siena, ochre, van Dyke, bright blue and dark violet – were glorious. It has some similarities to the Egyptian, though that has nephrite green or turquoise instead of blue, and the ochre is warmer. Afterwards I didn't bother going back home to Scandinavica to eat. Instead, Regina Backberg and I went to your Barilaristorante on Via den Cerchi before plunging into the Ufficies, where we spent the whole afternoon. I'm not really interested in the baroque or rococo, and I don't get so carried away any more by those Dutch magnifying-glass still lives and minutely detailed portraits or those lifeless, petal-like, S-shaped madonnas on a gold background. Veronese, Giorgione, Rembrandt and Rubens, along with Botticelli, were the best things I saw there. In the evening, after I said my goodbyes to Regina who is off to Nice, I went to a little café with the Enckells and drank vermouth. Today I went to a big Medici exhibition, and the chapel of that same dynasty with its Michel Angelo sculptures and their library, plus the cathedral museum and S. Lorenzo. In a little laffka I found watercolours in tubes and bought 20 of them. They'll be good for me and Mama to have this autumn. All this art can be quite draining sometimes. You get this weird sense of the fantastical number of artists employed through the ages on an even more staggering number of works of art – and all you see is better than anything you can ever hope to produce ... Well, I don't know why, but sometimes it makes you scared of the whole profession. Dashing from one gallery to another here, vaguely worried that some critical development in the political situation could send me home, I can't get on with my own work – but I'm collecting up everything I see and consciously spending longer on anything that could have a positive effect on my own painting. I'm longing to go and see some modern stuff too, eventually. I hear that in Rome there's currently an exhibition of young artists' work.

Tove's coat of arms with crossed pencil and pen and heart. Her caption reads 'contd. in next letter – 2 hrs later – hip hurrah'.

SATURDAY P.M. 29 APRIL –39

My beloved Papa and Mama!

I happened to be sitting on a chair when I read your letter, otherwise you could very likely have knocked me down with a feather. Madonna mia, the blood rushed to my head with surprise and delight. 12,000! And not just because of the money – I have more faith in myself now, and a fresh urge to get down to work and show them they weren't wrong about me. I'm quite sure I'll be able to borrow a brush from the Enkells and paint my anemones tomorrow. So now I shan't be leaving here on Monday after all, and I no longer feel guilty about the shoes that pinch! Magari! I could have sent much posher presents with Sigrittan. And that letter from you both made me so happy, I wasn't expecting anything as I set off to the Ferma in the rain after the Bargello museum and looked for any signs of life. When I saw there was a letter I was so enchanted that I started to laugh, went straight to Donnini at Piazza Vitt. Em. nearby, and ordered the most luscious thing I know, iced coffee with cream. And now I've turned into a capitalist I shall invite the Enckells out tonight and drink your health in "Tears of Christ", as recommended by il professore. The "rhythmic" picture is a birthday present for Mama on 1st June and Papa, you can choose whichever you want and like best. – Never, with the possible exception of when I went off to Brittany, have I had a letter from you at such an opportune moment, when I badly needed one. Now I know all is well with you (assuming Mama's cold clears up quickly?!) and that Polon has passed his exams. – And I also think it's now completely justifiable for me to take a room on half board for a whole 30 l. and to buy some new shoes in Rome. I don't think I shall need more than half the money, and even on that I won't have to worry about my travel and accommodation and can even let my hair down now and then. So I expect I'll be home at the start of July now that I'm <u>obliged</u> (!!!) to be abroad for two months. Looking forward to Rome enormously. Look after yourselves, all of you, and hugs to each of you in turn. – Expect I shall nip over to S. Guiminiano and Assisi sometime.

your own Noppe.

laffka, also lafka: Shop.
12,000: TJ had won third prize in the Finnish state art competition.
Magari!: Of course!

1 MAY –39 [*Florence*]

Beloved!

On this day last year I sat on my own in the Bois de Boulogne eating an apple in the rain and thinking of you. This time it's vermouth with the Enckells, but I'm sending my thoughts in the same direction. I spent all afternoon painting the flowers I picked in Certosa but fear I haven't achieved a great deal. Tomorrow I'll go up onto the terrace and start on landscapes, and that's all I'm going to think about while I'm here. I can fuss over still lives and interiors when I'm back home. I'm convinced I shall be able to work once I find the impetus and get going.

This morning after I'd been round Palazzo Veccio I bought a whole set of materials, 12 little panels, oil, brushes and paint, paper, crayons and a little paintbox – all for 180 lira. So that was a pretty cheap way of establishing myself as an artist, wasn't it? Enckells have been in Venice for a day and it's nice to have them here again, even if I really only see them at dinner. Our evening out was very pleasant, Lacryma Christi and asparagus in a little eating house with lots of kittens running round our legs. We agreed to drop the titles when addressing each other, and later I had a look at Rabbe's sketches. – I spent a whole morning rambling through the Pitti galleries and the Bobolito gardens, then I went to Porta Romana and caught a bus to Certosa monastery. It was extremely attractive from a distance but the interior, or what we were allowed to see of it, seemed to me somewhat marred by all the gaggles of tourists being led round and the monk droning the lesson. I went to fortify myself with green liqueur (1 lira!) afterwards and then took a random walk up a high hill uncrowned by any of the kind of tourist sights that feature in Grieben. It was lovely and peaceful. The valleys with their little houses crept ever lower, the track that wound between grey olive fields and red clover meadows rose ever higher to a tiny chapel, no bigger than our dining room, where there was a monk going round lighting candles in front of the simple images of saints. I picked as many flowers as I could carry, thinking to myself that these hills could very well be the "cassia-scented" ones of the Song of Solomon. And the only people I saw were pairs of lovers. When the sun went down as a mass of dark-blue clouds towered up in the east it was wickedly beautiful, all warm pink, ochre and endless shades of green. – Now there's a radio starting to play some inflammatory speech so I'll go back down into town. Buona notte!

2 May. I've decided now that I shall leave for Rome, via Perugia and Assisi, because the Florentine climate is far too capricious. You've hardly started painting before your subject's obscured by a curtain

of rain, and as soon as you've packed away it clears up, only to pour down again just when you've got everything ready to go out into the wilds. Thorsen, the proprietress, says it's always like that in Florence, right through to mid-May when summer abruptly begins. So as I 'd reached the last thing I wanted to see, Belle arti, I shall leave for slightly more benign climes today. I met Gerda Thesleff in the afternoon and we went out for coffee together. Ellen's quite poorly, apparently. And Sigrid was very ill here for a while before they went home.

I'm sending a letter I received yesterday. I shan't answer it, but feel vaguely worried. Damn it! What could they mean? Anyway, time to send off this letter. I'll write from Rome. Love to everybody from me.

A big kiss x your own Noppe.

PTO!

Rabbe was up at the Ufficies yesterday with his canvases to get them stamped before he leaves the country. They asked him to state the total value of the pictures and he said 5,000 l. The gentlemen stared at him as if paraffinised and then burst into hysterical laughter. In the end one of them, with tears in his eyes, managed to stammer out: "Well, shall we say 300 then?" Rabbe was highly amused. Priceless story, isn't it! Kisses!

Tove

Grieben: German publisher of such titles as *Griebens Reiseführer* and *Griebens Reise-Sprachführer*.
paraffinised: TJ is playing here on the similar sound – and even more so in Swedish – of the words "paralysed" and "paraffinised". Possibly a family joke.

ROME 8 MAY. –39

Beloved Papa and Mama! And boys –

Sitting waiting for my spaghetti in this cheap little some-thing-somewhere after four hours going round a big exhibition of modern sculpture and painting. Overall I find the sculpture better, the quality is more even. But they can paint as well, oh yes. I hope I've learnt something from it all, even though the result at present is mostly making itself felt in my legs. This morning, thank goodness,

I bought myself a pair of flat, boat-like shoes with air holes and other finer points, healthy and practical, so even if my feet look like a German's, I can traipse unbelievable distances without getting tired.

The man in charge at "Flora", a square little chap with a pug face, white hair and jet-black beetle brows has moved me from room 13 to 11. He was incredibly proud to be able to give me his "most elegant" room. I tidied up the elegance afterwards and bought new drinking glasses plus a soap dish, and like the chipmunk in Snow White I cleared a round patch on the window, and discovered that the sun shines straight in there in the mornings! I can also look down over the little triangle of the Piazza (del Biscione), just along from the fleamarket at fiori, where there's a terrible hubbub in the evenings round all the little cafés, and where they sell flowers and puppies in the mornings. The room is pink with St. Antonius above the bed, a stone floor and a bed you have to climb into from a chair. I like it. Perhaps you could send a few letters here, (not registered mail. – I always keep my valuables on me), i.e. to Albergo la Flora, via dei Biscione 6. I'm so enchanted by Rome that I shall probably stay several weeks.

The modern exhibition halls here are amazingly grand. The one I went to today had at its centre a bar and café (that would be something for the Kunsthalle at home) and music, a fountain in the middle, and above it you could look up to the sky through a big, round opening. One side was constructed in terraces of glass with indirect lighting and mosaics, and the water dancing down in countless little cascades. Something else that impressed me very much was Forum Mussolini, an enormous sports hall where I go every Sunday morning. The swimming pool (where I splashed about for 2 hrs.) was magnificent, with mosaic on the floors, ceilings and walls, a café and all sorts of diving and jumping paraphernalia, which rises to the right level automatically. The whole of one wall was a window, the other had vast marble staircases going up it, and the bottom of the pool was turquoise with mosaic flowers. And while I'm on the subject of all things modern in Rome, I must also tell you about the huge Mostra Minerale, where I found myself par hasarde while I was out looking for some ruins.

As big as a world exhibition and quite exhausting, but interesting. They had reconstructed a proper marble quarry, for example, complete with workers and machines for polishing the stones, a tower for drilling for oil, and two mines. Everywhere there was the roar of machines. A fountain sprayed out quicksilver rather than water (you were allowed to dip your hand in it), and there was gold, and mosaic makers and glassworkers producing little spun-glass animals. And they showed everything made out of Italian minerals, from flying machines to cannons and the most delicate goldsmithing.

Home again. The museums are shut today so I've concentrated on churches. If I had unlimited funds to decorate a church, I would use modern art to make it as gorgeous as the old ones. Contemporary sculpture and painting, glassware and mosaic, textiles, metal, marble and gold. Alongside all those studies of the female form, futurist works and tendentious "men of power" at the sculpture exhibition, and a stylised interpretation of the figure of Christ that wasn't at all traditional. As I stood there wondering whether "the masses" here could worship such a naked, modernist image as readily as the old ones, a workman came up, knelt and kissed the knee of the sculpture. I found it very touching. –

Today it's really hot, which I'm enjoying after all those cloudy, windy days. I got myself a "faglio da giorno" from the piloce, who didn't bat an eyelid even though I was supposed to go there three days after I arrived. They take everything with equanimity here. I like that. And I went for a look inside the Pantheon and climbed up the monument to Vittorio Emmanuele. I also saw the dungeon where St. Peter was incarcerated, Matti Haupt's exhibition (there's so much to see here that it got a bit swallowed up in all the rest) and took another stroll round Foro Romano which I think is wonderful. It's the blend of the modern and the ancient that captivates me, and I've never seen that anywhere else to the same extent as here in Rome.

I still appreciate the charm of travelling alone, except in the evenings, when the customs of the donna romana force me to retire early to bed or to look out of the window. An anschluss in the street always leaves me agitated and depressed. The museum attendants are also very energetic in following me arround, they must find their work very boring. Unfortunately they're very boring themselves – whether their job is the cause or the effect, I can't say. Anyway, I get out and about as much as I can and file everything I see in lots of pigeonholes in my head. Sometimes it quite wears me out – but I enjoy it. I'm very glad I moved from Patricia, I'm freer like this and it's cheaper too. In other respects I find it pretty expensive living here, but now I've settled down and "set up house," things will probably be more normal.

Tomorrow I'm going to Karttunen's after my Vatican tessera. Hope she'll take me out one night as I'm stuck with being only a donna! – Every day I think of you all and every evening I hug you goodnight. – Best wishes to Impi!

your own Noppe.

P.S. If a parcel should arrive from here, just put it on my sleeping platform. It will either be some bits of rubbish I don't need, or presents I'd prefer to give you when I get home, because it's fun having "tuliaisia" the first evening.

Do please send me Okkonen's criticism!

Tove.

<u>Send me a detailed report on how Mama is.</u>

fiori: Campo dei Fiori.
"faglio da giorno": Residence permit.
piloce: Joke family name for the police.
Matti Haupt's exhibition: Finnish sculptor Matti Haupt.
anschluss: TJ uses the word in the sense of an (inappropriate or unwelcome) approach, a proposal to keep company with someone, an erotic invitation.
Karttunen: Liisi Karttunen, a historian and correspondent who worked at the Finnish legation in Rome.

In Rome, Tove Jansson meets two young Danes – Hans Jensen and Nils Ferlow – and they travel together for part of her trip. She goes with Jensen to Capri, where they later part company.

17 MAY. −39 [Rome]

Beloved Papa and Mama!

It's late, but I can't possibly go to bed, the warm breeze is blowing in with the distant hum of the city and the whole sky is bright with stars above the market place. Finally the hot weather has arrived.

And <u>how</u>! I'm enjoying it, but not galloping round at such a pace as before.

Mama's card arrived yesterday. I really am awfully glad Per-Olov's taking a trip before he sets to work on the Latin. I expect the boy is in his bunk on the boat right now! – Yes, I found a very pretty necklace of turquoise beads for Emmely, which I sent off together with a letter to Ingmar. – It's nice that you aren't at all worried about me – the hotel, which I viewed with some mistrust at first and reserved my judgement, has turned out to be entirely honest and friendly beneath the grime. (some of which I've rubbed off) It opened about 100 years ago and when you scrub here and there, old paintings and finest marble emerge. In keeping with the custom here I pay my 8 l. every evening, tutto compreso. Once I suggested paying for a week, but this confused and embarrassed the proprietor, and it eventually dawned on me that he couldn't do multiplication! (he let me pay for 3 days. He could cope with that!). I'm still seeing curly blond Jensen and a friend of his, Ferlow, who's a doctor of dead languages, spends his days among ruins and goes to bed at ½ past 8.

One evening when Jensen and I were mooching about we found a funny trattoria in a cellar and went down for a mezzo. We were drawn to an inner room by the tones of a haidar and were utterly charmed when we went in. The owner was standing in the centre, beating time, and the others were dancing ring dances and waltzes by turns, changing ladies when it came to the chorus and laughing and shouting with delight. It was like a children's Christmas party. Jensen and I were so taken with the atmosphere that we danced kasatschka in the middle of the floor. The owner beamed and gave us wine. There were old men and women, and little children of about 6–7, and they all carried on in the same high spirits until the clock struck 2. I thought the whole thing much more fun than going to a palace of dance or a variety show. Jensen was in seventh heaven – the poor chap has been feeling very gloomy here in Rome, and lonely. He was meant to be coming here on his honeymoon but it was all called off at the last minute, so he came on his own anyway. We've been swimming at the Foro Mussolini and we saw a completely ghastly gymnastic display on the sports field, went to the art gallery at Pincio and with Ferlow to the Vatican again. We've also sniffed the historic air of the place where Constantine fought his mighty battle, at Ponte Milvio, but there were so many modern shops there that I felt no sensation at all. Ferlow, on the other hand, was genuinely excited.

Now I shall sleep – Buona notte!

Next day.

Letters from Mama and Per-Olov, both lovely, made me so happy! But right now I'm fuming; can you imagine: I was going to make "dinner" with flowers and wine, a cold buffet, candles, fruit and cheese for Jensen and Ferlow and had already invited them – and then I find out that no being of the male sex is allowed to enter the rooms of a signorina here, not even a family member who comes at twelve noon! What fine imaginations they have. I always feel as if I've been pelted with dirt after something like that happens – but we're going to console ourselves with a trip to Tivoli instead. – Yes, wasn't "the co-op social" a bright idea! To be honest, I knew in advance it would be as dry as dust but I went there to see if I could find someone as all alone as me to see Rome with. We shouldn't rely on others but take action ourselves, openly and frankly, and that's what I did when I just went over and introduced myself to Jensen, who looked the friendliest, and started to chat to him. Before that I just sat at home some evenings waiting for L.K. or Haupt to ring. At any rate, Karttunen sent a card with a very nice invitation to the Järnefelts' for tea – I'm off there in an hour.

It was such a relief that Mama's angina was so short-lived – they can be hellish sometimes. So no more stomach trouble, then? – Well, I have the address of the Thesleffs' seaside resort, it's called dei Marmi. I plan to stay here another fortnight, I can afford it – and somehow the city's assumed a new charm now I can discuss what I see with someone else and am not left cursing to myself about its shortcomings. So it's probably best (though this isn't definite) to start addressing things to the main post office again at the end of the month – or maybe Naples? Because I'm going there first, with detours to Capri and Pompeii. Then I'll have to see how things go. Over time I've grown more and more wary of planning too far in advance, someone or something generally turns up and draws a big black line through it all. – No, I don't put myself under such pressure any more. After 10 days or so I always tend to calm down and then "see" less, but more clearly and rewardingly. But try as I might, I can't get away from that initial sense of the trip being a gift that mustn't go to waste but I have to exploit with energy and ambition to prove myself "worthy". Is that stupid?

As regards the grant, didn't I already write to say I only need the first instalment? I still don't know if it will be best to send it to Naples or here to Rome so I can pick it up on my way back. I'd prefer it in lira, maybe as cheques? I thought I'd come home at the start of July – or around the 15th. Unless the "grant period" is 3 months? I'd very much like to know. I shall enjoy going in Polon's smart new canoe – I'm <u>really</u> glad he was able to buy it. And very much so, to judge by his letter.

I think that, for the moment at least, I would rather show what I've done in my own country than in Sweden. If the Young Artists' exhibition happens this autumn, that is – and I can <u>definitely</u> exhibit <u>at least</u> 8 or so pictures. Fed up with twos and threes. Whether they'll manage to send back my stuff from Gothenburg in time for the autumn show is another matter, of course. (I've always prefered both–and to either–or!) – Today the Pope blessed the whole nation for the first time. Including Jensen and me. We went out to S. Giovanni in Laterano where the crowds had already been waiting for hours, sitting on the grass in the shade of the trees with the bread and wine they'd brought. The place was swarming with servicemen in swanky uniforms of a dozen different kinds and monks in black, white, rusty brown and crimson. After endless splendid and symbolic preparations, music and prayers, the Pope came swaying along on his throne under a fluttering canopy, and stopped on the middle balcony which, like all the surrounding buildings, was decorated with banners in the colours of Rome and the papacy – yellow and purple, white and yellow. The people shouted and clapped and held their children up to the Pope, who rose majestically to his feet and blessed everyone. Most of them fell to their knees. Hundreds of doves were released from their cages on the roof of the church, the monks cheered and threw their skullcaps in the air and the musicians played la Giovanezza. It was very festive and joyous – but quite solemn too, we thought. Now I must get along to the "ministerial tea" rooms!

Evening. Lots of delicacies. Tea like flowers, Turkish cigarettes and Greek nuts and sandwiches like postage stamps with cheese that you had to hold in place with your thumb to stop it sneaking off. The minister and family very amiable and surprisingly trim, given all the entertaining they are called on to do. They knew vast amounts about all the unfamiliar people coming in, none of them sure what to do with their hands, even knew that I had exhibited at the Society of Illustrators, and made elegant and polished conversation with each and every guest for a set number of minutes. Matti Haupt and his impresario of about 25, sporting side-whiskers and 1890s-style starched collar, were also there. They were so full-blooded and bursting with confidence, and illustrated their art criticism and philosophical flummery with such wild gesticulations, that the back fell off a fine old gilt chair. They said life was composed of divine follies and that what made an artist was simply knowing everything, working and not asking anyone's advice. Matti Haupt has never sought advice from anyone. Rome is the only place to live, surtout la notte, but Greece isn't bad either, as long as you know what you want and understand. I understood nothing but still enjoyed myself no end. Then I went to the Spanish Steps and looked at the sunset, and home through the balmy blue twilight. On the way I came across a Cine Variety and went in. It was hard to hear with all the screaming babies and people cheering whenever the baddie got thrashed. Ah, madonna mia, what a city! Now they've laid out long tables down in the piazza for several dozen laughing and singing signore, the womenfolk are hanging out of the windows scolding, the cats are fighting and the bats are skimming past my windows.

Buona notte carissime – hugs to the boys and good wishes to Impi.
your own Noppe.

tones of a haidar: Tones of an accordion.
"the co-op social": In an earlier letter, TJ writes that "the Swedish church's social gathering" with recitations and music sounds like "Pellinge co-operative society, but perhaps it will be all right."
the Järnefelts: Minister Eero Järnefelt and his wife
la giovanezza: Giovinezza, the unofficial Italian national anthem 1924–43.

POMPEII 4 JUNE –39

Beloved everybody!

I'm lying in bed drinking Cognac Medicinal as the Pompeian moon tips over the mountain ridge beyond the garden and the tsetse flies come swarming in along with other creepy crawlies (Hr. Beck found a "bedbug" yesterday), high-spirited after the flaming-hot day. Even as we were driving up to Vesuvius yesterday there was something wrong with my insides and now I've diagnosed it as a slight dose of gastric flu. The kindly Danish couple who arrived recently (del Sole is a Scandinavian boarding house) have piled up half a medicine cupboard on my bedside table, so tomorrow I ought to be able to launch myself at the ruins with fresh enthusiasm. But after that I suspect I shall have had enough of them, and will go back into Naples. Jensen and Ferlow make a detailed study of every single inscription and potsherd, lugging a whole library along with them, and they're so learned and energetic it makes my head ache as I run after them like a little dog and always have to take everything "in order". – and then I long for a letter from you.

Of all I've seen, Vesuvius is certainly the highlight. We set off at 6 in the evening and drove up the new autostrada, which was only finished two months ago. It zigzags almost all the way up to the summit, and then you walk the rest of the way with a guide. Way down in the valley you could see the lava from the 1906 eruption towering up round burnt-out houses and, the higher you went, the wilder and gloomier everything got, the villages and Capri and the sea disappearing in the heat haze until everything was just a confusion of gravel and fabulously intertwining streams of lava, like a snakes' wedding (they were able to set a piece of paper on fire by putting it on lava that was 15 months old!).

We went up the rim of the old crater and down into the cavity from the centre of which Vesuvius hurled red-hot rocks high into the air, and huge plumes of fire at regular intervals. Everywhere you could see it smouldering in the cracks, yellow-green with sulphur, there was a rumble beneath your feet and it grew hotter and hotter. A little newborn crater, 4 days old, was sending out streams of lava right up to our feet, and behind it all the sun was setting amidst the brown vapour. We were allowed to light cigarettes on the lava, the guide holding it up to us with a metal rod, and we sat and looked at the splendid sight until it got dark and the whole thing looked the very picture of Dante's inferno.

Down below, lights came on round the bay like strings of pearls, and on the lower slopes, in the villages – but ancient Pompeii lay there like a black stain. The curious figure (as grimy and picturesque as the most dedicated tourist could wish) sitting by the crater making ash trays out of lava with a soldo coin in the middle came down with us in the car afterwards, a few others hanging on the side. It was the last trip of the day, you see. They bellowed O Sole mio all the way down, making the car shake, and told us in a terrific mixture of five languages about their families, sweethearts and exploits – past and future. The driver attempted to make an arrangement for the next day and, on failing, tried to sell me Vesuvius wine instead, or extract a promise that I'd go to a hairdressing grandmother of his for a perm.

<u>Monday.</u> Today I'm fit and healthy again, perhaps thanks to the cognac, which tasted ten times worse than castor oil, now one's become a meek drinker of wine. I was up by ½ 6, left the Danes to their ruins and took a long walk along tracks between the fields, down to the sea. After an hour I came to a flat, sandy beach where the expanse of the sea was spread out in front of me, with Capri

silhouetted on the horizon. On the way, incidentally, I had a proposal of marriage. A bearded farmer invited me to sit up on the back of his rattling cart, pulled by a horse with red velvet ear-cosies and a pink silk bow on its forehead. The usual questions followed: Signora or signorina? Travelling solo? German or student? and once I had given honest answers, the conclusion was clear, as usual, though he got to work a bit more suddenly than I was used to. (disregarding the hairdresser who tried to kiss me in Rome when I shut my eyes so as not to get hair in them!!!) The farmer took out his wallet and showed me its bulging, grubby contents and innocently asked if I wanted to stay with him in Naples forever. I laughed so much I could scarcely get down off his waggon.

– The water was so salty I could almost lie there with my legs in the air, and warmer than August in Pellinge. As I was the only donna taking a bathe, a lots of boys gathered round me, all singing sole mio and asking if we had bikes in Finlandia, and if I was travelling solo etc. I got so tired of it I said my husband lived in Pestum and I was travelling with a lady's companion, studying Etruscan vases and ethnology. That calmed them down a bit, but sole mio accompanied me all the way home, where I arrived burnt as red as a lobster and feeling as if I'd been soaking in brine. Tomorrow I'm off to Napoli if the bedbugs haven't eaten me up by then.

– 6 June.

Napoli. A letter and a card from home! I'm sitting on a balcony with the whole Bay of Naples below me, on the fourth floor – and watching the twilight come sweeping in over Vesuvius. It's so beautiful it's positively alarming to think of all the lovely things that come to us undeserved.

Napoli has not been a disappointment to me. I think it's magnificent. I made the journey this morning with Mr and Mrs Beck, who brought me to their boarding house. Otherwise I don't think I would have got a room anywhere, because the town's full of Spanish troops, tens and thousands of soldiers, and there's a huge parade here in the morning.

Mrs Beck and I immediately dashed to the National Museum, but they whisked us out after an hour, so we went to the Duomo and strolled up and down the narrow alleys of Napoli, where a new

Italy came alive for me, motley, shrieking, dirty and wretched beyond description, but captivatingly charming at the same time. We bumped into a procession in which a giant-sized saint was being carried round on a litter adorned with roses and Madonna lilies, followed by a brass band playing a – military march! Semi-naked, gutter-grimed urchins by the hundred, priests with candles and standards, barefoot women and shouting soldiers. Now and then the procession would stop and a man would climb up a ladder and pin a 10 lira note onto the saint's garment – and along with the gift a folded note on which the donor had written their request. And then the saint would sway off again beneath the washing lines, accompanied by brass music, whooping and laughter. It was glorious.

Well, and then I went to the ferma. I saved the letter right until I got home and read it here on the balcony.

I can't say <u>how happy</u> I am that Einar is coming to see us. Mama, beloved, <u>isn't</u> it wonderful? Of course I want to be home for that. I'd intended coming in the middle of July in any case, but perhaps it will be earlier now? Naturally I'd be contentissimo if they could come after the 15th, but am happy to travel a little faster if they can't. Here's the route I thought of taking. (not confirmed, I admit – but broadly correct) The day after tomorrow, Thursday, I shall go to Pestum early, and if the Danes have had enough of their ancient remains they will jump on my train In Pompeii and come with me. We'll come back from there that evening because they say the malaria and typhus run riot there after 5 o'clock (!) and then continue our journey, with shortish stops in Salerno, Ravello, Amalfi and Positano to Sorrento, where Ferlow will probably peel off and Jensen and I go on to Capri. My new address is ferme in posta, <u>Positano</u>, and I've given that to the main post office here, as well.

If Hans's money lasts, he'll stay a few days on Capri, and we'll go back to Napoli together – if not, we'll part company there. I only expect to stay a couple of days in Napoli, then I'll go to Rome to pick up my luggage and potter on to Orvieto. From there, after a day or so, to Siena and S. Guiminiano with rather longer stops, and then a day in Pisa. After that it's possible I may have a slightly more extended stay in Forte dei Marmi which is a little way up the coast from Viareggio and finally try to do a bit of proper painting. (The Thesleffs' address) After that, if I still have the time, urge and money to see Nizza, which has always held an allure for me, I shall go there for a while – if not, then straight up through Germany and home. Don't you reckon that's a good itinerary? I think it would be too much to go to some "cooler country" as Mama suggests – I can't digest more than Italy in one go – that alone is pretty strong fare!

It was terrific to hear about Per-Olov's "Big Day" in such detail. As you can imagine, I was with the boy on the day and would have loved to hop over from Rome for that and Mama's birthday! Those marks are splendid. Lasse's are very good too. Hugs to them both from me, and tell them how proud of them I am!!! – I'll gladly send the three canvases to Gothenburg if you want the bother of them – how nice to go there in Papa's company! Thank you for Soc. of Illus. criticism, pleased with the reproduction. Good night all my loves – I kiss you in my thoughts.

Your own happy Noppe.

TOVE JANSSON WROTE SHORT STORIES ON HER TRIP TO ITALY. One is set in Verona, one on Capri. The story "Aldrig mera Capri" (Never Again Capri), describing a donkey ride up to the village of Anacapri, was published in the magazine *Julen* (Christmas) in 1939.

11 JUNE –39. POSITANO

Beloved Mama and Papa!

It seems so long since I wrote – in Napoli, yet only a few days have passed. But they have been so intense that I feel I've lived here on the south coast for ages. When I took the train from Naples I was quite tired of museums, had wandered around M. Nationale from opening time in the morning until four o'clock when they kicked me out. I ate my packed chicken and cheese from the boarding house behind a Venus, a very difficult operation as I had no tools and was obliged to gnaw away every time the visitors turned their backs!

On the way to Pestum I missed the Danes, but they turned up in the temple from a different direction a bit later, so we strolled around the deserted landscape all day. Pestum isn't exactly attractive, an empty plain with bare ridges of mountains on the horizon, stark, silent and scorched, and just a few clutches of whitewashed dwellings – but the temples lend beauty and stature to the scene. They were built in 600 BC and are so well preserved that as you approach them from a distance, their warm ochre hues standing out against a bright blue sky, you feel it wouldn't be all that strange for people from that time to suddenly step out from between the pillars or come walking along the paved roads which they themselves built and which run from the wild meadows right down to the sea. – But the coastal stretch from Salerno to Positano is still the most magnificent of the whole trip. We took the bus to Amalfi because Ferlow's leg hurt, as a result of tripping on a bone at Pompeii and falling over, or so he said. It wouldn't surprise me, the way he kept rushing about with his nose in his "führer" and ferreting in the most unlikely places. He looks like this – and here's Jensen. [*The illustration is lost*]. There was minor squabbling between them the whole way because Jensen had wanted to go on foot, but then we all got bus-sick and went quiet. The road was stunning. It followed the gigantic cliffs into every cleft and round every projection, almost tying itself in knots. Below a stone barrier about half a metre high it was a sheer drop to a sparkling sea, bright green along the shoreline and paler in the shallows, with brown patches of the seaweed visible far out in the water and the sails looking like bark boats. On the other side of the road, the mountain rose just as steeply, dotted here and there with clumps of olives, figs and unfamiliar flowering trees, until it was cloaked in ragged clouds and heat haze. Darkness fell very quickly, and down below, in an expanse of soft cobalt that blurred the horizon, legions of lights were lit in the fishing fleets.

As we passed we glimpsed walls of buildings, the occasional woman carrying a sack of cement (!) on her head, her legs braced like two rigid pegs, a barking dog, a heavy-set man on a miniature donkey, almost obscured by panniers of vegetables, a brightly lit trattoria with youths hanging about the doorway – and all at once Amalfi lay before us, just round a bend, a collection of lights straggling up a mountainside bisected by the river's fall, the majolica-tiled dome of the church gleaming in the lamplight. The young people of the town strolled to and fro along the short seafront promenade in a steadily flowing throng, a group of men on the piazza, and the sand of the little strip of harbour covered in brightly coloured fishing boats and bathing huts on stilts.

Capri.

So silly that when it's one thing straight after another, each new impression overlays and disturbs the other before I've had time to compile a reasonable letter.

Now I'm so full of Capri that Amalfi, which was closely followed by Positano's even more remarkable scenery – has been pushed back as no longer current. In fact, they're all very alike each other in vegetation, terrain and colour, the only difference being that Capri is entirely occupied by tourists who lend the whole place an artificial but dazzling sheen. A chunk of typical Italian landscape is in the grip of north European customs, spaghetti and formaggio make way for "egg and baken" and "gefüllte mælle speise", dark suits for shorts and espadrillos, trattorias for bars, "Sole mio" for the latest popular song from Berlin. The women boldly wear trousers and merrily practise their Italian on beautiful if dirty fisher-boys from Marina Grande, and the men dress as robber barons with red sashes round their middles, Viva Villa sombreros and sandals with thick cork soles. The local population displays no surprise. It picks its way unperturbed across the fashionable kitchen midden of the noisy piazza with its gypsy chapel, drooping palms and stacks of souvenirs, just as it did in Amalfi and Positano; with bags of cement and enormous bundles of grass on its heads, baskets of fish and huge amounts of wine. Cheating the tourists wherever they can. And they seem to do it very well. Luxury hotels everywhere "mit schöner Aussicht, am Meer", Aussichtspunkt, 3 lira, Eselfahrt 20 lira, 5 o'clock tea, Andenken, dernier cri de Paris – vero frascati – "wild, romantisch" – nur 50 lira!

I am pretty flabbergasted but accept it all. I've ended up in a newly built Germania hotel that smells of fresh distemper, thickened soups and sauces, and Aryan cleanliness. My room is white and brass with razor-sharp lighting, its window looking out over an unbroken line of sea beyond a bare, roughcast terrace. Way down there, the funicular crawls upwards like some kind of straggly red beetle, bringing more tourists, always more. They swarm out onto the piazza, jostle on the terraces to see the lights of Napoli and the vague outline of Vesuvius, spill over the bathing beach and go jolting off with cries of delight in a plumed coach pulled by miniature donkeys. (Wild romantisch!)

<u>13th</u>.

Now Jensen and I have paid our dues to romanticism, too – we rode on donkeys up to Anacapri to see a religious procession! My donkey was called Michel Angelo and Hans's was Tiberius. Both had occasional bouts of joie de vivre (the donkeys, that is) and set off at a wild gallop with hoarse bellows of aaa–ii–aaaa, leaving the donkey driver to run after them, dragging on their tails! The local people had a good time and so did we. Then we went round the Certosa monastery, and after that I waved farewell to Hans Jensen in Marina Grande as the tourists frantically snapped up their last souvenirs and the radio of the coastal steamer played "Non si scorda mai".

I, half concerned and half intrigued by my new solitude, took a walk in the drizzle along a narrow winding track that hugged the steep side of the mountain and then descended through the vineyards to a deep green bowl between the cliffs – Bagno Tiberia. The gaudy bathing huts and canoes, the tables with their flowers, the palms, the sun terraces – in the rain and utter silence they all seem strangely out of place. The Capri built up by the tourists loses its life and meaning when they abandon it – the closed bars are more dismal than a populated graveyard! Here I sit in lonely majesty in a deckchair, writing to you. Behind Vesuvius the skies are clearing, perhaps we'll have nice weather tomorrow. [...]

I shall potter along the beach a bit. Hugs to the boys, my darlings! I'm sending you all kisses in my thoughts.

Your own Noppe.
Best wishes to Impi! Address: Ferme in posta. Siena.

S. GIMIGNANO 20 JUNE −39

Beloved everybody,

P.S. <u>23rd</u> card from you!

It's pouring in San Gimignano. Beneath my window, the whole valley is wrapped in thickening grey gloom and rain is spouting from the gutters of legions of tiled roofs. I'm sitting in bed with a quarter of white wine (which I brought with me from the dinner table, against all the rules) plus 4 pairs of holey stockings. Tomorrow I shall go on to Pisa, determined to make time to lean at an angle in the tower, and then to Marmi. There I shall rest my legs, do a lot of laundry, get my finances and correspondence in order, finish off my sketch books and, as the saying goes, gather my impressions. My impression of this rocky little eyrie is of magnificence. Everything in the town is exactly the same as when Dante, Savonarola and Boccaccio lived here – from a distance it looks like a fairytale castle with its seventeen towers. Rich families here would show off once upon a time by building high towers – each one a metre or so higher than its neighbour. There are said to have been around thirty before the most distinguished family lost its temper and pulled down most of the others'. I arrived last night on the bus from Poggibonsi, a terribly drab, boiling hot, silent little town where people and dogs were asleep in every street. I booked myself into "Cisterna", one of the town's two hotels. It was extremely difficult getting into the museum, a door had rusted shut and the attendant couldn't find his uniform cap, which he absolutely had to have on. He spoke with regret of the old times before 1928 when there were still tourists, especially the English – who spent money. "And now, politics keeps them away. Well, we've got the Germans instead. Sisisisisi, they're fine. But they don't pay for anything." (His comment explained why it is that if you leave a shop without buying anything, you get a politely sarcastic "auf wiedersehen" as you go!) Lingering by the iron doors as I came out, he told his whole life story, before slowly closing them at last and taking off his cap.

In St Agostino I was shown around by a melancholy old "padre" who also sat for me. He described the content of every picture in great detail and his language (the best Italian is spoken here in Toscana) was so beautiful that I often forgot to pay heed to what he said simply because I was listening to the music of his language. Everyone seems very friendly and calm here. No trains, cinemas, cars or shops. But the "dolce far niente" atmosphere is more tangible and makes me want to protest.

And then – moving on at 5 in the morning on the bus to Poggibonsi – a train to Emboli, another to Pisa. There I had another proposal of marriage, from a young winegrower – well, you can see for yourselves what he looks like! [*A photo enclosed with the letter has been lost*].

It's a hopeless problem for me, the way they manage to fall in love in half an hour and never tire of wearing out their adjectives. The worst thing is that I simply can't take them (at least not the ones I've come into contact with) seriously. I get the impression we mean more when we say "it's a shame you're leaving" than they do by proclaiming that their hopeless, undying adoration will kill them piano, piano, in an abyss of nostalgia. We had our pictures taken in front of the leaning tower. Unique shot. Completamente a la maniera turistico. Slightly dazed and with a pleased but embarrassed grin. Campo Santo is splendid, especially the "Triumph of Death". The whole piazza with the cathedral, campanile and baptisterium are among the loveliest things I've seen, by the way. At four o'clock I went on to Viareggio and then by tram to Forte dei Marmi. It's so nice to finally unpack all my things and not have the faintest idea when the next train leaves. This is a pretty place. A plage about ten kilometres long, fringed with villas and hotels, and a tiny little town. Not too many tourists and no inflated prices. When I got here I went into a bar and asked if they knew of a relatively cheap albergo. The entire clientele instantly gathered round, vastly interested and gesticulating wildly. They agreed on a private casa and took me to its door, jabbering away. And now here I am, renting, initially for four days = 30 lira (cheaper than Campo dei Fiori!) a little blue room from which you can see out over the sea above the treetops. It's wonderful to be free of those pre-journey nerves, and all those stockings, and Grieben!

<u>Next day.</u> I've consoled myself for your continuing silence by lazing on the sand all morning, like a person of independent means enjoying some recreation. There are no sharks here, they say. But I'm afraid to leave the shallow water even so, because in Capri they grinned at my unease too, and then I found out four children had been eaten up a short time before, not far out from the beach. – (The Duce sometimes graces Marmi with his presence, so it is a very distinguished place.) On midsummer's eve I shall hire a boat and set to sea with wine and cheese. Missing you so much.

A big, big hug from your own Noppe.

P.S. Have my parcels arrived? There should be 2, plus Mama's paints. When are Einar & co. coming? You haven't gone and sent letters to ferme other than those I told you to??? Say hello to Impi. How goes it with Polon's Latin and Lasse's swimming?

<u>Midsummer's eve</u>

Thanks for the card!!!

It made everything twice as nice and bright. Stupid to worry of course, but you know the sort of wild fantasies one falls prey to when there's no word for a few weeks! I'm very happy to hear that Papa is entering the fountain competition – there's no one who makes them more graceful and beautiful. I hope it won't eat up too much of your Pellinge stay!

It's blazing hot – today a heat haze and between twelve and three you feel completely feeble. Lovely to be beside the sea, so I've escaped to the right place just in time! I was out in a "boat" yesterday and hunted for a shark but didn't find one. I did however find a very pleasant gentleman, more sympathetic than the mosaic workers and winegrowers I've had contact with so far, and I went for dinner with him. Sign. Lucio also likes "lazing on the sand" and hails from Rome. So this evening I can mark midsummer in company, which I'm very glad about. La nostalgia, veda. I've paid for a room for a whole week, because I really like it here. No need to send any scholarship money because I've still got loads of money – 2,200 lira and the trip home from Stettin is already paid for. And I'm not spending much here! But I'd very much like to have those 100 marks in francs, if I decide to fit in that trip to Nizza. Do you think I can, or is it insane? But I'll have to see. For now I'm doing little sketches and swimming –

and am very tanned, with bleached hair, and have shed my entire skin twice over! Terribly happy though I miss you all, all the time.

Just think if Ingmar and Emmely came to see us too! What fun! Pellinge is wonderful when there are a few more people around to come along on outings and go swimming. Now I wish you all a bellissima midsummer and send my very biggest

your own Noppe.
Best wishes to Impi!
And Kalle and family.

Sign. Lucio: He and TJ met again in 1948 when she was visiting Florence with Sam and Maya Vanni.
Kalle: Kalle Gustafsson from whom the Janssons rented their summer cottage.

TOVE JANSSON'S LAST LETTER FROM ITALY IS DATED 28.6.1939. It consists of three pages; the fourth and final page is missing. From Italy, she went on to Paris, before returning home via Germany and Stettin.

VIARREGGIO 28/6 –39

Beloved Mama!
I'm sitting on the sand – in a fresh breeze and sunshine, writing to you. I've come in to Viareggio, partly to sort out tickets and money, partly to escape Lucio's imploring doggy eyes over breakfast. It is as you say, five days is the maximum – then you wish you'd preferred your solitary spaghetti! Ah well – I shan't be in this country for much longer. How lovely it's going to be to hug each other again!

The information I got from CIT was pretty negative, but they were friendly and helpful. I'm not allowed to take more than 50 lira (!) out with me because I've got travellers' cheques, and they weren't prepared to change them – because I hadn't spent six months in the country. What's more, we're apparently not permitted to send any money at all by letter!!! But. I can change some lira in France, even if it means I lose a bit, and who on earth can know how many soldi I have on me when I cross the border? So it's all going to work out fine, without my having to worry too much about defrauding the Italian state. And I've ordered my ticket here – as far as Stettin, with 60% through Germany. Besides, I don't think they're going to find out you're sending me francs, but you can always stop the exporting until I tell you I've received the letter. And anyway, I don't need any more for now, ça va trés bien! And you mustn't be at all concerned or worried that I'm coming home via Paris rather than Nizza as I'd first thought.

I had a terribly nice letter from Samuli who's working in Chevreuse, with a level-headed and unusually pleasant addendum from Hebi. They want me to spend the July public holiday with them. I can't deny I'd enjoy it enormously, and I could stay there, near town, and paint with Sam. Marmi's very good of course, but apart from the bathing beach there isn't anything to detain one for very long.

As regards Hebi, to be honest I'm not the least bit worried any more.

I don't know if it's the trip that has helped me develop a greater, and cooler, self-confidence but I think in these months I've made great strides in Gordin's "healthy egoism". My dreadful, misdirected deference to everything and everyone has suffered considerably as a result of having to elbow my way forward among people whose main aim is to live off tourists and cheat them as far as possible, from one town to the next, and of perpetually going on the offensive against their conviction of women's inferiority.

I feel strong and cheerful and don't ask the whole world for advice. So I hope and believe it's satisfaction you feel, more than anything else, at my doing what I want. For emotional and practical reasons, I am initially opting for my old hotel – 56 r. Monsieur le Prince, Hotel Medicis – you know, until I see what Samu's landschafter look like. Write to me there! It's going to be lovely to feel the free and easy Parisian atmosphere around me again. Don't tell anyone, but I was much happier there than in the Roman! I'm going there at the start of July and then home straight after the public holiday. – Yesterday there was a strong wind here and the waves over the sand banks were huge. I danced in them for two hours until I could hardly move my legs, the only bather on the whole beach. Storm clouds and just magnificent. Other than that there's nothing new to tell you except that I advanc- [*letter ends here*]

Hebi: Herbert Rosenfeld, a good friend of Sam Vanni's and TJ's. See letter to Vivica Bandler 16.1.1947.

*"I am never alone when
I talk to you"*

LETTERS TO EVA KONIKOFF
1941–1967

Eva Konikoff.

"YOU'RE RIGHT, I'M YOUR BEST FRIEND – AND I ALWAYS WILL BE," writes Tove Jansson to Eva Konikoff on 16 December 1947. It is over six years since Eva Konikoff, whom Tove Jansson sometimes calls Konikova, sometimes Koni, moved to the USA, but their friendship endures in their letters. It is as if the distance between them brings them closer together.

Tove Jansson and Eva Konikoff (1908–1999) meet in the late 1930s – Eva Konikoff is referred to in a letter to the family when Tove Jansson was on her Italian tour in 1939 – and she moves in the same artistic circles in Helsinki. Among their artist friends are Tapio Tapiovaara, Sam Vanni, Wolle Weiner, Eva Cederström and Ada Indursky. One of their meeting places is the textile and interior design store Hemflit, where Eva Konikoff works and from which Tove Jansson receives various commissions. One of these is the composition of new fabrics, she tells her friend in a letter in 1942.

Photographer Eva Konikoff was born in Helsinki and came from a Russian-Jewish background. As a child, she lived for a while with a relative in Novgorod, probably at the time of her parents' divorce in 1916. She had one brother, Abraham, called "Abrascha", and later acquired two half-brothers when her parents, David Konikoff and Rosa, née Tsibuleffsky, each married again: on her mother's side Ruben Kamtsan (b. 1918) and on her father's, Boris Konikoff (b. 1922). Abraham later changed his surname to Karno (1938). Eva Konikoff's family and brothers are mentioned in the letters, particularly her younger half-brother Boris. At the start of July 1941, Eva Konikoff goes to the USA, only weeks before the outbreak of Finland's Continuation War. Finland has been allied with Germany since the end of the Winter War in March 1940. On 22 June 1941, Germany launches its major attack on the Soviet Union (Operation Barbarossa), and after the Soviet Union launches attacks on coastal defences and bombs towns in southern and north-eastern Finland, Finland finds itself at war on 25 June. The events of 22 June are described by Tove Jansson in a dramatic letter from Pellinge, dated the same day: "Then the news came on the radio down at Kalle's. Papa just came in and said 'Well that's it then'. Nothing more was said, we just each of us went and got on with packing our own essentials."

Eva Konikoff goes first to stay with her uncle, Joseph Konick. There is no direct explanation in the letters of Eva Konikoff's reasons for emigrating, but she is clearly seeking new directions in her life and profession. The political situation is very fraught and for anyone hoping to get away it is a matter of leaving while one still can, before the borders are closed. "I'm glad you made good your escape – after the war things could get distressing here in so many ways", writes Tove Jansson after receiving her first letter from her friend in the USA. Eva Konikoff is as free as a bird and wants to move on, according to Tove Jansson's later characterisation of her. That image recurs in more specific form in the short story "Brev till Konikova" (1998, Letter to Konikova). "Once you said you felt like an albatross and I thought that was laying it on a bit thick, but now I understand better."

When their correspondence starts, in June 1941, Tove Jansson is twenty-six. For the young painter, Eva Konikoff represents freedom, strength and will and she often writes about the resilience of their friendship, the mutual candidness that binds them together. They see each other outside Helsinki circles, too. In the summer of 1940, Eva Konikoff visits Tove Jansson in the island community of Pellinge where the Jansson family rents a house each summer. The following year, Tove Jansson starts a painting of her friend, entitled "Eva". The model sits legs apart, hands clasped, her arms resting on her legs; she is looking to one side, not posing. A free woman, that is Tove Jansson's perception of her friend. After Eva Konikoff's departure, she repaints the background and changes the light. The picture is shown just once, at the Young Artists' exhibition of 1942. The artist subsequently makes a gift of the painting to the sitter.

The first letter from Eva Konikoff reaches Tove Jansson in August 1941. Postal services during the war are unreliable and many letters are returned to sender unopened. There is also censorship to contend with. "I don't think you've received any of the letters I've sent over the past few months – but it's been a joy for me to talk to you anyway", writes Tove Jansson in January 1942. She is a scrupulous correspondent and numbers the letters for the sake of good order.

Tove Jansson's longing to see her friend is evident in letter after letter, but they do not meet again until the autumn of 1949. On that visit, Eva Konikoff is also a guest at a meeting of the Amateur

Photography Club in Helsinki (15.9.1949), speaking on the subject of "photography in America and showing her own picture collection" according to the minutes. The minutes also note that the "interesting pictures, which differed in some respects from Finnish perceptions of artistic photography, generated lively discussion." That same autumn, Eva Konikoff takes a series of pictures of Tove Jansson in the studio in Ulrikasborgsgatan and Tove Jansson comments delightedly on these in a letter in February 1950 (23.2). They meet on several other occasions in Finland, and on Tove Jansson's round-the-world trip with Tuulikki Pietilä in 1971–1972 it is Eva Konikoff who books their hotel in New York. She also visits them on Klovharun a few times. But Tove Jansson's dream in the late 1940s to go and visit her friend in New York is never realised.

In her letters to Eva Konikoff, Tove Jansson writes about herself. The letters turn into a diary, written to "Koni", and through them, she creates someone "to talk to". This is an expression of extreme closeness and Tove Jansson uses it again and again: "I seem able to talk to you about all my great joys, all my agonies, everything going on in my head – there's no one else I can talk to as I do to you" (August 1946). In her letters to Eva Konikoff she writes of her wish to dare to live her own life, her quest for an identity as an artist, as a social and sexual being. But in her choice of lesbian love she finds no support from her friend. When Tove Jansson writes of her plans to go over definitively to the "ghost side" (ghost being used as a synonym for lesbian) in the early 1950s, she makes it clear that this is her own decision and no one else's: "I think I finally know what I want now, and as my friendship with you is very important to me and is very much founded on honesty, I want to talk this over with you. I haven't made the final decision, but I'm convinced that the happiest and most genuine course for me would be to go over to the ghost side. It would be silly of you to get upset about that" (28.2.1952).

The letters to Eva Konikoff chart the changes in Tove Jansson's life from her time as a young painter in wartime Finland to the hectic existence of the famous Moomin author in the 1950s and 1960s. Here we find probably her most candid accounts of life during the war, encompassing both family and friends, reflections on the theory and practice of painting, declarations of principles in the art of painting self-portraits, and accounts of the emerging, developing world of the

Moomins. One of the letters contains what is probably Tove Jansson's earliest introduction of herself as author of the Moomin books.

The correspondence extends over twenty-five years from 1941 to 1967 and comprises some hundred letters. The intensity of the letter writing declines with time and distance, but the friendship endures. At the same time it is clear that the correspondence changes in content and becomes more sporadic. The frequency and length of the letters is most marked in the 1940s; in the war years, Tove Jansson sometimes writes two or three letters a month, but later the intervals grow longer and there is a period when they try keeping in touch by means of postcards. After 1951 there are only about ten letters. Eva Konikoff is clearly the one most keen to keep the correspondence alive. On St Lucia's Day 1962, in her penultimate letter, Tove Jansson writes:

> You know what, I strongly suspect nothing can come of our correspondence, which we have restarted so many times. With great Solemnity and Resolve and Explanation!
>
> Instead, let's do this: occasionally when the spirit moves us, a little card like this. That doesn't tie us, it's a fleeting smile, a signal that we haven't forgotten, though time and distance fracture our intimate contact.
>
> Is that *all right*? I think so.

The letters to Eva Konikoff became the material for one of Tove Jansson's last short stories, in her collection *Meddelande* (1998, Messages). Alternative titles Tove Jansson experimented with are "Portrait of a Friendship", "Early Friendship", "To my Albatross" and "Just Before the War". The idea was to write a novel, but the material was hard to work into shape. She went through the correspondence and wrote notes on scraps of paper that she tied up together with the bundles of letters. The notes might read "checked through; some transferred, leave the rest" or "checked through – unusable", or simply "twaddle". But what recurs in her drafts is the impossibility of writing about the war – which she describes as the hardest time in her life. "Old letters are dangerous, and it's hard to fathom that all of that no longer exists unless I breathe life into it – and I can't", says one of her notes, made in 1993. Later she writes: "I visualised a book about the Winter War and Eva's brave new life in America as background, and it would have been illustrated with her terrific photographs of Harlem and Manhattan. Then Helen Svensson came and said: how about boiling it down into a short story? That's not the first time she's helped me when I've got stuck." (Letter to Boel Westin 9.3.1998).

Tove Jansson got her letters to Eva Konikoff back from her friend in the USA. Like the correspondence with Maya Vanni, the addressee was urged several times to burn letters – "Kisses and please, burn my letters" says a letter written on 28.2.1952, for example – but we do not know whether any really were burnt. The letters that Eva Konikoff wrote to Tove Jansson have not been found. But the letters from Tove Jansson to her friend Eva Konikoff can be read as living conversations, even though only one of the parties speaks.

* * *

10/6 –41 H:FORS TO EVA KONIKOFF
ADR/ JOSEPH KONICK. C/O SYLVANIA HOTEL. BROAD &
LOCUST. AT JUNIPER. PHILA. PA.
– FROM TOVE JANSSON. APOLLOG. 13, H:FORS FINLAND.

The whole of Hemflit and Gylling send their greetings! (Getting the table soon.)

Dearest Eva!
Now I know from Pergament's telegram that you've safely arrived in the new country, and can write the letter I've been postponing, out of childish fear of tempting fate.

Eva dearest, I've been following your whole journey! Twice I was gripped by terrible anxiety, thanks to people's baseless rumour-mongering. Now it's all fine and I'm glad you have left this whole merry-go-round of ours behind you – though I miss you, enormously, every day. I got your letters on Åland, and cycled a long way so I could read them in peace, to a hillside of birches with drifts of wood anemones and placid sheep.

In my studio I found you everywhere in the things you had given me, there are so many places in town where you still walk beside me – and to start with I was often on the verge of ringing you when I felt like a chat. And Tapsa ran after a girl the whole length of Alexandersgatan because she looked like you!

But of course there isn't anyone like you! It feels empty without you, Konikova. As the train carried you away I had a feeling that we would meet again very soon. And I still don't think it will be too long. In Karis I overtook Issi who was on his way to you, but hadn't time to talk to him – chuckled to myself; I knew he would come! And then I found myself on Åland, leading a peaceful existence in which the frenzy of Helsingfors just melted away.

I sat shivering in an empty sailors' hostel as the foghorns wailed in the harbour. The very next day I went off to a remote part of the island, where I spent long days strolling in the birch-dotted meadows and along the beaches. All at once the weather turned warm. I borrowed a dilapidated little rowing boat that had to be bailed out after every 20th oar-stroke and then pottered round the coast stark naked, made fires and cooked food, painted, went swimming (it <u>was</u> cold, the floes of ice were coming in from the sea in great log jams!), read the legends of Paul and generally felt I was living in paradise. I saw neither houses nor people on my excursions, but in the evening I sat in the inn and had a leisurely chat with Villebisin about drought, leaseholds, cows and the injustices of the world.

[...] The sun shone day in and day out, I ate card-free and got a tan, and Villebisin's unruffled calm crept over me. But in the end the superintendent's conscience got the better of her and she went back to Mariehamn to look after the exhibition. Just a single picture had sold – a little Carlstedt, but the Ålanders' own works, which they had mixed in with ours, sold splendidly. No wonder, as their prices were in the hundreds and ours in the thousands! And besides, they have such "natural colours", you see! As consolation I was invited to dinner at the town's smart clubhouse, and then I gave myself a present of two of those charmingly romantic shell boxes I used to long for when I was little. Then I left all the pictures I painted on Åland unframed at the exhibition, finished painting the last one at the sailors' hostel in the hours before my boat was due to leave, and put Åland prices and names on them, like "Fog Lifting at Lotsberget in Geta", in the most shamelessly literary and unartistic way. But it worked! "New ÅLAND views!" announced the newspaper. Direct from our landscape! And "Fog" sold on the spot, along with another canvas, to the Collections. So now I'm almost immortal, and my trip is paid for! The newspaper wrote really nicely about the way I "practised my cherished artistic craft on their cherished island." (How horribly easy it would be to get rich.)

Back in Lallukka, Ham and I felt the urge to get away from home and work, so the gents were dispatched to Pellinge to dig the soil and we went to Ekenäs to meet Prolle and celebrate Ham's birthday. It was a cheery, festive little trip, which we made the most of in every way. Prolle instantly showed us his latest short story, which was the best thing he had ever done – but too long for a newspaper. So we solemnly decided that he should start work on a short-story collection. He looked hale and hearty and was pleased to have been selected for a radiotelegraphy course, which he's very interested in. In July, when Ham's free, he's going to put in for a week's leave with us at Pellinge.

We've sent Lasse to Jullan's for June, to their place in the country outside Åbo, where he's busy swapping stamps with his uncle, collecting butterflies, and has to our dismay started writing another novel. He went up to seventh grade unconditionally, thank goodness! Papa is busy with another fountain, which is going up in the courtyard of the new building beside Bronkan and Lyhty on Espen. He was ill the other day and was overwhelmed with anxiety. We'd been at Ragni Cawén's 50th birthday party, where everyone was dressed up as Orientals with their faces painted brown, and laid their gifts, food and wine before the guest of honour's throne, above which I'd painted big angels carrying horns of plenty. It was a very lively occasion and Papa came home in the morning without his coat after roaming round town with a friend. They drank some arrack punch and then dashed out for a long Sunday family walk. And when Papa started getting stomach pains I assumed he was growing old and couldn't take much any more! I do so much hope my papa Faffan will never fall <u>seriously</u> ill – he would never cope!

The day after tomorrow I'm going out to Pellinge – with Carin! There's no one there until midsummer, after all, and then she'll come back in again while I stay to receive the rest of the family.

She's intensely looking forward to revisiting the island where we had such a good time together back then and I think she needs to get away from that Brandö café for a while. She's moved her stuff there from Fernanda and now devotes herself mainly to cooking for the Weinars, while all the melodramas of that hot-blooded family crash daily around her poor head. She was shattered and very down one day when we were at the swimming baths, and assured me most definitely that she was going to wait not six months but a full year before her wedding. (I don't think it's ever going to take place) Wolle's doing nothing to win her over, control himself or try to adapt – and when he sees fit to be in a bad temper, the whole of Brandö Manor shakes. But Carin is taking on as much work and drawing as she can get. She did a really lovely cover for the anniversary edition of "Seven Brothers". She's sticking to it, not giving up even though she has to battle, not only for him but for work and painting and freedom. She hopes she'll be able to change him. (<u>Can</u> you change someone??)

Rosa's got to go to a sanatorium over the summer. The doctors claim the problem is not so much her lungs as her nerves. She doesn't <u>want</u> to get well, she says. She's bitter, irritable, with violent mood swings. On top of it all, she's fallen in love – and it's her first time. Poor little girl! She asked eagerly after you and sends her greetings – as does Karin.

Today I was out at Samuli's with a little picture and had a look at what he's been painting. Loads of new canvases, mostly of Maya. Nothing completed, but solid and promising. We took a stroll to Taru across the bridge, but it was a quiet walk and the conversation didn't really take off – except when we got onto art. We're slipping further and further away from each other, I'm afraid.

But I've grown closer to Tapsa. His strength and sensitivity are things I've only gradually discovered, and it's taken me even longer to realise what he means to me. We often talk about you, and he sends you warm wishes. Turtis, too. (Elvi is unavailable again). Tapsa has had a huge job, illustrated poems of Edith Södergran for Söderströms. He's made them light, ethereal – nothing of his usual heavy style. They're very good. – I've also got a commission, from the rubber industry this time! 2 big marquetry pieces, made of rubber. I shall take the job to the summer cottage with me. I'll write to you from there next time. Mama and all the rest send their very best wishes! Everyone who knows you sends greetings, and thinks and says nice things about you. And that makes me feel glad and proud to be your friend. In my thoughts I'm hugging you – hard – and wishing you all the nicest things I can imagine.

Be happy, Eva!

Tove.

P.S. Jukka's married now. I only got your last letter when I was back in H:fors so I wasn't able to look up Isa as I'd otherwise have done. – My cousin Meri from Åbo has a job in a bank in H:fors for the summer. I'm in deep water there, because we have to spend time together for the sake of the family, but we don't get on at all. Seldom was there a less compatible pair of cousins! But now I'm off to Pellinge. Bye!

Let me know what date my letter reaches you.

card-free: During the war, Finland introduced ration cards for a series of foodstuffs and other products.

Villebisin: Old man Ville.

superintendent: TJ had been appointed the superintendent of an exhibition of Helsinki artists in Mariehamn on the Åland Islands.

Jullan: Julius (Jullan) Jansson, Viktor Jansson's brother.

Espen: The Esplanade in Helsinki.

Carin: Carin Cleve, TJ's friend from her time at the Technical School in Stockholm, has many pet names; in the letters she is referred to as Cajsa, Caj, Caja, Cajso, Cajo and Clevan.

Wolle: Wolle (Woldemar) Weiner, artist, stage designer. TJ sometimes writes "Volle".

"Seven Brothers": 1870 novel by Finnish author Aleksis Kivi.

Rosa: Rosa Linnala, a fellow student.

Maya: Maya Vanni, see Letters to Maya Vanni.

Tapsa: The artist Tapio Tapiovaara, her fellow student at the Ateneum in Helsinki.

Turtis: The author Arvo Turtiainen.

Elvi: The author Elvi Sinervo. Both she and Turtiainen were members of the left-wing Kiila group and opposed to the Continuation War.

BORGÅ STOR-PELLINGE SÖDERBY. 20/6 –41
[Place names later crossed out]
TO MISS EVA KONIKOFF. JOSEPH KONIK.
C/O SYLVANIA HOTEL.
BROAD & LOCUST AT JUNIPER. PHILA.PA.
FROM TOVE JANSSON. APPOLLOG.
13 HELSINGFORS. FINLAND.

Mama and Papa send greetings! As do Impi, Carin, Volle and Rosa. – On Åland I sold two of the things I painted there – one to the museum in Mariehamn. I previously sent you one airmail and one ordinary letter.

Dearest Eva!

Now I'm all alone again, and the sun is back and the sea is a mass of white geese. Cajsa and I were up before six and rowed down parallel to the mainland in a heavy swell and with a broken rowlock – one oar shattered and we got lots of blisters on our hands! But I came in smoothly alongside The Lovisa and Clevan was up the ladder like a streak of lightning. Just think, this is my eighteenth year here yet I've always let Kallebisin do that manoeuvre – just because Faffan said it was too hard! Stupid.

Now I'm going out to tidy the plot and make the house look nice for midsummer. The bog myrtle has come up in the marsh and the meadow flowers are finally appearing. Tomorrow the family will be coming out here. I so look forward to seeing them but it was a bitter disappointment that Carin had to leave before they got here. We had such a happy week together – and it pained me to have to send her back to the hell of Brändö. Because it must be hell, from what I can gather. Volle is very erratic and spoilt and curtails her freedom with his envy and egoism, and the atmosphere out there is thick with opposition and family scenes. They have scarcely a single interest in common. I know now that she only sticks to him out of sense of responsibility and regrets the whole thing bitterly. Poor little Cajo. She's bought her "freedom" with new bonds – but I wonder if it will be long before she breaks those, too. She's grown stronger than I thought she possibly could.

Almost every day at this time it's been rainy or overcast, and the last two days a dense yellow mist rolled in from the sea to settle suffocatingly over us, obliterating everything. It made us quiet and listless, and Carin said it seemed "the will of Fate", somehow. And she was right, actually. But in the background there was a more palpable unease, a sense of waiting that was worsened by the mist. There have been a lot of rumours going round for a long time – enough to make me shy away at the sight of any other human being in the hope of hanging on to some semblance of calm and some of the pleasure of being out here with Cajo. There's been alarm in the air everywhere, everybody knows so much, and yet nothing ...

One day when we were busy digging a channel from the bog in the diamond valley, a pilot turned up all out of breath with an express telegram from Volle. When we dashed up to telephone he was in a complete panic and wanted Carin home right away. The ass had rung Ham several times and put all sorts of nonsense into her head, so I had a very anxious letter from her. About Prolle, of course. Oh, these people! Can't they leave us in peace for this short time we might have for enjoying summer and freedom! Caj was hopping mad with him and stayed put, of course. But the rumours grew and it was as if a big shadow had passed over our summer.

Abbe took Ragni's new sailing boat over to her in Köttboda and we were allowed to follow behind in the motor. On the way home the wind really blew up, it was cold and grey. In the middle of the bay a motorboat came towards us, full of earnest Pellinge men, it stopped and brief orders were barked out to us, which we were to pass on. It was like the primitive relays they used for messages hundreds of years ago. Abbe went off the same evening. – I had a letter from Tapsa, he isn't in town any longer either. A melancholy, yearning sort of letter. Written as if it's all over already – about how he's been fortunate, and is thankful for his life. And grateful to me.

And now I'm walking around outside and it's all so exquisitely beautiful that one simply can't grasp how people <u>can</u>. One finds oneself living with such intensity, every hour of the day, like no summer before. And yet I still believe – when I let reason speak – that it's nothing. The whole summer will probably be as lovely as it is now. We shall meet again – all of us. Prolle's coming home on leave, I shall take the boat into town and see Tapsa again. He wanted to come here with us – I felt dreadful having to say no. Why can't we sometimes throw aside prejudice and stupid discretion and accept whatever pleasure comes our way and try to love each other even better, even more warmly! When we know so little of how long we will be able to keep each other. –

Cajo and I had a sauna yesterday. I went up the hill on my own to cut a birch switch because Carin was scared of the horses. The sky was coppery red and the sea yellowy grey, and there was a strangely becalmed sense of anticipation everywhere. After the sauna we solemnly lit one of your candles and made tea in the cottage.

22.6

Sitting aboard the Lovisa as she heads towards town, fully loaded – perhaps the last trip she will be able to make. It's been a peculiar day. Ham and Faffan came out yesterday evening to celebrate midsummer, we had a lovely, happy evening unpacking all the goodies they brought with them and inspecting the garden plot, Laxvarpet and all the preparations Cajso and I had made indoors – and a peaceful, sunny morning of "just being" and letting all the glory of summer stream over us. How we've learnt to enjoy everything these days! We can't just take it for granted any more – it has to be seen as a gift.

Then the news came on the radio down at Kalle's. Papa just came in and said "Well that's it then". Nothing more was said, we just each of us went and got on with packing our own essentials. We left the cottage with its fine array of flowers in every room and the rugs still down, and we finished off by watering everything on the plot. Whoever harvests it in the end they do need it, those poor little things that are just shooting up in earnest. Ham stayed completely calm and went round humming and talking about everyday things. But she was white under the eyes.

It took us several hours to toil through the woods with all our luggage, stopping for a rest now and then. It was hot, with mosquitoes. And so beautiful. White bog myrtle in all the marshes, new flowers coming into bloom. The elks were grazing on the meadow at Hempeltängen. I had to turn round halfway and dash back for the ration cards, which I'd forgotten.

[2 illegible lines]

I haven't really taken it in yet. At Pellinge jetty there were lots of people waiting to lug all their hastily assembled possessions onto the boat. And now here we sit, engaging in small talk and waiting. It's the first time I haven't felt glad to come into town from Pellinge.

But there's one thing I'm glad about – and that's you being over in America!

25 June.

Hi, Konikova! It's 7 in the morning and we are sitting in the air-raid shelter feeling sleepy. The evening we returned to town, the first warning sounded; we'd hardly had time to make a cup of tea and get off to sleep. So now we're back in the old routine of going with Jorma to inspect what stores we have in the building, the group with guard duty and the ugly old clatter of boots beside one's bed. Ugh. And as a strange background there's the summer, sunny and glorious.

The day before yesterday Tapsa rang, just as he was about to climb aboard the bus with the others to go "somewhere". He was terribly down, could hardly say anything on the phone. – Carin's going home, having had a series of panicky telegrams and telephone calls from Siri. But she'll stay as long as she can with Volle, who's volunteered as a medical orderly, to make their time together as warm and pleasant as possible. Fernanda has already left. Yesterday I was out on Brändö and went for a stroll with Cajso, Volle didn't want to come. He has no enthusiasm for anything now. It's hardly surprising Carin generally finds it so tedious out there. [...]

– Out on Brändö they had kittens, black-capped, miniature versions of Mosse. In a fleeting moment of madness, I brought one of them with me in a box, fixed to the handlebars of my bike. It was a real nuisance to get home, because it kept poking its head out and ripping holes in the box. But it proved a true success. Papa, who's busy with his fountain, abandoned work to crawl around on the floor and play with balls of paper. Impi provided a descant, mewing along in delight, warmed some milk and was very touched. And Ham was also
[2 illegible lines}

I'd intended borrowing it for two or three days – but it looks, may the muse preserve us, as though it's going to be longer ...

Gylling's desk has arrived and I had a sort of nervous shock when I saw the thing, it was so much like a director's desk in some ghastly office. The man had painted it a dreary dark-mahogany colour instead of light walnut. All my things shrivelled and died beside it. I rushed out and bought all sorts of paint strippers and steel wool etc. to add to your paint remover and methylated spirit and then I scrubbed away at it all midsummer long. So now it looks about 100 years old, covered in spots and patches, the wood all roughed up; Ragni would be absolutely ecstatic about the piece of junk and Gylling would be appalled. Now it fits in with the studio and doesn't turn me into a director. – Terribly long air-raid warning, this one. There are big bangs outside. –

27 June.

4 air-raid warnings before breakfast. It's all underway in earnest now and one dreads the news. Things are hot where Prolle is. Mama is tired and depressed. Little Mosse lightens the domestic mood a bit. Lasse is still at Jullan's. I've been slaving over the Garm seaside issue to take my mind off things.

Koni, I miss you! But everything will be all right – it has to.

Fondest love

your friend Tove.

PS Lasse writes from Jullan, sad and lonely, saying he wants to be with us. Faffan thinks he's better off staying put, but around Åbo is where things are worst! And of course we want to be together.

Lovisa: The name of the ferry that the Jansson family took to get to the summer cotttage they rented in Pellinge.

Kallebesin: Old Man Kalle, Kalle Gustafsson.

Laxvarpet: A bay where TJ's brother Per Olov and his family later had a house.

Siri: Carin Cleve's mother in Stockholm.

Garm seaside issue: TJ was a contributor to *Garm* (1924–53), a Finland-Swedish political and literary comic magazine. She first had a drawing published there in 1929. In the 1940s, TJ was its main illustrator, producing both comic drawings and pointedly political ones.

4/8–41 BORGÅ. STOR-PELLINGE. SÖDERBY

Dearest Eva!

I assume you haven't received any of my letters, as I've heard nothing from you – but I can't help writing sometimes all the same, when I'm particularly longing to have you with me again. Perhaps we'll each get a pile of letters when the war is over and be able to follow what each other been up to better than if we had exchanged summaries of everything that happened. And how many impressions and events there must be in your case! So many people have phoned to ask if I've heard from you it's made me feel so glad and proud to have people suppose I'm the one with "the latest news"! When can I start writing English to you, *my dear old miss*? And when can I dare to start dreaming about coming to you – because that is a thought, a resolution, I have not relinquished in any way! Here at Pellinge, where Lasse and I have now been for a week, I sense your presence so vividly. Everywhere I walk I remember the way it was for us in this same place a year ago. Two of the happiest weeks I have ever experienced at Pellinge!

5th

Just at present an idiotic blocked nose that I tried to get rid of by going for a swim has turned into a really bad cold – I only crawl out of bed to throw something edible in the pot occasionally but am otherwise reading a humorous tome by Jules Verne, found in pieces (the book, that is) by Lasse in the attic. I lie here looking at the birch tree outside my window, which rustles like a thousand silk petticoats – the sea is a greeny-black and the first rain has arrived. It's been terribly dry and hot here, the grass around the house parched to yellow, the water from the well rank and unpleasant, mould and maggots in everything, enough to drive you mad. And in the forest, on the common, big burnt areas left by those airborne oafs and their firebombs. It's wonderful to hear the wind and the rain again.

I can bring you good news: Prolle's safe from the blasted Russians for the next three months; he's been sent to some westerly town up north, to do the R.U.K. course. You'll understand how taken aback I was when they rang from H:fors to say he was passing through! Ham had him for a whole twenty-four hours – and in a few days' time she's coming out with Impi and taking the whole of August off! It's too wonderful to be true. We were worried when we didn't hear from him for so long, but then we got a letter saying he'd been sent north of Ladoga and was pushing forward to the front line through devastated villages full of dead bodies. It hit Ham terribly hard. She went up onto the roof terrace and refused to come down, or eat. The tension in the family was awful, an atmosphere charged with political differences about to explode. After one clash I brought Lasse back here with me, because I think it's up to Ham and Faffan to sort this out, if two such different outlooks on life could ever rub along. All I can do is shut up and keep out of the way, but there's nothing to stop me thinking what I like. It <u>was</u> nice to come out here, like closing a padded door on a busy city street. To take a break from all that naive rumour-mongering, all that political provocation, all those monologues, and from seeing all those people the war makes mean and desperate – I buried myself in the solitude and silence and wished it would last forever. The trip out here was a lively one; in Borgå there was an air-raid warning just as the bus was fully loaded, but the leisurely driver refused to let us leave until the post arrived. When it came about 10 minutes later he calmly started the wood gasifier and we jolted off between the piles of rubble left by the previous bombardment. The bus was seething with nervous anxiety – but we got out of the city before the planes came over. In Pellinge they had already reached the village with their bombs – when we, after waiting a couple of hours in [*deleted by the censor*], boarded a military transport vessel that took us home, we could hear the thuds in Sauna Cove and see them chasing firewood-sellers' boats across the bay.

The planes come roaring in over our heads on a daily basis, like death's black cross in the heavens. At night I lie listening as they drone over the sea or climb at dawn to clear the treetops as they make for the mainland.

One day, one of them went down and dumped its load in the sound between us and Rödholmen – another time they attacked one of the pilots carrying a cargo of firewood from Nyttis – presumably thinking it was ammunition. He saved himself by jumping into the water under the boat, but if he hadn't held on to painter as he did, the swirl of water caused by the bombs dropping would have dragged him down. Yesterday I heard that Asta Kajunas' brother had been killed.

Tapsa's last letter, a couple of days ago, says they're being sent to [*deleted by the censor*] to relieve the others. He's written almost every day (when they weren't actually engaged in combat), delightful, encouraging, loving letters. Ham sends them to me from the studio so Faffan doesn't see them. It's a shame – but these days I have to keep everything to do with my private life and my friends hidden from him. We've nothing more to say to each other.

If the war doesn't claim Tapsa, I want to keep him. A new urge has been growing inside me for something lasting and stable, something warm that one can rely on – I'm tired of episodes and violent love affairs. Tapsa and I know what to expect of each other, there's infinitely more to it than the sexual aspect, and our correspondence and the war have brought us closer in a wonderful way. He's taught me not to be scared of life. If he comes back, I will be the one (with everybody here at home) being brave and cheerful and trying to help him forget "what no human being should have to see". I'm tired of having to fight for my friends and absolve them from accusations – I want to be left in peace with Tapsa. He is one of the nicest, most unselfish people I've known, he is my route to greater growth, peace, joy and warmth. I'm grown up now, and as my obligations increase, I also have a right to a life of my own. –

Lasse and I have spent our time here pottering around doing a thousand little jobs that have lent this summer the illusion of being like other years, even though the great shadow of war has always been lurking in the background.

We cleaned and repainted the sailing boat, went fishing – which yielded minimal provisions – collected horse manure and went diving for seaweed out on Sanskär, watered the plants with seawater, picked blueberries and made frantic attempts to tame the garden which after 5 weeks of neglect had twisted itself into a more or less impenetrable jungle. We haven't been able to get over to the islands – only to Nyttis. Lasse is ideal company, quiet but cheery, and ready to do whatever I ask of him. Abbe, who's in camp on one of the closest outer islands, sometimes pays us a visit in his motorboat, and works the whole night of his leave on his half-finished boat orders. Fanny has been going around grumbling to herself about the "ryssin" ever since that day she almost dropped dead from fright on [*deleted by the censor*] as the bombs came down just offshore. She and Freya dashed off into the forest like streaks of lightning. She spends long hours looking out of the window at dawn, the eyes in her long sallow face expressionless. Old Kalle goes calmly about all his little tasks or just stands there looking out to sea, and Lasse flaps about the place with his butterfly net. The leisurely uneventfulness of it all started getting on my nerves for a while – but now I just think how lovely it is.

The other day they sent search parties to comb the island for Soviet spies who had parachuted in – I later heard it was on account of "secret signals", markers just inland along the coast. I have to report to my deep shame that these markers were my way of staking out a new path to Sauna Cove last summer! And now they'd pretty much sown panic in the village! – At the top of a tall pine just by Laxvarpet I've installed a little platform – from there you can see through a sort of green window out over the sea. Childish nonsense, I know – but it still gives me a sense of secret satisfaction and elation. It's late evening now. The rainclouds are chasing across the sky and the forest is murmuring. In the distance there's something wailing: a siren perhaps. It's sombre and beautiful. I'm sitting here shielding the light from my torch and writing. Huge, huge love – Eva! How wonderful it would be to hear how things are for you!

Tove

P.S. 6th, had a card from Tapsa.

Ada hadn't managed to get an entry permit for Stockholm by the time I came out here. Samu's painting at Munksnäs for all he is worth, but I shall leave them in peace because it just depresses me, having no contact with them. From Carin a melancholy letter from Stockholm that she wrote ages ago. Rosa – did I already say this? – is in hospital with tuberculosis. That's all I can tell you about our friends.

R.U.K.: The school for reserve officers. Elsewhere referred to as *Rukken*.
Abbe: Son of Old Kalle [Gustafsson], from whom the Jansson family rented the summer cottage.
Fanny: Sister of Kalle Gustafsson.
Ada: Ada Indursky, fellow student on TJ's course at the Ateneum.

23/8 –41 EDENS NÄS

Cheerio, dear old missus!

Today I got your first letter, a good three months after you left! It <u>was</u> good to hear from you, almost like talking to you again. I read your letter with a torch under the covers on account of the "pesky flies", as the first real storm of the autumn raged outside. Konikova, I'm so glad you like it in the new country! Just you see, you'll find more than you expected beneath the surface of the new people you're going to live with.

You really must have felt pretty bewildered those first four days – a whirlwind of new impressions and people dragging you off in all directions. As you see, I've a very clear picture of your new American appearance! Just imagine if you could go to New York, Eva, and find a job there. Somehow I'm sure you're going to be happy in America and find your feet there. I'm glad you made good your escape – after the war things could get distressing here in so many ways.

It was sweet of you to write so soon, though you must have been terribly tired once the excitement of the journey was over. And fancy you, in the midst of so much that's new, taking the trouble to ask me about those little details of all our lives here at home. I hope that by now you've had some of my letters? I sent the last one on 6 Aug. Now there's only a week of summer left, and after that Ham and I will go into town and leave Faffan, Lasse and Impi (and Mosse of course) to reap and gather into barns in September. Faffan only came out yesterday, because he had a hard job finding anyone to make the plaster cast of his naiad for the Bernsow building. He's been toiling away at it all summer and seems tired, thin. I was a bit taken aback to see that he's starting to go grey – somehow it's natural for Ham to go white, but Faffan must always keep his brown thatch. Maybe because he's a boy, despite his years. It'll be nice to know he's out here in his fish and mushroom paradise. Ham and I are going to be a carefree, female, politics-free household in town. I think she's been able to rest a little these three weeks – she's cheerful, has energy for everything; a wholly changed Ham since we heard Prolle had got into Rukken. He rarely writes because they've so much work they have to be given leave to cram for their exams at night. Their officers are crazily fierce and the drill is tough. The course is bound to be cut short, I reckon.

Lasse has devoted his whole summer to his big, burning interest: butterflies. Jars of larvae, stretchers, sheets of glass, jottings all over the house. It's nice to see how completely and patiently he can get absorbed in something. He's been wonderful company for me. I don't feel lonely here any more, by the way – I even relish being left in peace and get annoyed when people turn up outside the house. I often take a walk to Laxvarpet and climb up to the platform in my pine tree and sit there for hours, writing and reading or just looking out of my green window at the sea.

I've painted very little, but I'm not worried. I've treated these weeks as a gift of tranquillity and delight after that dismal, hectic time in town. Perhaps also as something I need, in view of everything one might have to face this autumn.

Every day there's a letter from Tapsa waiting in the village. Warm, encouraging, very beautiful and loving letters. Only once did he write in utter despair, broken down by all the appalling things he's experienced and seen around him. It was when they'd been sent back behind the lines to rest, and with the tension lifted there was nothing to stop him thinking and all the horror and senselessness of war came crashing over him and filled him with terror at the idea of going back. He also wrote about a medal he'd got. But the very next day he's calm and cheerful, with faith in the future and the human race, and "my hands that are now being used for destruction will no doubt soon be back to doing what they long for – creating and building up."

Initially I was very afraid of losing him, and would paint horrifying pictures in my mind, imagining great emptiness and loneliness to come. I tried to make my letters sound happy so as not to deflate his confidence – and after a while it stopped being so hard to keep my anxiety out of them. I believed he'd come back and I wrote from that point of view. It's very satisfying to know that my letters were a help to him. I've gradually started feeling less impoverished, my emotions are stronger, more honest. Sometimes I think that if I can only love enough, it must preserve him for me. [...]

We've had violent storms here these past two days, coming straight in from the south. The sea throws up debris: bits of boats and planes, lifebelts, clothes. The constant faraway rumble of cannon, the flares blaze into the darkness and the pesky flies go roaring over. At first I used to run out to the privy when they came, the only place I felt safe, childishly enough – but now I don't bother any more. Last week Faffan was here for a couple of days while his naiad dried, and when it was time for him to go back we rowed him over to the mainland at night to avoid the pesky flies. It was brilliant!

Over the sea the thunderclouds were gathering, standing out sharply in gleaming bluish-white against a night sky reflecting the red of distant lightning flashes. Off we glided with a brisk wind behind us and arrived at dawn, delivering Faffan before going on to Ragni Cawén's, where we stayed all day. As we were having a swim, a pesky fly we hadn't noticed in the sound of the surf came droning in at low altitude. I splashed to shore at lightning speed, the others stayed in the water. But it only made a pass above our heads and continued with its load. We set off home in the night in a south-westerly storm. Took it in turns to row, keeping in the lee of the islands. It was ghastly and grandiose, black and boiling, the crests of the waves luminous white under a magnificent, starry sky. When we finally put into Sauna Cove after several hours' rowing we felt our way ashore and huddled there in the open air under a wet old horse blanket. Froze like dogs for a couple of hours and then went on, in a desperate state. I've no idea how we got round the point, I was disgustingly seasick. And to crown it all I had to spend two days in bed, back and stomach ache. What a feeble wretch I am!

Other than that the days have passed calmly and uneventfully – filled with the collecting of berries and mushrooms, seaweed, manure and roots. I'm trying to learn English and gradually picking my way through the language. You must be learning fast now you hear it around you all the time and <u>have</u> to speak it.

Sometimes I get such a strong urge to go off to some place where they speak a foreign language and nobody recognises me. It's sickening to think of all the wonderful places on earth one will never see – as the days just plod by. One day I shall go to Brittany with Ham. And one day I want to see America, Mexico, New York, California. With you. But this is certainly no time for dreams. We have to take each day as a gift, as it comes.

I'm keenly anticipating your next letter. We all send our greetings, lots of them. I do wish you the very best, Konikova, and don't ever feel homesick. A big, big hug

your friend Tove.

"pesky flies": The Russian bombers.

28/9 Abrascha rang, and sends best wishes! As does your mama.

Eva, dearest –

My drawing is in the press to dry, so I've stolen a moment to talk to you – just as I would have run up to see you for fifteen minutes if you'd been here.

You know that when we're missing someone our feelings can stay calm and even for a long time, but suddenly ignite for some entirely insignificant reason. That was what happened as I went past Colombia the other day – I went in and sat down at our table, where we sat on one our last days, and felt rotten, and really missed you a lot.

I sat there one day with Arno, too, having bumped into him on the street. He was home on a few days' leave, had been there on the Isthmus and talked about his extraordinary luck with an expression of surprise and reverence. He's off to Terijoki next, to a job in transport, so maybe one painter is thereby spared for his canvases, at least in this war.

He was tremendously happy to have had a card from you, and I filled him in on the rest of the American news. He kept coming back to you as he was talking, couldn't say enough about how splendid and radiant you were at the goodbye party in your room. And he sent his – warmest – wishes.

The war has claimed another painter – Hageli. It's awful – and still seems inconceivable. He always seemed so exceptionally alive and was such a life-affirming person. I'm glad now that our past spot of professional bother was sorted out last spring and that I went to the art school. "Make peace with your antagonist while he is beside you on the same path." But maybe Hageli was spared from following the curve as it turned down, he was able to leave while still at the top – before any possibility of his hopes being dashed so he ended up old and bitter.

Yesterday I had a visit from a little soldier – Boris. He was home on weekend leave – and you can imagine how much I appreciated him making time to pay a call on Ham and me, though he had so many people to see. It was a completely new Boris I saw before me: animated, talkative, liberated somehow, and more self-aware. He told us about the work camp where he's been, gave us a surprisingly lively description of the various kinds of lice they encountered (colour, shape and character), while there were big notices, decorated with sprigs of birch and announcing "Cleanliness is the army's foremost virtue", pinned up amid all the junk. He talked about people he'd met, about the work – offered his own views and criticism – and I was charmed, and thought: if only he writes to Eva the way he talks, she'll realise this young man is going to be all right. The whole boy seems to have woken up. Don't worry about him – after a.u.k. which takes at least six weeks he's going to try to get into Rukken, or he might get work as an interpreter. A friend has already recommended him and told him where to apply.

Prolle's course ends on 1 Oct and then it'll either be the front or bark orders, i.e. it'll be his turn to boss the new little Rukken recruits about. If it's the latter I'll be ready to sink down and howl out loud with gratitude and relief. As it is, worry takes hold; you may ostensibly be living a normal everyday life, working as usual – being cheerful, but there's a permanent dark, burrowing background of anxiety and lots of horribly graphic pictures in your mind's eye, hard always to keep at bay.

25/9

But Prolle himself would rather go to the front – first because it seems easier to him than being sent for crushing into the unbearable atmosphere of excessive militarism, and then because he "needs to see and experience the war to have a firmer and more factual basis for his opinions on it". O that dear boy, he's the same as ever!

His friend Stige who was in England and the North Cape with him was sent back to H:fors because of an intestinal haemorrhage and came to see us before he was sent out there again. It was desperate to see him trying to hide his dread of going back. They'd asked for volunteers, lined the boys up and asked 10 to step forward. Nobody moved. So they were subjected to a blazing speech – "it wasn't at all as dangerous as they thought – it was really nice, you got bravery crosses and iron crosses ..." And wooden crosses, chimed in somebody from the ranks. It was set to turn into a real scandal. Then they called them in one by one, and that way they persuaded them to go "voluntarily" ...

Tapsa's forging his way through the marshes somewhere over towards Petroskoi. They haven't had any post for several weeks – and when we don't hear from him, I persuade myself the useless postal service is to blame. I really miss him – and wonder if he'll be very changed when he comes home.

I met your papa today when I went up with invitations to the exhibition opening. We talked about you – of course! And he sent his most heartfelt wishes.

The menfolk are still at Pellinge where they seem content and have started catching lots of fish. We'll have them home in a week – and Impi will take over the housekeeping, which despite a light touch from me and Ham is still quite an irritation. We're up to our ears in work and hardly move from our desks. In the mornings we feel like something the cat's dragged in! But thank goodness for work!

I've had a number of books from Söderströms now – the most interesting has a particularly "thrilling" title: Black Eroticism. And I did the drawings to match, so people will be rushing to get the book, even though it's a good one! The publisher, who is a bit short-sighted and very absent-minded, thought he had met me in the market square and treated the poor doppelgänger to some earnest comments on the sales potential of black eroticism. She fled in dumb panic!

At the moment I'm busy with a commission for Stockholm in multicolour print for Folket i Bild's Christmas number. Storm Petersen from Denmark, Blix from Norway and Högfeldt from Sweden are also part of this Nordic four-leafed clover, each of us contributing a humorous picture. Stenman, the art dealer, went and told them I drew the best comic pictures in Finland, and I've been working very nervously for fear of falling too short of that accolade. I finally finished my various drafts this evening, just in time, because Rosa's coming for a couple of days' séjour from Kivelä sanatorium tomorrow – and I suspect she'll want to make the most of her time!

Other than that I've backed away from folk as much as possible, filled with a single, overpowering urge, to be left in peace to work. It's really only Volle and Ada who ring me, both of them feeling alone, but strictly speaking they only interest me indirectly, Volle for Carin's sake, Ada through you. She's got a job doing something decorative for Artek now – which doubtless suits her better than free drawing and easel painting. Volle's had a letter from Carin that has upset him a lot – she writes quite brusquely that he certainly doesn't mean as much to her for the time being as Siri, who's making superb efforts to get back to health and needs all the help she can get.

Good Lord, poor Volle could do with help himself, he's not a well man and Caj is the only one who can help him get there. But when it comes down to it, they'll have to help themselves! As long as Caja is brave and bold enough to help herself to happiness and finally do exactly what she wants! She's given up the studio now and started at the Academy and is doing some kind of course with the women's voluntary defence service. And she's putting down roots over there.

Sam is taking part in this year's autumn exhibition at the Kunsthalle, where he's also on the jury with Lönnberg and Yngve Bäck. So no solo exhibition for the time being.

I sent in seven canvases of which one, a little still life of flowers, was refused. The portrait of Ada really lifted the collection, it actually still has something of what I first saw when I started painting her. And there's a big spray of flowers in strong colours, new in that the pot is on the floor and I've got the interior in the composition so the flowers don't look so pretentious. A little sketch of the cliffs outside Pellinge and the canvas Carin and I painted at Nyttis. It's quite muted, a soft greyish-green, motionless, scrubby forest where three Fanny figures are out picking berries in the twilight. Also a natura morte and a summer night with moon and all that stuff, which drove me a little bit crazy because half the picture would insist on being in daylight. It's damned difficult painting golden yellow cornfields at night! A railway crossing beyond the fields with the melancholy edge-of-town attributes of gasometers, factory chimneys, closed goods waggons, solitary buildings. The girl on the road is luminous white. – The week before submission day was a bit hysterical as usual, the canvases were up and down onto the easel and I was convinced not one of them except Ada would be finished in time. I went and messed up the background of your portrait, so I'll have to save it for the spring. It's such a relief to have handed in the pictures, now the critics can chew on them as they will! – Goodnight Eva – now I shall fall irrevocably asleep. I have a storybook to do tomorrow.

26/9

Best wishes from Rosa who is here for five days and seems so fit and well and blooming that I'm starting to be convinced she's genuinely getting better. Another letter from Tapsa at last. One of his brothers has been wounded – in the face. They've had a hard time; scarcely a third of the men have survived. He writes about his despair as he is obliged to accompany one young boy after another right to the end – and not be able to help. He wrote of Nelimarkka: "That was the life of a wonderful young person and one of the best painters, snuffed out entirely needlessly. I love the questing kind of youth that he represented. Nothing is as sacred as young life, yet that is what is being so insanely thrown away – on both sides of the front. I am speaking across borders and each and every one of us here feels the same – in this common suffering we feel no hatred. Nor do we bear hatred when someone carries out a brave feat that is our undoing. We openly acknowledge the bravery. That is why you at home find it hard to understand life here – if you let hatred colour your vision. Cowardly devils can be sadists – but they do not feel comfortable here."

Evening. – I feel tired today and work is going slowly. Tired of waiting, perhaps ... But I've got to work hard and earn some money. I've just foolishly made a hole in my "fortune" by yielding to my old temptation in a moment of weakness, the blue fox cape. At Steinbock's, 2,325 marks. It's beautiful – and as always when I buy myself something, it's with thoughts of Tapsa's return and wanting to look smart for it. Do you remember how often you all used to grumble about me looking such a mess!

27

I've handed in the last job now – until the next one – in a few days' time – and I shall try to paint a bit. But today's Event is that I've found some potatoes. We're going to need coupons for them now, thank goodness. I went to the exhibition opening with Ham, in cape and curls and all that stuff, and grinned and talked like a machine to loads of unimportant people. That was that. They seemed to like my paintings, and they were reasonably positioned. Samu good as usual, but tends to repeat himself in that yellowy-green colour he's started to adore. We've got Rosa coming to dinner today. Ham sends her regards. God how I long to sit and talk to you, out of reach as you are, and to be spared talking rubbish to all those people I've no interest in! I'm hugging you, hard.

Tove.

Colombia: Café in Helsinki.

Arno: Arno Ahtaja (formerly Ahlgren), a fellow student from the Ateneum.

the Isthmus: The Karelian Isthmus, retaken by Finland from the Soviet Union in 1941, with heavy casualties on both sides.

a.u.k.: School for Junior Officers.

Stige: Stig Landgren.

Kivelä sanatorium: Presumably Stengård hospital in Helsinki.

Lönnberg: William Lönnberg, teacher at the Ateneum.

Nelimarkka: Eero Jaakko Nelimarkka (1919–41), son of the artist Eero Nelimarkka.

He wrote of Nelimarkka: TJ quotes the letter in the original Finnish (here translated from the Swedish).

H:FORS. THE STUDIO. 22/10 –41

FROM TOVE JANSSON. APOLLOG. 13 H:FORS. FINLAND.

TO. MISS EVA KONIKOFF. C/O KONICK.

6100 NTH. 17 ST. PHILADELPHIA PA. U.S.A.

4 SHEETS OF PAPER. CENSOR, PLEASE DON'T DELETE

ANYTHING, IT'S ONLY ME! TOVE.

I've had 6 of your letters, starting with the one I got on Åland. This is the tenth time I've written. Have you received them all?

Dearest Eva!

Your letter written 24/9 was waiting here in the studio when I came to talk to you – having scarcely budged from my drawing job all day except to eat. That's how it's been recently – I feel like an Indian ink machine and am starting to think everything around me is drawn; nothing but lines and planes.

It's so nice to come back after that to my quiet, peaceful studio. The rain is pattering on the skylight and I've only put the little lamp on so I don't have to worry about blackout curtains. I pour a glass of Mesimarja and put on my dressing gown and feel glad about the job I've done, the solitude and your letter.

It was so lovely to hear from you again!

My poor dearest Konikova, to think of things being so difficult for you over there. The isolation and routine work. Your descriptions give me a pretty clear picture of life over there, the glitter, the toughness, the bustle, the opportunities. But I don't think you're one of those who'll be trampled down – you will break your way through, and one day will be able to shape your life the way you like it, your own work and people you care about. I think you're doing the right thing in taking yourself off to New York. Perhaps your relatives will be able to pull some strings. But don't let them tie you up with them! It's just as well, I'm sure, for you to keep your uncle at a bit of a distance – it must be quite a hard balancing act with him as things stand.

I'm glad you've at least got another human being you can talk to, young Madway. And you will find more, Eva! If you learn the language and can leave your loathsome kilometre machine.

No, I wouldn't be "disappointed in you", or surprised, if you got married. Why not! You long to have a baby and I'm sure you would make sure it had a fine and wise papa. Of course you'll find somebody you can be fond of.

It's so sweet of you in the midst of all your new merry-go-round to still worry about us and take an interest in every detail of what happens to us. It's not as difficult as you think – although lots of things have run out, we've got quite enough to get by. We are doing just fine at home because we've had quite a few food parcels from the family in Sweden and thanks to Harriet Linnala's brains and resourcefulness we've loads of potatoes. You eat your American food with a clear conscience, dear heart! Your papa got it wrong about Ham and me and a trip to see the uncles. We didn't go to Sweden, it was just that she went to Uncle Jullan's in Åbo to bring Lasse home. It would be simply splendid if you could send the boy stamps or even butterflies! He's a proper little professor for his 15 years, goes to the public library every morning regular as clockwork and sits there poring over butterfly tomes. At the moment he's busy on a book that's going to be about a new and simpler method of examining the poor wretches. He slogs away from morning till night and does the most minutely detailed illustrations. His book for boys is due out for Christmas; we've already been given the cover to work on.

Ham's in the midst of her busiest working weeks now and I sincerely hope things will ease off soon – she looks terribly tired. Sometimes I find time to help, but generally my days brim over with my own work.

Ham doesn't buckle, though, and she isn't downhearted. Because Prolle's still in the R.U.K. where the course is now over and is continuing with practical exercises with his comrades in arms, you see. To that end they've been decked out in madly smart fur coats, new underwear, boots, uniform – everything tip-top to show what the country can achieve. They call themselves the mannequin company and have worked their way up out of the bootlegs they were stuffed into, dashing off to the canteen and cinema now they're free of drill for a few days. In two weeks' time we'll have him home for 5 days' leave – then he's off to the front. And I don't think the war's going to end very soon, not any more …

[…] Faffan is working on a grave monument (Lord knows there are enough of them, these days). The mood has lightened – and little by little I'm realising, with relief and some degree of pride, that my efforts to control myself and hold my tongue aren't blunting me or burning me up as they did at first. I no longer feel the need to explode – I think "internally" and no longer feel it's so dreadfully important for everybody else to share my views, or even to let them know I don't share theirs. Sivén who invited me out to dinner at the Royal after I gave him a painting for patching up my teeth brought me together with a couple called Carlander, and there was some discussion. That was when I noticed that I'd learnt something. One of our topics was the Jewish question, which always used to send me into Feuer und Flamme. This time it was the other person who got worked up and gave himself away, while I weighed every word and rejected anything he could argue against. I was so happy to go home knowing I'd given as good as I got and made him less certain.

It's 11 o'clock now, so Tapsa won't be coming. I haven't seen all that much of him, you know! He's running around on that blessed leg of his (the piece of shrapnel – Finnish - is up in his thigh) to all his friends – in the grip of a fix idé: he wants to find somebody to write a book about the war. Not a war book in the traditional spirit – but "something authentic that will help mankind and make it not all have been in vain". We were at Hagar Olsson's one evening, and he alternated between shaking her and getting down on his knees to make her promise to write that book before he goes back – and she was half flattered, half angry and very unsettled. That evening he was drunk for the first time – his friends had been plying him with alcohol since the morning and Hagar finished the job. For the first time I saw how terribly he was suffering after all he had seen, all the faces that would not leave him, how confused he was and how helpless. Good God, what state will he come back in next time! He's rushing around and talking, talking – talking far too much – and I'm scared. Yet at the same time, as I sit drawing, I feel so very glad to know he's treading his thousand paths, resuming old discussions, welcome everywhere. Women often ring me when they're trying to get hold of him – that makes me chuckle to myself. He's the way I wanted him to be, now; that apologetic doggy look has gone, he doesn't ask and isn't so biddable – a bit more self-assured and aware. Now I love him, and now at last the freedom I have always given him feels like a boon – though he hasn't needed it until now. The first twenty-four hours were ours alone. He was here incognito, came straight to the studio with flowers, an icon, rysskorvirke, sugar, war souvenirs. He was so tired, and lay down for a sleep while I mended his clothes and boiled macaroni for breakfast – I felt I was part of some odd domestic idyll. And happy.

We had a celebration dinner with wine and your candles, Impi had cooked a bird, with corn on the cob and berries. I wore my dark red silk dress and he – the only time – his medal. It seemed such a solemn occasion that we hardly said a word as we sat there chewing on our bones. Just to think that he's one of only 10 left out of the 200 who left from Kottby in June.

It's wonderful to see his face light up as he wakes and realises he's not at the front.

23rd

He sends you his very best regards, as does Ham, and Rosa who's going to a sanatorium in Sweden. She's better. I haven't seen the Sams since they were with me at Lallukka – and other than that I've seen nobody but Volle. He's finally got Carin to promise to come here for 2 weeks after Christmas – I expect we're in for the final showdown that she hasn't dared risk until now. I sold Ada Indursky's picture to the Art Society lottery. Critical reactions have been fine, except those who yap on as usual about my lack of "feeling".

A big hug. I miss you so much!

Tove

Mesimarja: Arctic raspberry liqueur

His book for boys: Lars Jansson's debut book *Skatten på Tortuga*
(Treasure on Tortuga)
rysskorvirke: Some kind of Russian food or drink substitute.

TOVE JANSSON MEETS THE ARTIST TAPIO TAPIOVAARA, KNOWN
as Tapsa, at the Ateneum. He crops up in her notes in 1937.
Tapsa comes, Tapsa goes, she writes in 1939, and that describes
the nature of their relationship. In long letters to Eva Konikoff,
Tove Jansson writes of dashed hopes, fervent yearning and the
betrayals of infidelity. Their love bears the stamp of wartime
conditions: brief encounters and painful farewells, always in the
knowledge that this could be their last meeting. The relationship
also brings the question of independence to a head. He wants
children, but Tove Jansson is against the idea. Her intention is
to work and make art, and she does not want to bear children
who could be sacrificed in a war. In a letter on 1 November
1941 she develops her thoughts on the price of love and sets
out a feminist programme. It is all about men's war, the terms
of which she refuses to accept. In notes made in October the
same year, she has already formulated her ideas. Her relationship
with Tapio Tapiovaara comes to an end in the spring of 1942.

27/10 –41 THE STUDIO.
FROM TOVE JANSSON. APOLLLOG. 13. HELSINGFORS.
FINLAND.
CONTAINS 5 SHEETS OF PAPER.
TO. MISS EVA KONIKOFF. C/O KONICK.
6100 NTH. 17 ST. PHILADELPHIA PA. U.S.A.
<u>WRITTEN IN SWEDISH</u>.

Dearest Eva!
    All my commissions have dried up – as suddenly as tropical rain.
Perhaps another shower is on the way, but just at the moment I feel
bewildered, like a fish out of water – and appreciate what a help
that work has been to me although I moaned about it taking all my
days from me.

For what would I have done with them, had they been mine?

I know that now, as so many times before, you would have dropped everything to come to me because something was wrong. That's why I'm writing to you – the writing is a help in itself. It's so quiet and dark here and the clock is inexorably ticking away my time, the last three days – and the lift goes endlessly up and down.

Konikova, how strange life is, when it comes to it. It all repeats itself, and everything is just a boomerang that comes back. And it's hard, hard not to get bitter, hard to see the point, hard not to be scared.

I wrote to you a few days ago – about Tapsa and my celebration – about the way he was running round town to see his friends and talking, talking – about being glad that his ideas and his friends filled his time and stopped him remembering – I knew I was there as a warm, safe background. I wrote about how rarely he came round, always in the mornings – and finally stopped, about how I went up to Socialidemokraatti and Toini Aaltonen confused me with her talk of people I didn't know, about how I finally went to find him because I was afraid he'd talked himself into trouble. The same evening he rang me and asked me to come with him to see Hagar again. All those unfamiliar and dangerous names were burning their way into me; I was worried and asked him tentatively if he ought not to watch out for himself, if he could blindly trust them. I mean to say, Toini had told me they laugh behind his back at his naivety, his sky-blue idealism "two circuits of Kaisa Park, a bit of idle chat about culture and enlightenment and he'll believe anything, do anything."

He was angry, "someone's been sticking their nose in where it's not wanted".

I told him that I'd just been glad to know he was with good friends who liked him but that it hurt me to know he was spending his precious days on people who gave him nothing and were only a danger to him. And I thought – they've no right to exploit him now, show off "the hero from the front", pump him for painful recollections to feed their own craving for sensation or to create material, hector him for illustrations before he's killed and their commissions risk being left incomplete, squeeze all the strength out of him before he goes back – and then to mock him.

He gave me the letters he received at the front for safekeeping, and none of them wrote to him except Elli Tompuri, Hagar, the family and v. Hellens. Nobody felt the anguish, nobody loved him. He's mine, and they've no right to him.

Of course he defended them loyally, and what could I say? I had to stay silent. As we turned into Hagar's street he suddenly said: I've been stupid. I laughed to lighten the atmosphere and said – it's not that bad. Maybe they give you more than I know. The main thing is that you're content. Is it stupid to care for one's friends?

No, it's not that, he said quietly. I went on with my banter – well, what can you possibly have done? Been sleeping with girls, perhaps?? We'd reached the front door of Hagar's building and he answered "Yes".

It was a delightful party as you can imagine; by the end I felt I could hold up a job in the theatre. The trams had stopped running so we had to walk the whole way in the rain, from right over at Tullbommen. We talked about the weather, I think. But there was a bitterness rising in me that knew no bounds and I was so full of unkind words that it scared me. But all the while I was remembering I'd promised myself not to give him a single unhappy minute in the short time he might have left to live, I remembered how the previous night when I couldn't sleep I'd written a kind of verse with no rhyme – like when I was seventeen – where I tried to convince myself it didn't matter where he was, or with whom, as long as he was happy. I recalled him twice leaving me with a smile, doing everything to stop me feeling bad that I'd fallen in love with someone else. I remembered the red carnation he gave me then, a symbol of freedom – and how I always used to say it was his turn to go – whenever he wanted – and I would smile as he once had. But at the same time I thought of all my anguish and waiting, the way I fought down my fear and my weariness with life for his sake and forced myself to write hopeful, positive, strong letters every day, when I thought the world had turned into a stinking pit. I thought about the detailed plans I'd made for what we'd do together when he came, and how none of it happened – with me. I felt my old fear and bitterness creeping back because I knew another person – maybe more – was helping him now, and that he didn't need my courage any longer. And I thought of all sorts of stupid little details – Espana unplayed, the tin of sardines unopened, the toothbrush he hadn't used …

And I felt myself going completely numb and empty inside and I lay beside him with no inclination, incapable of lifting my hand in caress.

He said nothing, laid his head on my breast and waited. And as I felt his warmth it all came bursting out and I wept as I seldom have. He tried male excuses: I was drunk. It was the protracted sexual abstinence. – And with that, all my conciliatory feelings were gone, because I realised that from our first evening, which I'd considered a sacred ritual, he'd gone straight to her. He couldn't even wait two miserable extra days, because he'd come at a time of the month that wasn't good for me. Didn't he think women could feel the same level of desire, and have a right to, without being whores! (like Kajus, another "MAN" said). He made the naive objection that he'd thought I was doing it for him. I blew my nose and howled, and snarled that he had the temperament of a lukewarm bath sponge compared to mine – and all at once I saw the funny side of the matter. But I forgot to laugh, just as I'd forgotten my lovely poem, and turned my back on him and made a few remarks about men in general.

He wasn't upset. I feel cheerful, he said when he went in the morning – and because I thought he'd be back in the evening I magnanimously said he could go to who he liked, I wouldn't wait, freedom etc. "as long as he was happy" – like the chorus of the song. But he didn't turn up in the evening, and I did wait, even so. I waited for three evenings because he'd said he loved me and because I decided not to try to comprehend that strange race, men, but to console and forgive them, that being the mission of that even stranger race, women.

But I couldn't sleep, and that's never happened to me before. But I didn't dare take anything for it – in case he did come.

Today I went out and bought a red carnation. – (there's no denying I've always liked grand gestures as much as he has) and planted it, with a message attached, in his room.

It was a very pretty letter, no overstatement, and I almost felt proud of it. I realised what he wanted was a baby, but I definitely didn't want to give him one. And he had to go back to the front, anyway.

(That was my way of glossing over the sadness in the situation.) And to round it off really nicely I promised to carry on not being scared, in spite of everything.

But it's a lie, of course. I am scared. Life is grim and dreary and empty and I can't paint.

But like hell am I going to produce cannon fodder, even so! When men stop killing, then I'll bear a child – but I know they never will stop.

And now I'm going to take some sleeping powders after all, and I embrace you and thank you for letting me talk about this typical interlude on the home front.

So long, my dear old american missus!

Tove.

PTO!

28th Oct.

Today Prolle rang to say he's coming on leave 8th Nov, and Wolle to say he's going up to Petsamo to dig. More drawing jobs from Toini Aaltonen and Garm. I shall shortly be illustrating an English textbook by Prof. Reuter.

I was up at the Kunsthalle to fetch my canvases – 3 of them have sold, in all. Most recently the flowers, to Prof. Björkenheim. So now I'm nearly 7,000 marks richer. Stupid that it doesn't make me feel happy. But yes, of course. I shall come and see you one day. Strange that it will all just go on, we will paint, travel, love, grieve, collect money, buy things, grow old ... whether we want to or not. Ham sends warm regards.

Hug.
Tove.

29th.

Today he sent me orchids – "live well, dearest" – nothing else. He leaves tomorrow. I shall paint them.

Socialidemokraatti: The newspaper *Suomen Sosialidemokraatti*.
Toini Aaltonen: Editor, translator and critic.
Kaisa Park: Kaisaniemi Park.
Hellens: Doctor Arno von Hellens, Tapiovaara's childhood friend.
Kajus: Musician Kaj Kajanus.

I NOV. —41. H:FORS.
CONTAINS 4 SHEETS WRITTEN IN SWEDISH.

Eva dearest!

Tapsa's returned to the front now. Lots more happened on that score after I wrote to you about my carnation "gesture", but I understand less than ever. I only feel – well, in fact, that I feel nothing and have no other urge than for someone else to relieve me of all responsibility and choice so I am spared having to say things and do things. Or – for me to understand. There's an awful lot I've got to understand before I can go on.

And because of course I will go on with everything, painting, talking, collecting money, waiting, brooding, eating, going about, meeting people – since no one is going to carry this responsibility for me – I still have to try to understand. That's why I'm writing to you. Perhaps things will grow clearer if I write. You don't have to understand, or help me. You've nothing to do with my burden. But you can listen and I know you're my friend.

The day before the one I'd worked out he'd have to leave on, I threw all pride and big gestures overboard and rang him at home. They seemed used to it and promised in a resigned, bored-sounding way that they'd ask him to telephone me. While I was waiting I painted his orchids, those beautiful, twisted, wax-like ornaments that looked so out of place in my studio. And then he was there, on the phone, promising to come and say goodbye. I sat there and went through everything I wanted to say, trying not to feel so uncomfortably noble and artificial. Conciliatory stuff – the wonderful parts cancelling out all the rest, gratitude and forgiveness, that I understood him and wasn't bitter, but loved life and would go on being brave, "God be with you" and "Don't worry about" ... But all the while I had the feeling God was laughing at me. And I <u>was</u> afraid.

It went very well. I said it all and didn't lose the thread. It was like being in the theatre. Then he said – The thing is. I'm not going to the front. My friends have got me another job. It was as if I'd written a pompous obituary and its main character had suddenly popped up, grinned knowingly and said "Stop! Are you sure you want to drivel on like that now I'm not planning to die after all?"

I couldn't believe it was true, simply sat and stared. Swear you're not joking. Is it absolutely definite?

99% definite, he replied. And now – I must dash. Got to have breakfast. I'm already late.

Breakfast, I repeated like an idiot. Is there somebody waiting for you? I still felt sleep-dazed and empty, and experienced a sudden pang as I remembered the pure intensity and honest joy that filled me the first day he was back on leave.

And I only gradually took in the fact that this wasn't the last time I would see him. That he would go on living and didn't need the last rites from me. And that infused me with verve and passion, I woke up and felt the urge to fight and said, Fine. I haven't had breakfast either. I'll come too.

Tapsa looked scared, but then started to laugh and shrugged his shoulders. An absurd exhilaration came over us. We held hands, ran for a tram that was already on the move and laughed all the way to Alko.

She was big and platinum blonde and very made-up and seemed kind and pathetic. She'd been waiting three-quarters of an hour. We had a friendly chat about bread coupons, children and cod, and how terrific it was that her husband was going to get some leave and how dreadful that everywhere had sold out of nail varnish remover. Tapsa said nothing, toyed with his food and grinned. After two hours, she wanted us to come home with her for coffee – but by then my elation had drained away and I didn't feel like it. I wanted to go to an exhibition. That fine theory about the child he wanted to have before he went back no longer held water. I didn't understand a thing and I was tired. […]

In the evening I set the table for tea – the first time I've done it without listening for the lift – and for the first time, he arrived punctually.

But nothing was the same as on that first night. I was filled with a sense of distaste, with fear at having grown so niggardly. Instead of warmth, of our uncomplicated old togetherness that asked and demanded nothing, there were only bitter memories, brooding and uneasy thoughts. I withdrew and he felt entirely alien to me. First I have to understand, I said. The most important things. Yes, I had to understand. That his letters meant nothing, that I was not needed just then, when I had plucked up my courage and positivity for his sake, that he loved me yet still let me wait every night and knew he was doing it, that God was love even though He exacted vengeance and much, much more.

Tapsa said nothing. I lay there mulling things over gloomily and felt somehow it was very urgent and I had to hurry. I understood less and less. He fell asleep and I was terribly lonely.

Suddenly I had a feeling there must be one thing that could transform horrible back into beautiful, and it must be if people loved each other enough. Enough to understand – or not worry about understanding – and not just forgive but also forget. I woke him and tried to get it all out of my brain and said Tapsa, I've forgotten everything. Let's just be happy.

It wasn't so important what he felt for me or what he'd done – the main thing was for me to love him enough. He smiled at me and hugged me. Then he went back to sleep and I lay there trying to feel full of love and nothing else. But I found no peace, I wasn't happy with myself. Everything that makes me not want to get married came back to me, all the men I've seen through and despised – and the Faffan pressure at home – men's whole, loyally preserved and protected pedestal of privileges, the glorification of their weaknesses in just as many unassailable slogans, the lack of consistency and consideration in their whole puerile fraternity, asserting themselves without a hint of nuance and banging their big drum from morning to night. I hadn't the money, the time or the inclination to get married! I can't find the hours to admire and console and pretend it's not all just a false front! I feel sorry for them, yes – but I don't want to give my life for a performance that's so transparent to me! I see the way Faffan, the most helpless, most short-sighted of us all, tyrannises the whole house, I see that Ham is unhappy because she's always said yes, covered up, given in. Given up her life and got nothing in return but children that men's war will kill, or turn into bitter, negative people. I see what will happen to my Painting if I get married. Because when all is said and done I have in me all those inherited female instincts for solace, admiration, submission, self-sacrifice. Either a bad painter or a bad wife. And if I become a "good" wife, then his work will be more important than mine, my intellect be subordinate to his, I shall bear him children, children to be killed in future wars! And at the same time I shall see through it all, and know that I acted against everything I believed in.

If we are just together – without any claims on each other's work, life or ideas – then we can carry on being free individuals and not get on each other's nerves, neither of us need be subordinate. – But, can I talk about love, I – when my own concerns take precedence for me? That must mean I'm not loving enough. I pay nothing, and therefore I shall get nothing. Everything went round and round, the hours passed – towards morning I fell asleep, to be woken by the telephone while it was still completely dark. A woman as usual, asking for him. Everything felt dirty to me somehow – and God was laughing at me even more.

We made tea, played España, as per the good old ritual, I mended his sweater and then he left. He was off to find out about that job on the home front they'd promised him.

He rang me in the evening, and said very quietly and wretchedly: "I was wrong. It's the front, after all." I asked if he had time to see me. Yes, he was at the station now. We walked round the dark station and I tried to be cheerful. He got his papers and found out when the train was due to leave. But that gives you several hours! I said. I'd thought of saying "gives us several hours" but my trust wasn't what it had been and I held back. I knew he would go to Alko. He walked with me to the tram – and I went home.

So that leave was over. Now I'm waiting for Prolle's. As far back as I can remember, I've always been waiting for somebody or something. – I remember the expectation – but only rarely the fulfilment. Perhaps I waited too much? Perhaps I expect too much of life? What can I demand of other people – as someone who gives nothing? A painter of genius can demand – but my canvases don't give enough. And yet – I expect them to give me something. To give me back my pleasure. You're going to write to me that it will come. That I already paint unusually well for someone so young. That it will all be all right. Once the war's over. Maybe.

A lot of things are behind me, a lot of things have stopped hurting. Much remains of pleasure, travel, success. Perhaps even, some time, understanding. It's just that I'm so tired. And alone, as every human being is. I hug you and thank you.

Tove.

Alko: The state-owned alcohol store.

Dearest Konikova!

I'm sitting at Colombia to write. I seem to remember we were here this time last year. – As now, I'd just handed in my canvases for the "clearance exhibition" at the Ateneum. – I sometimes feel as though I miss you more than Tapsa – even if it's childish to measure you two against each other in those terms. Yearning can take a thousand forms. But what I most need just now is a person of my own sex and my own generation, someone I'm close to. There's Carin of course – albeit in Sweden – but even though she's a wonderful friend to whom my heart will always be open, she lacks something that I've found in you: wisdom of insight, life-affirming strength, a permanently burning flame that even in moments of depression, and unconsciously, lends others its fire. In this time of total upending of all concepts of justice, of morals and ethics, it's hard for those who still haven't stabilised their attitude to existence – for young people – to find a foothold.

Under the pressure of being obliged to keep quiet, anxious about their own little circle, everyone hunches more deeply into their shell. The great events unfolding around us, rather than widening our horizons, have shrunk them into petty stubbornness, we get manically hooked on the phraseology of misdirected nationalism, on slogans, boundaries grow less and less flexible, logic goes out of the window. But the old prejudices and principles continue to be defended. In a chaos of monologues, all contact becomes impossible within a people that was already so reserved and pig-headed. People shout and argue, or shut their mouths. – I've chosen to shut my mouth. – except for the times when I meet Ham in No-Man's-Land and talk to her.

It's only now that I start to appreciate your distaste for turning thirty that time you and Sam were in my studio on your birthday. I thought then that you were afraid of losing your youth; your young face. But there's more to it. These years are marked with a deeper sense of alarm. This is the period when we are supposed to take up a stance in life, adopt the right position – while we are still pliable.

These are the last years in which a basic outlook, a job, an opinion can be exchanged with the careless confidence of youth for the boundless riches of possibility and time, But time isn't infinite – only now do we notice that the possibilities have to be sifted and sorted – we can't embrace them all, we have to choose. For we no longer have the stamina to do it all and we demand more than skimming over the surface.

Studio evening. It's confusing that as a background to this new-born expectation of greater depth and stability, and a definitive position on life, the whole world is in chaos. A world where all that we thought best, found just and sound, is no longer venerated and so much that we repudiated has been raised to become the rule of law.

Of course we try to cling on to what we believe in. But we can feel very lonely. Perhaps we always were – but only notice it at moments like these. But what's hard is to go on trying to be positive, calm, trusting, to quell every tendency to bitterness, which it would some-times almost be a cowardly relief to burrow down into. – I probably wouldn't write about all this if I weren't seriously attempting, and even believed I would be able to make it through all this.

I have made attempts, some of them childish, to be a bit more austere in, to bring a bit more spiritual economy to, my existence. So as not to squander my energy for painting I've turned down a couple of drawing commissions – for the first time. I must start studying anatomy. And be even stricter about saying no to people I allow to take up my time out of sympathy or habit. And never to worry whether I'm popular or not, whether they think me intelli-gent or not. What does that matter, if I'm not living a life I myself consider dignified?

My honesty and lack of restraint in letters to Tapsa, without a safety margin for the first time, was also an attempt at stability. I'm sick and tired of changing who I like the same way I might unpick a sock. I wanted to burn my bridges, trust entirely to feeling for once and not leave any doors ajar.

It went badly. I forgot that he too might have doors. But I intend to carry on with what I think is right. The gloss has worn off it – but perhaps I shall give us something else instead.

The days are short and grey. Everyone goes round in their own little space, waiting for peace and delivering monologues on the war.

Prolle writes often. The most important place in the house is the hall mat where the letters arrive with their soft thud. I love that boy so indescribably. But the tremendous anxiety of the summer has turned into burdensome waiting, quite calm. I haven't the stamina to keep screaming inside for so long, I push it away, carry on working but shrink from the things that bring the outside world up close: newspapers, the radio, the phone, the newsreels. They churn up everything that's smouldering away deep inside. But my head isn't in the sand, I'm intensely aware, at every moment, in every part of myself. [...]

It's been a long time since I slept in the studio. I shall enjoy it. Wolle left a little while ago. He talks about Carin differently now. There's uncertainty, resignation – he assumes he's going to lose her and is trying to get used to the idea ready for whenever she's brave enough to tell him the truth. I feel so sorry for everyone who loses the gloss, the sense of trust! But I suppose that's the basis on which we all gradually have to put together something resembling a real person. I understand Samu now, when he suddenly took the radiance and charm out of his pictures and started the heavy work of rebuilding everything from the bottom up. "I'll put the gloss back afterwards, sometime ..."

You're in New York now, so I hear from your papa via Abrascha. And coping with the language and with a job in prospect. Good for you, Evotschka!

A big hug
Tove.

19/12 –41 H:FORS. THE STUDIO
<u>TO</u> MISS EVE KONIKOFF C/O H. HANSEN
258 RIVERSIDE DRIVE. NEW-YORK. U.S.A.
<u>FROM</u> TOVE JANSSON. APOLLOG. 13. HELSINGFORS, FINLAND.
<u>WRITTEN IN SWEDISH. 3 SHEETS.</u>

Dearest Eva!

Today I put Mary and baby Jesus up in my studio. She's sitting on a white island made of the stones and shells you collected in Pellinge. (Which Rosa and I then laid at your feet on Sanskär!)

A big clean-up, white paper collars round all the candles I can muster, some ginger snaps in the shape of Christmas goats, made with syrup we got from Sweden – here they send it all to the fronts.

It's snowing outside – non-stop for several days now. The storm's blown the drifts into razor-sharp ridges – like up in the mountains.

Tomorrow I shall make my Christmas visit to the Samus. They've lost half their name now, poor things, and are just called Vanni. Maybe it's practical. I went into Hemflit and passed on your best wishes. Before I left I was seduced into buying a blouse, shocking pink, and a wide blue skirt with tiny mauve polka dots. A summer skirt. Just because I didn't need it! Your purple check blouse was there and Ham and I both said at the same time "Koni!" – Incidentally it's no fun going to Hemflit any more, now you're not there with your big, welcoming smile.

20/12.

Wolle just rang, black as night, and bitter; Carin's visa has been turned down, not only in Sweden but also here. If he knew how much greater cause he has to be gloomy! Caja's letter to me sets out the whole Weiner problem, with wailing and gnashing of teeth. His epistles, in a perpetual state of emotion and made of wishful thinking, bring her close to tears and make her fear breaking it off even more. She didn't want to do it by letter; that seemed cowardly to her, too casual – but in words. She applied for her visa from a sense of duty, but dreaded the thought of living with him again out at the café, and knew it would be too cruel to say anything in those few days, with him likely to be called up to serve in Petsamo very soon after. She dared not say anything to her mother about the visa, for fear of hysterical scenes and a relapse.

So, as you can imagine, she was glad the visa wasn't granted! And there was Wolle getting me to run around and look for other possibilities. So I did. It's damn tricky trying to steer a path between those two, be in the confidence of both, listen to both and talk without betraying their opposite number. At the moment I'm happy for Carin's sake and sad for his, and pretty fed up with the whole thing! It's a bloody liability, getting actively involved in other people's business. You have to walk a tightrope and stay neutral as best you can. –

Lasse's got hold of a chap at the Zoological Museum who's promised to write a foreword to his butterfly book and talked the whole thing over with him for several hours. They tested it out today at the Z. Museum by getting 4 classmates, all complete novices at butterflies, where each was given a critter to examine, using the Jansson method. The result was 87% definite identification. The girls managed 100%! Lasse's up in the clouds with excitement, living among his tomes. Ham's addresses to Ryti and Mannerheim are finished now, and stupendously lovely. The best things she's ever done in that line. She, Faffan and I all have our work on show in Lallukka's assembly room; it's the inmates' first exhibition. (And they are the main visitors to it, as well!) Tandefeltskan dismissed us with "The Jansson family is exhibiting – of course". How offhand! I think she's starting to get a bit doddery. Art and genealogy haven't much to do with each other!

Though actually – damn it. In my canvas (116 x 189) "The Family". I can't tell you how I've battled with it, every hour of daylight. If I can knock it into shape, I'll make a copy for you. I hope there won't be many drawing jobs this spring, so I can finally get time to paint!!!

I had two "patrons of the arts" here today. The first, small, timid, shabby and insignificant, found what she wanted at once and almost threw her arms around my neck with joy at "owning such beautiful, beautiful paintings". (!) The other, elegant, talkative, affected and brazen, she picked and chose, haggled and nitpicked for 2½ hours, before making off with one of my best still lives for 1,300, – 3,000 was the asking price. Even on her way out she was still fretting that I'd "swindled" her. I let her have it for the shy little one's sake. How funny people are!

21/12.

It seems rather too much like a diary, writing you a bit now and then, all in the same letter – but I so much like leaving my work for a little while, as if for a chat with you. – You know Eva – although it's true that we have our own will and ought to be able to steer ourselves wherever we want, there are times when what happens to us (I mean within us) is like a powerful, inexorable ebb and flow that we can do nothing about. It's so awful to wake up and realise the ebb is on its way. All this autumn (may Allah shroud it in oblivion) has been one big undulation, up and down, I've been constantly working my way up out of depression and I'm tired. You know how it is when you finally think you've found a balance between extremes, tense and anxious the whole time in case anyone or anything dislodges you from your hard-won composure.

My paintings turn out so strangely. When I do self-portraits I invariably, however hard I try, end up with such a rigid and sardonically superior-looking face, and when I tried to make myself look alive and happy in "The Family", it suddenly turned into you. It's odd, that picture, I wonder if I can ever show it – it's too obvious. My intention was for Ham, turning round in her seat, to pass on the rhythm of the painting to me, and my outstretched arm (putting on a glove) would transmit it to Faffan – who by his entry into the room would direct interest back to the centre where the boys are playing chess as a calm foreground. Instead Ham looks as if she's been startled by something, or is trying to keep me there in some way, I seem squashed in by the cupboard and nobody can really believe I can get past Faffan who's blocking the door and also incidentally looks as if he's discovered someone in flagranti and has a kind of helplessly imperious expression (if you can imagine that combination) as he clutches his newspaper. Everything's cramped and unharmonious except for Lasse, who looks like himself, gentle and natural. Prolle ends up as a sort of unreal dream figure with no expression in his face, however I try. Good grief, imagine what a meal Raffo would make

of that picture. But I'm going to get rid of the distorted atmosphere by use of colour. Yes, damn it, I will!

Prolle's friend Stige has got tuberculosis – they'd sent him back to the lines after only a few days in hospital to get over pneumonia. Maybe a sick boy is better than none at all.

Tapsa's been awarded another medal, just escaping with his life after a series of violent battles. Currently another long break in his letters. But I simply can't go on worrying in the same way. It's a case of blunted feelings and listless waiting now. Prolle writes to me often. Sometimes I think he's more than a brother, he personifies everything I admire and believe in among our youth of today – Prolle is almost a concept. One might say an ideal that I don't want destroyed. May he come home again – unaltered!

It was splendid at Samu's yesterday. Red wine, schnapps and cognac, cakes, coffee, cheese, chocolates. That side of things is always very lavish now, you see. It gets a bit trying, never being able to see them without a posh party. The Renvalls were there too; Ben's just been allowed home. All very pleasant and friendly. And yet it makes me melancholy. Must pull myself together. I'm the one being silly. – Sam asked me twice if I'd seen the announcement of his name change in the paper, but I just said "Yes". Essi was rather snide: So couldn't you change it to Lehtonen now? Why would I? "Well, then you can tell them your name used to be Vanni, if they ask!" – Boris has written me a terribly sweet letter. He's going to be an interpreter now, thank God. He sent his best wishes and said you're never out of their thoughts. And I had a Christmas card from your papa, too. Just imagine Boris sending him <u>pancake</u>!

26/12. Quiet evening in the studio. I've arranged my new Christmas books, a lovely blue cushion from Lasse is on the bed – proof all around me of people's thoughtfulness and generosity. I sometimes think we should have ten Christmases a year so we remember what it means to be enfolded in warmth – how much we depend on one another, remember how the joy of giving can help us, too. Christmas was much happier and brighter than I'd dared hope. It was actually Stige who brought the real spirit of Christmas in with him – he suddenly turned up at my studio – on sick leave. I was so glad that I took the boy in my arms. Then we had a cup of tea and listened to Beethoven, which he'd been yearning to do. He had tears in his

Cover design for *Garm*, Christmas 1941.

eyes. – The tubercles aren't definitely confirmed yet, he's got to have a more thorough examination. But I do hope he won't have to go back – I don't think he could cope with it. I happened to have a runty little tree with a star in the studio, which he took home with him; his family, who weren't expecting him home, hadn't bothered with Christmas at all.

Our tree had snow crystals in it this year, white covered with shiny cellophane. They looked lovely, slowly turning and glittering in the light. Ham read the gospel from the Doré bible she had as a present from Lasse. The old language was so beautiful. I'm going to sleep now Eva, I'm so tired after being out skiing with Lasse all day.

With all my heart I wish you <u>a Happy New Year</u>.

your friend Tove.

Tandefeltskan: Art critic Signe Tandefelt.
Raffo, sometimes Raff or Raffu: Rafael Gordin (b. 1904), family doctor
and friend of the Jansson family. In 1935, Gordin became a specialist
in nervous disorders and mental health, and the following year he set
up a private practice in Helsinki. Eva Konikoff was part of his circle
of acquaintances, and clearly asked after him in her letters.
Renvalls: Ben Renvall and Essi Renvall, both sculptors.
His name change: Until 1941, Sam Vanni was called Samuel
Besprosvanni.

THE WAR YEARS ARE A TIME OF PERPETUAL CONFRONTATION
with Viktor Jansson. He is pro-German, anti-Communist
and makes no secret of his aversion to Jews, infuriating Tove
Jansson. Their opinions are entirely at odds and the ensuing
scenes and political arguments are often referred to as "clashes"
or "crashes". By 1942 she is renting a room on Fänrik Stålsgatan and working there. In September of that year she leaves
Lallukka and moves in there.

27/1 –42 [*Postcard*] SENDER: TOVE JANSSON.
FÄNRIK STÅLSG. 3 A 20 HELSINGFORS. FINLAND.

Today several of the letters I'd sent to you were returned – it made
me really sad. It's been such a big help to talk to you – to know you
could follow everything that happened to us here at home. I'll try
a card this time – maybe that will get through. Would you like the
letters anyway, once the post is working again, or shall I burn them?
– Yesterday I submitted your portrait, with repainted background, to
the Young Artists, a landscape, a big, pungent canvas – "Nachspiel"
(have to see if I get in trouble for it) and 7 graphic prints. I've got
a job from Hemflit, designing two fabrics, and lots of other commissions, too.

Letters from Prolle and Tapsa recently. Boris is an interpreter now.
I felt ill this morning, could hardly speak and planned for a week
in bed. But when I tried getting up – it all blew over, just like that.
I suspect myself of deliberate suggestion so I can "hide" under the
covers. Koni, I'm so tired. Sometimes I feel a jolt of pure rage that

really scares me, so I run to the studio and do some scrubbing or write verses (!) and then try to be as pleasant as I can in the evening. We're all rather on edge, in our own way. Did you get the letter where I told you that Gordin's in town these days?

31.1.42

We've had the big clash that I've feared and expected for several years. This time it's final. Faffan and I said outright that we hate each other. I feel very sorry for Ham. But I don't feel any guilt, or sorrow, or anything. I feel like a stone. It would be nice not to have to go on living but we carry on, of course. I wonder how I shall organise things now. It'd be sheer hell to go on living at home, but I suppose I shall have to come round for my dinners, for Ham's sake. Damn the war.

Tove.

[*Postcard*] SENDER: TOVE JANSSON.
FÄNRIK STÅLSG. 3 A HELSINGFORS FINLAND

9/2 –42.

Can't help writing to you though I scarcely believe even these airmail cards will reach you. Since the family crash, things have been awful, in multiple ways. Now things are rolling along without too much friction again. Got to compromise for Ham's sake. – have my dinners at home and try to talk about uncontroversial topics (there aren't many!) and be agreeable in the evenings. I so much wanted to write to you, miss you such a lot! I felt completely lacking in initiative for a week, mostly didn't even bother getting up. Then various things happened to show me I had to take responsibility again, work, put on a cheerful face. To force myself not to be antisocial, I took a supply job at Central School as a drawing teacher. 30 unknown Finnish pupils, all adults. I took valerian, brushed up my Finnish and was scared stiff. Arno's come home and taken over now, thank goodness. Then I went to the party at the Guild, also in the spirit of educating myself. A very odd party. Oh Eva, fancy not being able to send you more than a postcard!

Your picture at the exhibition was well received – I put a high price on it because I want to keep it for myself – <u>something</u> of you. I've sold a number of pictures. Financially speaking I'm in rude health. Ulla Sukkari sends best wishes – she's called Mrs Hjelt now. I shall go and visit your mama soon. Abrascha and wife are coming here to the studio in a few weeks' time. Your brother Ruben is getting married before long. Good news from Boris so far. Prolles's been moved a bit back from the front and is hoping for leave in a couple of weeks. Tapsa's in Petroskoi – for now. Wolle wasn't permitted to travel to Stockholm with the exhibition as we'd planned. He was terribly disappointed. He comes round pretty often, gets me cigarettes, theatre tickets and is terribly kind. Lasse, who's been made editor of the school newspaper, has done a really great job. Ham's been awfully down since the crash, but I've managed to get her calm and cheerful again. The atmosphere at home is gentle and cautious. Everything's been said – I'm not in fear of another altercation. But it feels empty. An endless compromise, an endless balancing act, when one wants an "either – or"! I put my arms around you and miss you so much. My very warmest best wishes.

Your friend Tove.

20/3 –42 [*Postcard*] SENDER: TOVE JANSSON. FÄNRIK STÅLSG. 3 A 20 HELSINGFORS. FINLAND.

Dearest Eva!

It's the day submissions have to be in for the spring exhibition and I can't bear to look at my one entry, "The Family", any more. I've built myself a new picture shelf and put all my junk into the new corner cupboard, and I've rearranged all the furniture so it's as neat and tidy as a hallway to heaven. It'll be nice to start on some entirely new things, <u>without</u> any more exhibitions and in a fresh setting. And I suppose spring will be coming – though it's still only –15°. Though I'm a bit nervous about the spring; I know one feels everything more keenly then – I haven't really taken it in yet that it's over between Tapsa and me. He had another fortnight's leave – and like last time, I scarcely saw him. He'd been in town several days before he rang me, claiming he was calling from the station. And there were a lot of other clues to make me realise I've become some kind of "Duty and obligation" for him. He knew I was waiting evening after evening, felt bad, put it off until it was a nightmare and impossible to go at all. That's how it must have been. The last night he rang me from his lady-friend's, drunk, and asked if he could come. We cleared the whole thing up on the phone, kept it friendly and workaday. I asked him if he wanted to be free and he was touched and grateful. "It's too much!" So I let him go. It's all very peculiar. The fact that we spent the whole war trying to keep each other's zest for life going with our letters, often writing every day, talking about all the lovely things we'd do when we could be together, and that he loved me for seven years – and then when he gets some leave he goes to that painted blonde from Robertsgatan and is grateful to be free. But there's one thing I know: I <u>have</u> paid my debt to him. Haven't I, Koni. I miss you so terribly. The last letter I had from you arrived sometime in the autumn. Do you get mine? Are you happy over there?

Tove.

11/4 –42 [*Postcard*] SENDER: TOVE JANSSON.
FÄNRIK STÅLSG. 3 A 20. HELSINGFORS.

Have you read Lin Yutang: "Importance of Living"?

Eva, dearest! Just got home from Samu's and want to talk to you about what Samu was going on about: that my drawing makes my painting too graphic and they're incompatible ... It upset me. Perhaps he's right. Perhaps I'm half and half in other ways too – the daughter, the painter. You know – everything at home. It should be something free and happy and simple ... I wish I could go away – completely, go south – and I yearn for someone shrewd and lively, like you – someone to rely on. Or just to drift, to "be" – do you remember us talking about it once? No duties or obligations. Or success. – Guess what, I bought Beethoven's violin concerto, Schubert's 8th unfinished and a Bach toccata and fugue. They're wonderful (And expensive!)

Boris paid me a visit while he was on leave. Letter from P.O. today – fierce battles in which he's had the whole command – losses. It's starting now – "spring". People so tired, off-balance, everything's about food and politics – "The Family" at the spring exhibition was a shameful blunder; I shan't show anything else for a long time. Paint in peace, doggedly, try to get somewhere. It's got to be now. Studying Italian, doing a series of Christmas cards, illustrating a book. Maybe it disrupts the painting ...? On Easter Day there were yellow flowers hanging on my door, a card: "Demobbed!" It was Tapsa. Curious to think of him in town – finally away from the front. Stupid, the whole thing. But it was only right to give him his freedom. – Wanted to talk to you about Carin. You see, a couple of months ago I sent her a huge cry for help, totally impulsive, not to say uncontrolled, I was at rock bottom and needed someone, frantically. She never replied. Only now, a letter full of excuses about work and having a cold. And you know, I felt awkward, wretched, stupid, naked. Like when you scream for help and the other person, cringing with embarrassment, looks away and changes the subject. She's right, we've got to be "civilised". But the thing is, I can only send her impersonal, entertaining letters now. However I try, that's the way they turn out. Writer's block! Yet she doesn't notice the difference ... I was out and about with Tito, Liv and a few others for 2 days. Tremendous. It made a nice change. – You're so often in my thoughts. Wonder if you're lonely over there? (Have you read Carson McCullers: The heart is a lonely hunter? Horrid book). Hugs.

Your Tove.

Liv: The writer Liv Tegengren.

20/4 –42 [*Postcard*] SENDER: TOVE JANSSON.
FÄNRIK STÅLSG. 3 A 20. H:FORS.

Dearest!

Today I had dinner with Tapsa, who rang and said he had "spring feelings" and wanted to be out in the sunshine. He's always done that at this time of year, probably didn't want to spoil the ritual. Afterwards, coffee and Beethoven in the studio. Peaceful, very nice.

It looks as if I'll be able to be his friend, just as he wants, and I'm glad about that. He's entirely back in civilian life now, drawing for W. Söderström, a permanent position. (3000 a month.) Turtis still in clink. I'm very happy that Ham and I are going out to Pellinge at the start of May to tidy the plot, do some planting etc. When Faffan comes out I shall go back in again because somebody always has to be in town keeping in touch with Prolle. Really looking forward to spending time there with Ham, just the two of us. Perhaps it will be as wonderful as it was in Sept. She and I have pasted all her caricatures and books into two big albums, a huge job. I paint outside every day now, and I've got some new paintings in the studio, too. There's something new in them – and they're not graphic, so to hell with Samu!!! An idiotic couple came up to buy a canvas today, trampled around among the paintings: "It won't do them any harm", turned their noses up at everything. Sold 4 pictures to the Björneborg exhibition at the Salon. At my door one night I had two soldiers of the kind I don't like, you know, but they had greetings from a friend in Estonia. The music in my studio made them feel homesick, poor things – they had nowhere to go so I let them sleep here and went home. Strangely enough, Faffan wouldn't take them in ... So much for female logic. Illogical, but often more sound than the male variety. I trusted the people, not the idea – he the opposite. But I still didn't want to be seen at a restaurant with them – to Faffan's annoyance. O, Koni, I do so long for a sign of life from you – or just to know that you get my cards. But I expect you aren't able to write. I feel lonely – but cheerful and confident again, now the painting's going better. That will carry me over everything else one day.

Your Tove.

Turtis still in clink: Left-wing radical writer Arvo Turtiainen was held in protective custody during the Continuation War.

29/4 –42 [*Helsingfors*]

Eva, dearest!

My first try with a proper letter again. It's warm here now; I'm going round in your coat with the bobbly bits and your shells are between my windows. The skylights have been cleaned (first time in 15 years). And the light, blue night is shining in on me. Boats are tooting in the harbour again as I stand outside to paint, and one day the cranes came flying back, in their wide skeins. There's something strange about those birds – whether they are coming or going, they ignite wild restlessness and yearning in me. And – I felt almost moved that they made the effort to come back – here.

Tapsa popped up to the studio to show me his new suit, he's so used to me in spite of everything that I have to be part of whatever happens to him. So we exchange unreliable versions of what we've done, seen and heard – before he leaves again – but don't tell each other what we've been thinking, not any more.

Ina Colliander is trying to make friends, Volle's grown very dependent on me, colleagues come and go and little girls are allowed to borrow the studio for their young men. I never go to them, but I accept them all.

Constant fighting in the north, no chance of the post getting through now the thaw's set in. When I'm outside painting I can hear the salutes being fired at regular – and such short! - intervals over at the cemetery, it makes me shrivel up inside. The Collins have lost a son, as have so many of our friends. At home it's like a well of silence, everyone shut in with their own thoughts. I slink away like a dog to the institute, the studio, the docks. One evening Ham and I went to a concert, the young virtuoso had to play 4 encores before the applause died down. The blunted apathy of winter has given way to an intense receptivity to everything, people listen, see and feel all too acutely – maybe because of the endless waiting. The spring offensive has started now –

[*two lines blacked out by the censor*]

I was happier than I have been for quite some days as I sat there restoring a little lightship, a model boat made of metal (45 cm) that I paid a lot of money for in a fit of juvenile transgression in a junk shop. It was constructed with great expertise, affection and patience, with tiny doors and hatches, winding gear with cogwheels and chains, bells and whistles, sleek lifeboats (named Eugéne, Lucio, Jacques Ferencz – and Lucio's even got a silver trim!) and anchor. The main light is working, and to port and starboard I've mounted little lamps, green and red, plus one in the cabin, and a little storm lantern with wire wrapped round it on the roof. When they're all shining in the darkness it's like being on board at sea – among the shadows of davits and struts on deck. They took me two days, the eighteen little double blocks with balsawood pulleys ...

Raffo ran into me as I was coming along with the ship, and he laughed. Maybe he saw it as a flowering of my masculinity complex! – I happened across Kajus one day and we decided to be friends. His latest mistress even comes here sometimes. I like her. I'm seldom "with" all these people, I listen to them, and watch. But you're always close, and more alive than they are. I know you often write to me in your head even though I can't receive any letters. I wish you all good things, Eva!

Tove.

Collins: The family of artist Marcus Collin.
The spring offensive has started now: At the end of April, the Red Army mounted large-scale attacks on Finnish positions at Svir.
A model boat: This is the one Tove is pictured beside on p.487.
Eugéne, Lucio, Jacques Ferencz: A humorous detail; TJ has named the lifeboats after her male friends in Paris in 1938 and Italy in 1939.

17/6 –42 PELLINGE
TO: MISS EVA KONIKOFF. C/O H. HANSEN
RIVERSIDE DRIVE 258 NEW-YORK. U.S.A.
FROM: TOVE JANSSON.
FÄNRIK STÅLSG. 3A 20 HELSINGFORS. FINLAND.
<u>WRITTEN IN SWEDISH</u>.

Dearest Eva!

For once this is a happy Tove writing to you. I'm on my own out at Pellinge and intensely at home with the absolute silence, with being able to wear the scruffiest, comfiest old rags and divide up my day exactly as I like. In these white nights one can go to bed and get up whenever one likes, anyway. There's a stiff breeze this evening and it's storm-red over Sanskär – I've just had my dinner: little pancakes that I ate one by one as they were ready (the only proper way to eat pancakes – and what's more, no washing up!) and I'm now going out to plant the last things in the garden. Beside me

I have Taidekorttikeskus's little bear series; cards to rival your Mikky Mouse – a domestic equivalent, you see!

It was a very sound idea to bring my work out here – but I haven't made a start yet! The native hut and the cave are uppermost in my mind, with its current childish bent. But why shouldn't I be allowed to crawl behind reality for a while and just be happy after this long and awful time?

A month ago, when I last wrote to you and was out here with Ham, I made a bit of a start on the new hut before we went back in to work. I pulled down the old shack with the straw roof out at the point at Laxvarpet, and the timber from that plus what I scavenged from the beaches out at Tunnis were enough for the new "house". What are these atavistic nest-building instincts that constantly beset me? However infantile it may be, I always so much enjoy this work, sawing, lugging, chopping, hammering and digging. Maybe because – unlike my painting – it always turns out as one had imagined, a quicker and more tangible result.

This is what it looks like, my latest flight from reality. It's built in such a way that the cave opens up like an inner room, the back wall isn't covered but allows you to look up the rock face and see a patch of sky. I got some tar for the walls down in the village, and the roof will be of wood shavings. There are primitive, multi-coloured spikes protruding from under the edge of the roof, the window is of woven willow, and outside stands a totem pole with a wildly grimacing goat face, its beard and horns made of twisted roots. There are similar root systems topping the poles at the entrance. The palisade will be made of light grey branches, dried in the sun. I've put ladders in, leading all the way up to the top of the rock, and over to the right I'm busy digging out a particularly promising ravine. Inside there's an earth floor with flat stones and a set of steps up to the cave, where I've scattered shells on the white sand, and on its walls I'm in the process of carving out mammoths and other animals I've faithfully copied (from prehistoric finds). In the hut there's a wide, comfortable seat covered with my big goatskin, and raffia matting on the walls. My china Madonna tries discreetly and in vain from the depths of the cave to outweigh the savagely proto-barbarian atmosphere. The local population seems a little bit crazy, but interested. Lisbeth from Odden comes sometimes and talks about dance and young men and

In a letter to Eva Konikoff 11.9.1942, Tove Jansson writes: "I've started on a portrait in a lynx boa. I myself look like a cat, with my yellow skin, my cold slanty eyes and my new smooth hair in a bun. And a firework display of flowers. I don't know yet whether it's good or bad, I simply paint."

smiles down on me in a wise and patronising way. She's sixteen now and tells me "what it's like to be young" – which "the rest of us have forgotten" – the "new age is totally different from back them when we were young ..."

O Koni, if only you could be here – you, at any rate, are young enough to feel at home in all my "palaces"!

Tomorrow I shall ring home – and I'm already dreading it. All the rest of it will come sweeping over me down the wires. Maybe I'll be called up for compulsory labour? It would serve me right, antisocial old painter, to spend the rest of my summer in some turnip patch! [...]

1st June we celebrated Ham's sixtieth birthday, a hectic and happy merry-go-round. I decorated the boys' room all over with flowers – in the middle of the table was Faffan's marble bust of me as a little girl, and hanging on it a picture from me. Lasse gave her a terribly expensive bracelet – his latest passion is studying precious stones – his ambition now is to take up chased-work. He buys cameos, opals etc. in little junk shops, borrows books to bring home, goes over to discuss things with Lindroos. With the same fervour he devotes to everything he does. (That one's definitely going to be your most difficult child – said Raff. Hmm.)

And then earrings, silk stockings, books, a giant copper pan for spring water at the cottage, teacups, wine glasses – candles and a cake we'd spent ages saving for. Wine, cigarettes. The next day we had to write 90 thank-you cards for flowers and telegrams – all day long a stream of people to be plied with port, Madeira and coffee. They ended up colliding with the dinner guests all dressed up to the nines, which was rather awkward and had to be dealt with by lots of tactful grinning – and then the dinner ditto were herded into the boys' room where they had to sit and meditate. By the time we finally got to eat (after a lightning change of outfit in the bathroom), we were completely limp. Very late by the time we got to bed. But it was a splendid day – and the best thing of all: a letter from Prolle saying he would now be able to rest.

The next day Ham was in such festive spirits that I persuaded her to buy a lovely squirrel cape, straight, dark and exceedingly beautiful. A lynx happened to slip in for me too – I was in festive spirits as well.

And Eva, you were part of it too – because we served the guests' coffee with your bottles of cream, which I'd been saving up! Ham sends her thanks!

And then it was back to the usual routine and intensive Taidekortti production. Lasse went to Åbo, Faffan got to work on the Kramer fountain, Ham on her books. I must actually get back to the grind tomorrow as well. But there's sunshine and sea here – and carving mammoths _is_ more fun!

A heartfelt hug, Eva. You are always with me. Be well.

Tove.

Tunnis: The island of Tunnholmen.
Taidekortti production: In 1941–42 TJ designed a number of sets of Christmas, New Year and Easter postcards, and some with humorous animal pictures, for the publisher Taidekorttikeskus.

TOVE JANSSON'S DECISION TO MOVE AWAY FROM HOME develops over the summer of 1942. She has had her own studio for short periods before, but when she moves to Fänrik Stålsgatan 3 it is definitive. The time has come for the liberation she has dreamt of for so long. Two years later, she moves into the studio at 1, Ulrikaborgsgatan.

14/7 –42 (THE STUDIO)
2 SHEETS. WRITTEN IN SWEDISH
TO MISS EVA KONIKOFF.
114 WEST 21ST. STREET. NEW YORK CITY
FROM: TOVE JANSSON. FÄNRIK STÅLSG. 3A 20.
HELSINGFORS. FINLAND. TEL. 49849.

Eva dearest –

You have a new address now. Which doesn't tell me anything except that you're no longer looking after Hansen's brat ... Your family has had a telegram, from Philadelphia. So at least you exist! Leaving me to imagine the rest for myself. And I do, often, long stories. And they mostly end with me being there too. Goodness, if only I were! Just at the moment I'd give three exhibitions with canvas stretchers and the whole works to be able to have you nearby.

Your family is fine. Boris no longer has a dangerous post – the others are out of the army, David on holiday. He had – how incredibly generous of him – included my name in the telegram to you. He knows I'm close to you. I'm to send regards from Bärlund and Ulla Hjelt who's had a little girl – and from Clevan. She's finally broken it off with Wolle, who I had sitting here in my studio yesterday, subdued and bereft, but strangely calm. They all turn up here. And talk. I like it. But you're the only person I could give some of myself to in return.

It's bells and whistles here again, Prolle's on two weeks' leave, with the Freedom Cross for "calm and measured conduct in battle". We've already spent a week of it in Pellinge – it was happy and enjoyable, and Lasse joined us as well, from his time of misery in Uncle Jullan's garden in Åbo. (To which he isn't going back. The question of camp remains open.) Faffan melts when his "Klucke" comes – however much he may go on about his "third, antisocial misfit of a child"!) One day Prolle went in his canoe to fetch his friend Stig, who stayed with us for a few days. The boys went sailing and fishing, did some target practice, and generally idled about, whistling under their breath. One time they, Ham and I went out to Tunnis and made little houses in the sand. – do you remember ours, Konikova. The war was so far away. And yet – soldiers' leaves are like spring – eagerly awaited and delightful, but always too short, always so immensely melancholy beneath the joy.

All my postcard sets are finished, may the muse be praised. And I'm longing to start painting. Really start. Next we've got the gathering in of berries, leaves, roots, mushrooms and fish – but after that it's September. And then!

Eva, I'm leaving home in September, moving out, with my ration cards and wardrobe and the whole show. I've told Ham and she can break it to Faffan at some suitable time. A very ordinary little scene gave me the last push. This has been growing for so many years, so much torment, guilt and duty, so many inconsiderate outbursts arising from far too much misplaced effort to be considerate, so many bridges of reconciliation, too weak to carry the everyday traffic, and all that brooding! All of a sudden I just knew I couldn't bear it any longer, not for a single hour – I knew part of me would break, somehow. And I knew I'd never become a happy person, or a good painter, if I stayed. I'm trying not to dwell on how it is for Ham. Heart problems and Prolle and everything – I mustn't think about it. I stare back at the happy week when I was alone at Pellinge and try to recapture some of that wonderful peace, and find I'm thinking: you'll have that now, always. Of course it won't be as easy as that. But it's the right direction. Ham knows it.

I think Raff would be pleased with his "dream patient".

You know what, my cave suddenly seemed so pointless. Perhaps I hacked my belated childhood deep into its galloping mammoths once and for all – and there it can stay, with the pirate's gold in a glittering pile among the shells in the sand. The palisade of sun-bleached grey branches was never properly finished, and there's a bit missing from the paved courtyard and the wall up to the totem pole. But I got the roof covered so it doesn't rain in on my goatskin, and I managed to plant all the wild flowers. Some bones and a sun helmet that the sea threw up, a floor of sand and rounded stones, a blue lantern and fantastical negro emblems on the walls in the hut, white anemones – damnation – it's hard after all to see some of it go. Like when I come across old Teknis drawings, wild and moody extravaganzas, and laugh and wonder: what was I thinking of? And then with a slight pang: I've forgotten. I've no access to that blossoming world of dreams any longer – I'm trying to establish myself in the real world.

And it is a shrivelled sort of establishment sometimes. It especially doesn't like fine adjectives. I'm sure I used too many in one of my last letters to you. That bit about not making do with an illicit peek but actually sitting in the stalls and paying. Well, I took the illicit peek anyway – when it got too hard to be without the spectacle, and now it looks as if I'm going to have to pay after all – with a fine on top! Could be a false alarm. Or perhaps something that could be sorted out if I tried. Don't know why I'm leaving it and just waiting. Wondering whether, if it was a girl, I'd keep her and move to some more kindly country further south – and if it was a boy, he could have the little soldier-to-be. Totally and utterly. – A kind of strange, calm "can't be bothered" is growing in me, with a strong sense of loneliness and fear. Since I decided to leave the family, everything's changed, choice of words, thoughts, even tastes.

I played Beethoven's violin concerto, the adagio, which I used to love best – and didn't like it at all. And enjoyed Bach for the first time – that's just one example. It's as if something's happening to me – not as if I'm the one taking the action. Sometimes I even forget my ambition. The field is open for everything, I've done a really thorough clean-out but not put anything back in its place. Maybe one only becomes a painter once one has – oh – I don't know. I miss you so much, so much.

Tove.

25/8 –42. STOR-PELLINGE.
FROM TOVE JANSSON. FÄNRIK STÅLSG. 3A 20. HELSINGFORS.
FINLAND.
TO: MISS EVA KONIKOFF.
114 WEST 21 ST. STREET. NEW YORK CITY, U.S.A.

Eva, dearest!

I've rowed out to a tiny island off Tunnis, with velvety smooth rocks and bright blue bugloss growing in the cracks – it's peaceful, sunny after a long period of mist or wind. The seabirds fly screeching over the water, and away in the distance, the cannons rumble on. The storm boats are passing on their way in to the mainland. Tonight, planes are going over in steady waves and there was gunfire above Helsingfors from eleven to four. It's hard to reconcile the war with a day like this, an island like this. I came here to pretend to be happy, on one of those achingly perfect days that summer produces at the very last minute – but instead I feel nothing but a tremendous sense of melancholy. In a few days, you see, I shall be going into town, the studio, my new independence. It's like diving head first into unknown waters – but you do know they're cold ... To do battle with painting again, run up against people again, build that existence without the family which I've been fighting for, and for such an age. Of course I long to set off. But it's a little bit like before an exam. Oh Koni, if only you were there!

I've toiled like mad all month to gather in food, and Impi's preserved, salted and dried all the berries, fish, roots and leaves I've carted home. It's a little gesture for the family. I enjoyed roaming about the forest, being out on the sea – but at times I felt frantic with nerves about my painting, which has been at a standstill all summer. I've had a panicky feeling I shall never get going again. It's always the way – once I've "taken the plunge" I just find myself painting anyway. I know this. But I'm still scared. And breaks can be dangerous – they're rarely "like the arm of the spear thrower pulled back for the throw".

I've spent some of my evenings marking and folding away the linen I had from Ham for my birthday. I thought with a little chuckle of your impressive linen chest that made me tease you so much. The boys gave me a beautiful pair of touchingly pricey gold earrings with opals. "Is one of the gentlemen engaged to be married?" the shop assistant asked Ham. "No, they are for a sister." "Are there really such brothers?" she said, and tears came to her eyes. Well yes, there are. Things are quiet in Prolle's sector for the moment. Lasse's at a friend's. The forebears are in town. One Saturday when they were coming out, "Lovisa" ran aground in the fog and they had to spend an adventurous night out in the skerries. I wonder if there's been an air raid in town tonight. I expect I shall find out in due course. Soon I shall make my way back from this island – the last outing I shall have time for. Then I shall pack, and pick leaves for making tobacco substitute. – Thank you Eva, for a chance to talk. I'm going down for a dip now. *So long!*

30th.

Came to the studio straight off "Lovisa" – the town is in beautiful summer mode, and mystical in the darkness. And there are bombsites scattered around the centre. They're wild now, the Russians. But it still feels peaceful here. And in my own studio, with my work around me. All my stuff from Lallukka has been brought over here and the place is rammed full. How am I to cook – where shall I keep my clothes? But it will come right, I'm sure. It will all come right. Oh Konikova, I'm free, free! Love

Tove

LETTER NR. 3 1943 10.2.43
TO MISS EVA KONIKOFF. 21 ST. STREET. NEW YORK CITY, U.S.A.
FROM: TOVE JANSSON. FÄNRIK STÅLSG. 3A 20.
HELSINGFORS. FINLAND.

WRITTEN IN SWEDISH —
PLEASE, PLEASE, DEAR CENSURE — LET HER RECEIVE THIS
LETTER!!! THERE IS NOTHING ABOUT POLITICS.

Ham sends her <u>very</u> best. She's fond of you.
Don't forget me.

Dear friend Eva!

I've been feeling like a potentate today. In bed with influenza, cooking my meals in a horizontal position, surrounded by tulips and books, directing my genuine French cleaning lady who's turning the studio upside down and drying out my half-dry paintings without my having to lift a finger. She's seizing the chance to speak French and playing rumbas and disparaging the whole of Lullukka with relish and conviction. She just found my private pipe – so I shan't be spared in future, either. Anyway I shall send it, the pipe, to Svenka Grönwall. While he was back on leave he came up to the Guild's anniversary celebration, a shabby affair with too many people sitting at the wrong tables and telling each other lies. Svenka and I both found the whole thing excruciating, so when the crowd was turned out at around 12 we came here and sat talking until five o'clock. It was nice to talk to someone with a bit of sense – and I was glad, too, that contrary to expectations he hadn't taken umbrage at a letter I sent with his Christmas parcel, which was hopelessly crammed with civilian life, its little details and, well – trivialities. He ticked another colleague off roundly for a similar letter about our exhibitions etc., said we were putting on airs here at home and forgetting all those who are fighting, somewhere out there ... I understand his bitterness – but he should also try to understand the oppressive anxiety and desperation underlying our little everyday concerns and squeezing the life out of our paltry socialising.

My phone's been ringing all day, and I've been touched and surprised to find so many colleagues eager to bring me flowers and stuffed cabbage rolls. Especially the Jansson "academy", Wolle, Joyce Swanljung and Andsten (a giant of a man with a large beard and small, subtle paintings), all of whom have worked here now and then, for lack of a studio. But when I'm ill I have to be alone, firstly because I'm such an unaesthetic sight, secondly because I need peace and silence beyond measure. [...]

15th

I've still got my cold and feel like something the cat dragged in. Expect I caught it at that Grankulla party of Atos Virtanen (married to Stenman's daughter). I was behind the bar there, concocting "explosive Manhattans" and assorted other fabulous cocktails (out of simple basic ingredients) for about 60 people, mostly literary types, musicians and actors. It was nice to get away from snooty artists and I'm planning to insinuate myself into these new circles from now on, so I don't end up with scurvy of the mind.

There was a violent snowstorm that night so I huddled up in a corner and woke just in time to wash the glasses the next morning. How much I would enjoy talking to you about all these different people, many of whom you know, to give you a colourful picture of the incredible way the party started to unravel. But the letter would be too long. The censor ... And it's never really the same when I haven't got your living face beside me – when all it can be is a monologue sent off into empty space.

Things were pretty lively over the city tonight, for the first time in ages. Restless little Pan is home on leave again and came round one evening – a bit drunk to help him get over "his respect for me" and bearing a bunch of yellow flowers, and he proceeded to sit on some of my gramophone records and break them. I haven't seen him since – expect he took fright in some way. Tapsa shows up occasionally, harried by all the people trying to exploit him, holds my hand and talks shyly of dividing himself into small pieces and not having time to live.

Young Lasse is working on his book until late into the night. He had a party the evening we were all at the Guild, I provided wine and rumbas. He only invited girls. "They're much prettier and softer. And for once I'll be able to have them all to myself!" He's priceless.

20.2 –43

Lasse's finished his butterfly book now, and given it to the best entomologist in town for comment. We'll have to see!!! I'm well again and working every day. I'm sending three canvases to the Artists' Guild 50th anniversary exhibition after all, because it's sure to draw huge crowds and being seen can be a good thing. My canvases are more painterly than before – this time they won't be able to call me an illustrator!!! I'll have to show those at my solo exhibition in the autumn, even though they're no longer in the first flush of maidenly youth. – They've most likely sent Prolle on extended patrol because he's their best distance skier, and I'm extremely worried. Ham waits expectantly for the post three times a day and is totally drained. I keep ringing home to enquire. Faffan is annoyed, cross because she's worried (and – possibly – because he is, too) and I had a crash with him today. About my friends, as usual, and out of loyalty I defend them against his attacks. Out of loyalty? Habit, perhaps. Would I grieve for any of them – beyond you – if they disappeared? I don't believe I would. I'm blunted – and yet so convulsively susceptible to everything. I've decided to call little Pan just an episode. I've a new lover now – you don't know him. – I turn down all drawing jobs and seldom leave the studio. I work until it gets dark and sometimes I party with wine and dancing, all by myself. I reckon what I'm doing now is what they call "burning the candle at both ends". That's how it feels, Koni, Eva dearest, pray that there will be peace.

Your friend Tove.

Svenka Grönwall: The artist Sven Grönvall.
Joyce Swanljung: Fellow student at the Ateneum.
Andsten: Ricki Andsten.
Atos Virtanen: See Letters to Atos Wirtanen (p.257).

10. 44. H:FORS
SENDER TOVE JANSSON. ULRIKABORGG.
1. A THE TOWER. HELSINGFORS. FINLAND.
TO: MISS EVA KONIKOFF. MR. SALETAN.
70 FIFTY AVENY. NEW YORK CITY. U.S.A.
<u>WRITTEN IN SWEDISH</u>.

Dearest Eva!

I can't help writing to you again – we have peace, so perhaps we'll be able to send letters to America before too long. Next year, maybe. I shall hold on to the letter until then; it still shows that I was thinking of you. Oddly enough, Konikova, you felt more alive to me all these years than any of my other friends. I talked to you, often. And your smiling Polyfoto cheered and consoled me and shared my good fortune when nice things happened. I remembered your warmth, your vitality and friendship, and was glad! At first I wrote often, every week – but after about a year, most of the mail was sent back to me. Carried on writing even after that, but they were often such dejected letters that I didn't bother saving them. Now there's such an impossible number of things I want to tell you that I don't know where to start. Koni, if only I had you here in my grand new studio and could give you a hug. There's no one I've longed for as much as you these past few years.

It's magnificent here, don't you agree? A tower room, as lofty as a church, nearly eight metres square, with six arched windows and above them some little rectangular ones like eyebrows, up near the ceiling. Piles of mortar and cracks here and there, because it's still not fully repaired after the bombing, and in the midst of all the debris, an easel. A huge Art Nouveau fireplace with ornate scrolling and a comical old door with red and green glazed panels.

A studio one could spend a whole life beautifying if one wanted to. And next to it an asymmetrical, whitewashed room where I can keep all my female clutter, all my soft, playful, showy, personal stuff – with two windows up near the ceiling. 1, Ulrikaborgsgatan. The Tower. Hageli's old studio. Some part of his cheery, adventurous soul is still lingering here, I can sense it. Slightly melancholy. – I'm glad and grateful that my grand Studio Utopia has become reality. And I feel the urge to paint again. Wake up in the mornings and remember – first that the boys are alive – and then that I've got the Studio. (and then Atos!)

Lasse came home from the military academy a few days ago, demobbed – tomorrow he turns 18. Oh Koni, to think that he never had to go to the front! Now he dashes about the house, whistling, has lots of irons in the fire: he's writing a book, studying Spanish, doing scarily big business in postage stamps, practising taxidermy on caterpillars and devising new systems for the examination of butterflies. And he's incredibly proud of his uniform, dear child. He passed his university matriculation last spring, on special study leave, along with the queen of his heart, Erica von Frenckell.

Peo's at a field guard post somewhere in a bog, and we're still a bit worried they might send him up north to scour Germans out of the country. If <u>only</u> I could write about politics – but it's important that you receive the letter in one piece! Maybe a time will come when the dam is allowed to burst and we can say <u>whatever</u> we want to one another about our thoughts and opinions. Peo is a lieutenant now and has been wounded twice; the first time by a piece of shrapnel from a mine in his leg, the second by a splinter of a grenade in his arm. Thanks to the grenade we were able to enjoy a bright and happy summer month at Pellinge together, just as the fiercest fighting broke out along his front. When he went back, he didn't find many of his comrades left. It must have felt appalling. – He's engaged now to a very sweet, lovely, feminine little creature called Saga Jonsson. Her father runs a building business. She's tremendously like Peo in her quiet, kindly discretion. Peo <u>might</u> take a job teaching English at the girls' school just opposite Lallukka. If he wants to. A year ago he declared it was too late for studying, he just wanted to get away from here – travel, sail, live. Write about what he saw, take photographs. I understand him. Five years of his youth have been taken from him. But I still thought – well. Back then he could have got that scholarship to Oxford. He wanted to study philosophy. But, Konikova – the only vital thing is for him to be happy! These years have shifted so much of what I thought was fundamental in my attitude to life.

Before, all that mattered was for my pictures to live on when I was gone. That's important now, too. But more powerful than the longing to be "great", to be famous, is the longing for joy, for happiness. For <u>a whole year</u>, Eva, I haven't been able to paint. The war nearly did for my desire to, in the end. It took me time to understand that it has to be a road, not a destination. What I want now is for my painting to be something that springs naturally from myself, preferably from my joy. And I want to be, I will be, happy. As I am now, Konikova. I'm going to make up for these lost years many times over. They've been so dreadful. But now I don't want to think about them, write about them. – You know, just seeing Ham's new, calm, shining face brings happiness. We're caught up in the influx of autumn drawing jobs at the moment. I'm only taking on the work that interests me. The other day Samuel asked me to recommend him for a drawing job – he needed the money. It's the first time he's been forced to do that. He and Maya were in Stockholm for a few weeks. We meet at events now and then, and all get along very well together. Maya is a dear, wise person when you get to know her a bit better. [...]

I hope to meet up with Rafael Gordin some time, once he's a civilian doctor again; I should like to show him that his "healthy egoism" is finally starting to bear fruit. – Konikova, what a pathetic summary (of a fraction of what's happened) but I expect I'll be able to give you the subtle shades eventually. For the censor's sake – goodbye. And lots of love!

Ham sends warm wishes.

from Tove

Hageli's old studio: TJ took over the studio in August 1944 from the artist Olga Nordström, who occupied it after Hjalmar Hagelstam was killed in 1941. The tower was damaged in the intense air raids of February 1944. TJ spells the street name differently in the heading and in the body of her letter.

13.10.44 H:FORS
WRITTEN IN SWEDISH. FROM TOVE JANSSON.
ULRIKABORGG. I A. THE TOWER.
HELSINGFORS. FINLAND.
TO MISS EVA KONIKOFF. MR. SALETAN. 70 FIFTY AVE.
NEW YORK CITY. U.S.A.

Good morning Konikova!

How lovely to be able to talk to you again – with some hope of you eventually getting my letters. You're not quite so distant any more. World peace can't be so far off, and the doors to the outside are opening again. First for the letters – then for us! I've never dreamt and planned as much as in these past few years. Not as a game – but as an absolute necessity. I've travelled round the world and come to a stop in Morocco at Westermarck's villa beside the sea. Warmth, Eva, colour! Atos and I thought of setting up a colony there for artists and writerly folk and maybe only going back north for the beautiful pale summers up here. And to America, Koni!

You'd like Atos Wirtanen. He's as sparky as you are. Full of untamed zest for life, with a dazzlingly clear mind. I've seen him angry, but never depressed. He's no taller than me, a creased and rumpled little philosopher with a smile even wider than yours. Ugly, cheerful and brimming with life, thoughts and utopias. And self-esteem. He's quietly convinced that he's pretty much the finest brain in Finland at the moment (or maybe even all the Nordic countries, he sometimes wonders!) His great prophet is Nietzsche, on whom I've heard endless disquisitions, so I'm starting to get a bit tired of him. But Atos is very busy writing a book about said coryphaeus, in which he replaces Wille zur Macht with the will to form. Hopefully this – the book – will help to free him from his grand ideal so he can create more freely himself.

Atos is a Member of Parliament, a social democrat, 38 years old, and has been extremely politically active these past few years – the enfant terrible of Parliament, and taking delight in everything that smacks of plans, intrigue and mystery-making. Like a boy. But as a fully grown human being he is unswervingly honest, a genuine, "proper" person, as Raff would say. He's generous, but loathes giving and receiving presents. Loves parties, but hates the traditional kind, never wanting to mark birthdays, Christmas and so on. His amused dismay when I came to wake him dressed as Lucia last Christmas! He has no understanding for sympathy or sacrifice or melancholy, sadness. He's more or less the man I was longing for when I grumbled about all the "doggy eyes", all their imploring, self-effacing, guilt-laden looks. We met at a big party out at Grankulla at his house (rented) among a host of politicians, artists, journalists, actors. It happened fast – we were so obviously suited to each other. He didn't want to get married either – he's been scared off by his three-month marriage to the Stenmans' daughter Maja.

There's a lot of talk about us, of course. And Faffan is angry. Ham understands me. And Eva – what an enormous relief; she's made it clear to me that she understands the nature of our relationship and doesn't think it wrong. For the first time I'm not bothering to conceal things and sneak away – I'm so proud of him! And of course

I shall have to pay the price – but I can afford it. (What miserable little hyenas people can be – some of them.)

Atos Wirtanen hails from Åland, and his 9 brothers and 3 sisters are all quite simple people. Sailors, navvies – a wild clan, getting into fights and stealing each other's women.

Wonder how he happened to be the only one to get the special intelligence chromosomes. His books of aphorisms are good – and his poems too. But I don't think he can give himself free rein in a really comprehensive philosophical work until he gets out of politics.

This summer I had a wonderful week on Pellinge – the only purely sunny one, in all senses. The parents came too, and Atos, Peo and Saga. Every day was like a blissful dream. Uncomplicated, happy. Crawling out of the tent with Saga and rowing to fetch the philosopher from Sanskär. The others stayed in Kalle's little summer cabin – we've had to move out of the bigger house. That's now occupied by the young master, Albert, and his wife and little boy. Every day we made long, adventurous forays to the outer islands (we ignored the mines), bathed in clear green rock basins, in the surf, in the moonlight, in a gale. We rambled in the forest and around the inlets along the coast. Atos was enchanted and stopped in wonderment at every step to lose himself in endless philosophical musings on a crevice in the cliff, a spider's web he couldn't mend, a lichen on the mossy rocks, a bird's egg. It was like discovering Pellinge all over again. Peo and Saga went round quietly, holding hands. Any expression of sentiment is inimical to Atos. He's never told me he's fond of me – and I'm sorry about that. But the important thing is what <u>I myself</u> am capable of feeling. –

[...] It's late – I shall get off to bed. They way things are now, in eager anticipation of the next day, not yearning to be away from it all for a night. I embrace you in great friendship. All the best to you.

Tove.

Westermarck's villa: Philosopher and sociologist Edvard Westermarck's villa near Tangier. See Letters to Atos Wirtanen.

4 MARCH −45
FROM TOVE JANSSON. ULRIKABORGSG. 1 THE TOWER
HELSINGFORS. FINLAND.
WRITTEN IN SWEDISH.
3 PAGES TO MISS EVA KONIKOFF.
MR SALETAN. 70 FIFTY AVE. NEW YORK CITY. U.S.A.

Dear Eva!

Now the door to America is opening, maybe in a couple of weeks. I wonder whether all my letters will find you. I shan't send you a bundle of melancholy wartime letters. That time is past. – Here, spring is arriving, very gradually. In the sunshine there's dripping on all my fourteen windowsills and reflections of the sun are dancing around the whole tower and making it hard to paint. The rain comes straight through the plasterwork of the ceiling and streaks the walls, and in the mornings it's not +1° in the studio any longer, but + 6°, and 9 in My Room.

It's so nice here now, a profusion of colours and objects. I shall draw it all for you some time. (Once the censor stops suspecting it might be a camouflaged war map!)

At present I'm busy with a collection for the spring exhibition at the Artists' Guild – those last nervous weeks when the canvases fly up onto the easel and down again, looking wilder with every passing day – as do I.

Atos spends most of his time on campaign trips, or holed up in meetings half the night. I really do feel like a politician's wife when he gets home at 4.30 in the morning or I have to go down to the station with coffee and sandwiches! That impertinent Sigrid Schauman has taken each of us aside in confidence and asked us "what we're waiting for" and why we don't "do something about it". The muse be thanked that Atos has a sense of humour! But there's no doubt that people in general are getting used to it, accepting the state of affairs and always inviting us jointly to things. Though some rascal's giving people my number and getting them to ring early in the morning and ask for Atos. It's stopped annoying me now: I'm far too proud of him for that. – Samu's been laid up with jaundice for six weeks but he'll gradually take on his teaching duties at the Free Art School. He had an exhibition of drawings that attracted some attention. – Tapsa got the sack as a prison warder because he kept treating his charges to trips to the cinema. Recently he's been putting on the Russians' exhibitions, going to their parties and generally spending his time in circles I have no contact with. We came across each other on one occasion, at the Guild's Runeberg party, and we danced a waltz. If we ever meet in heaven I'm quite sure the first thing we'll do is ask the angels to strike up a Viennese waltz! The lady of his heart nowadays is a ceramic artist – a pretty, dainty little creature. He isn't in employment any more, but is his own lord and master as he always wanted to be.

Carin Cleve writes in a rather melancholy way that "one's thoughts just go round in circles, somehow" when everything is just a dreary cycle of housekeeping and cooking, looking after her baby son, washing and cleaning. They have no social life and her husband gets home very late. What's more, their finances are in a wretched state – sometimes she can't even afford to send me letters. Even so – I think she's happy. Mostly about her little boy, whose development I find described in detail whenever I get a letter from her after a gap of many months.

Wolle Weiner has signed a contract for another year as a theatrical scene painter in Vasa and is as gloomy as the night.

Peo got the English-teaching job as soon as he was home from the front. He's also been giving private lessons and going to Uni. Lasse changed course and gave up his biology; now he's doing the same as Peo: philosophy, history of literature, and English. Peo has written a collection of short stories, which Söderströms will publish this autumn. I think it's good, though it has the subjectivity and melancholy of youth. It's probably going to be called "Young Man Walks Alone". The main idea running through the book seems to me to be a development from proclaiming of the importance of self-sufficiency and solitude to gaining an insight that one does still have to live with, and for, another person.

Lasse is also going to try to get his Stone Age dictatorship book into print – and I shall be publishing a story, which I'm currently illustrating! I shall send you the Janssons' combined literary efforts when the time comes! And, by the way, wouldn't you like your box of books sent in due course? Lasse's been a little sober because the Frenckell girl went and got engaged in Stockholm – but his friendship with the Hjelm lad seems to have helped him over it. They're writing a crime-fiction novel together – like the brothers Goncourt – and it's going to pay for their round-the-world trip! Peo's trying to get hold of a boat for a honeymoon sailing trip with Saga this summer. (20 March. He got the boat, it cost him all his army pay plus the money he's scraped together from teaching.) My own plans, now that they can be put into practice, extend further than that: down to Morocco, Tangier, where Atos and I hope to rent Westermarck's villa. Maybe we can set up an artists' colony there. We also dream of buying Äggskär at Stor-Pellinge and renovating the abandoned pilot's cottage. You remember, where we found the dead baby seabirds and myriads of swallows' nests in the lookout tower.

I scarcely dare believe it could happen – but we've already made enquiries at the Maritime Pilot Administration. I suppose it will eventually become rather impractical, us not being married, but until we're forced into matrimony we'll just try to stick together anyway. I know now how Atos feels about me – that's important. A couple of months ago I told him about my match (well, spiritual mismatch) (P.S.: the seascape painter) in the last years of the war, and for a while after I'd met him. To my immense surprise he was far from philosophical, quite jealous and wild in fact, and for a few days I thought I'd lost him.

But he came closer to me after that – oddly enough. I'm glad, though.

That previous contact flared up when he was on leave, one week when there was intensive bombing, and then I grew strangely dependent on the man. Because, I think, he was someone who for the first time in my life allowed me to experience the body at rest and satisfied. In spiritual terms we were poles apart. I found it hard to leave him and didn't want to, though I could sense the balancing act between his domain and Atos's making me feel frayed and tense. In the end I had to choose, of course. Bringing on a nervous collapse or some such bloody nuisance. And infernally enough, it timed itself to coincide with my studio-warming party for 35 people, and settled in my stomach. It put me very much in mind of that wretched thing you once got – do you remember, when you were beside yourself about Samuel and rang for Raff in the middle of the night. I was given morphine, and now there's a story going round town that I've turned into a morphine addict and was so drunk that I couldn't stand up at my own party!! Well, they enjoyed themselves anyway, thank goodness – they were still drifting out at six in the morning, taking what was left of the booze. They're sombre memories, all these. Now I want nothing else but this new, serene affection I feel. Just occasionally, increasingly seldom, I experience a strong yearning for those dark, dangerous years, which glides swiftly over me like a black cloud.

I must finish now – this letter's getting too long. I send you a big hug, Eva. Perhaps a letter from you will eventually find its way here? How happy that would make me. Ham sends lots of good wishes. All my best!

Tove.

the Janssons' combined literary efforts: Besides Per Olov Jansson's collection of short stories, the other publications were Lars Jansson's adventure book *Härskaren* (The Master) and TJ's *Småtrollen och den stora översvämningen* (The Moomins and the Great Flood).
the Frenckell girl: Erica von Frenckell.
the Hjelm lad: Börje Hjelm.
studio-warming party: The party had been held some time before, in December 1944; TJ gave an account of it in her letter of 10.12.44 to Atos Wirtanen, who was away on Åland at the time.

IN JULY 1945, TOVE JANSSON GOES TO ÅLAND TO VISIT ATOS Wirtanen's family and the area where he grew up, round Saltvik north of Mariehamn. They are intending to discover Åland together, although she initially travels there alone. Atos Wirtanen arrives ten days later. But another motivation for her trip is the need for solitude. When Wirtanen leaves Åland at the start of August, Tove Jansson stays on for several weeks. She is hard at work on her second Moomin book, *Kometjakten* (*Comet in Moominland*).

12.8.45
WRITTEN IN SWEDISH. FROM TOVE JANSSON.
ULRIKABORGSG. I.
HELSINGFORS. FINLAND.
TO MISS EVA KONIKOFF. 46 WEST. 17 STREET.
NEW YORK CITY. U.S.A.

Eva, dearest friend!

Your first letter, dated March, was like having you very close – I felt happy, sad, full of longing and warmth. To think that you, too, missed me so much these past years. To think that you, too, wrote letters that were never sent when you felt lonely! The war years were certainly wretched, I hope never again to go through that terror of waiting to hear from the boys. But things must have been just as hard for you, of course – feeling lonely and homesick, and struggling with the language, with work.

I'm so happy, Eva, that you feel you've found a new homeland, where you've got friends – and I know you'll make those wherever you go – and that you're not missing your old home any more. I do hope Boris will be able to come and see you. Now he's on his own, I'm sure he'd like that. I've thought about you all the time, about how hard and desolate it must have felt when you got the news about your father.

I received your letter of 2nd May and a card a few weeks before that, and they complement each other to give me a more complete picture of you. You may well have changed, and be standing with both feet on the ground – but you're still the same. How could whatever lies deepest within us, our essence, be peeled away! Ever since you were a little child you've had to go through more than it takes to create a 100% cynic and realist, but you're still as I love to remember you. More realistic, yes – but not materialistic, less sentimental but still idealistic. I've changed too, in the course of these years, grown more mistrustful and self-assured. It does no harm.

This evening I'm sitting here in Åland in my little room next to the sauna, burning the last candle stump I've saved, with the crickets holding a concert out there in the August night. I really miss you right now! I've lots of male friends, but none of them could even half-fill your place, and Carin's slipping further and further away into her family life. I've already written to you about our friends, Tapsa's marriage, Samuel's teaching job at the school of painting and the child they didn't have, the Renwalls' divorce, Lönnberg turning into a complete negativist and falling out with everybody. Arno and Raffo Gordin have entirely disappeared from view.

Lasse abruptly abandoned biology and switched to studying philology. Now Ham has written to tell me he's thrown his studies overboard entirely and is going round as black as night, melancholy. I had a panicky letter from him, asking me for new ideas for short stories, so I'm trying to see what I can find for the boy. Poor thing, he's so unlike Peo and so like me. Black periods followed by ecstatic ones, and forever falling in love. Peo goes through existence calmly weighing things up and observing them, and very seldom takes a wrong turn. They're happy, he and Saga – and they thoroughly deserve to be!

He's publishing a collection of short stories in time for Christmas, and Lasse an adventure story. Perhaps you'd like them, and the children's book I've got coming out?

Faffan is definitely the one of us all least changed by the war. Perhaps he's just sunk a little deeper into his bitter brooding and his feeling that he stands alone against Ham and me. Poor Faffan. And poor Ham! I've gradually shifted away from them, but will never be able to live entirely my own life while Ham is still alive. Her need for me is so boundless – and the muse knows she is half my heart as well.

She's had a difficult summer with lots of work in the heat, Faffan down with diphtheria, Lasse's Weltschmerz and a young cousin from Sweden with recurring stomach pains, unaccustomed to the poor food, plus Impi in the kitchen going through every 50-year-old's bouts of desperation.

Meanwhile I've been here on Åland since 10th July, roaming about in a spell of work and a need for solitude, feeling like a deserter, but I've gritted my teeth and decided to stay anyway.

There's a great sense of melancholy here as summer comes to an end. Quiet days as I drift around the small fields and pastures down by the sea, paint and never meet a soul. (except an angry bull once, who attacked my canvas while I perched up in a puny little pine tree, quaking.) And I'm thinking about the autumn, exhibitions, friends, family – everything I shall have to immerse myself in again. And about Atos and me. Sometimes I love him so much that it almost hurts. At those times it seems so simple and natural to get married. It wouldn't really change anything, we'd live separately, as we do now. But whenever he's off on his trips to the great cities of the world to give philosophical lectures, I could go with him. He's not bothered about children. He's something of a genuine one-off, something meteoric and absolute, I don't understand why he feels no urge to continue himself, only to complete and clarify his intellectual life. He's the sort of person who makes me understand (which I've never done with any of my 100 and one other loves) that it would be very hard to marry anyone else after feeling his joy, his free spirit and intelligence. This scares me, but makes me feel proud and secure. I know he's scarcely capable of loving in the way we mean when we talk of loving. He cares for me just as he cares for the sun, the soil, laughter, the wind. More intensely, but in the same way.

Nietzsche is his Great Idol, and that pest of a philosopher has gone and written somewhere that a married philosopher is always ridiculous. *Well, there you are!* I'm content with things as they are, it's just the future I'm thinking of. For now, my thoughts are running along completely new tracks, and I sometimes wonder if I shall be able to die without having Atos nearby. And children? This war has taught me one thing, at any rate. Never sons. Never soldiers. Maybe it's become a bit of a fixed idea – but I've seen too much ever to risk it.

Eva, the idea of coming over to you has taken a firmer shape since your letter. Why not! We were going to go to Mexico together, go south. And just like you, I would dare to go anywhere and do absolutely any sort of work. And we would be happy on our expeditions! This is still all a long way off, I know, but my longing and conviction are strong enough to wait.

If at some point you were able to send me some paints, as you so kindly offered, these are the ones I use:

Important	*Less important*
Kremser white	Cadmium red pourpre
Cadmium yellow	Siena burnt
Cadmium orange	Siena natural
Cadmium red (light and dark)	Ivory black

Ultramarine (dark)	Light ochre
Cobalt (light)	Mars violet
Vert emerande (emerald green)	Alizarin madder lacquer
	(dark and pink)

But I can manage for now on what I've been able to come by. And please, send me the little book of the letters you wrote to me! – How terribly lonely you must have been in that big house in the country. Imagine you putting up with it for six months.

It was pretty miserable that for the years that were probably our most difficult, we weren't able to write to each other. But knowing that you were there and thinking of me was often a help. May you have good health Eva, and may you cope with your irascible uncle and find a more interesting job. May you not be disappointed in Ramon, either – may you be happy! Greetings to your two best friends from me.

Tove.

when you got the news about your father: David Konikoff died in 1945.
Ramon: Ramon Cordova, to whom Eva Konikoff was married for a time.

1 OCT. 45. WRITTEN IN SWEDISH. 2 PAGES.
TO MISS EVA KONIKOFF. 46 WEST. 17 STREET 11 N. YORK.
FROM TOVE JANSSON. ULRIKABORGG. 1 A.
HELSINGFORS. FINLAND.

Dearest Eva!

Today I lit the first fire of the year in the studio, because it's already down to just 8° in there. I can hear dripping on the tower roof again and the ships are hooting out there in the dark – spring sounds. But not worrying when it's winter that lies ahead ... It was the disinfector who brought the coal for me. He'd heard that I was cold – so he turned up one morning with two sacks of coal! There are some wonderful people, in spite of everything. And do you know what he did – (I gave him a picture he liked) – sent flowers to thank me! A remarkable gentleman, incidentally. It's made him something of a philosopher, having to go though people's flats, offices and lumber rooms so thoroughly – and every disinfection a voyage of discovery for him, as lives are unrolled and stripped pretty much naked. And he's seen people's faces, too. He was a telegram messenger for quite a few years. It's the workers and the aristocracy who bear a blow with the most dignity, he said. We talked to each other for a long time, and he was more interesting than a lot of my friends.

The Young Artists' exhibition has formally opened. Just think, Koni, I was hung in the middle gallery for the first time, with the older and more experienced artists. It feels funny to have come to that … I simply hadn't noticed I wasn't so young any more, but there it is! (They're even considering buying one of my still lives for the museum, so then I'd be "immortal" to boot! Cheers!) Fellow artists who reverently step into my cold tower say "One would have to be a young painter to have …" But anyway – life seems to me to grow richer and more intense with every passing year. I not only understand more but feel and see more. Perhaps the very fact that one learns not to try to understand <u>everything</u>. That one's emotions are not invested in too many people, too many things – and one doesn't see only what is pleasing to the eye.

Samuli came rushing up to the studio one morning and sat and talked for several hours in his old, frank way – oh, how long ago that was! It's a difficult time for him. And even more difficult for Maya, poor little thing. She's in Stockholm at the moment. He was reproaching himself in all sorts of ways. Talking about how he works, deaf and blind, in a kind of frenzy, for weeks on end. And while that lasts, nothing else exists for him. Not Maya, nor his friends. Perhaps his talent lies precisely in that single-track intensity of his. The heedless fury that's driven all the geniuses' wives to despair. I can understand them! (And, may the muse have mercy on me – I understand their husbands, as well.) To scarcely get a word, a friendly sign, a caress – to scarcely dare tell him dinner's ready. Sitting alone in a silent house, week after week, maybe for months, waiting for her husband to relax, a reaction period in which he notices she exists again! To put up with that, Samuel said, she has to love my work more than herself, more than me. But I've seen her eyes go black with hatred when she looks at my paintings. They're fond of each other. But how are they to get through this!

Sam is firmly convinced that in the three years he spent being a "good husband", he got worse as a painter. (His pictures were worse, a bit, but I thought it was on account of the war – we all found it hard to paint then!)

Now he has indisputably taken a leap forward. But he felt he'd lost a great deal too. The friends he ignored in his working period aren't interested now he's emerged from his studio for one of his intermissions. And Maya, who knew from experience that it would come after the exhibition, went to Stockholm to let him see how alone he was. He was certainly going crazy with loneliness when he came here! And wondering if the pictures were worth what he'd sacrificed for them. And what Maya had had to give! My poor friends. I always thought this was a women's problem – when she's in a creative profession. Sometimes the man has to choose too and Eva, it's a horrible decision!

Atos was here for dinner today. And it was so strange to hear him use more or less the same expression as Samuel, "The Concept". The unimportance of any event external to that – Indifference to everyone and everything apart from the life within (Painting) And goodness me, don't they both let their shirts get filthy when they're living free range!

But. There's a big difference. When Atos tumbles in at some hour of the night, sleepy and with his head full of politics – or abstract ideas – he talks to me. He lets me share it, even if I don't understand it all. I must admit I'm sometimes not all that interested in what this or that social democrat said – especially right after an embrace – but imagine if Atos said nothing. If he just retired into his own world and left me even more lonely and desolate than one is afterwards, anyway. If that happened, I'd jolly well be off to Stockholm too! (If I could.)

Can you believe it, I've had another proposal. A young painter, Siegfrid, aged 27. A gawkily persistent boy, his pockets perpetually full of poetry, and I'm sure he'll make a good artist one day. Just like Ricki (the seascape painter), with whom he shares my old studio on Fänrik Ståhlsgatan, he's a strange mixture of weakness and down-right hooliganism. A foundling whose bloody grim childhood was followed by a rag-tag sort of young adulthood at sea – and five years of war. I wonder if there's any poet who he doesn't know and whose best work he can't recite – and his own poems aren't bad. He's sold three canvases at the Young Artists' and can afford to get his trousers and watch out of hock!

Now Eva, goodnight. It would be lonesome without you to talk to sometimes. I wonder how you are this evening. Whether you were able to forgive Ramon. Not for what he did – but for being that kind of person. I wonder if you're happy. And I wish it, very much indeed!

Tove.

10 Oct.

A break for a rather action-packed interlude. Lasse, poor little boy, tried to run away to South America with a mate of his – thought they'd <u>sail</u> across. They only got as far as the Gulf of Finland before they were shipwrecked, but they're safe. I'll write again later. A kiss! Oh, and I've become "immortal". Cheers, Eva.

disinfector: a pest-control officer from the local health authority whose job was to disinfect people's homes.

26 OCT. 45.
WRITTEN IN SWEDISH.
TO MISS EVA KONIKOFF. 46 WEST. 17 ST. NEW YORK, U.S.A.
FROM TOVE JANSSON ULRIKABORGSG. 1 A.
HELSINGFORS. FINLAND. 4 PAGES.

My best wishes to Ramon!

Dearest Eva!

I really miss you this evening. The rain is dancing on the tin roof of my tower and I've pulled my electric sun as close as I can. The studio looks huge and gloomy at night and now that it's full of 4-metre-high lions and tigers and monkeys, glaring from every corner – it's almost creepy. I'm busy with the decorations for a big artists' gala taking place on 3rd November, and I've now spent nearly a month cursing the responsibility they've heaped upon me. It's going to be

Facsimile of the handwritten letter (26 October 1945). It includes a night-time sketch of the outside of Tove's building and a sketched floor plan of the studio.

Noah's Ark, Hagelstam's old idea for a new *Noch eine Nacht* that never happened. I painted the Ark and Mount Ararat in the scenery workshop at the Swedish Theatre – they're over 11 m high – and the brontosauruses even taller. May the muse have mercy, I'm starting to see animals going in two by two both day and night. It's going to be in the courtyard of the Adlon Börs hotel – and in the restaurant we're having Noah's vineyard with grapes and leaves by the thousand. This Bacchanalian popular entertainment has been organised by a Swedish art foundation, which has appointed me as animal painter. The waiters will be wearing donkey ears and tails, and I shall delight in yanking the latter with a "Waiter, a beer" – and consider it compensation for my work. Acquiring the materials took ten days – and it's all got to be painted in <u>watercolours</u> – and easel painters have an incredibly easy time of it – well, never mind. Let's talk about other things, I'm going mad with this silly menagerie Here is my study from outside, with all the 14 windows alight. And here is the marvel seen in bird perspective.

4 Nov.

Eva, dearest friend – I've had two more letters from you – with loads of new things to talk about – and a parcel is on its way to me! And what a wonderful parcel! It's as if you know exactly what I like best. And I absolutely must protest when you call jam, cigarettes, figs, tea, coffee and cocoa "practical items"! They're luxuries, Konikova, and will gladden my existence for a long time to come. It's so nice to think of having some treats to offer Atos when he comes. But you've got to go carefully, Eva, and not put yourself to too much expense on my account. I know you're not particularly rich – especially at the moment, while you're looking for new work.

Of course it would be wonderful to have any kind of clothing you don't wear any more, Eva! Do you remember the brown, buttoned coat I bought off you for 100 (!) marks? I've been wearing it ever since and it's been very useful. Now I'm wondering whether to turn the fabric and combine it with the best bits of my old brown fur to make a winter coat for Ham. Thank goodness I bought a yellow fur, muskrat belly, on the proceeds of my solo exhibition – but there are none left for her now. Since you ask so eagerly, a pair of woollen stockings, or any other kind, would be lovely to have – it doesn't matter in the slightest if they've got the odd hole! (Ham is size 38 (shoes) I'm 37). There have been no stockings here for many years. We manage pretty well, by the way, though we do look a bit shabby! Ham has had an awful lot of book covers this autumn and is quite tired. But in spite of that she came to the Noah's Ark party, in her sky-blue evening gown. Faffan didn't join us; he's become more and more of a recluse – burrowing into his newspapers and not wanting to see a soul. [...]

Eva, I have to tell you: I could have got the Paris Scholarship from the French state. But I didn't apply. I can't leave Atos! That's rather alarming, isn't it! You ask, Eva – and yes, I would marry him anytime. <u>But</u> still live here in the studio. I don't think the philosopher fancies embarking on matrimony, though. In your letter you touch on a problem that's been very topical for both of us recently. No, Konikova, it's not that we're starting to get old, afraid of being left on our own, keen to find "*security*". Not you and I. Nor do I think it would be so impossible for us to rise above the awkward incidents and inevitable gossip that can't but follow when one lives openly with a man one loves. And it's easy to end up as a *part-time job* even if one has married him, isn't it? There's something that lies deeper.

Up to now I've been a single person, who has taken great care over safety margins, and I've always kept that kind of private life carefully hidden, keeping it as a rather embarrassing luxury, alongside my work. Now I don't care about the margins any more. I don't want, and never will want, to have anyone else but him. Until now, the thought of potential loves to come has always been <u>thinkable</u>. That's been a bit sad, perhaps, but also comforting. Now my burning wish is never to have another love affair – it seems inconceivable. And I can't, and don't want to, hide away what I'm most proud of, which isn't just luxury-on-the-side any more, but something natural, essential, a big part of my self and my life. It would be like not daring to show your eyes! And that's why it suddenly seems so obvious that we should also show outwardly, legitimately: we have chosen each other. Besides which, it's a token of appreciation of the other person to want to marry him or her. You close off the retreat route, or at least make it more difficult, you admit "I intend this as my definitive choice, and am acknowledging it openly in this way". I'm very tired of this half-heartedness, my own half-heartedness. But, Eva – one thing. I know I would accept a so-called secret marriage with the same joy; the knowledge that he's chosen me for his whole life. (naturally apart from anything that could later divide us, split us up.) It's a matter between Atos and me – the outside world isn't at all as important. Of course a marriage would be more practical, one wouldn't have to be on one's guard, holding one's breath when there's a ring at the door in the morning instead of simply opening it and saying: Come back later, my husband's still asleep. For example. And we could enjoy ourselves at the same parties, go on the same trips without having to beat about the bush at stations and hotels.

Yes, I thought Ramon would change his mind again, once he'd had a chance to ponder and keep you under observation. And now you have doubts ... I very much wonder how you've organised things between you. I sense you were a bit dampened by his monologue on the ridiculous inventions of the bourgeoisie. Because in your case it seems to me so totally natural for you two to get married if you like each other. I mean, he's almost always with you, virtually lives there, and you sew, cook, work and toil for yourself and him. So wouldn't it be a simple little gesture to give you his name as well?

Tell you what, Eva, I have two minor suggestions in the major problem of "unmarried wives". 1. Combine the titles Mrs and Miss into some kind of equivalent of "Mr". (At any rate it would make those unthinking children who get married to become Mrs calm down a bit). And the scorn directed at a "Miss" who is a mother might lessen. 2. Give children the mother's name. (At least there's never any doubt who the <u>mother</u> is!) It would be no more than right, because she has all the actual work of them and has carried them inside her. I wonder whether that anxiety about not having the right to a lover's surname is an instinctive desire to safeguard any future children. Well, who knows? Let us leave these difficult matters in the hope that the whole thing is a bit better managed in, say, three hundred years' time.

What a relief, Eva, that you got away from your bad-tempered uncle. It's amazing you lasted as long as you did. I suspect he's going feel quite lonely, but attempting to stay on with people who have such a dreariness about them reduces one's spirit to tatters. Oh Eva, isn't loneliness (and bustle?) the greatest curse of our age? That throng around us, people, contacts, relationships – yet deep inside, cruel and silent loneliness. I've lost count of the eyes in which I've read longing for <u>real closeness</u>, real contact. If I, with so many beloved and loving people around me, can feel it sometimes, how must it be for those without friends or family members!

I really hope you find a new job, something with beautiful objects around you – which I think you need, to be able to exist. I'm eagerly awaiting your photograph, and Ramon's (I shall send you mine and Atos's.) I've sent you Garm – and you'll have the books as soon as they are out.

But the cutting you talked about wasn't in the letter. I like hearing you talk about the art exhibitions! I think, like you, that surrealism was a very temporary phenomenon. Perhaps influenced by the sudden rise of new psychology, everything subconscious being dragged into the light. Surrealism is a twisted, suggestive world – seductive but, for me, without potential for development. A gown so sensational one can only wear it for a single season – a single party!

The impressionists, that's where you'll find my masters. Their best works thrill me more than anything else – a Cezanne still life more than some vast, pathos-filled painting or crucifixion scene.

I'm definitely an art snob, Eva. L'art pour l'art. You write that Dali "only works for himself". Who else is one to work for? As long as one is working, one has no thought for others! One tries to express oneself, one's perceptions, create a synthesis, clarify and liberate. Every nature morte, every landscape, every canvas is a self-portrait! Then, when one exhibits – of course it's nice, sometimes necessary, for the work to be appreciated, to bring someone pleasure. I detest art with a serious message.

The war has given rise to a lot of that, of course, some of it good <u>despite</u> its tendentious aspects. Here, so far, all I've seen is this: Some painters' work has grown colder, darker. Others defiantly opt for wholly Romantic motifs. A number are coasting on nationalism. We'll only see the real effect of the war in a few years' time, maybe. The reaction can't be the same as after the First World War, at any rate. Then, artists turned from all naturalism and classicism to ruthless violence. We've taken that as far as it can go ... But anyway, every artist portrays not only themselves but also their time. Do we know the face of ours yet, though?

My canvases are praised, admittedly, but in a rather cold and respectful tone – while there's lively criticism of my "restraint and lack of emotion". They're not good, but they get <u>better</u> with every exhibition. The rest does not concern me. Maybe I paint too much with my brain (though my heart is in despair over every picture), but most of the spontaneous talents here paint with their stomachs. Oh yes.

And you asked about various of my friends.

Boris, above all – I haven't seen him for an awfully long time – not since last summer (spring?) I don't think. I do hope he makes it to America! (Oh Eva, if only I could come over there with Atos – and Ham – and live there!) Carin Cleve hardly ever writes. She feels shut in by all her domestic cares and spiritually blunted. Poor little thing. Their finances must be their biggest worry. Her husband also has his first wife and two children to support. In the Renwall saga, I think Essi's keeping the children. She seems bright and in fine spirits, and Ben's found a bashful, clingy, pink-and-yellow type who's the absolute opposite of Essi. Arno's working in the same way as he was before, and I think he has a teaching post now. He asked after you very keenly and wanted your address. As for Elli Tompuri, I'm only in touch with her through Tapsa, and he's entirely disappeared from view. Hagar Olsson has published a book about Karelia, tendentious stuff, too literary and laboured for me. But on the whole I admire her as much as I did before. Verho is a painter with an open, placid face, quiet. You once said how much you liked him. A thousand hugs from me to you, Eva!

Warm greetings from Ham! [*Part of the last line is illegible*]

Hagar Olsson has published: TJ is probably referring to the play *Rövaren och jungfrun* (The Robber and the Maid), which appeared in 1944, though the description is more reminiscent of *Träsnidaren och döden* (The Woodcarver and Death), 1940.
Verho: The artist Yrjö Verho.

14.5.46. [*Helsingfors*]
TO MRS EVA CORDOVA. 46 WEST 17 STR. N.Y. 11

Dearest Eva!

Thanks so much for the photos of you and Ramon! (I think I possibly like your everyday pose just as well as your grand-style photo ...) I have the feeling I'd like him enormously if we met. He has that warm vitality, that likeable look – those kind eyes! When shall I see you again Konikova, I do wonder. When Atos embarks on his big utopian trip to Asia, and I don't want to stay at home on my own? Some spring when the boats are tooting their horns too much outside Brunnsparken? I'm not bound by employment or family – no, wait – of course I'm bound by family. I can just see Raffo raising his eyebrows! I went to keep Ham company on her way to work, now I'm sitting in the studio and the sun is creeping from one picture to another. They've all been repainted since I got back from Sweden. More self-confident, angrier, more "slovenly". God, how I loathed them when I saw them again! This profession is sheer agony sometimes. You know, days when you just wander around, nothing gives you the urge to paint it, nothing comes to life, the hours go by, measured by the school clock across the road, every failed blotch of colour makes you feel tired to death – in the small of your back. You hide away under a blanket, doze uneasily for an hour, think you'll try again, scramble up and stare at your canvas – and then it's dusk. Sometimes something emerges. And then you're overtaken by this anxious fervour, you can barely squeeze the paint from the tube, and feel a nervous sort of power ... If a picture suddenly gets that "something", a promise, an intensity – you can stand at the easel furiously redoing canvas after canvas. Then the empty days return, nothing but a waste of paint.

And people drop in, saying they don't want to disturb you in your "painterly ecstasy". Anguished anticipation, more like it. But I do wonder why the painter in literature is always a "cheery chap", a whistling lily of the field. I mean, I understand that art can never be based on coercion, duty, liability. There may well be despair, but there must also be desire. For me, that desire isn't there from the word go. It sometimes arrives once I've toiled away, tried again and generally run riot, arrives as a huge sense of breathless tension – if that can be called desire. And they call me light, write that my work is frictionless – competent, popular! Well – I don't seem to be as popular any more, thank God. Exhibitions go abroad and people scheme, making advance lists of those not to be included. I want to say to hell with success and ambition; they are a tie and a hindrance. And yet, I still can't help that bitter little sense of grievance. But one increasingly learns how utterly unimportant being appreciated is. It's something one has to learn! To be part of things, visible, making an impression, what does it matter. I've got a solo exhibition this autumn, that's enough. – I have less and less appetite for social life, parties. I'm happy in my beautiful tower and have almost scarily little need of company. It's a blessing when several days pass without the phone ringing, and no need to go out and buy food. Ham and Atos and occasionally writing to you, that's sufficient. Plus work and books. I'm illustrating the second Moomin book at the moment, a charming and peaceful job. Atos is in Stockholm again. I'm glad not to be in Sweden! God preserve me from that sort of social merry-go-round, I was never alone, it was rarely quiet, and the vanity of the world in the shops drove me mad. No wonder it was impossible to paint a single thing.

26th. [...] We're sailing out to Pellinge on Ascension Day, for five days. On the boat Lasse took when he tried to run away to America. Atos can't come with us, too many meetings as usual. He's been in Stockholm again and he did actually, as I'd quietly hoped, buy me a piece of jewellery for the first time. Not, alas, the sort of thing I had romantically imagined, a ring for instance, but a little china <u>ox</u> with staring eyes! So like him, the dear donkey!

28th I've looked over my canvases and would be ready to exhibit them any time. At Bäxbacka's in the autumn. They're freer, brighter in colour, Koni! I'll be damned if I'm not a good painter after all. The "illustrative" element they referred to has entirely gone. And the "grey-on-grey" look that came over the pictures during the war has vanished, though I remain very interested in the colour now I've discovered it. I know I've made progress, let the pests write, scheme and talk as they will. I've been expecting this opposition for a long time; I got off to far too good a start for it to last.

I'm glad to hear that Garm finally reached you. I shall send you more issues, some of the earlier, more political ones if I can. You're very welcome to publish what pictures you like, wherever you like, it makes me happy and proud. And it would make me happier still if you'd be so extremely kind as to keep the fee for yourself. I don't expect it will be much – but you and Ramon can always use it go out for a special dinner for us all!

On that subject, I had a good long laugh about your diplomatic mother's party for you and Ramon. She truly is splendid! May she now send you several tons of furniture as a token of her goodwill. – I can understand you not wanting to put pressure on Boris on the question of his trip to America. I tried not to, either, though really I felt like shaking that youth and shouting Go, you young idiot! Åbo will suffocate you! Be bold while you have the chance and are still young and unattached! – And you, Eva, are considering a trip to Paris at some future date ... Surely that would give me the opportunity to meet you both! My friends there? I'm afraid they're probably scattered round the world, or dead. Jews, Romanians, Armenians, Hungarians ... There's one Parisian you'd both be very interested to meet, but I only know him vaguely. Monsieur Grosset, photographer, a delightful, cultivated gentleman. A friend of Maja Stenman's (perhaps more than that), who was here during the war.

I've posted off your books as printed matter, there'll be more to follow in due course – I've a whole suitcase full of them. Ham sends very best wishes. She's been terribly ill with flu, her temperature up to 40°. But perhaps above all with overwork, not being fit, her heart. I was dreadfully worried about her for a while. Impi's still in hospital, it's been five months now ... but she's nearly well again.

Do you really reckon, Eva, that Moomintroll could be published in the USA? That would be tremendous. I've a troll coming out for Christmas again. What if Lasse could translate them and then someone in America could put some life into the language? Write and tell me what you think.

And let me know what you think I should do with Raffo's letters. Send them to you or him, burn them, read or unread? And do you want a catalogue of your books here? There might be some you don't want, and I can give them to Boris. Warm wishes to Ramon, my dear. A tight hug from me.

P.S. Your letter to Ulla Bärlund was good. Bye!

Tove.

P.S. We've really enjoyed your English magazines. Once we'd read them, Ham and I cut pictures out of them for our cuttings albums. They're a big help in our work!

since I got back from Sweden: TJ spent virtually the whole spring with relations in Gothenburg and Stockholm.
the second Moomin book: *Kometjakten* (*Comet in Moominland*) was published in the autumn of 1946.

19 JULY. 46. [*Pellinge*]

Dearest Eva!

So I'm out at Tunnholmen now, the sun is setting, red against a dead calm sea of violet-blue. The writing paper fell in the sea, as you can tell. It's restful out here. Just the seagulls screeching and the chug-chugs puttering placidly on the horizon. They are funny, those boats. Like the corncrake, you never see them yet they're there, somewhere out of your field of vision.

A life belt and a bread basket with a little sculpin in it were lying in my bay. Both bearing the Russian star. This sort of stuff gets washed ashore all the time ... I walked round my island, scrunching through seaweed that the evening sun had stained ruby red. Floats, birch bark, dried reeds and sun-bleached driftwood edged the shore like a garland, and everywhere there were bright yellow plumes of loosestrife and blue bugloss. I can ramble around here in nothing but my skin, with my hair all tousled. And I've brought no mirror and no way of telling the time.

The tent is small but very smart, with a base and a mosquito-mesh door. It's pitched right out on a little promontory, which the elements have worn smooth, and it's almost the same colour as the rock. Tomorrow I shall start work. If only I had you with me! You'd like living here and cooking up food between the big stones. Together we'd explore the little islands out towards the open sea.

sculpin: a small spiny fish, also known as the bullhead or sea scorpion.

THE REST OF THIS LETTER, HALF A PAGE LONG, IS DATED
"19 Aug cont.d." It has therefore been inserted into the letter

below, as a continuation of its 19 August section. In it, TJ describes the aftermath of being given notice to quit the studio.

14 AUG. 46. [*Pellinge and Helsingfors*]

My dearest friend!

I've seen Sara now and found out lots of new things about you and Ramon, and I felt quite close to you during our conversation! What a beautiful blouse you sent me! It goes brilliantly with my suntan from Tunnholmen, and I really like the way it's cut. Thanks, loyal friend, for providing so many golden moments these past few years! I love your coat, and have bought myself a new autumn hat to go with it – <u>proper</u> blue felt. Right now I'm sitting outside the shop waiting for the milk, the sun's going down, red in a fierce south-westerly gale. Atos has been here for a couple of days, fine weather, perfect sunny days – our summer holiday. After endless postponements for meetings, trips, editorials and lectures I managed to abduct the philosopher, and Peo sailed us out to Pellinge to the accompaniment of singing, almost running aground, and holding forth on everything under the sun.

I had with me crayfish and birthday rockets, the first fireworks to come in since the war, and in the evening we lit a fire outside before I, in the dignity of my 32 years, strolled off to the tent at Laxvarpet.

We spent the next two days almost entirely at sea. I don't think you were ever out at Kummelskär. It's about twice as far from Pellinge as Tunnholmen – a splendidly wild and rocky island with two navigation markers and two little lighthouses. It was mined and out of bounds for the whole of the war, so I was immensely pleased to see "my island" again, the one I like best of all.

Lasse, Atos and I spent the night there, rolled up in the sail in the heather. The island is high but bare, except for a dense thicket in the middle, all tangled together by the gales, and the rocks are clad in some spectacular seashore flora. As I was lying there, looking up into the mass of stars and listening to the gale, I was seized by a powerful urge to actually live on the island – or own it. Laying claim to Ägg-skär, as Atos and I had dreamt of doing, seems to be absolutely out of the question on account of the anglers, so we've had to abandon <u>that</u> idea. But, *you see*, I must always have something to dream about. Perhaps I could get us Kummelskär, as it's the island furthest out to sea, unsheltered, with no chance of fresh water, no soil and no forest. One would have to take lots of bottles of Vichy water, and boil seawater, too – I expect in due course we'll be able to buy tinned goods again, and the boat could be drawn up on rails of some kind, as there's no harbour. You'd love the sheer drops, ravines and lagoons on the far side, where the swell throws up surf even in calm weather.

That night we went up onto the tallest cliff and saw the thundering sea, white in the moonlight. It was scarcely real – the island looked like a lunar landscape or a dream. Abbe's going to pull down his old sauna – I could buy that and reassemble it out here just as it is, with windows facing the sea and blue weatherboarding. <u>If</u> I can get permission to be here. Everyone always has a thousand objections and is so discouraging and mocking, but I'm sure you understand me – you and Ham – and hope I will contrive to get my island!

Yes, this week I've been pretty far removed from my exhibition and my anxieties about it. It's going to open on 5th or 19th October, may the muse be with me! Last time I was here taking a look at Tunnis I managed to get a few charcoal sketches done. It'll be the first time I've exhibited freehand drawings. As for the canvases, I'm still messing about with the 30 from the early summer, spring and winter. It's better for me to concentrate on them than to aim for 50 like three years ago.

Peo's out here again, stocking up on fish for his family for the winter. Peter's first word was "hi". Modern, eh?

Lasse's here as well, but staying placidly aloof from all the hysterical food gathering in the knowledge that he'll be in the army from October. We're growing ever closer to each other, I feel – we like the same objects and topics of conversation, have similar imaginations and often the same plans and ideas. We pitched the tent at Laxvarpet and we read until late into the night by the light of our last candle stumps, recommending our books to each other. Erika v. Frenckell was here for a while. I'm glad that Lasse has her. It might be good for him.

Faffan's been an angel since I wrote him that letter after a clash over politics; a conciliatory letter in which I tried to explain that I'm actually apolitical and not "setting up a front" against him. That

I'm upset about what's going on in Europe mainly out of a universal human sense of justice and that I'm not capable of political theorising and have no appetite for it. That we must try to get on with each other and remember everything we were able to keep after the war, in spite of everything, try to build something up again for the sake of peace of mind in our work, try not to wear each other to shreds with gloom, defamation and bitterness. –

And if rocket-propelled missiles are eventually going to blow us to smithereens along with everything we've done, I want to be as calm and happy as I can <u>now</u> and work in peace.

But today he was black again and full of negativity, homing in on everything difficult, sad or deranged in every event and utterance. The way one does when one is deeply unhappy, disappointed and bitter. It's such a pity for him, the war has shattered his nerves. He now even talks of fishing and mushrooming, which used to be his greatest pleasures, as a duty and a nuisance. [...]

19 Aug.

In town, nearly autumn. This was the first night it was too cold with just a blanket ... Peo and I sailed over from Pellinge, a wet and stormy trip with our baggage swimming in oil and salt water ... But Peo is first-rate, always calm and kind. We took in more and more of the sail, and in the end we had to take refuge for the night on a little island. How simple they are, the setbacks nature gives us to do battle with – being freezing cold, wet, afraid of capsizing, seasick, hungry ...

But now I really do feel sick, since getting that little note on squared paper two days ago from the new company that's taken over this block, giving me notice to leave my tower, the studio. You can't do battle with regulations, companies, documents, authorities!

19 Aug cont.d.

A hotel and restaurant firm wants to rebuild the whole attic storey where my tower is. I can't do anything, but hope Atos will be able to help – or perhaps a lawyer I know. Though it's not very likely – I punched him on the nose once when he tried to kiss me at an after-party. It's dangerous to own physical objects, grow attached to them! If the best I can hope for is that they give me a standard little room instead of my castle – where will I find room for my enormous work table, my newly prepared canvases, the sculptures, the huge bookshelves I'm so proud of, and – I can't help smiling – my four-poster bed? I've tried to build up a home, and ideal studio in the tower I've been dreaming of all my life, and thank the Muse for every morning. And then a bit of paper torn out of a notebook arrives, and I'm to clear out to wherever I like on the first of September. So much for the social life, the civilised city life I've always held as important. Maybe one should live on remote Kummelskär, on one's own land, which only a new war can take away (it's in the mine-laying zone) and not own anything to make one dubious about leaving the door open for fishermen and anyone who happens by and needs to get warm when one isn't there. Now what is to become of my exhibition on 19th October?

Oh Konikova, I try to take things the way Atos does, laugh and shrug my shoulders. At ambition, at beautiful objects, at having a Home one is always embellishing and making more personal – but I'm weak, I can't do it. Yet!

When I dream of a simple little shack on a bare rocky islet, it's not because I scorn space, warmth, lovely things, company, the glitter and bibelots of life – but just a Romantic craving for contrast. – The way I'd enjoy, say, wandering about the docks one day in a shabby raincoat and drinking my own health in raw spirits in a disused goods wagon – and the day after that, in a hat with roses and a veil, skip playfully through an abstract discussion at some restaurant. An asocial aesthetic snob, as Turtiainen, Tapsa's friend, put it.

Perhaps this is my allotted portion. To finally be driven from happiness in the ostrich's hidingplace of my post-war years, to the others, those who still have to live in air-raid shelters or lodge in tiny rooms off other people's kitchens, bombed out ... Does it serve me right, Eva? Will it make me a better person? (But like hell will it make me paint better, having to work in a corner of poor Faffan's studio!). Since the war I've closed my eyes to everything, only tried to be happy, to find peace for my work, to fill my surroundings with lovely things and my heart with dreams of moving forward. Never back – hardly even seeing the misery that persists everywhere – or the threat, the one about which Faffan always assumes the worst. Perhaps nobody has the right to isolate themselves in private happiness? But oh, Eva, I feel such a strong urge to build. Work, home atmosphere, a relationship with another person I love. Before the war I couldn't, during the war I wasn't allowed to. Now I want to! But I've never cared about the general work of building up society. Only what can be achieved alone, the way I built that crazy, childishly fantastical grotto in a desperate flight from reality during the war …

You know, Eva, I seem able to talk to you about all my great joys, all my agonies, everything going on in my head – there's no one else I can talk to as I do to you. I'm not putting a burden on you – am I? I think, I know, that the way you always listen to whatever I tell you is like the embrace of a friend.

Tove.

20 Aug.

Ah Eva, how happy your parcel made me! Coffee and tea! Unpacking it felt very festive – and I'm wearing the spotted dress as I write. You should see what a nice fit it is; it doesn't need a single alteration. And the trousers are extremely interesting. Even my Junoesque hip measurement is made to disappear by their streamlined American cut. If I ever become the owner of Kummelskär I shall walk its cliffs in your trousers, snug against the south-westerly! I was especially touched that you'd thought to send me powder (a well-chosen shade!) and cream. Woman cannot live by grain and wool alone! You dear, thoughtful friend, how will I ever be able to thank you for all your presents. Today I'll have macaroni for dinner, but I shall save your tin of tongue for Atos and me one Sunday. And I'll give one of the soaps to Peter, he's allergic to the soap we get on ration here. How many different things one can do with rice! I feel so rich, Eva – but richest of all in my knowledge of your friendship, which stays the same in spite of the distance and the length of time that separate us. My longing to see you again is growing stronger and stronger. When will it be, and where. In your country, in mine – or France? Do you know what, if I get thrown out of my building and lambasted at my exhibition I shall jolly well feel like leaving, without the ballast of the tower and the heights of fame! I could come to you, why not!? But it isn't so easy to get away from this country when one even has to kick up a fuss, and for months, just to travel to Åland!

Evening. I've sent out distress signals in all directions – and it's simply wonderful how many kind people and friends there are who really are doing all they can to help. And the muse knows I'm unworthy of it. But, however things turn out, it's heartening not to stand alone with one's troubles, and the fact that people care for me is something to treasure. [...]

Hugs and farewell, Eva, my dearest. If the worst comes to the worst I shall put up my four-poster bed on Hesperia Esplanade over my American tent, which I also bought entirely by accident. Alack, you possessions! A kiss from your friend Tove.

Peter's first word: Peter Jansson, Saga and Per Olov Jansson's son.
bibelots (French): Trinkets.

TOVE JANSSON HAD MET VIVICA BANDLER IN DECEMBER 1946. In the year that followed, many of her letters are about this new relationship, her overwhelming passion and great disappointments. See Letters to Vivica Bandler.

A WEEK BEFORE CHRISTMAS –46.
[*Helsingfors*]

Dearest Eva,

Something has happened to me that I realise I have to tell you about. I'm so happy, so elated and relieved. You know I feel like Atos's wife, and I expect I always shall.

But what has happened now is that I've fallen madly in love with a woman. And it seems to me so absolutely natural and genuine – there's nothing problematic about it at all. I just feel proud and uncontrollably glad. These last weeks have been like one long dance of rich adventure, tenderness, intensity – an expedition into new realms of great simplicity and beauty. Vivica is Erica v. Frenckell's sister, three years younger than me. It was actually Lasse and Erica who had been saying for ages that Vi and I might get on well together, and one day they brought her to the studio. I saw a tall dark aristocratic girl with a prominent nose, thick straight eyebrows and a defiantly Jewish mouth. She is blind in one eye, but the other is clear, dark, penetrating. A mop of short hair and the loveliest hands I've seen. She's such a gorgeously feminine creature, and one day I shall paint her as she is, chiefly as a profusion of fruit and blossom in full bloom.

One evening we went to see The Song of Bernadette and walked home in silence, deeply affected. Two days later I went to a party at their place for the French minister, and when everyone had left we stayed on and danced. That was when I realised, as we were dancing. It came as such a huge surprise. Like finding a new and wondrous room in an old house one thought one knew from top to bottom. Just stepping straight in, and not being able to fathom how one had never known it existed. We took a trip to their estate in Tavastland and stayed for four days. What conversations, Eva! Like finding the best I had in me refined and explained. Time has rushed wildly on, dragging with it one inner event after another. You'll never guess, all my bitterness towards Faffan has suddenly gone! We joke – and are comfortable together. And you know what, I'm finally experiencing myself as a woman where love is concerned, it's bringing me peace and ecstasy for the first time. And I know I can go on and find even greater sweetness. You see, I'm no longer afraid of the dark outer reaches where the "seascape painter" led me. It's being able to talk about everything, and not feel ashamed any more. It's my friends staring at me and asking what's happened to me. I'm new again, liberated and glad, and with no feelings of guilt.

I don't think I'm entirely lesbian, I have a very clear sense that it can't be any other woman than Vi, and my relationships with men are unchanged. Improved, maybe. Simpler, happier, less tense. Atos has been away and will be back tomorrow. And tomorrow Vi is off to her husband in Stockholm, and then travelling on via Denmark and Switzerland, where his parents are – before spending the whole spring in Paris, where she'll be directing a film.

It's dreadful for us to part just when we've found each other, but we have our work, of course, and can safely wait. There may be great difficulties lying ahead for us. The others don't understand, you see – they haven't experienced it. The backbiting has started creeping in. But I don't care. I'm even ready to lose Atos now.

The fact is, Eva, that just now I can't write any of the things I intended to. Your art magazine, which I wanted to analyse, Christmas, the family, my work, my friends. I'm caught up in this one big joy and agony.

Eva, life is so tremendously rich!

I embrace you. All the best – everything you wish for yourself and Ramon!

Your friend Tove.

her husband in Stockholm: Kurt Bandler.

15.3.47 [*Helsingfors*]

My dearest friend,

I've been worrying for a long time that you might be ill, or cast down by some sad event. But then today it arrived, your parcel that I've been so eagerly waiting for. You sent it off ages ago, of course, and a great deal can have happened to you since then – but it was still contact with you. Eva, I felt so festive as I unpacked it here on my own! I was absolutely delighted with it all, the lovely clothes, coffee, tea, cocoa, cigarettes! How funny that you happened to send plums, of all things. They are more or less the only thing Atos really <u>craves</u>, and I'm always trying to get hold of some and hang onto them somehow. Now I'll be able to make us a spaghetti dinner when he comes back from his trip to Vasa – but I shall save the apricots for the summer. My Kummelskär plans have advanced to the extent that I think I can get permission to build on the island, that the boat is ready, that I was able to get nails – truly phenomenal! It's the timber that's the problem now, we aren't allowed to buy anything without a licence to build, which of course I can't get. But this will resolve itself. If I dream and act intensely enough, it <u>will</u> happen!

I'm so pleased with the soap and face cream! I generally look an absolute mess, because the stoves play up on a daily basis and refuse to eat their peat dust, which they spew out over the studio in black clouds. It's a bit warmer now at any rate, I've survived my last bout of influenza and the snow is crashing down from the roof of the tower in great avalanches and melting on the windowsills in the March sun. I'm wildly happy that spring is coming, more so than ever – and about the days growing lighter, filled with intense work as they have been since the start of the year. I'm very tired, and nervous about the frescoes at times – but I enjoy having one big job and finding that I can concentrate on a <u>single</u> task after all. The result just <u>has to be</u> good. Not only because my colleagues are all fired up with indignation that the commission went directly to me without any sort of open competition beforehand. All this unpleasant talk that chips away at one's ability to work and one's peace of mind! There's nothing to do but isolate myself in my tower and carry on, taking no notice. Perhaps one day they'll say I got the commission from v. Frenckell because he's Vivica's father. I mustn't take any notice of that, either.

Eva, how thoughtful of you to put in those sewing bits for me, darning wool, some tape for my skirt! All the things I can't get. It was lovely to put on a pair of stockings without <u>holes</u> – the others were nothing but darns that I could barely hold together. Dearest – you definitely are the most wonderful friend a person could have. You're short of money, have a crazy amount of work, many years and half the globe divide us, yet still you go on sending me presents. Every day my hands touch something you gave me, and every time a happy, warm little feeling comes over me. – I think the black dress will be just the thing to wear for those mysterious cocktail dos they have in the circles Vi is introducing me to. Last time I noticed I wasn't the same as all the rest, and there's no need for that. I hate it when people think "she's an artist, so she has to be (or is allowed to be) different! Clothing shouldn't be a badge of one's profession. (And not just a badge, either – but <u>my</u> way of dressing – though not an "artistic" one.) I simply love the blue suit. You may not believe it, Konikova, but I look really rather pretty in it. I've had an idea for a cap to go with it – with something red in it – and on more formal occasions my blue hat, which I wear with your coat. How lucky I feel! I pulled out one top after another, one gorgeous colour after another and tried them on in turn, dancing round the studio in your grey trousers, which have kept me warm all winter.

If only I could take you in my arms right now and thank you, and you could see how glad and happy I am – and how smart I look! We could have a celebration meal together (do you remember that one we had, just the two of us, in your old nest?) and then I'd show you my work and get your verdict. It's coming on slowly, but steadily.

18th.

My assistant Suihko and I have finally been able to get hold of two-year-old limewash and brushes and powdered lime from Sweden, the half-scale colour sketches are done, and one of them drawn on the wall, full size. In between times I shall take on beer labels and glass paintings to stabilise my rocky economy. I shall use the big honorarium coming my way this autumn to try getting to Paris. Vivica's back from her month of directing there and started making our September plans. If only it works! Surely we'd be able to manage for a month or two over there.

And you? How far ahead are you and Ramon looking as you make your Paris plans? It would be too good to be true if they coincided ...

Atos will be travelling this spring. Political invitation to Oslo and Copenhagen – then he goes on to London, Paris, Berlin, trying to get his Nietzsche book translated. He's also talking about his big trips later on. Politics is starting to get on his nerves. Sometimes I think he's serious when he says he'll give it all up for good. We see little of each other and I find now that I very readily slip into his tone of camaraderie, don't miss Those Words and feel no need to utter them myself. If he asked me to marry him I would, of course, but not with the stirring sense of joy and solemnity I'd have had before.

There are enchantments, Eva, or miracles if you prefer to call them that. But they happen quickly. It's over now with the one that so transformed me before Christmas and gave me such wonderfully candid courage, a joy and strength that meant I could tackle anything and made people wonder what had happened to me. When Vi came back, her initial tempestuous passion was over, she had had an experience in Paris that now lay between us. It is gradually fading and is of no consequence – but it exists. At first I was confused, disappointed – everything seemed to take on a strange and ugly face. But now I've had time to think and understand. That regeneration isn't lost, it's still there. But there will be no more instant enchantments, I will have to fight my own battle to lure out that free and happy person within me who suddenly spoke, moved, painted and loved in a fresh, new way.

We're no longer in love in that radiant, self-evident way, there are always complications – anguish and irritation and jealousy – and the constant need to conceal it!

It's going to be hard. We're going to lose friends. Feel torn, hurt one another. But we'll only grow closer to each other, I know, and I believe, helping each other become "truer" – and perhaps happier people.

Right now we've both got more work than we can cope with, and assignments that take us just a little beyond our ability. The first film, the first fresco – and a host of minor tasks. Things will calm down. If we can get through this period – the Monday morning after the party – then it will be all right.

Vif is terrified her little sister Erica will find out she's a borderliner. Strangely enough, Erica and Lasse seem to have had some kind of relationship. Lasse broke it off on his last leave, and I'm sure it's an indication he's now gone over to the "rive gauche". He knows about Vi and me, but nobody else does. Yet.

Sometimes I'm very happy, Konikova, and feel brave and rich. Then everything comes crashing down and I feel like my own frightened observer. But I am going to be happy, that's for sure – for sure!

Yesterday I had *bad news* about Kummelskär; they won't allow any building because of the herring fishing. But I've opened negotiations for another island! I must have my island, and I <u>will</u> get it.

Good night, friend. Did you get my letters? Including the one I wrote before Christmas?

Do you think you could write me a few lines sometime? It would make me so happy.

frescoes: See Letters to Vivica Bandler
Suihko: Niilo Suihko.
"rive gauche": "Left Bank", a term for homosexuality.

THE NEXT LETTER IS DATED MIDSUMMER EVE 46, BUT THIS must be a mistake. Tove Jansson is writing about events in the spring and early summer of 1947. She and Lars Jansson have been offered the chance of leasing Bredskär, after her vain attempts to lease Äggskär, Tunnholmen and Kummelskär. They sign the contract, valid for fifty years, on 26 June 1947.

MIDSUMMER EVE 46 [*should read 47*]

Eva, dearest,

We had been planning for ages that when Lasse came out of the army we'd go out to Pellinge for two days and try to buy our island.

I imagined what a nice trip it would be, what great fun, but as time went by I also looked forward to it for another reason. Lasse's the only one who knows I'm bisexual. This spring has been the most insane muddle of disappointment, despair, excess and various different attempts to repair things that had irretrievably fallen apart, and by the end of it all I was just so tired. All I wanted was for someone, something, to help me decide – anything at all, in any way, as long as I didn't have to brood on it any more. I longed to be able to express what was grinding me to pieces inside, in some light, informal, matter-of-fact way – and get an answer, a bloody hell – or it'll pass – or get yourself out of that pile of shit – or you've been an absolute ass – or don't give up, you'll win in the end if you stick at it. Anything, however small – as long as it's kindly meant!

Things got off to a bad start. The evening before we were due to set off, Vivica wanted me to meet her best friend, Göran Schildt – a meeting I'd anticipated for ages, ready to win him over, be a credit to her. I was very nervous and had prepared, as if for an exam, the cheery, light style I intended to maintain. He would presumably be all eyes and ears, because he knew everything about Vivica and me.

It was as if some strange urge came over me to thwart my own plans, demolish my gains just as I had made them, work against my own interests. I knew I was too tired for drinks with Sam during the day – but it was such a relief to go out for a drink with someone again, and I invented an excuse, namely his first prize in the Ahlströms' fresco competition. But I wasn't in great shape by the time I dashed back to the studio in the evening, and ran out of time to prepare things, or to titivate the place or myself for the party as planned. And I hadn't reckoned on Vivica wanting to bring her lover with her, plus Maya who is her latest interest.

A sparrow and a mouse saved us from the embarrassment of the introductions. The sparrow came flying out of the stove, black and wretched, and just after that the mouse scuttled from the woodpile in a state of delirium. – I liked Göran Schildt very much. Elegant, slim, with a bright, intelligent face and a balanced reserve that didn't conceal the warmth and essence of him. But we felt shy because Vivica had told us both too much about each other. Little Koskinen was as lost and confused as the sparrow in the stovepipe, said nothing, smiled and stuck close to Vivica.

Maya was quiet and wide-eyed, too, and Samuli flopped and slurred and didn't care that he was drunk. Perhaps it was a good party – but for me it felt like a series of convulsions. Vivica danced with Koskinen, Maya and me by turns and deployed her charm in overbearing outbursts. She was off to see her husband in Stockholm the following day and was elated and stimulated by being the centre of a tangle of relationships. After twelve my cheerfulness started to stick in my throat, I came out with stupid comments for fear that suddenly no one would have anything to say, and all I could think about was that Vivica was going away and that she had my studio keys in her pocket and I didn't know if she planned to use them for my sake or Koskinen's. We hadn't spoken to each other. As Göran was on his way out, she quietly asked if Vannis were going home for the night and I answered far too loudly "I'm sure they are. You two can stay here if you like." Göran slipped out in a trice and Vivica went all rigid and stood staring at the wall. I'd gone and acted against my own wishes again – I knew Vivica hadn't asked for Koskinen's sake this time and really wanted to be with me. That damn pride of mine always gets in the way.

So the two of them left, and Vannis just sat there looking on. Suddenly the room was full of anxiety and I rushed to the telephone to call a cab and get rid of them. But I didn't make it in time and the hysteria came crashing over me in all its disgusting uncontrollability and I dissolved into tears. Maya came over and held me, quietly and sweetly, and I think she got Sam into the studio before I blurted out that I'd had an affair with Vivica and just couldn't bear hearing all the details of her new partners any more and pretending to be glad and interested, and didn't want to be part of it any longer and all the other crap I talk when my nerves give way. Hush, Maya said kindly, don't say anything. Samuli came in and said the frescoes were finished now, and he could well understand me being tired after all that and needing a rest in the country. Then they left.

I forgot to pack all the things I'd meant to take on my trip with Lasse, the jam and chocolate and all the other treats, and went to Lallukka in a horrible travelling outfit even though I knew Lasse was going to dress in his best. And I must have looked pretty ghastly all round when we set off in the morning. I couldn't control myself and started going on about the night until I noticed he'd clammed up and didn't want to hear.

It's always worst in the morning. Even before I've groped my way up to the surface of consciousness, I have an uneasy sense of something being wrong. Then I wake up, recognise myself, remember everything and realise I've got to be part of a new day, right through to evening. And the machinery of my brain slowly cranks into action and starts champing on the usual subjects, back and forth, going over the same words, events and gestures until I could scream. After the frescoes I've no work to feed into the machine and it's running on empty, ticking over on the dregs in the tank until I feel like puking myself up. Vivica rang in the morning and asked plaintively why I was so angry with her, she'd been no worse than usual. I stupidly answered that oh no, I wasn't angry, just tired, your train will be leaving, have a good trip, be happy. And I knew then that I'd bungled my role again, pricked her guilty conscience, lost an immense amount of all I'd fought for. In Borgå I tried to ring her back while Lasse and I sat staring over a dismal celebratory meal but she had guests and couldn't come to the phone. What would I have said? I don't know. Maybe used the pretext of telling her to put the safety chain on if she took Koskinen to the studio because I'd given a spare set of keys to a colleague so they could go and paint there. Maybe sounded all cheerful and talked about the island and how much we'd all enjoy it there, or joked about the day before and the Vivica Society we could set up for all her lovers, with me as chairman and monthly meetings and annual reports on the 28th when no one can do anything anyway!

She'd have laughed at that, been amused and appreciative, and her sense of guilt would have subsided. Or maybe I would have said don't be upset. We love each other, don't we. We must try to be glad and not make life hell for each other. Let's each have a wonderful trip and come back for your book, which I shall illustrate.

I was just tired, and sick of everything, as Lasse and I walked to the bus, and I thought let me be ill and not have to talk and be cheerful. Never talk anything to pieces again, let others take responsibility.

It was rather funny. I developed a sore throat en route, and by the time we got to Tirmo I couldn't say a word, only whisper.

I wonder if there is any greater poison than a sense of guilt. That was what made the time before Christmas so wonderful, almost sacred. She took away my anxiety about so many things, Faffan

Tove Jansson on Bredskär. Late 1940s.

and Ham, my masochistic tendencies in sex, that ambitious sense of duty that's driven the pleasure out of my painting, and she freed me from the timid, old-maidish prudery that makes people think I am, or pretend to be, naive. Those three weeks were one long hectic dance of bliss and ultimately she not only gave me hope, but also the assurance that one day, through her, I would reach the apex of the sexual act and finally be at peace and feel that I was a real woman after all. She felt freed, too, by the fact that we were so fond of one another. From the anxiety of trying to be a man, because it's as a woman that I love her. And the fact that I perceived her as an artist as a matter of course, not as an agronomist or a failed minor writer – that I never for a moment saw anything unnatural in what we were doing. In all my life I've never felt more natural and proud.

[...] I'm going to send you photos of my frescoes. I painted them in a hell of a rush, but I think they're good. Especially the second one, which I did when I wasn't happy. The one with the trees.

Perhaps sometime I shall come to count this spring as one of the most positive, in the same way. In spite of all the pettiness, weakness, drama and lack of self-control. Perhaps it's better than the three weeks before Christmas, which Vivica never mentions.

I believe I was right when I told her "it wasn't me she missed so much, but herself, the way she was then". This is no different. It's a continuation. Perhaps a logical one. Glimpses of miracles flash by just so one fights to make them gradually come true. So far nothing's succeeded and I've understood nothing. But perhaps it will come. Before the war I thought one lived to do things that were as right as possible, and after it to try and be as happy as possible. Perhaps one is simply meant to work and live in as dignified a way as one can. If it can be done.

Tove.

Göran Schildt: Author, art historian and critic.
Koskinen: Irja Koskinen, later a secretary at the Lilla Teatern theatre in Helsinki.

10 AUG. 47. H:FORS.

Dearest Eva,

I lost track of your letter. I'm sending it now, to complete my lesbian lament. The poems, too – though I barely remember which ones you've already had. You are silent and so far away – and I wonder how things have been for you and Ramon. Perhaps you are going through a difficult time, my friend – or working too hard, otherwise you would write. At least I know you often write to me in your thoughts. That will have to do.

It's a long leap from last time again. After two bloody awful weeks, the glass paintings were done, Ham crawled out of hospital – far too early, as it turned out – and her brother Torsten arrived from Sweden. Another hectic week of sightseeing in town, and then we all went out to Pellinge, except Faffan who stayed with his reliefs and only went out there today. A few hours ago I waved Torsten off on the Stockholm boat, and my heart was full of genuine blessings for his séjour here.

Our two Pellinge weeks have done me a power of good.

Almost every day he, Lasse and I were out on Bredskär, the little island I've finally been able to lease for the next fifty years. It lies to the south of Tunnholmen, with just a narrow strait separating the two, and the whole sea beyond.

Do you remember Tunnholmen? That was where Rosa and I built little houses in the sand while you were asleep. But Bredskär is at the other end of the island. There's a little sandy beach there too, and rugged cliffs round the outside. Quite a lot of trees, flowers along the beach, bird cherry, rowan.

Thanks to Torsten we're going to have a house on the outer rocks 4m x 5 with a single room, three windows. He brought nails over from Sweden and was on hand with advice for Lasse and me while all three of us were building. To start with I was barely even interested, just feigned cheerfulness for Ham and Torsten's sake. But the work, not to mention rounding up the materials, was harder than I'd imagined. And all of a sudden I noticed that my thoughts weren't just running on empty any more but were engaging themselves in earth for the floor, roof trusses, joints and calculations. I was worn out after whole days of lugging stone and wood, clearing ground, putting in posts, sawing and hammering. I slept dreamlessly and ate like a horse. I got more and more interested, and took pride in every obstacle overcome. This is going to be the house for my friends and my solitude. Its name is Wind Rose (= compass). Lasse's going to write his book there in September, Atos is coming some *week end* or other when he's too tired. And lots of others.

We now have all the upright timbers in and the roof trusses up, and two gable ends weatherboarded. I got the roof timber through a sugar transaction, but there's still no proper floor and no roofing felt. I'll send you photos of the island and the house in the autumn – perhaps you'll feel like coming here at some juncture ...

I suspect that this time has done my poor body good. Before I went out there, the X-ray plates of my lungs were pretty much covered in black speckles. But now I only feel the occasional stab of discomfort and I'm not as thoroughly tired and listless.

And yes – there are certainly stabs of another kind as well. Sometimes that anguished old dream comes back, always the same; the last evening with her before I wrote the letter. Then I build like a thing possessed to wear myself out and avoid dreaming, avoid thinking. So I'm building two houses: an external one, and an internal one of calm and indifference.

This evening I'm in bed in the studio again – and missing the nights in the tent on Bredskär. Here, the walls are still steeped in

Lars Jansson on Bredskär, 1950s.

the melancholy of last time – the city seems horrible, somehow. The spring and early summer are crowding in on me – all the bad things that happened then. These last weeks while I was writing your letter, my self-control entirely gone, coming up with all sorts of mad exploits so as not to have to think. I would go to three cinemas, one after the other, or get drunk, or sleep with people I happened to meet, or seek out any old *bore* to talk the time away. It was extraordinary that the glass paintings turned out as charming, humorous and elegant as they did. Sheer force of manual habit. – It doesn't worry me that my painting's ground to a halt, it barely interests me at present. I want nothing but peace.

I'm going out to Bredskär with Lasse on the next boat and won't be back until October. The address is Borgå, Stor-Pellinge, Söderby. He and I are on good terms again, now that I've cheered up. My embraces and best wishes for all good things, Eva. *Good luck to you.*

Tove.

If you write sometime and care to have the rest of my poems, do send me the first words of the poems you've already had, I can't remember which ones I've already sent. There ought to be about 30 of them.

the glass paintings: TJ's decorations in the student hall of residence Domus Academica in Helsinki.

1 OCT. –47 [*Helsingfors*]

Dearest friend Eva,

Your parcel has come! Yesterday I got back to Lallukka from Pellinge and we had a big unpacking session and mannequin parade. The brown dress will be fabulously useful this winter, because in-between dresses for town are just what I need most. It's lovely! It will be a very good fit in every way if I just let it out a little across the chest. And the shoes fitted Lasse – that was lucky, wasn't it! He sends his best wishes and also says thanks for the pale-blue wool shirt, which was too big for me. He was delighted. I'm sitting here writing in the mustard-checked jacket, teamed with the brown skirt. My dear friend, you've pretty much renewed my wardrobe! [...].

For most of September I was alone on Bredskär – an unbroken stretch. I did a bit of drawing, got the house finished, cleared the overgrown places in the trees, wrote poems and some Moomintroll. Immense peace and a slight sense of desolation, especially in the evenings. It blew a gale almost the whole time and the wind really whistled through the house, out on the point. The sea spraying up all around, and the strangest illusions of voices, steps and music in the wind. Particularly the acoustic phenomenon of rhythmic fiddle music before I drifted off to sleep, which was a bit disturbing. It makes you a different person with different thoughts, living alone with the sea and yourself. I discovered that I like solitude (at least for three weeks!) but am incurably afraid of the dark. The sun had scarcely gone down before, despite all my resolve, I was putting covers over the three windows and turning the mirror to the wall. It's a shame, really, because there's been moonlight, and the northern lights. And I started talking to myself like some old biddy! One time I nearly lost the boat in the storm, and another day the sparks from the chimney set fire to the moss. After that I didn't dare cook anything for a week – which was how long the s.w. lasted. – at ½ past 2 one night I managed to row all my stuff over to Pellinge just as the wind was changing. It was absurdly magnificent and sombre. The northern lights, grey dawn and an enormous swell, a clear starry sky. And a great illuminated steamer, sleeping at anchor between Tunnis and Odden.

The evening before I left, Atos suddenly turned up – to "bring me home". I was pleased he'd come. A long, expensive, awkward trip for a few hours on Pellinge, even though I was about to come home. We walked round the beaches in the gale and took a smoke sauna.

It's strange to be here again. I'm still in the transition phase and the studio feels a bit alien to me. But it's not unfriendly, not hostile like last time I was here. Perhaps I can start painting again.

I'm busy with the Moomin series for Atos's paper.

I shall be criticised for moving to the left. (Which they'll all believe I am, of course.) But it doesn't mattter. Atos is so happy and enthusiastic about the idea that I can't say no.

Lasse's got a job on the radio: he's translating 10-minute *short stories* and doing interviews. Working 9–4. It's given him a boost to get a permanent job. In the evenings he works frantically – until late into the night – on a historical novel he's entering for a literary competition. He's started writing poetry, in English. I'd like to send them to you. They seem good to me. – Ham's stomach is better. It was terribly nice to see her again. Lots of work, as usual. – Once I'm back in the swing of life in town, I'll write again. Lots of x x x x to you and Ramon and a big hug

from your happy friend Tove.

the Moomin series for Atos's paper: See Letters to Atos Wirtanen.

16.12.47 [*Helsingfors*]

11 photographs in the envelope.

Dearest Eva!

My friend, I was terribly pleased with the slippers. Quite apart from the fact that the old ones were worn out and cold, and these so pretty and as warm as birds' nests – I was so glad that you'd thought of them and sent them – in the midst of all your work. The parcel notification card was waiting in the studio, where I haven't been for a week; you'll appreciate its walls felt chilled and dusty and dead. And then you were here to receive me with a pair of slippers! You're right, I am your best friend – and I always will be. I know I haven't written since the early autumn, yet I still feel you are the only one I have the urge to write to, and never ever with a sense of obligation. Tens of letters have been sent off, and lots of parcels to sort-of-friends, and all of them with roughly the same contents and the same words. My relationship with you, on the other hand, is so different from all the rest that I wait to talk to you until it's a pleasure, something I wouldn't want to miss. So you'll get this letter long after Christmas.

Your mother will be writing to you to say I've got a licence to send you the big portrait in the blue skirt, the one you sat for at Fänrik Stålsgatan. When we realised she was thinking of sending you your portrait of Samuli too, though, we decided to let you choose which you wanted. They're both pretty large for a small flat – but maybe you'd like both? The licence can be used for any canvas you like. Possibly you'd like Samu's now – its colours are better – and mine later, and it could also be that the customs duty you'd have to pay would be too high.

Your mother brought a photograph of you, and we realised your face is growing more attractive, the older you get. And she gave me something to look forward to: the possibility that you and Ramon are coming over to Finland if you can afford it.

You can imagine how happy that made me! Just to think of being able to show you the studio – and Bredskär! Of talking to you again, seeing you, walking around with you and just being. I'm sending a bunch of photographs of my immediate surroundings, I'll send some more of the island later.

I'm wondering whether to go out there early, in the spring, to finish off the verandah, inner roof and weatherboarding. And then stay there for as much of the summer as I can. Lots of people have talked about coming out to visit, but you know how few of them actually will in the end. Atos, too. He wrote to me from Poland, a lovely little letter that made me happy. Short and cheerful and as honest as he is himself. Said he could have written in Stockholm, but longed to make a serious job of it, once he was by himself. He'd like to come out to the island for a while, just with me. He said his spring would involve intense political campaigning, he was going to start another newspaper, in Finnish, but it would be one final campaign. Said I was with him on his journey and that I was a part of him. Not that usual talking-to-a-little-child tone he so often used to adopt. Just before he left on the trip I broke down and said we should split up because after all the only thing keeping us together was force of habit and feeling tolerably comfortable together. He didn't want to, had nothing in particular to say.

Apart from the past week, which I devoted to family parcels, cleaning and Christmas presents at Lallukka, I've been trying to get a few paintings into shape in the studio. The first part of the autumn was just hopeless; I did things that were far below the standard of my canvases a year ago, wasn't in the mood and couldn't concentrate. At the end of November I finally started to get somewhere. Patches here and there that actually looked like painting. There are a couple that could turn out to be all right, but I somehow feel incapable of judging their quality, as if my entire will has slipped out of my control. At times I think they are worse than ever, at others that I'm working in an entirely new way and didn't notice myself crossing the old boundary and moving on. The worst thing has been this complete lack of relish for anything I do. I assume it's the result of playing someone other than myself all through the spring in my attempt to win another human being. Swallowing and lying and feigning all that unruffled banter. Then putting on a cheerful face for the family's sake and for our Swedish guest, and systematically trying to kill off my feelings for the very person I was fighting for. It's hard to be kept dangling in mid-air between woman and man, and when you finally realise you've got to be honest, and nothing but honest – then you're left not knowing what is real.

It's all turned into something that has little to do with "happiness" or "love" – oh, all those words – only work and peace of mind. When Vivica got back from France and called me, I was ecstatic.

We haven't seen each other much since then, and it's a long time since she came. Nothing's happened, nothing's been decided. Sometimes it's *small talk*, or a flare-up of the same bitter old misunderstandings, the beginning of a conversation, an attempt at warmth. I was prepared for absolutely anything, for going on, for making do with friendship, for meeting only now and then to talk and laugh. But I've got to have someone to help me shape all this into something other than frayed torment and uncertainty.

She said, I don't know. I haven't the energy. I've no appetite for anything. So I realised that there isn't, nor ever will be, such a person to help me. And however much I would like to help her with her coolness, her vulnerability and distrust, her lack of productivity, I just can't, any more than she can me. We've turned into two people in some kind of relationship, who can't quite be bothered with making an impression on – or caring for – each other. It all feels so lifeless, though violent reactions can erupt at any time. For example, I mentioned that I'm doing a Moomin comic strip for the children's corner in Atos's magazine. She was beside herself at such betrayal and made violent accusations. I ought not to have defended myself, but I did – and the result was a huge argument out of all proportion, ending in tears on both sides. There, you see, that's what is untenable and unnatural about a lesbian relationship. Not the morality, not the anatomical aspect, not the social issue. But the fact that a difference of opinion, a confidence, a joint venture, in fact anything the two of you try to forge can never maintain its equilibrium. In a dispute between a [*the following line is illegible*] her softness, perhaps thanks to his composure. Between two women, those complementary aspects are lacking, they both tend to overreact. I assume the same happens with two men. An infernal sense of melancholy and powerlessness afterwards. It's like building a house of cards, when it collapses for the nineteenth time you feel like hurling the whole pack out of the window.

Now I've done something and (as with everything else) I don't know if it's brave or just the opposite, exceptionally cowardly. I wrote to Atos and asked if he thought it would be a good idea for us to marry each other. If he didn't fancy it, we could simply talk about other things when he came home. He'll get the letter in Stockholm on his way back.

When I sent it off, something really nice happened. The dialogue with Vivica that's been going on in my head ever since the early spring stopped. That terrible rumination on everything we'd said, could have said, should have said, haven't said. Bottled up and chewed over, day and night. I hoped I'd get the chance to tell her everything that had been weighing me down when she came this time, and thus be free of it. But she didn't let me say a thing. It served me right for being so self-absorbed, but I thought it was the only thing that would help me through. It would help me understand something important, and after that we'd become friends, real friends.

I think I'm hoping Atos will feel like marrying me. We could have separate homes the way we do now, and not change how we live at all. Probably he wouldn't even alter his attitude to me – though perhaps he might lose his vague sense of guilt

[*following line missing from copy*]

But I imagine that as a "symbol" it would mean a lot to me. Why – I don't know. I know less and less, in fact. But perhaps I'd feel calmer and more able to work. And not keep yearning to be over on "la rive gauche".

So that's that. I could write about the monkey and various odds and ends happening at Lalukka – no. That's what I've been doing in a whole batch of "Happy Christmas letters". But when I write Happy New Year! to you, I mean it with all my heart and wish it most sincerely. Regards to Ramon!

Tove.

I wrote to Atos: See Letters to Atos Wirtanen, Undated, 1947.

4.1.1948 [*Helsingfors*]

Dearest Eva!

I'm lying in my studio at the moment, proudly surrounded by sixty newly prepared canvases and getting through a bad cold. Impatient to be up again, because my urge to paint has come back. Admittedly the new things I've done are less exhibition-worthy than my earlier stuff, but with more potential for development. Broader, simpler, more painterly. I think. In fact, it doesn't matter. The return of my urge to paint is the only really important thing.

I'm pleased to be able to tell you that Atos and I will be getting married sometime this spring. He answered my proposal letter the way only he could. "Tove, is it true we aren't married yet? I thought we were, we must have neglected to do it somehow. It's just a formality, of course. We really must get round to it before too long. People will start suspecting we don't get on with each other." I chuckled over that letter for quite a while and felt absurdly light and glad. Everything was suddenly so simple, there was no need to brood any more.

I was wondering earlier whether I'd been particularly brave or particularly cowardly. I'm pretty sure it was the latter. If I'd been fully conscious as I proposed that he was the one I loved, then that would have been very brave. But I didn't know, merely wanted to save myself. In some way. But that doesn't matter either. It happened to be right. It must be right, because it made me so happy and I still am. I shan't tell anybody about it until we're actually married, if then.

It is, as he says, just a formality, but for me it has symbolic significance and is a bigger thing than he imagines. Anyway, I wanted to write and tell you, the one who has accompanied me along these tangled paths this past year. Of course I'm under no illusion that it will be a smooth ride along the high road from now on – even if I genuinely believe I shall never feel the inclination to be anything but faithful. I've found too much inside me that's strange, and there could very well be more. My hatred of her hasn't been tamed, and I must turn it into honest kindness. It's dangerous to be afraid! And I suddenly feel a little bitter to think it was all so unnecessary and nothing but destructive, tearing things down. I must try to find the good aspects that were there before. Oh there's so much to sort out ... But it doesn't matter that much, as long as one finally has a sense of calm. Eva, just imagine – if I could make my paintings look the way I see them before I start work – I think I'm falling asleep. A hug! And all the best.

Don't you think I shall be an odd sort of politician's wife?

Tove.

In 1948 Tove Jansson went to Italy and France with Sam and Maya Vanni. See Letters to Atos Wirtanen and the introduction to Letters to Maya Vanni.

2 april 48 [*Helsingfors*]

Eva, dearest

your letter got here just before I'm due to leave – in four days' time. I seem likely to spend those days doing battle with a tiresome attack of angina that swooped down on me last night. I can only whisper and feel tired out. Sofen got home in the middle of the night. Oh no, Eva, I wasn't feeling hurt by him any longer – only for a couple of days. And I had no regrets, either. Sometimes I forget that normal standards can't be applied to him – but I'm learning more and more. These years – is it 5 now? 6? – have been entirely necessary for me to discover him – and myself. Now I feel we can gradually think of getting married without suffering any major reaction or disappointment later on. He mentioned it himself en passant. Said I wasn't to come home too late, because once we'd entered a state of matrimony he wanted to go out to Bredskär and write. You're right that anything one does honestly can rarely be ridiculous or cause harm. And that one should avoid getting one's confounded vanity involved. I always get ticked off if I do, and told to turn it down a bit if I give way to pathos or get all dramatic and officious. Everything's going to be fine, you'll see.

Atos was pleased. He'd had a letter from Tomas Mann, to whom he'd sent his Nietzsche book. Tomas Mann was quite enthusiastic and wanted to get it published in Germany.

Sofen's been perpetually on his travels for some time now, with quick stops here sometimes for a couple of days. Since I last wrote to you I've spent virtually all my time dashing round making preparations for my trip. Transit visas for 6 countries and applications for currency plus permission to buy the ticket – outward and return – in Finnish money. The latter was granted after a good deal of argument as an exceptional favour, but I drew a blank on the currency. So the dashing about this past week has been all about subsistence down there. If nothing else works, I shall try to take on drawing jobs for some comic magazine. Sam managed to lay his hands on a bit of currency, but Maya couldn't even get travel money. We're going, all the same. In spite of angina and the bank.

I've got a really sore throat. (Wash your hands when you've read this letter!) I simply must talk to you before I go, though it's hard to collect my thoughts and my writing looks like spiders' legs.

Today the first spring rain has arrived.

You must sometimes miss the slowness of our spring. It's the loveliest thing we have here … It's a pity when it turns hot all of a sudden. It's so nice to go about in a sense of expectation, to watch things as they change and sense everything as it awakens in the air. I can't tell you how happy I am that you haven't given up the idea of coming over here, after all. I <u>know</u> we'd enjoy being together on the island. I know you and Sofen would like each other and not be disappointed in each other. I shall joyfully wait and wait for the day you come – and if you can't get the money together, I'll come to you. Because I'm starting to think it's been quite long enough since you vanished. I've never really got used to not being able to ring you any time of the day or night, or dash straight round to see you if anything happened ... Luckily we've had the letters, but it still isn't really enough. My friendship with Eva Wichmann, the author I think I told you about, has grown stronger. I'm glad about that and grateful for it – and surprised; we only found each other after I'd given up my long-standing hope that things would get a little warmer between us than just intellectual teatime chat. But whoever comes and goes around me, I miss you in exactly the same way as I did the day after you left.

I was terribly pleased you liked the picture. Imagine my happening to send something that cheered you up when you were feeling lonely! I was afraid the picture would just seem big and oppressive in a little apartment.

You must have had a very hard time after the divorce and his stupid selfishness. I agree with you – if these are the things that are meant to enrich our lives, they can keep them. Isn't it strange that right after such periods of disillusionment and dirt-grubbing, one's life-affirming flame can burn twice as brightly. It's only natural for you to give your lonely body what it demands. It's so awful when it becomes your enemy.

Evening. Stuffing myself with sulphur, every cigarette tastes like filtered aspirin. (quote from Torsten)

So you've been building a house too! Well done them, for putting together their new Photo League themselves. You'll have lots to tell me when we meet (just not about Berenice Abbott). I haven't received the photos you referred to and am wondering whether you've sent them off or not. Will recent events have a very detrimental effect on your photographic work? Have you got the equipment you need, or did Ramon take it all with him? You bet I understand how anxious the inactivity makes you feel, with nothing getting done and nothing going well! And the agony of never being able to summon up enough concentration.

It comes in waves, all that, periods that pass but don't feel any easier for it. I'm sure it's quite natural for you to feel *down* at present, after all the negative things that have happened. Pretty typical, I think, for your mother to feel personally hurt by your divorce.

Next day. I feel a bit more human now. I'm living in a sort of cloud, but today it isn't a feverish one. It's to do with not being at home any longer, but still not on a journey. In between. I'm sure I embarked on big journeys much more naturally and nonchalantly when I was 20. Am I getting old, timid and nervous? Or has our era just become bureaucratic, suspicious and complicated? I'm sure everything will be all right once we get underway ...

Has your family gone barmy, expecting you to feed not only them but also all the old aunts and poor wretches in the world? I actually think they'll manage fine, so just ignore their emotive little conceits. (That was entirely in the D.R. style!) Do you know what D.R. is? It's a secret society Eva Wichmann and I have started, "The Rude Ones", devoted to vigorous, straightforward freedom of action, not worrying too much about the feelings of others. We have our setbacks, of course – but it's getting better. Society crest: a steamroller. I'll ask Eva if you can join too. Ham is our honorary member, with the honorary title "Worst of the Lot". She's very proud. She reckons she's turned hard and selfish (Hmm.) since she read Forrester's [*above the line*] Foster's? A Passage to India, in which she felt a particular affinity with "Mrs Moore". This *missus* gets completely fed up in old age with consoling, feeding, marrying off or taking any kind of interest in anyone but herself, and dies an egotist, furious and quite content. Ham has now decided to become another Mrs Moore. She has my blessings for (but also my doubts about) the venture!

I'm waiting with great interest for the magazine you promised to send. The books you've sent have always been important, in their various ways. We all read What Makes Sammy Run. I found it perceptive, genuine and violent. Even the illustrated short stories, though built more on effect and sneaking sideways looks. And the magazine of modern American prose – great!! No, Dorothy hasn't answered Lasse's letter and poems, but on the other hand the paper (Viking?) he sent them to for forwarding has written him an extremely courteous letter. Explaining that D. Parker is very short of time, etc. You know what, if I was the Great Woman, and received some (really quite good) love poems from a young man in Finland ("the other side of the globe") in my own language with an adoring dedication, I'd damn well send a few lines in reply. Don't you think? But it could be that a much larger proportion of humanity than one might think goes in for amateur verse and sends it to poor Dorothy's *deeply understanding mind* ...

Yes, Trollkarlens hatt is due out from Schildts for Christmas with 40 illustrations in pure black and white, no wash drawings. A new, smaller format. I had to delete two chapters to make it cheaper to publish. It's been a tremendous rush to get it finished before I go. While the Swedes (may lilies of peace garland their path) were staying with me, I got most of the illustrations done, so the time wasn't entirely wasted. [...]

Lasse and V's sister have found each other again. He and I were in Sibbo the other day to take a look at the houseboat. A majestic craft, 14 m. long. Now Lasse wants to start a shipping company and bring it into service! So I suppose I shall have to wait a while to paint it green and fit a figurehead to the prow. He's also found another boat he wants to raise capital for. Would you like a share in Amalgamated Jansson & Wirtanen Houseboat Owners?

Various kinds of cloud are now descending on me, and I send you a big hug of farewell. I'm having all my post directed to Lallukka, and they'll send it on to Italy from there. Ham sends warm wishes. She really does like you, Eva!

A big angina kiss from your friend

Tove.

Sofen: Short for "Filosofen", the philosopher. One of TJ's many pet names for Atos Wirtanen.

the picture: TJ had sent Eva Konikoff the portrait she had painted of her.

Photo League: Radical association of American photographers, which was fighting for its own survival after being blacklisted by the authorities.

Forrester's: E.M. Forster.

What Makes Sammy Run: Novel by Budd Schulberg.

Trollkarlens hatt: Published in English as *Finn Family Moomintroll*. This was the first Moomin book to be published in English.

9 APRIL 49. [*Helsingfors*]

Dearest Eva!

It's spring, finally, dripping and sparkling and things seeming Different, more feasible, more obliging. The last time I wrote to you was from Kotka, where I painted seven metres al secco for the children in February. And with this letter I'm enclosing the photographs Lasse took, before the work was entirely finished and touched up, I admit – plus my mug with its *new look* ... (as captured by Peo). Since then, I've mainly devoted myself to oils. I'm in some kind of tiresome transition where everything I've done up to now seems poor and alien to me, and I'm trying to find my way to bigger, calmer planes with fewer lines.

It's hard; hardest on the days when things grind to a halt and I feel as if I've never painted before. Periods like that tend to mean I'm moving forward, so I take it calmly – now.

You know; there are times of relentless *"summing up"* in one's work and existence, when there's simply a need for a good clear-out before one can be happy with one's job and oneself. I've tried to discover on my own account where the root of the "pleasure – duty" problem lies, because that's presumably where things got knotted up at some stage. I've shelved all the ego analysis for now, but I think it was useful to devote a few days to that kind of self-absorption. I based the whole thing on dreams, Zsondi analysis (lasts a year, 6 sessions with Dr Parland in Nickby – more like a parlour game than anything else), on going through the pretty ghastly diaries of my youth and on being as honest as possible in one's assessments. Plus – your "Wasteland" book, which actually gave me *the first hint*. It all seems to hinge on a false ambition; something that ought to be natural expression and need, (work) has become a means for achieving entirely different things. So no wonder I feel like puking in my paintbox!

One thing I really was pleased about was having the opportunity to get closer to your and Peo's work. I was selected as a (painter) member of the five-man jury set up to judge a big photographic competition in which the towns and clubs of the country are involved, to mark their sixtieth anniversary. We deliberated until 12 for the best part of a week, and I learnt more about photography than I had in my entire life before. I thought of the wisdom you'd passed on to me when you talked about your job, and though initially timid I was soon fighting like mad for anything I considered *first class*. The pictures were divided into groups: landscape, figures, portrait, still life, other images. Peo won first prize in the still life category. It felt like a lot of responsibility – and for weeks afterwards I saw everything in black and white and found photographic motifs everywhere. It's a splendid art form, photography! But in my view it's still burdened here by traditionalism and sentimental attitudes. To what extent do you think retouching, any kind of editing, faking or trickery should be allowed?

Lasse's latest craze is book covers. It's almost spooky: whatever he alights on it turns out pretty good – but once the initial wild enthusiasm that makes him work all night has worn off, he leaves it behind him just as casually. He's currently taking sketching classes at the art school, and has mastered lettering better than me and been offered a job by Otava, the publishing house. Before that it was an illustrated children's book. I've realised it's not primarily ambition that drives him – he wants money, and money that will allow him to do the things he enjoys – when it suits him. There's lamentation from all quarters that "such a gifted boy is frittering away his life – he ought to take a degree – he ought to write regularly ..." I understand him, and appreciate his ambition in an area where I struggle: the ambition to be happy, rather than appreciated. He's been round at the studio a lot, often eating and sleeping here. He's built a little temple from wood and plaster, with sweeping front steps, pillars and a domed roof – in which will lie the head of a rose, containing a ring.

Proposal of marriage to Erica, Vivica's sister. She appreciated the gesture, but not him – or not sufficiently to marry. I don't know if he was relieved or disappointed. He'd planned to take her south; he wanted them to settle in Polynesia or some other sun-drenched group of islands.

I think Erica's too national to ever agree to go with him. The inhabitants of this country, including the Finns (though they are reluctant to admit it) are like the wolverine among his birches, his lakes and much-loved but unlovely towns, and start feeling homesick almost before they've left.

Lasse turned up the other day burdened with maps, facts and figures about currencies, steamer tickets, etc., and lots of information about the archipelago to the south west of South America. He'd found out who the consul of Tonga is and sent him a letter to ask whether it would be possible to *settle down* over there. He asked me if I wanted to go with him. Why not. The only thing binding me to Finland is Ham. It's a strong tie, but when the day comes for it to break, I'm ready to leave. After her, Lasse is the person I'm most fond of. Nobody apart from her is directly dependent on me, sofen and I are drifting quietly and calmly apart. As for my work I can, like Lasse, take it with me – and maybe over there I shall finally realise it doesn't matter in the least whether the Artists' Guild in Finland appreciates me. In five years' time I shall be forty (unless a new war has reduced us all to a pulp by then) and it's time for me to secure myself against the greatest sin of omission I shall have to regret when I die.

We'd travel via New York. Quite a few years might go by before it happens – but then we need time to save up half a million. And now we're wondering whether you'd be terribly kind and go to a travel agent to ask:

1. The cheapest price for New York—San Francisco
2.   — " —   San Francisco—Honolulu
3. If foreigners are allowed on   — " —   and to visit

But as far as I understand it, Lasse imagines us spending the rest of our lives there. And why not? By the way – Konikova, didn't you, too, have southerly plans? I feel as if no disappointments can ever really hurt me now I've got this wider horizon.

In a few days, Kerstin will be coming to spend Easter here. Then I'll write to you again. My very warmest wishes.

Tove.

Kotka: TJ painted a mural with fairytale motifs in a kindergarten in Kotka.

Zsondi analysis: The Szondi test, developed by Hungarian psychiatrist Léopold Szondi. It is a non-verbal personality test, based on pictures and photographs.

Dr Parland: Psychiatrist and author Oscar Parland.

your "Wasteland" book: TJ is presumably referring to T.S. Eliot's *The Waste Land*.

Tonga: The Polynesian plans came to nothing. The governor of Tonga sent a letter politely explaining that they could not take any more new settlers, partly because of lack of homes and materials.

Kerstin: TJ's cousin, Kerstin Hammarsten

THAT AUTUMN EVA KONIKOFF WAS IN FINLAND. She visited Helsinki where she and Tove Jansson met up.

30 NOV 1949 [HELSINGFORS]

Dearest Eva!

I wonder if my letter was there to receive you in New York – my idea was for it to get there first. I'm sure that in due course you'll tell me about the crossing and everything, and how you found your house and friends when you got back – and yourself! I currently have the peace and quiet in which to tell you about everything here, having been laid up for three days with an insufferable cold, bursting its banks in all directions. Isn't it dreadful, Eva, when you've been dashing around and working away for a long time and everything's settled quite nicely – and then you have to lie on your back and reflect for a few days and all the gloomy notions you thought you were rid of come over you again! I was so aghast at myself that I staged a cure for <u>one</u> evening from sheer force of will and went to the Authors' Union comedy revue and dinner to which I'd been invited. I was so hoarse I could only whisper, but the next second I was on the phone to the hairdresser, speaking clearly and distinctly! You know?

Today I feel worse than ever, but "mentally" *all right*. Lasse acquitted himself well on stage, we gave him some freesias, and he was very perky with Elisabeth as his partner at dinner. Ham came to the performance but was too tired to stay for the party. They gave me a terrifically good seat among the guests of honour, which was deeply touching. I don't normally care about such things but it <u>was</u> an act of kindness that did me good. Atos turned up too, sporting a beard and a jacket, he and Amos, (Andersson) sat there larking about together, and Putte Fock looked so beautiful it took your breath away.

One evening when I was really missing you I went out to Munksnäs to see Putte. There's something the matter with her, she has dangerous, lonely thoughts and I'm worried about her. I'm sure we can become fine friends, but I'm so nervous about the possibility that I approach her very cautiously – and rarely.

Carin Cleve finally wrote me a letter – from a nerve clinic where she seems to be having an extremely nice time; free from her manic husband and her mother, who is now discharged but hooked on morphine, and still entitled to practise as a doctor.

One evening I went out to the Vannis to look at Samu's abstract paintings. He's got a portrait commission in Paris – from Helo, and was delighted he'd be able to spend a couple of months there (that's a secret for now). My portrait will have to wait for a while, because Sommarschield is off to the Canary Islands all of a sudden. At least I can order Ham's coat; my fee, any day now – then I shall have to sort out the picture as best I can in the spring. Wolle thought quite well of it when he was here, though, and I made various changes that really improved it a lot.

You'll never guess what, the Society of Illustrators has bought three drawings from me for a total of 9000 marks. For its collections. I was so pleased I paid them three years' subscription in arrears and, while I was at it, the August tax bill I found in my pocket last week, to my horror. So now I've paid off <u>all</u> my debts! What's more, the state has developed a (belated) guilty conscience and sent me 4000 they had overcharged me. Fantastic!!? So that'll cover December's rent. Hurrah! And how are you managing with yours????

Kenneth turned up yesterday, presented me with bedside bacon and flowers and was noble and concerned. I feel unbelievably ridiculous and cross with myself whenever he pops up, and wish he wouldn't do it. I'm still a little in love with him, and it makes me dejected, seeing him. He now plans to stay in town until Christmas, *dam'it*! At any event, I've asked him to relieve me of all his stuff when he goes to Kairo, on the pretext that I've got to move out of the studio. Because I don't think I shall find it particularly cheering to trip over his painting things, underpants and dressing gowns around the place on a daily basis. He's coming back in May to exhibit at Hörhammer's.

One evening I was invited by the Frenckells to the Olympic Committee's *tea party* at the City Hall restaurant. The frescoes hadn't changed much, but I had; I could look at them without distaste. (One day in the not too distant future I shall be able to view Green's underpants with the same lofty composure!!) 30 women journalists from America were on the guest list and various interesting cultural figures. No cocktails, worse luck, just tea and buns. Vivica brought me together with a minister's wife and a female author (Windslow?), who with an incredibly metallic sparkle of teeth, shiny jewellery and bits of mirror glass in their hats expounded on their leopards and Pekineses and were generally extremely bewildering. Windslow knew Al Capp, so I shall now amuse myself by sending him my Moomin book, via her – and he'll see there's a sort of Schmoo in Finland, too!

They wanted to go to the theatre, so Vivica got us into Nicken's box for the last act of *Taming the schrew* and asked me to see the bigwigs home in the Frenckells' car. But they stopped off at Kämp for cognac on the way and kept the car waiting so long it drove off. We had to take a taxi to the American legation but the driver refused to take their traveller's cheque. Luckily I had enough money but then had to walk home, hence the influenza.

Apart from that, nothing very exciting has happened. Oh, yes! An old friend I hadn't seen since the winter war came up one evening, filled with gloom about his job in an advertising agency, and having no studio. We sat talking and drinking whisky, both of us equally morose and frozen, and he didn't leave until the following morning. I felt happy and liberated afterwards. He was tender and intense. We're scarcely likely to meet again. – At the theatre they've had their first on-stage rehearsal, and I thought it went well. (Touch wood.) I've been hard at it 9–4 in the scenery workshop for nearly two weeks now and the wing flats will be finished before long. Tomorrow I must crawl out of bed and go over to see what they've been up to. Welche has been reassuring, whereas angry Agnes in the costume workshop is in the grip of violent loathing for me, so I never dare go there in person to say what I want done. Whether I survive the premiere or not, it's been a stimulating and enjoyable project.

And I'm rewriting the Moomin memoirs, by the way, and finding it almost as onerous as writing a whole new book. Trollkarlens hatt has apparently been surprisingly successful in Sweden – so I must make sure the sequel isn't a let-down.

The snow's arrived – with blizzards – and the whole city is white and cold and the lights are on almost all day. You escaped from the winter in the nick of time! I wonder if it was very rough for your crossing? Boris said you looked awfully tired when you set out.

1 Dec.

Today I dragged myself up but feel so lousy that I'm not going to the theatre. I rang them, and Sauvola (the real scenery painter – Welche never <u>touches</u> wing flats) was off sick too. So Nicke will just have to explode when not everything's finished by Friday. But I think we'll get there, even so.

Yesterday the father of two Moomin-admiring children from Vasa came up to the studio. He wanted to show me a thick book of drawings and paintings they'd done. All copies, big ones, of my illustrations, painted with enormous affection and reverence. I was deeply moved, and equally so by the accompanying letter. I've always felt a bit silly, writing my stories – especially since the invitation to the Norwegian picture exhibition came – Moomin illustrations! But a visit like this helps one to see things the right way.

My dearest, I hope that today you're not feeling as snowy-snotty-rotten as I am, but can, on the other hand, share in feeling the sevenfold strength of the wakening "in spite of everything" that's starting to move somewhere in my feet.

This letter, which I'll send off by normal post once I'm out and about again, will no doubt take weeks to get to America. So in case I can't write again before then, I wish you as nice a Christmas as possible in the company of some person, or several, you enjoy being with. Lots of big hugs, and all my warmest wishes!

Tove.

with Elisabeth as his partner at dinner: Written above the name Elisabeth are the words "Not Erica?"

Amos: Businessman and newspaper proprietor Amos Andersson.

Putte Fock: Ulla Fock (née Stenman), wife of art dealer Eric Fock. TJ sometimes spells the name "Foch".

Helo: Finland's ambassador to Paris, Johan Helo.

Kenneth: The British portrait painter Kenneth Green borrowed TJ's studio in the summer of 1949 and they had a short relationship.

Al Capp: Al Capp's cartoon strip *Li'l Abner* included a character named "Schmoo".

Nicken: Nicken Rönngren, head of the Swedish Theatre in Helsinki 1919–54.

Welche: Stefan Welche.

DEC. 49 [*Helsingfors*]

Dearest Eva!

I'm on the train to Grankulla to do Atos's mother the honour of a 75th birthday visit. I dashed to get here after an exceptionally hectic day at the theatre. Tomorrow we've got a technical rehearsal, which means all the flats and props need to be ready. We open on the 28th. Since Sauvola died and Wenche washed his hands of the play I've had to toil away in the scenery workshop with an apprentice, who spends most of the time on theatre posters. So you'll appreciate what a rush it's been!

But anyway, I'm now so stimulated by the theatre atmosphere, in spite of all its nerviness and jealousy, that I don't care if I have to run all sorts of messenger-boy errands as long as the play is ready – and good.

Vivica's done great things with the direction since I last wrote, the costume workshop is at loggerheads with me – I really don't know why – but I'm starting to *go along* quite well with the workshop and scene shifters. Even my old enemy Welche's started calling me either "kid", Tove or Moominmamma, which I take as some kind of peacemaking.

The students Vivica's working with have turned out very well and are friendly and pleasant. Gerda Wrede is as sour as a lemon – she sits there watching rehearsals with her face all puckered up and then leaves without a word. Professional envy, maybe? I'm going to miss this colourful period when it's all over – whether it's a flop or a success.

I'm trying to find a bit of time for Christmas too, by the way – running home to bake some ginger snaps, wrapping presents and applying the sealing wax, queuing to post off parcels to Sweden. It gets quite expensive, of course, because the Stockholm relations, too many to count, have sent lots of food parcels, in spite of Ham's polite request for everyone to be sensible this year and dispense with the presents. You see – it's sad to receive without being able to give in return. Seeing as it's them.

But now I've applied for a big scholarship – the first time for 10 years – so I'm pretty hopeful. And tomorrow I'll get my advance on the play.

Kenneth is leaving in a few days' time. I reckon I'm fairly much over him already, but I shall feel even more relaxed once I know he can't *pop up* with his own key whenever he likes. I roared with laughter the other day when I came into the studio and found the epilogue in the middle of the floor. A huge pyramid of papers, discarded painting gear, clothes, letters, dead flowers, etc., crowned with his old shoes. The closing vignette of *my Green period*!

Unto, my fellow student from our time at the Ateneum, gave me a bigger present than he realised that night he suddenly turned up because he was so depressed about his advertising job. I can't honestly remember if I mentioned that episode? He came back again, which I was surprised by. And even more so by the fact that he introduced something purely lyrical, and a great tenderness, into this for me non-emotional affair. I think the thing that touched me most was the fact that he made the bed the next morning. No one else has ever done that. He's intensely Finnish, full of inferiority complex and diffidence + urge to assert himself. Often drunk. Slim, with an attractive figure. Consumed with longing to carry on painting – but without the courage to try again.

Now it's the day after the day after Christmas Eve – a quiet evening before all the theatre business starts again. Heavenly Canaan, how glad I am that Christmas is over. Nice, of course, as always – but it's been so hard to find time for everything and everyone I wanted to ... and then feeling guilty because Ham had to clear up on her own.

These days off have finally given me a chance to clean the studio and decorate it for the first-night party with the actors. And I had a letter from you!

I still don't know how you found your home and your friends on your return – or whether you got over your mental block about work – and whether, now that time and distance have put your Finnish months into perspective, you've been able to be reconciled to your innermost problem – so many, important things!

The description of the crossing itself gave me a powerful picture of your anxiety. How well I understood how you were feeling! Just like when a precious, much-anticipated long-distance call has come through and it's only after the miserable three minutes are up that you realise what you ought to have said and the way you ought to have said it. Yet you're so convinced you got it wrong.

I don't think you have any idea what you gave us. If you gave the others a fraction of what I received, you gave them a lot. I often admired your self-control and your ability to listen and re-immerse yourself in a world that must have grown very alien to you.

Eva, if you're feeling dissatisfied, think of everything you had to struggle with here. Your electric family atmosphere, your cheerless childhood and defiant, introverted youth, all the memories, a desolate room, unrealistically projected expectations, a new and tough working environment, everyone's maliciously watchful eyes – and then you yourself! And much more besides – I imagine. Don't be downhearted, my dearest friend; you came through it so very well – it's just that you can't see it all in a proper light yet. And later, when the mud settles to the bottom – how I wish you might then see what I believe: that the trip brought you something positive, after all, some kind of solution, or insight – or perhaps the realisation there no longer <u>is</u> anything that needs solving at any cost.

Rehearsing *Mumintroll och kometen* (*Moomintroll and the Comet*): the director with a sheaf of script pages, the author with a broom, and the mask-maker with a Moomin head. Drawing by Tove Jansson from *Nya Pressen*, 1949.

You belong to America now, I think, that's where your air is, your work, your friends, your <u>new</u> memories. Which grow stronger with every passing year.

Today there was news by telephone from Stockholm; Kerstin and her brother Bengt and another cousin, Ulla (Einar's) are intending to come over for the premiere. I was deeply touched and flattered, but at the same time my brain started working frantically: where are they to sleep, how will I find the time to spend with them if they arrive early ... But it's going to be all right, where there's a will there's a way. Delightful idea of theirs, wasn't it? – We've now had the dress rehearsal, and it went so dreadfully that we've high hopes of the first night. So they say. Snufkin overslept after a party and didn't turn up at all, the lighting went entirely to pot, props were missing, all the acting was poor. Nicken thundered. <u>But</u> – he laughed as well. (Blast – wish you could be here right now.)

By Christmas Eve I was absolutely shattered, I've been slaving away at the theatre twelve hours a day recently, often without proper meals. It'll make a nice change to paint a peaceful old still life again – but how I shall miss the theatre!!!

Gebers in Stockholm sends me very encouraging letters about my next book (which I haven't had time to touch) and wants the play to come to Sweden. Wouldn't that be great? But Vivica would have to come along as director, I'd refuse otherwise.

On the painting front I've had little success – drew a blank on the scholarship. I suspect they think I'm rich – (or the truth is that they dislike my pictures!?)

Peo has collected your lamps and sends grateful thanks and best wishes. My lovely big one stopped working yesterday! Treacherous object. It's the best lamp I've ever had. Lasse's carrying on with Hannele's classes and also giving lessons to Atos, who's making amazing progress but doesn't give a fig about the grammar. We meet regularly if not often, and there's an easy-going warmth between us. Fock's art shop has opened and Lasse's there every day, and enjoys the work. His short-story collection "Jag är min egen oro" [I am my own unease] is finished now. Good, I reckon – a big step forward.

It's late at night – must sleep because of work in the morning. Snowstorm outside. A heartfelt hug, wishing you all the good things imaginable. Eva, do write even if you're feeling *down* and disappointed, fed up with everything. I know.

Love, Tove
Best wishes from Ham!

Unto: The artist Unto Virtanen.
Gebers: Hugo Gebers Förlags had published *Trollkarlens hatt* in 1949
and was the Moomin books' publisher in Sweden thereafter.

23 FEB. 50. [*Helsingfors*]

Dearest Eva!

First and foremost, some good news.

I can keep the studio! I finally plucked up the courage to ring – and was told that they're putting up a brand-new building for their school after all. They'll give me a one-year contract, but wouldn't go any further than that. I went straight from the phone to get out a dozen canvas stretchers and start nailing and preparing – a job I'd kept putting off. And cleaned the W.C. – had an urge to paint … You understand how it feels. I was no longer a guest in my own home.

You've had a long wait for this letter – and have sent me two in the meantime. Ham and I spent ten days at the Frenckells' place, Saari Manor, at Vivica's invitation, so Ham could rest her stomach. Three days at Pellinge, funeral. Albert's (our landlord) brother died of cancer. No older than I am. Ham came too, enduring the dismal, freezing journey by bus, car, sledge, and finally on foot across the ice. Faffan and I stayed for two days because we realised Abbes wanted company.

I've done some more work for the theatre, two sketches for the authors' revue. Stromboli, in wild lava colours, spewing out chiffon veils with the help of an electric fan, and Kontiki, a great deal of trouble, and by the time it was ready it reached right to the top of the proscenium arch. A tall, greenish-white wave, with a raft (three-dimensional) balanced on its crest, and an enormous amount of rigging. Plus a giant shell (3 m) in the background, from which a mermaid will emerge. Welche's still cross with me, so I was obliged to work in a narrow, draughty corridor under the carpentry workshop.

And then – apart from various other drawing jobs – I illustrated the whole of Moominpappa's memoirs, about 40 pictures. I thought about you all the time, "talked" to you, and really wanted to write – but hadn't a moment. I'm starting to feel out of my depth with all this Moomin business. Thank God I don't have to defend myself publicly in the papers any more – but there are constant interviews and book events, I make stupid mistakes in commercial agreements, which then have to be sorted out, and the whole thing gets out of hand. Moomin china, Moomin films in special viewers and *what not.* And then the Moomin opposition, good grief – all those aggressive types who pick quarrels with me over that poor troll. And caravans of children ...

But now I shall try to be strictly factual and give you all the information you want – because even though *I'm terribly fed up with the critter*, I can't think of anything nicer than him getting a foothold in America. His "mistress" definitely wouldn't be too far behind him ... You're a marvellous friend, Eva, being prepared to do this for me. Kisses and hugs from me! May it all go well!

All right. Let's see to the facts.

1. Jansson, Tove Marika, born 9.8.1914 in Helsingfors. Studied arts and crafts (decoration and graphic art) in Stockholm 1931–33. (The Technical School.) Studied painting in Helsingfors 1933–1936. (Ateneum.) Study trips to Paris 1938 and to Italy 1939 and 1948. First exhibited paintings in 1937. Besides painting, also a cartoonist and illustrator. Exhibited publicly in Helsingfors, Oslo, Göteborg and Stockholm. Awarded a travel grant in 1938, first prize in the "Ducat" competition 1939 and third prize in the State Art Exhibition 1939. Two solo exhibitions in H:fors.

2. Painted an al fresco mural (13 m in length) in the assembly room of Helsingfors City Hall and an al secco mural (c. 10m) in Kotka for a room where the workers leave their children on their way to the (paper?) factory.

3. Moomintroll was actually created by my maternal uncle, Prof. Einar Hammarsten. (who does Rockefeller-

funded research on isotopes at the Karolinska Institute in Stockholm.) (professor of medical chemistry, has lectured in America) When I was very young and always hungry and stayed with him in Stockholm, I used to help myself to snacks from the larder at night. He did his best to convince me there were "moomintrolls" who would come and blow down the back of my neck – they lived behind the stove in the kitchen. I got the idea for how Moomin looked from a tree stump in the forest that was covered in snow, which was hanging down like a big round white nose. Started writing the first Moomin story in 1944 [*44 crossed out, changed to 38*] when I was feeling depressed and scared of the bombing and wanted to get away from my gloomy thoughts to something else entirely. (A sort of escapism, to the time when Ham used to tell me stories.) I crept into an unbelievable world where everything was natural and benign – and possible. Then I went on writing whenever I felt like it, for my own fun – generally only when I was feeling carefree and cheerful. The books have no particular purpose, neither educationally nor in any other way – and nor does the children's Moomin play – which various irate letters to the newspapers have labelled tendentious, or to be precise, "demoralising" for children! (The one signing himself "Bewildered Father" mistook the metamorphosis mixture for whisky and "begroked" for a swearword along the lines of "bloody". "Metamorphosis mixture" is a magic potion that turns everyone "opposite" – it's given to mean and nasty people.)

4. The next book comes out this year and will (very likely) be called "My Stormy Youth", Moominpapa's Memoirs. Schildts publishing house (where I went when Söder-ströms backed out of "Trollkarlens hatt") rang the other day. They asked if they could act as agents for all three of my children's books with a company that was asking for Finnish children's literature. Through this company the books will (perhaps!) be published in Norway and Den-mark. A Dane wrote to me recently, asking to translate the books into Danish. The company's going to get in touch with him. Jarno Pennanen has offered to translate one (or

more, I'm not sure) into Finnish and get it published by Otava, through a lady with very good contacts there.

Elisabeth Porch's translation of "Trollkarlens hatt" into English is now finished and will go off within the week to a publisher in London who saw the illustrations and expressed an interest. That translation's been a wretched nuisance. She started it to teach herself Swedish, and the idea of actually translating the book only came to her later. For that reason, the language in the early part is pretty stiff and literal – not "thought" in English. Kenneth said *it needed brushing up*. So (via Vivica) I got hold of the wife of the British Council here, Margaret Washbourn, and got her to go through the whole thing, and both she and Liz were fed up with Moomin and with each other by the end of the process. Margaret's work turned out freer but more banal; she took all the personal expression out of it. Liz, on the other hand, was *awkvard* [in TJ's English] and personal. So Lasse and I had to go through it all again – and next week we cooks will all meet again to make sure the broth's in order. Would definitely have been better to let Warburton (who translated James Joyce's Odysseus) take it – which was what he wanted. But by then Liz had already got it and I couldn't go back on my word.

5. Sent Dramaten (at their request) a set of parts, some photos, programme, costume and stage design sketches, and heard no more from them. When I got your letter I phoned dir Hogland there and asked if they could send back the material (except the parts) because I needed it for another purpose. They replied that they liked the play and might possibly put it on next Christmas. But nothing's at all definite. And it's taken them until now to send back the photos.

6. So I'll be able to send photographs of the play in three or four days' time, by airmail. I'll also put in the cartoon strips, which Peo will photograph. I wanted Lasse to translate the captions into English and photograph them too, overlaid on the originals, but he hasn't had time what with his classes

and the art shop. Lasse will have to translate them later, and I'll send them on after the strips.

7. Same thing with the reviews – I'll send them as soon as Lasse finds time to translate them. All the material might even reach you at the same time.

8. As for Al Capp, now I've got the address I'm sending him Trollkarlens hatt (that's the one with the best illustrations) along with a letter saying how I discovered his Schmoos and was tickled by their similarity to Moomin, and how enchanting I find his animals.

9. In Liz's book [*added later:* transl.] the names are mumintrollet – Moomintroll, Snusmumriken – Snufkin, Tofslan o Vifslan – Thingamy and Bob (Eng. expression meaning roughly "pass me that – whatever it's called – from over there"), the parents, Moominmamma, Moominpappa. Sniff = Sniff, Snork = Snork, Hemulen = Hemulen.

I think I've covered the most important points now. If you write anything, say less rather than more – no unnecessarily boastful facts. You know. I just wrote down what occurred to me – you can pick and choose.

And finally, I want to say how absolutely delighted I am with the photographs you took in my studio. They're the most authentic pictures to have been taken here, both of me and of the studio. Everybody likes them. Eva, thank you, *congratulations*. If you really did want to give me enlargements – or copies, of some, I'd be tremendously glad. A picture like that one of me by the window would be so nice to give to a friend who wanted a photo. A <u>completely</u> natural picture. And what's more, I even look quite attractive, don't I? Just think, I've never dared let anyone take a picture of me in profile before. Maybe one of the window photos (16, 12 and 8) no. 8 is best. Do you think I could have a couple of that one? And after those, I'm also delighted with no. 14, with me standing in profile beside the easel. Excellent light and movement! The studio pictures are first-rate, just a shame I'm pulling such a face in them. No. 4 has such brilliant tones and composition. I'd really love to have that one, and no. 17, and two where you've managed to incorporate the baldachin into the composition – especially rhythmically in no. 17. I bet you're pleased with the pictures where I'm pouring coffee and looking like a sulky boy. No. 11 is good, with the dark face against the pale canvas. No. 16, too, with my head bent in front of the easel. What do you think of them yourself? Do write! [... *Last page missing*]

Eva Konikoff's photo of Tove Jansson in her studio in Ulrikaborgsgatan: "a completely natural picture ... I even look quite attractive."

Ham and I spent ten days: See Letters to Vivica Bandler, Unknown date in a snowstorm. 1950.

Started writing the first Moomin story: The date of writing *Småtrollen och den stora översvämningen* [published in English as *The Moomins and the Great Flood*] was altered in the letter from 1944 to 1938 by TJ. She makes reference to the story in her diary in May 1944 with the comment: "Felt like tidying up Moomintroll's wonderful journey and revising it." She has "the Moomintroll book" finished in a couple of days.

Jarno Pennanen: Author and journalist, an emerging left-wing radical and opinion former.

Elisabeth Porch: Elizabeth Portch, Liz, who gave private lessons in English in Finland for some years. Lars Jansson was among her first pupils.

Warburton: Thomas Warburton, translator and senior literary editor at the publishing house Holger Schildts Förlags.

Dramaten: The Royal Dramatic Theatre in Stockholm.

dir Hogland: Director Claes Hoogland, dramatist and critic.

TOVE JANSSON HAS A NEW LOVE: BRITT-SOFIE FOCK, WHO works as a goldsmith. They live together for a number of years and Britt-Sofie Fock sits for several paintings. The pace of work in the early 1950s is intense and Tove Jansson is engaged on numerous artistic projects. In 1952, she does two frescoes for Fredrikshamn's "society house" or clubhouse, another fresco at Kotka and publishes her first picture book about the world of the Moomins, *Hur gick det sen?* (*The Book About Moomin, Mymble and Little My*). That year she also signs a contract for the Moomin cartoon strip with Associated Newspapers. "There's a lot going on all at once", she writes to Eva Konikoff.

28 FEB. 52 [*Helsingfors*]

Dearest Eva,

Thank you for your long letter! So in four days' time you'll be working again. I wonder if you found a better place than last time.

You know what, your whole letter was so much calmer and happier than for ages. Well, perhaps not happy exactly – but hopeful. It did me good to have another chance to talk to you for a while. I know now that the contact between us will never be broken again – even though the intervals will sometimes be long.

Perhaps it was a good thing Barney vanished. The way people, friends, seem to vanish in New York. It's not so easy here. One bumps into old mymbles, friends and enemies everywhere. It's such a ridiculously small world – and Finnish intellectuals and artists in particular are forever tripping over each other. And getting hopelessly tangled up with one another. There are so few of us!

Another group that's few in number is the lesbians. The ghosts, as we call them – and as I shall call them in my letters from now on. That might be one of the reasons why Vivica attracted so many people's attention. It seems to me that the world is full of women whose men don't satisfy their need for affection, eroticism, under-standing, etc. Lots of things a ghost can provide – though she can rarely provide respectable security and is over-sensitive = difficult in absurdum. It's not surprising you didn't connect with Vivica. She "shut down" and was quiet and impersonal in your company, because she sensed that you didn't like her.

You can definitely drop all your grudges now because she will never "*let me down*"! On the contrary, I know that she will be with me all my life as an utterly loyal friend and helper. And I realise now that I could never have received a better gift than that tough time when I was in love with her. It eventually made me into more conscious, more self-assured person and peeled away all those stupid, unnecessary ornaments of self-deception, restraint and naivety. I'm also very grateful to Atos – mainly for the intellectual strength he tried to give me. You probably know that we mymbled now and then, as friends – rather the way one might cuddle one's old husband – purely for the pleasant familiarity of it. Now I've rearranged things a bit and *made up my mind as to where to belong* – and definitely ended all emotional involvement with him – but the friendship part is still there, of course. [...]

In emotional terms, these last few years have been very shaky and uncertain. Constantly in the early stages of falling in love, masses of concocted feelings and disappointments, casual new liaisons and the renewal of older ones – and all the while that uncomfortable sense of hanging in mid-air, seeking where there's nothing to be found.

I think I finally know what I want now, and as my friendship with you is very important to me and is very much founded on honesty, I want to talk this over with you. I haven't made the final decision, but I'm convinced that the happiest and most genuine course for me would be to go over to the ghost side. It would be silly of you to get upset about that. For my own part, I'm very glad and feel intensely relieved and at peace. – These last weeks I've been almost exclusively with the one I've found, unfortunately just a short time before she goes off to France. We're both equally happy. I'm also working like a thing possessed – inter alia on a couple of portraits and nude studies of her. She won't ever be coming back here, but this time I've decided not to bury myself in grief.

And the day will come when I feel able to start looking round for somebody else I can be fond of. It won't be easy. And I'm afraid I shall look a little ridiculous. Can you imagine me making cautious enquiries of all ladies in collar and tie, or placing pathetic advertisements in Hufvudstadsbladet! "Who will take me to the distant shores of Lesbos!" The risk would be that they'd think I meant Esbo ...

But all that will come later. The main thing surely has to be feeling at ease with oneself and knowing what one wants.

I shall be painting my murals all spring. In a few days the two canvases, each 5½ m, will be dry enough to paint. I had two young-sters from the Ateneum here to prepare and stretch them for me at an hourly rate. ("Old Naturalist exploits impoverished young geniuses for work of Mammon ...") The 1:1 scale tracing onto the walls is already done. And the sketch for the Kotka mural sent in.

As regards the Daily Mail I'm still in correspondence with them about a Moomin cartoon strip. *Would be a good thing for the publicity of my books. Bobbs-Merrill writes about the possibility of toys, perhaps solid, perhaps balloons, based on my Moomins. But it is no more than an idea, I believe.*

The picture book I did over the summer is off to the printer's, and Warburton is dragging his feet interminably over his translation of the Moomin memoirs. And tomorrow I shall deliver a collection of 6–7 oils for the open exhibition at the Kunsthalle. There's a lot going on all at once. But I'm enjoying my work – finally, after so many hellish years of failure and lack of productivity. Time to get a meal ready. *So long* until tomorrow!

Next day.

Hello Eva – today I can't paint a single line or do anything sensible at all: the day before it has to be submitted. How very distasteful I find exhibiting! It's going to be a terrific relief once the canvases are in, even if they're then refused or harshly criticised. This is a sort of *"come back", you know, and I am terribly uneasy about it. Samuli, who now and then – twice a year perhaps, comes here and gives me critic, was rather positive, though. Dunno ... And the day after tomorrow I start painting my walls. You can perhaps imagine it hasn't been easy being in love with all that work around you. Time is simply melting away, you hardly dare to sleep – and though feel in a mysterious way stronger and more alive than ever before. I suppose I am happy.*

Peo's departure still isn't definite. Peter's had bad angina and been in the epidemic hospital, Peo's film is finished after a huge amount of work, Saga minds other people's children during the day to earn a bit of money. If they are able to go I shall be delighted to be able to help out financially for a change. And once in Canada, Peo will apparently find a wonderful job in his line of work. We'll have to see. Faffan's been brighter and hasn't been on the binge at all, not recently. He and I haven't exchanged a single unkind word for years now. I wonder what I shall do for Ham's 70th on 1st June. She refuses any kind of formal celebration and stubbornly insists on going out to Bredskär with me. But of course that just <u>won't do</u>! What about Faffan? Well, she says, that's the only present I want, to be alone with you on the island. Apart from that, she wants nothing for herself. I wonder how things will turn out. Kurt thinks we ought to go to Vienna with him for a week and Ham should then go on to somewhere like Florence.

Eva, your Mexico plans sound bewitching to me. <u>Of course</u> I'd like to. But it's a long way away, and lots can change. Why not ...? It seems some money will be coming my way.

Lasse's still at the art shop and doing business with varying success, but undoubtedly with increasing proficiency and salesmanship skills. And his interest in it definitely seems lasting. He's busy writing a novel about love, psychological.

As for Sam, he's become a tremendous bigwig in the art world, teaching at the Ateneum, sitting on lots of juries and committees, and is just as nice as ever, but with a much larger paunch. I suppose Maya has "calmed down", as you put it, they're getting *along* fine, but I think she'd quite like to do a bit more ghosting. I can very well understand that.

The dressmaker's workshop that wanted to buy my studio has backed out, but other prospective purchasers keep turning up for a look so who bloody knows what will happen.

Where the summer's concerned, I'm probably going to have another new cousin on the island, this time from Germany. But I'm sure I won't feel as free and easy as last year. The Kotka fresco has to be painted and in a modest sort of way I'm wondering about a solo exhibition in the autumn. – Yes, Impi's well for now, thank God, though one wonders how long it can last.

Non-figurative = non-figural representation is actually "abstract art". I share your view on that score. I can admire it while not actually "liking" it. But I do love Matisse.

Right then, hugs and farewell for today. Next time I write, a lot of my jobs will be over and done with, my Bitti will be gone and spring might slowly be on its way.

Kisses and please, burn my letters!

old mymbles: Former lovers, male or female. Mymbling is used to mean more or less the same as sleeping with someone.

THE ISLAND. 5 JUNE 52.

Dearest Eva,

thanks for your long letter – and for those glimpses of your February and April. Little Lynn and Howard, Rosa, Devora, Ada – I already feel quite familiar with them from your descriptions. But the most powerful threads running through your letters are those of work and the very lonely battle you are having with yourself. You write to me when you're frantic, when you're hopeful and when you're strong – and I'm glad of that.

[...] If only I could have you here for a week on the island! That's how long I've been here with Ham. When we came I was on the verge of tears from exhaustion and nerves, but now calm skies, horizons, the quiet and the gentle monotony of the days have wiped all that away. It's strange to think there was a time when I didn't "like nature". How stupid.

A few essentials are increasingly crystallising out. A few people, jobs of work, settings. It's as you say, one would prefer to have just a few desires (though those may be greater than ever?) and can muster no time or energy for anything superfluous.

I've often described Bredskär to you. You know everything that generally happens here, what I get up to, and that I'm happy on my island.

So I'll tell you instead what happened in town this hectic spring.

I had 4 big things accepted at the Kunsthalle, and I was lucky with the hanging, in the centre of a wall in the middle room. And better reviews than I had before the war. Maybe my painter's block will ease off now. The best canvas was a portrait of Eric Fock's sister Bitti.

Other than that I've painted nothing but the murals for Fredrikshamn – "The Beach" and "Seabed". Working full days most of the time – and they were ready a week before I came out here for Ham's 70th birthday, just in time to be taken to F:hamn for mounting on the wall. It was one hell of a final spurt. What made it such a rush was cartoon-strip business getting in the way, a chance that I didn't dare pass up. Mr Sutton (my Moomin agent in London) came over on the last day of April to agree a contract between Associated Newspapers Ltd and me, and I had to have synopses for 80 cartoon strips ready for him.

I finished them the day he came. In the evening a big May Day Eve party for him at the studio for 20 people, guitars and Finnish brandy, irate caretaker, balloons, intrigues, dancing and morning coffee, the whole works. And on top of all that, a May Day business breakfast at Kämp – disturbed to some degree by the restaurant being full of students, singing and dancing and climbing pillars, and children playing and most of the guests from the night before.

Mr. Sutton may have got a somewhat misleading impression of Finnish high spirits, but he certainly enjoyed himself. Admittedly he hid behind his grey English moustache when Vivica asked me to samba with her in the studio – but the contract was agreed and my synopses met with approval.

Mistrustful as I am these days, I surreptitiously found an expert in all the chaos, and showed them the contract, which proved to contain a significant trap. The clever wording seemed at first glance to say I would receive a certain % for cartoon strips sold to other newspapers, when in actual fact this only applied to television, broadcasting and cinematograph rights. And <u>they</u> will hardly apply in the case of strips. So I got Sutton to put in a clause about my right to a % for publication in other newspapers.

He's handling the % for rubber articles (!) in America for me. Had a try at raising the royalty, but failed. Benn's is busy with "Muminpappans bravader" [*The Memoirs of Moominpappa*] and a publisher in Switzerland is interested in "Finn Family". The Mymble picture book is now at the printer's here and has also been translated into Finnish. I'm firing off commercial letters in all directions and am amazed at the sheer volume of all the Moomin business. If the cartoons prove popular in London I shall be engaged for maybe 4 years to deliver one a day. Permanent employment – the first time in my life ... They want them quite large with lots of detail and keep changing things and raising objections, so it takes quite a long time to finish a whole strip. Here on the island I've finally had time to make a start on them – I've got to deliver them regularly, in bundles of six.

Where to put in murals and oil painting ...?

Just before I came out here, my sketch for the Kotka fresc [*sic*] was approved – it's to be done in September. I've fixed up some paper and started drawing the composition in charcoal. And in October the ballet Pessi and Illusia opens at the Finnish Ballet. With my stage sets, to be done this summer. So as you see, it never rains but it pours. I've opted out of jobs for the Sw. Theatre and the Junior Theatre and various illustration commissions. Only taking the things I haven't the heart to refuse, for the sake of the glory or the money. But no damn body buys paintings!

In July, Bitti's coming back from Paris and is going to spend some time on the island with me. You'll realise how I'm anticipating that and trying to get jobs out of the way beforehand. *Bredskär is a good place for stripmaking.*

6/6

(*and why not lovemaking too?*)

Uca's been in Paris for a while making arrangements for a film she might make here with Peo behind the camera. She met Bitti while she was there, and of course I was agog to know if they'd make contact. It's been preposterous always trying to keep them out of each other's way because Mary portrayed them as monsters to one another, played them off against each other and turned them into fierce enemies. They wrote eventually, and were clearly neither rivals nor antagonists any longer.

They were petrified of me, the fools, having gone and mymbled with each other! There was nothing for it but to laugh in my solitude. That pair who couldn't stand the sight of each other! This will simplify everything considerably.

Incidentally, most of the spring has been overshadowed by anxiety about my studio, which has been perpetually invaded by buyers. Last autumn the property value stood at 2,250,000 and gradually sank to 1,500,000. I applied for some new places they're building, without success, put out feelers everywhere, but the studio shortage seems insoluble.

I've been worrying about my tower for so long now that I began to get used to the idea of having to leave it, and even decided this was meant to stop me growing too attached to any one place – the moss really was starting to grow on me. So when I heard in May that it had been sold to a printing works I took it quite calmly. Just had to find out when they'd have the right to put me out onto the street.

So I rang every day to ask for their final decision; after all, I'd need to get myself a lawyer before I dared go off to the island. I could have risked my furniture being shifted out if I didn't appeal to the rent tribunal. And I couldn't do that before I'd had official notice to quit.

Every time I rang they gave me evasive and procrastinating answers, and after 10 days I started to think they wanted me out of town so they could do as they pleased. You see, 28 May – 8 June I had to be, wanted to be on the island to celebrate Ham's birthday with her. The pathetic little stretch of time a surrogate for our big trip that never happened.

Westerlund who owns the whole building and is selling the studio is a nasty piece of work – everybody says so. Through all the delay he waged a war of nerves on me until the evening before I was due to leave, when he admitted the studio hadn't been sold at all! But if

I could put half a million on the table the next day I could keep it and he agreed (after a fair amount of haggling) to bring the price down to 1,200,000. By then I'd been looking for a place for so long that I knew it was worth that, and I'd never get another one that big for that price. And the rent in new buildings is 25–30,000 a month. But at that point I didn't have a single penny to hand, having just given 100,000 to a friend who was involved in the protest of a bill, and 75,000, the emigration present I'd promised Peo, went on his treatment, and in the headiness of finally having some money (for the F.hamn paintings) I'd spent loads on Ham's birthday, provisions for the whole summer, lots of new clothes and work materials I needed + paid off all my debts and tax.

That evening, what with packing to go to the island too, really was a bit nerve-racking! The next morning, once I'd delivered 13 parcels to M/S Pellinge, I dashed to a bank and through some friends managed to get an appointment with the manager. To my surprise he said my name was good for half a million (they're not making any loans just now) and if I came up with two more rock-solid names I could have the rest as well. But not until after their directors' meeting on 9 June.

I rushed to Westerlund and told him it was all fixed. Then the ass demanded a 100,000 down payment, "otherwise he might let the printer have the studio while I was out of town after all!" At the last minute it occurred to me that my old paintings might have their uses after all. And the devil accepted them as a deposit! There was no time to get myself any "solid names", I'll have to do that on the morning of the 9th, may the muse help me, because then the boat left for the rose bushes.

And here we've marked Ham's 70th birthday with shells and leaves decorating the whole house, and a few wild pansies, because the rest aren't out yet. There was great deliberation about this 1st June. Right up to mid-May I thought I'd be able to treat Ham to a flight to Vienna and then take a little detour to Florence. Since the trip with Uca I've sworn I wouldn't travel anywhere in any form before I'd done it with Ham, and now she's thinking of retiring it would have been just right. I had the money, too, for once. But then Peo got this lung disease.

You already know that his emigration fell through because they found a harmless old calcification in one lung. In the very thorough examinations the authorities demanded, he also had to provide sputum samples as a formality. 6 weeks later he had some surprising results: he had bacteria and had tested positive. Since then he's been at Mjölbollstad Sanatorium in Karis (refused to allow me to fund the trip to Switzerland), being treated with the new wonder drug Rimifon.

It now looks as if he'll be restored to health over the summer. And there's a chance that the Rimifon (which has <u>only just</u> reached Finland) might also shrink or get rid of the old calcification, and thus also the obstacle to his emigration.

Imagine if he'd been allowed to travel, and was then taken seriously ill in Canada! He still had no symptoms at the time, and no idea there was anything wrong with him. Thanks to the investigations he found out in time. So I think we can only be thankful things went the way they did.

But Ham didn't want to go away on a trip, of course, while we still didn't know how serious his condition might be. Instead she said she wanted to go to the island, with <u>just</u> me, nobody else. It's all a bit absurd. In the end I persuaded her to invite Faffan along, but he didn't want to come – he feels hemmed in on such a small island.

At the last minute, Lasse decided to come too, and Peo took "leave of absence" and came with his family as a surprise on the morning of her actual birthday. I think she had a happy celebration, and things still are happy – a bit of birthday every day. Trips out to the islands, beachcombing, planting things, feeling at ease, relaxing after all our troubles in town. We've got to go back there in a few days. I do wish I didn't have to! Isn't it funny, Eva, that the worst thing I know; politics, overshadowed the first part of my life. Will business, my second least favourite, dominate the second part? Maybe in order for me to learn something – not to "run away". I've started (for the first time in my life) dreaming about money, and in the mornings I have to get up straight away, otherwise I start worrying about my bank loan. It feels strange ... And I'm an employee, too. Everything turns out rather the opposite of what one expected ...

And another strange thing, although I'm from a family line of clergymen, on the quiet I've begun to believe. It's hard not to when you start finding meaning in all sorts of things, and find you do receive help when you've been fighting the fight on your own account and then ask to be lent a hand.

This turned into a long letter. But I had a lot to tell you. Still more – but that will keep for next time. I wish you the best of everything, Eva!

Oh, and I don't know anything about Raffo. Wish I had some contact with him. Perhaps I'll try to get in touch ...

A big hug
Tove.

P.S In town. I got the bank loan! Faffan and Vivica put their names to it.

Mr. Sutton: Charles Sutton, head of syndication at Associated Newspapers Ltd.
Mary: Mary Mandelin-Dixon, journalist and playwright.
Since the trip with Uca: See Letter to Atos Wirtanen 3.4.1951.
Rimifon: Rimiphone, an antibiotic used in the treatment of tuberculosis.

IN THE SPRING OF 1954, TOVE JANSSON VISITS LONDON TWICE, the first time for a fortnight in March, when she works on her cartoon strips at Associated Newspapers in Fleet Street. She describes her experiences in a letter to Vivica Bandler dated 9.3.1954. A few weeks later, in April, she comes back with Ham. They are finally on their long-planned trip together, first to London, followed by three days in Paris, and then on to the Riviera. The cartoon synopsis she refers to below is "The Family Lives it Up", later renamed "Moomin on the Riviera". The trip also appears in literary guise in "Resa till Rivieran" ("A Trip to the Riviera") in *Brev från Klara* (*Letters from Klara*), 1991.

CAP D'ANTIBES. 7 MAY –54

Dearest Eva!

So we finally got away, Ham and I – and the whole trip has been as if my thoughts and dreams were coming true. It's been tranquil but happy, intense and liberating – and I'm deeply grateful. Back home Bitti's father is dying of lung cancer, but even that isn't pricking my Conscience in the old way; making me feel I should be somewhere else, consoling, sympathising.

Just now Ham is the right person for me to be with, not anyone else or anywhere else, and no one expects any work from me. Not even letters, and that makes it a pleasure to write to you, as I know you're following our journey with as much affection as Bitti.

Since I got home from that demanding fortnight in Fleet Street it's been the bank painting in the daytime and the cartoon strips in the evening, and Ham has been slaving like mad too. If one of us wasn't ill the other was, if nothing else, with anxiety about not getting away.

I didn't quite get the wall finished and only got paid 2/3 of my fee, but the problem was solved by Ham's bank presenting her with a large gift of money for "her contribution to making Finland known". Wasn't that fine praise? And someone unexpectedly repaid me an old loan. So here we are, sitting on a little sandy beach surrounded by jagged, grey-white cliffs with big clumps of unfamiliar flowers and bushes, and down in the bottom of the bay there's a glimpse of Juan les Pins and it's finally turned warm after several days of gales and torrential rain. Ham's collecting so many shells and stones that I've no idea how we're going to get them all home with us!

First we flew to London and spent five days there. For three of them we were completely left to ourselves, walking, looking, feeling free and just "being". We stayed in a hotel off Piccadilly, and from that sparkling, bustling centre we caught open-topped buses in all directions, from impoverished Whitechapel and the East India Docks via drearily middle-class Victorian Bloomsbury to Hyde Park where the magnolias were in bloom, just travelled on and on, absorbing everything like hungry sponges. In the evenings we fell asleep at 7 o'clock, both equally tired.

In Petticoat Lane, the English flea market, an Indian chief kissed Ham's hand and declared (in Swedish) that he loved her, we joined the throng in Zoot and Tussaud, Ham insisted on eating deep-fried lobster and bamboo shoots, and finally we dived in among all the gentlemen of Fleet Street.

There we drank champagne in the mornings and were chauffeured to and fro, everyone thought Ham was wonderful and they decided I only need produce one cartoon strip while I was away (I'll do double at the Island afterwards instead). And we each bought a cartoon-strip Dress!

Somewhat bedraggled, we flew on to Paris and checked into our hotel in rue de la Gaité where Ham and Faffan once had a studio. (Faffan didn't want to come on the trip, said he'd feel homesick.)

Their Atelier Impasse was exactly as it had been, Ham said, with its ivy, sculpture fragments and cats; the only change was that bits of abstract painting were visible through the decaying windows. We went to the little eatery where they used to order snails and walked to all the places we both remembered and loved, but only stayed three days. It's a little melancholy, perhaps, revisiting a city one hasn't seen for 39 years – especially that city, in the springtime.

Then we travelled straight down through France, taking the day train because Ham wanted to see the scenery. It was a pretty tiring journey and when we finally got to Nizza, we just tumbled into the nearest hotel. The next day it bucketed down with rain and the town looked oddly forlorn without its classic sunshine and beach-goers. So we decided to look up Eric Fock and his wife Putte who emigrated to Cagnes sur Mer. We had no more detailed address, so it was quite good fun trying to find them. They lived in one of those ancient old towns climbing up the hillside, with a medieval castle on top, where all the streets are sets of steps, with thousands of dogs and cats and centenarian locals whose legs are all crooked from only ever walking vertically. We wandered round in the rain in the maze of little streets, and all of a sudden the Focks appeared, walking towards us! After that we took it easy, with rum toddy and an olive wood fire in their casa (because it was perishing cold) and stayed with them for four days.

It was through Fock we found the pension where we now are, and will stay until we leave for home, travelling directly back by plane. We worked out that it would actually be cheaper for us to go for a kind of family discount return flight – thereby also saving a lot of time and seasickness.

<u>Later</u>.

After a very cold and salty dip with lots of sea urchins underfoot we walked the short stretch to the hotel garden where, as the only guests (the Expensive Season starts in July), we are sitting under a parasol drinking white wine while we wait for our meal. *(My, this is high life!)* This really is an amazingly cheap pension, considering its location on this fashionable coast, and without Bitti's brother we'd never have come across the little place, which is squeezed away in a corner and hard to find.

Le patron is huge and terribly friendly, and decorates our blouses with roses every day. When we first arrived he was distraught that his only double room was being painted and took us a bit deeper into the jungle of almost hysterically blooming foliage. We could stay in a villa whose owner was in Algier, while our room dried.

I hope it never dries! Through a little green gate in a hedge we emerged into a fabulous garden with palms, nut trees, oranges and a well covered in yellow roses. The whole garden is delightfully overgrown and guarded by a serpent, the only ugly thing here – a horrid little dog with a spiteful character, who we've christened The Woodlouse. Whenever he can he sneaks into the house and pees there!

Our villa is absolutely tiny, like something cut out of a picture book, white with green shutters, with a cypress at each corner. There are wild pelargoniums climbing up onto the roof, which starts at head height, the rooms are whitewashed and the floor is red-tiled. It's all just as I've been envisaging it ever since, as a young girl, I planned this journey with Ham. In the bedroom there's one big bed with just about room to climb into it, and red curtains.

When one wakes (we fall asleep at 9 o'clock and wake at 8, always simultaneously) one reaches up a hand and pulls back the curtain to reveal a yellow wall and a little snippet of picture-postcard blue sky, and knows it's a day for our bay. Then one falls back to sleep. We're living in absolute egotism, happiness and indolence. Juan les Pins is twenty minutes away but we don't go there, only for one day when we gaped at the exotically dressed people round the casino, the incredible luxury in the shops and the general air of Preparation for the Season. That's when the millionaires and those who have saved up for eleven months come here and spend the whole of August (according to our patron) running around the streets naked and paying 6000 francs for a bottle of champagne. The shops and Casino stay open all night and there's a general pursuit of money and those in possession of it.

I've made the most of the chance and started a strip cartoon synopsis about Moomintroll accidentally straying into this whole show and misunderstanding everything.

A bit of background: this entire coastal section is completely cut off. Scores of kilometres of "private", "beware of the dog", "reserved for (luxury) hotel guests". We spent a whole morning looking for a little strip of beach before retreating to our own solitary stretch of sand with an indignation verging on Communism.

I assume it's the same all the way from the Pyrenees to Ventimiglia, and luck must have been with us on our trip to let us have our own breathing space in paradise defendue.

How nice to be writing to you only about pleasant subjects again. My thoughts turn to you more often than you think, and I wonder how you are – how the encounters went between you and that unusual man with the bright eyes, who was so wise. Did things develop as positively as they started? Anyway – just write when you really feel like it, the length of the intervals in our correspondence doesn't matter much.

Did I tell you Atos was defeated in the parliamentary elections? Now he's more or less obliged to leave politics and has apparently started writing, for himself. Unfortunately I hardly ever see him, maybe he's a bit intimidated by, and out of sympathy with, my new "tendency". But I can wait.

Farewell then, dearest friend. Ham sends <u>warmest</u> greetings.

A big hug from your happy Tove.

ST LUCIA'S DAY –62. H:FORS.

Eva, *darling*,

A Christmas present from America came tumbling through the letterbox and sent my thoughts to you. Thank you!

You know what, I strongly suspect nothing can come of our correspondence, which we have restarted so many times. With great Solemnity and Resolve and Explanation!

Instead, let's do this: occasionally when the spirit moves us, a little card like this. That doesn't tie us, it's a fleeting smile, a signal that we haven't forgotten, though time and distance fracture our intimate contact.

Is that *all right*? I think so.

I've got just enough room to write that Lasse and Nita and little Sophia are in Spain, Ibiza, for the whole winter and spring, that Bitti Fock has had Lasse's room at Ham's this autumn and been working at Vivica's theatre, but is going back to the farm in Sweden after New Year, and that I'm having an exhibition in Tammerfors and am longing for spring!

Happy New Year, Eva!

Tove.

Nita: Nita Lesch, Lars Jansson's wife.
Sophia: Sophia Jansson, Nita and Lasse's daughter.

TOVE AND EVA REMAINED IN OCCASIONAL CONTACT DURING the late-1950s and at some points also during the 1960s. There are, however, only a few letters from this period.

29.11.67 [*Helsingfors*]

Dearest Eva,

This galactic picture is a New Year's greeting from my world to yours, not <u>too</u> dreadfully distant any more, since we were able to meet. That one evening meant a lot to me, the old warmth was still there and what was more, I discovered something new that was extremely stimulating.

It's a pity we're so far away from each other but there's nothing to be done about it. I don't think we should try to conquer time and distance through correspondence, it gradually becomes a "must". But we can still wish each other a Happy New Year and write about what the old one brought with it.

I've been wearing your earrings and necklace, which when it isn't on me adorns the vase where I keep my brushes. When I'm feeling poetic or bold I go around in your American hostess dress. But I don't have that many guests, only sometimes the handful of friends who're the absolute ... you know.

The family picture has changed in that Lasse and Nita have got divorced. Lasse's gone down to Ibiza where they lived for five years to sell the plot of land they bought to build a house on – and the car and the TV, and in a week's time he's coming back to Finland with Sophia. They're going to live in Lasse's old room at Ham's and next year Sophia starts school, she's going to the Zilliacuska. Nita's staying on in Torremolinos for the time being.

The galactic picture was the cover of the first edition of *Trollkarlens hatt* (published in English as *Finn Family Moomintroll*) in 1948.

I've finally got started on a new book after a break of quite a few years – four, five? But Moomintroll seems to have come to an end after "Pappan och havet" [*Moominpappa at Sea*], so now I'm no longer writing <u>for</u> children but <u>about</u> a child – for grown-ups. It's hard and exciting to be without the prop of Moomin Valley. And a great joy to have got underway and to be working for <u>pleasure</u>.

Ham is a bit worse and terribly tired. But we had a lovely summer, warm – with some big, beautiful storms – and she was better than for several years. Now Lasse's coming back home she need never be alone at nights again.

I was at Lehtovaara yesterday with some visiting children's author, and happened to sit at our table. I could think of nothing but you – you were so much more vivid. How are you?

Were you happy with your trip to Finland? Are we further away now at last – or closer?

All's well!

Tove.

I've finally got started on a new book: Bildhuggarens dotter (*The Sculptor's Daughter*) came out in 1968.

"I can see the ideas growing like trees straight through you"

LETTERS TO ATOS WIRTANEN
1943–1971

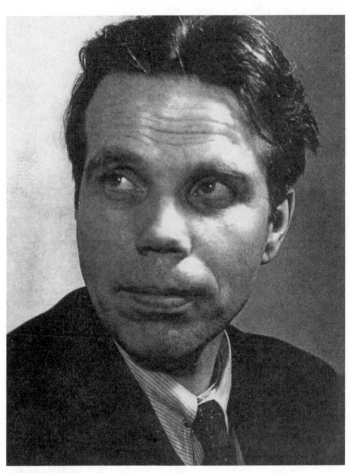

Atos Wirtanen.

ATOS IS "INCREDIBLY PRODUCTIVE AND THE ENFANT TERRIBLE of Parliament". Thus runs Tove Jansson's characterisation of Atos Wirtanen, author, politician, journalist and newspaper editor, in the autumn of 1944.

At this point Tove and Atos have been a couple for over a year. Atos Wirtanen is a philosopher with a great zest for life, as fond of parties as she is herself, and with a wide, generous smile. He is "brimming with life, thoughts and utopias". It is easy to be cheerful in his company, she writes earlier the same year. With Atos Wirtanen she feels free to work and to love, an ideal combination where Tove Jansson is concerned. Their paths first cross at an event early in 1943 and Tove Jansson soon becomes part of the circle that is in the habit of gathering at Wirtanen's house at Grankulla, just outside Helsinki. The group includes such literary figures as Gunnar Björling, Elmer Diktonius, Eva Wichman, Olof Enckell, Ralf Parland and Tito Colliander. When Tove Jansson is acting as bartender at a wild party there in February 1943, the two have not yet found one another, but a few months later, on 17 June 1943, she writes her new man on her calendar as "Atos". Over the summer, Tove Jansson is called up for three months' agricultural labour (a law passed in 1939 meant that all Finnish citizens aged 18–64 and liable for service could be put to work for the defence forces or the country's economic interests), and that is when she writes her first letter to Atos Wirtanen. She describes her daily toil in the fields and includes a drawing of the dream project they concocted the previous winter of the war: a comfortable and practical colony where artists and writers could work, somewhere in the south. One suitable location for it would be the villa in northern Morocco, near Tangier, owned by philosopher and socialist Edvard Westermarck. She does a sketch to put some flesh on the bare bones of their dream, placing Atos the author in a tower, and providing him with a hanging garden so he can write outdoors. She herself presides over a large studio, without vegetation except for what might be bunches of grapes round the windows. They put money aside for the colony over a number of years, but one day the box in Tove Jansson's studio is empty. The contents have been donated to a strike fund in the north of Finland.

Tove Jansson is not politically active like Atos Wirtanen, but they are both on the same side. He is oppositional, part of the radical left, and forced to go underground on several occasions. There is no mention of this in the letters, but a few notes in Tove Jansson's dairies allude to his political activities in the war years. At one point she writes of the need to find him a place to hide if there is a "coup from the right", and on another occasion she reports acting as go-between. With conspicuous pride she writes of having delivered "a secret document" for Atos, but does not reveal the recipient or the contents. Wirtanen later refers to Tove Jansson's involvement – her then studio at Fänrik Ståhlsgatan was on his list of potential hiding places – but in his account they are not yet well acquainted (*Politiska minnen* [Political Reminiscences], 1973.

Atos Wirtanen (1906) was born in the Åland Islands. He was a journalist (initially a typographer), author, philosopher and politician. He was named Atos after the Dumas novel *The Three Musketeers*, which had captured his mother's imagination. His brothers were given more ordinary names. Atos Wirtanen started his journalist's career at *Arbetarbladet* in Helsinki, where he had two spells as editor-in-chief in the 1940s. Later, he was editor-in-chief of the popular democratic movement's newspaper *Ny Tid* from 1947 to 1953. He was a Member of Parliament 1936–54, first for the social democrats, and subsequently for the popular democrats. He also presided over the Social Unity Party (which he founded) between 1948 and 1955.

At the time Tove Jansson and Atos Wirtanen first meet, he has published a volume of poetry (*Amor fati*) and some aphorisms, and he goes on to publish works on many subjects. Their relationship has an impact on Tove Jansson's writing in several respects. They do not seem to have discussed painting very much, but in her letters Tove Jansson offers some insights into her work as a painter. She writes about a coming exhibition, the sale of some paintings and a commission in a public building. She asks Atos Wirtanen to buy tubes of paint for her when he is away travelling. But their intellectual meeting place is the written word. In the letters they discuss Swedish writer Eyvind Johnson's Krilon trilogy (1941–43), as well as Wirtanen's work on his study of his favourite philosopher, Nietzsche – published in 1945 under the title *Nietzsche den otidsenlige* (The Unfashionable Nietzsche) – and Tove Jansson's work on the Moomin books. It is a proud "Moomin squigglemaker" who informs Atos that she has delivered the manuscript of her new book (*Trollkarlens hatt*) to Schildts in 1947. That autumn sees the start of the very first series of Moomin strip cartoons, in Wirtanen's newspaper *Ny Tid*, under the title "Moomintroll and the Destruction of the World". It is published in 26 episodes, from 3 October 1947 to 2 April 1948. Tove Jansson refers briefly to the plot of the cartoon strip in one of her letters (4.1.1948). She explains the background to the cartoon strip in the essay "Atos, my friend" (*Astra Nova*, nr. 2, 1996). Atos Wirtanen has plans for launching Moomin in the USA, but they come to nothing. He takes a close interest in her writing, even though his advice is perhaps not always the best. Tove Jansson's notes reveal that it is his suggestion to normalise the name Moomintroll into "little troll" in the book title *Småtrollen och den stora översvämningen* (which in English reverted to *The Moomins and the Great Flood*). There is no mention of this in the letters, however.

In the late summer of 1945, they plan a trip to the islands where Atos was born and grew up. They are to meet his relations, but Atos is in no hurry and Tove Jansson ends up researching family and places for herself. She is intensely engaged with work on her second Moomin book *Kometjakten* (*Comet in Moominland*). This book introduces the character of the philosophical Muskrat, a character who has often been linked with Atos Wirtanen. But the mournful muskrat, who likes nothing better than to spend his days in a hammock (in the company of Oswald Spengler), has nothing much beyond his interest in philosophy in common with Wirtanen. In one of her letters, Tove Jansson asks about their "muskrat", who lives in a patch of marshland near Grankulla, and this is evidently a reference to Nietzsche. "Atos went to the marsh and cogitated on Nietzsche", she writes in her notes in the spring of 1946. In her Moomin books, the Muskrat embodies the philosopher as concept.

The relationship between Tove Jansson and Atos Wirtanen continues until the early 1950s, at varying levels of intensity. There are breaks, and other lovers of both sexes (principally Vivica Bandler). Atos Wirtanen, too, has other partners during his time with Tove Jansson. Marriage is discussed at various points and proposals are made, but they never exchange rings. Atos Wirtanen eventually marries Irja Hagfors, a dancer, in 1954. By then Tove Jansson has been in a relationship with Britt-Sofie Fock, a goldsmith, for a number of years.

Tove Jansson and Atos Wirtanen remain friends, but they become less close over time, once they are no longer moving in the same circles. The few letters they exchange later on still, however, convey how significant their love for each other has been. Tove Jansson feels it is important to inform him when Ham dies, and later to tell him about her round-the-world trip with Tuulikki Pietilä. Atos Wirtanen refers briefly to Tove Jansson in *Politiska minnen* (Political Reminiscences) as a colleague at *Ny Tid* who contributes a picture story (the Moomin series) that is "among her most entrancing artwork".

But in the lovely letter Atos writes a few years earlier, when she sends him *Bildhuggarens dotter* (*The Sculptor's Daughter*), he pays her the greatest tribute one can give to a human being and artist:

> I hope you will continue this story of your life. You write for all ages. I am now getting on for 100 yet felt about 10 when I was reading you. You yourself are all ages, from youngest to eldest, and perpetually at the start of your life, which you have already lived many times over. There is a short and precise word for that: genius.

* * *

20.8.43 [*Måsabacka*]

Dear Atos!

Thanks for your letter, which eventually straggled its way out to Måsabacka. Glad your trip was positive. Yes, oaks. They're fine trees. Do you remember Krilon's reflections on oaks? I found it, the book you and Sam were talking about, and like it a lot.

The agricultural labour continues. My current watchword – the opposite of yours – is "back to civilisation!" Of course it would be nice, Atos, to see "crocodiles roaming free on a modern-day beach", but nicer still would be seeing the stooks of rye carried into the barn on an escalator and being free to get back to the traffic jams, electric sockets and a proper easel on castors.

I've started dreaming about painting at nights; the canvases are black and white except for the picture's darkest and lightest spots, which are in colour; the dark ones blazing hot and heavy, the light ones acrid and cold. But if I try afterwards to capture something of the picture's fickle yet absolute composition, simultaneously unreal and obvious, it just turns out as one of my usual + – o canvases.

I wonder if you sometimes get that sudden, intense feeling that you are on the verge of discovering something very important, and that all it would take is a bit more effort on your part to understand something fundamental that transforms, simplifies and explains everything. It could be a really fine picture if only one made that little effort – or is the phenomenon just a result of the brain being tired and getting jammed for a while?

As well as threshing, at the moment I'm learning the art of staying silent while being doused in a huge accumulation of opinions of every imaginable shade diametrically opposed to my own. She looks like this and has a peerless knack of making one feel like some kind of asocial luxury item. (which is also, by the way, starting to show its age.) – This evening the thunder is crashing over the fields and giving the monotony a good shake. I hope it will carry on tomorrow and give me a day in town. One grows so impatient – and so dulled.

What do you think about Guipuzcoa in the Basque Country? Sounds very nice. But Moroccan society interests me even more – so here's a project for you. The tower is reserved for you – hanging garden

at the top so you can write outdoors. <u>No</u> plants. Except perhaps for some grapes around the window.

All the best to you, Atos.

P.S. Vert emerande is the most important. I'd rather you skip the others. If it comes to it.

Krilon's reflections on oaks: A reference to Swedish author Eyvind
Johnson's Krilon trilogy, 1941–43.

28.5.45. [*Helsingfors*]

Dearest!

Today I brought flowery skirts and straw hats down from the attic, that's going to be my look on Åland!

Every morning I start looking forward to our trip all over again. In ten days' time I shall know whether they will give me a passport or not – if those snooty types make a fuss, I shall have to act as an assistant representative of the people, to punish them!

We've had some glorious days and I imagined you dashing around Stockholm (without a glance at the shop windows) and perhaps, I hope, finding time to get out to those oaks you longed to see but couldn't fit in last time.

Yesterday there was an awful lot of celebration – what did I expect? Eleven solemn gentlemen from the Society of Illustrators invited me to dinner with speeches and flowers for the lady; I dubbed them all knights and came home singing.

The Swedes arrived today: Olle, Kalle and Pelle, Hedberg, Åberg and Nordberg. Ham and Faffan took charge of Nordberg, and we are in the middle of a festive send-off for them at Ragni Cawén's.

Sitting in a corner with a puppy on my knee and a cup of Real Coffee beside me.

Not much of note has happened here otherwise. Except that I find you in anything I see that is full of colour, joy and vitality. Don't forget to make sure Maja gets you a new green hat!

All the best!

Tove.

PS I've been saving this special writing paper for a year, to use exclusively for love letters. Now I realise I ought to have written a poem on it instead. Perhaps that wouldn't have been a success, either!

But I am full of words and poetry and other kinds of garlands for the adornment of you and me. All of me is a dance tune about you, and I give it to you as a gift to be sung in the sunshine, with constant new words and melodies!

Bye-bye!

representative of the people: Refers to Atos Wirtanen's position as a Member of Parliament.
Olle, Kalle and Pelle: The artists Olle Nordberg Kalle (Karl) Hedberg and Pelle Åberg from Sweden.
Maja: Maja Stenman.

8.2.46 GÖTEBORG

Dearest solofif,

You ought to be here!

I'm lying on my stomach on a polar bear skin rug, listening to the ninth symphony (we must get hold of it!), out there a new city to explore and conquer tomorrow.

My youngest skiing and sailing uncle is out to dinner with his wife. The dog is dozing in a corner, on the walls there are ships sailing in all directions and tiny human ants climbing wild peaks.

The ninth is thundering over me and all is blessedly calm.

Did you get there safely with what little you were able to take with you? Are you up to your ears in politics again, do you ever have time to go down and look at our muskrat?

I miss you a lot, but in a cheerful, relaxed way. I know you will still be there when I come in the spring and that you sometimes long for me.

A plague on you, Atos! You didn't want my illustrations! I couldn't give them enough golden curls. Now I'm pinning my hopes on Fock and Pelle Åberg. How old do you think I shall be before my "craving

Atos (in the hat), Tove and her father, Faffan, enjoying a storm.

for things" abates? I shall probably still be sewing sequins on my slippers when I'm a wrinkled ninety-year old. (Maybe on yours too!!)

One evening I was at the Swedish women artists' monthly party, a peculiar event, extremely animated. And strange to separate the sexes within a single profession. It makes the atmosphere too homogenous.

A colleague from Finland, Rosa Linnala, has invited me to share her academy studio when I go back to Stockholm. I accepted with delight.

In that grey and untidy space, I believe I shall be able to work. No relatives or shop windows. Luxuriousness is all well and good, but having dived into it one does need to come up for air.

You must go to the studio sometime when it is warmer to inaugurate the four-poster bed. When you've been partying or want to be left in peace.

We must have a party when I get home to my tower. Give my regards to Sylvina Sylvarum and whoever else you can think of in our old crowd. And give Ham a ring sometime. As well as her two gentlemen she's now acquired a crazy Alsatian puppy to worry about.

All the best, Atos. HUGS.

                                                                    Tove.

solofif: A play on the Swedish word "filosof" (philosopher), one of TJ's pet names for Atos Wirtanen.
My youngest skiing and sailing uncle: Harald Hammarsten.

TOVE JANSSON'S PROPOSAL TO ATOS WIRTANEN AND HIS ANSWER are described in her letters to Eva Konikoff of 16.12.1947 and 4.1.1948. A more discreet proposal is hard to imagine; it passes almost unnoticed.

                    UNDATED [*1947, most likely December. Helsingfors*]
Dearest,

Thank you for your letter. It made me feel so happy and light. As if you had taken me in your arms. Today you are in Warschaw, crossing one border after another. You must be bursting with strong new impressions, I can see the idea growing like trees straight through you, and you coming back home to do battle and turn the right on its heads. Before leaving them to their fate and taking new roads that are your very own.

I'm standing on my head today, too, and am a proud Moomin squigglemaker! There, you see, it isn't so impractical to build rainbows after all! Before one knows it, one has used them to cross right over to America.

I have delivered the next Moomin to Schildts. Warburton read it through and seemed positive about it, according to Ham. We will have to see. Today a very small lady came to me and said she was circulating a petition at school: "Why hasn't a new Moomin come out?" To protest to Söderströms. I hope Appel will be impressed, I was!

Painting and thinking. Perhaps I shall be able to catch up so I can overtake myself. Perhaps I'm on entirely new paths and have passed my old latitude.

Longing to spread a new and happy forcefulness of colour, bigger and simpler than before. (+ individual explosions of capricious wealth of detail, where needed.)

And then I wonder whether you think it would be a good idea for us to get married. It wouldn't change our way of life, I don't think. If you don't want to, we can talk about something else when you get back. There's plenty, isn't there.

The city has dressed itself in its snowy beauty, and it is cold and clear. It's lovely among your spruces out there, I imagine.

The Janssons are going to the circus tonight. Do you think you will ever get to see the fight between the Bengal tiger and the boa constrictor? We <u>must</u> try to see a whale one day. Until then, the pike on Bredskär. Abbe has got hold of some timber for the weatherboarding and ceiling, so I shall go out early in the spring and finish building our house.

Interview as many kings as you can, and show them you're "no ordinary boy, oh no!" and then come home; because in a few weeks the days will start getting longer again. And to see someone who is very fond of you, namely me.

Tove.

the next Moomin: *Trollkarlens hatt* (*Finn Family Moomintroll*).
Appel: Bertel Appelberg, head of publishing at Söderströms Förlags.

4.1.48. [*Helsingfors*]

Dearest,

Right now I am lying here surrounded by sixty newly prepared canvases, getting through a mild dose of influenza and reading Stendhal. Moomin has reached the end of the world, after which a New Age can begin to take shape, exactly as we want it.

I delivered your message to the paper, and your regards to Eva who was so revitalised that she instantly wrote a new column. One evening we went to the Collianders' together; other than that I've been living a tower life and starting to feel comfortable in my painterly context. It paints itself into one's head and one lets the urge grow.

Everything has been smouldering away disagreeably for so long that I'm ready for a fairly major explosion. 60 canvases ought to provide the right amount of material, don't you think?

You enter the lists in many lands, musketeer! All the impressions and insights hurtling through you are of immense importance, but perhaps the most important of all is that you are able to be alone with yourself, even in the centre of Stockholm. I think – no, I know – that you will allow yourself a time like this every year, and that it will grow longer and longer. You've gradually discovered what a boon solitude can be if one is peaceful of heart and able to work (which amounts to the same thing?) Perhaps that very thing is the greatest happiness there is.

Sometimes I plan the island, sometimes the houseboat. The keel has been repaired, at a cost of 40,000; sold two canvases at the same time. (My first sale for a year.) Both the director and I were so pleased that we embraced. (He asked permission first.) And I might possibly get 50,000 for the glass paintings at the Domus Academy?

I'm afraid you'll find you have a very rich wife, but you can console yourself with the fact that I never stay rich for very long.

Sofen, you are the warmest, bravest and wisest person I know. And as for you being "difficult": it's like what distinguishes a bunch of flowers one picks from the florist's orderly, counted easiness. You see, there was a time when I wanted a proposal bouquet wrapped up in a cake doily, but I've learnt differently. Hopefully I shall learn even more in future, for it is certainly necessary.

Here it is cold enough for snow, and the sun has a slightly longer curve every day. In the mornings the room is full of friendly spots of sun and it's easy to get up. You are not so far away from me.

Would like to talk to you about how heavenly bodies come to reignite spontaneously, or those little creatures that dash around in pools of water. About all manner of things. You'll be so welcome when you come home, Atos.

Tove.

a New Age: a play on the title of Atos Wirtanen's newspaper *Ny Tid*.
Eva: Eva Wichman.
Domus Academy: The Domus Academica student hostel in Helsinki.

IN THE SPRING OF 1948, TOVE JANSSON WENT WITH SAM AND Maya Vanni to Florence, where they took lodgings and spent several weeks painting. From there they moved on to France, first to Paris and then to the idyllic little town of Chevreuse, just southwest of the capital. The Vannis stayed in Chevreuse, but Tove Jansson continued alone to Brittany, to the fishing village St Pierre.

13.4.48. VIA DANTE DA CASTIGLIONE 1.
DOTTORE MARANDINO. FIRENZE.

Mi caro sofo,

I should like to place you here, on one of the flower-covered hillsides, full of colours, buzzy insects and warmth – and send some other whale to make a speech in Finland. Every day I drink your health in the red wine you like so much and fall asleep with you as some unfamiliar bird sings a single, melancholy note over and over again, down in the garden. It isn't true that it's "too beautiful" here. It's just as beautiful as it ought to be, and entirely natural for us to be staying in a palace outside the city with tall, cool rooms and a prie-dieu for a bedside table. The hills climb up all around. I rise early and go out to draw, and Sam heads off in his own direction. The landscape has a completely new face here, with more vivid contrasts, intensely decorative. And before one knows it one gets carried away doing tourist pictures of picturesque scenes – I have to be on my guard to avoid being taken in. In the evenings we go out and buy cheap red wine, black and green olives, bread and oranges.

Now of course it's true that Italians of today dupe one in a perfect and rational manner, but at the same time are so brilliantly generous that one is entirely disarmed. On the train we met some curly-haired Neapolitans, beaming and radiating goodwill. They had as little idea as we did when the train was due to leave for Milan, but they obligingly invented a time for us. The upshot was that Maya and I almost missed the train, aboard which Samu was pulling his hair out and explaining in three languages that he had "lost his wives". The rest of the carriage was all sympathy, showering him with oranges and unreliable advice. Meanwhile, the wives' tram had got caught up in a crowd of demonstrators at Piazza del Duomo, where the whole of Milano (with prams) was listening to wild popular orators and the square was full of military vehicles. We leapt onto the train just as it started to move. To calm himself down, Sam bought a Chianti in Bologna, and the Neapolitans two, to outdo him. Everything they had, they shared with us.

The speedy journey down there made a deep and vivid impression. Particularly Germany, with its ravaged cities and grave people. The children ran shrieking along the railway embankment, catching the sweets and fruit that people threw out of the carriage windows. One little boy almost got run over when an orange rolled under the train. The passengers were cheery busybodies, just like on Högholmen. – eugh!

Switzerland went rolling by, a few concentrated hours of pure beauty – then came Italy's explosion of colour and warmth – a great wash of impressions that are only now starting to shape themselves into reflections. I think I want to stay here in Firenze, not travel about as I did nine years ago. Understand the landscape, develop a peaceful sense of living here and not chasing round after things I shall find on every street corner if I give myself time.

Our casa is up on the hillside outside Porta Romana. All the walls are drowning in great armfuls of luxuriant garden growth, every house is beautiful in colour and proportion, and the black spears of the pines position themselves with almost irritating precision exactly where they are needed in the landscape composition.

We get on well together. Prowl all over the city, making discoveries and being amazed. It's as if I have never been here before; I see things in a different way, nothing just brushes past, it all sinks straight in like water into dry ground.

Every day, aeroplanes streak across the city, spraying the streets with pink and green propaganda. It looks like confetti against the blue, blue sky – and seeing people grab them with shouts and laughter, one could so easily think the whole scene was nothing more serious than a carnival.

I have been infected by the general mood, trying to understand the temperamental speakers as they jig about in excitement, and reading the posters whose orgies of colour and outrage are splashed on every wall, every tree, every building.

The Germans blew up all the bridges, only Ponte Vecchio is still standing, amid the ruins of districts on both sides of the river.

A letter came from Ham, who writes that they have coltsfoot at the market. By the time I get home the August flowers will be coming up along the shore. I don't think Bredskär will appear any less beautiful to me for having seen all this.

It is wonderful for me to be given so much, to possess such quantities of friendship and love. Today I feel as if I lived in a horn of plenty. Greetings to my friends! A big hug.

Tove.

Raporto primo

Il buono Sofo. Make sure you ask Tove in your next letter:
Who is Fernandel?
— "— Antonio?
Other than that we are fine. With warmest greetings.

Sam

21.6.48 ST PIERRE

Kino vo! which is Breton and means: hello there, sof.

Just now your still faithful Tofsla is seated in the bar de l'Ocean by the harbour, drinking absinthe and thinking about it being midsummer and all that, and the quayside is a riot of blue-and-pink-trousered sailors and fishermen, carrying on in their strange semi-Gallic Celtic language; they ask me from time to time if I've done any "photographs" today, and why on earth the Finns don't rate the Russians. We're in a strongly Communist part of the country here, as I discovered at the lobster festival in Guilvinec. They took the greatest delight in attempting to knock a gentleman's hat off with soft fabric balls – and it was a star-spangled-banner hat. You could also amuse yourself by walking ten times round a post and then balancing your way along a rope to a packet of cigarettes, which no one ever reached, of course, or drinking red wine in tents decked out in green, crammed in like sardines in a tin – then there was a little propaganda, some dancing at the youth centre, some missing of the bus and a walk of eight kilometres across flat country, heading straight for my friendly lighthouse. Sky full, simply full, of stars and the breakers ever closer, and the mighty cross of light sweeping over and hurling itself towards me, past me and way out across the sea.

There's something enormously soothing about this flat, treeless landscape, the row of huddled houses by the sea, the expanse of ebb-tide beach with glimpses of blue in the far distance. A landscape of horizontal lines, barely in colour, but in a pronounced variety of shades. Lovely cadmium yellow moss on the low stone walls, seaweed in every hue from black purple to honey yellow, grey-white sand, the sun-bleached grass – and perpetual wind. All the waves of the Atlantic brought up short at this particular low beach – though there are sharks and whales further out – where Tofslan and others collect shells in the harmless shallows.

Talk of shells and offshore winds must seem very far removed from what you are working on now, which takes up all your time and all your thoughts. But they are on the island too, with us. The seaweed and the horizon, everything. Perhaps you'll be weary of speeches and crowds sometime towards the end of the summer, and feel like coming out there. That's why I'm sending you words of temptation

att man talar mycket eller ser många. Just nu blo...
liljor i potatislanden innanför murarna. Vindruvorna b...
med blanka blad och två låga äppelträd framför porten
Vid fiskhamnen och piren ligger båtarna röda och bl...
ebbmarken med skirande fiskmåsmoln, duddorna...
ker ut i gattet och tunga bruna nät ligger utbredda i
den. Kvinnorna sitter i sidigt svart och virkar i...
skuggorna. Och i allt detta vandrar jag omkring — de...
'riktigaste' landskap jag hittat på alla mina färder, o...
det som skänker en mest lugn. Om man inte hade
med sj själv kan det hända att den monotona öd...
heten skulle göra en utom sig — men annars stryker...
bara ut alla önskningars förväntningar och man
dagarna gå lika lugnt som regnet faller.
Tyvärr vandrar sedlarna också, så när går i jo...
får jag fnatta hem till mina egna domäner. Eva är...
lugnt stanna kvar i ateljén, för jag kommer bara att
mj tid att samla ihop arbetsmaterial, cement o...
mat, och sen far jag ut till Ön och stannar då...
tills vinterstormarna börjar. Har du en vecka ...
så är du välkommen dit — du kan säkert beh...
blåsa av dig alla dumheter du i detta laget varit...
gen att åhöra, av borgare och andra.
Sprid hälsningar till det gamla kolhos-systeme...
och var själv hälsad genom denna Valfisk av

Tov...

Facsimile of Tove Jansson's letter from St Pierre (21.6.48), with greetings from the whale.

from this coast, where the days go by without one speaking much or seeing many people. Just now, the lilies are blooming in the potato patches within the walls. Wind-torn bushes with shiny leaves and two stunted apple trees in front of the gateway.

Down by the fishing port and the jetty, the boats are at rest on the low-tide mud, red and blue among clouds of shrieking gulls, the chug-chugs are puttering out along the inlet and heavy brown nets are spread on the sand. The women sit in demurest black, doing their crochet in the shade of the walls. And I walk around in all this – the "most genuine" landscape I have found on my travels, and the most pacifying. If one were not at peace with oneself, the monotonous desolation might be maddening – but, as things stand, it just cancels out the expectations of one's desires and one lets the days pass as calmly as the rain falls.

Unfortunately my banknotes are taking walks as well, so sometime in July I shall have to hurry back to my own domain. Eva is welcome to stay on in the studio, because I will only give myself time to collect working materials, cement and food, and then go out to The Island, where I shall stay until the winter storms start. If you have a week free, you'll be most welcome there – I'm sure you can do with having them blown away, all those idiocies you'll have been obliged to listen to by now, from the right and elsewhere.

Spread greetings to the old kolkhos system, and greetings to you too, via this Whale, from

Tove.

Eva: Eva Wichman had borrowed TJ's studio as a workroom while TJ was away travelling.

IN 1951, TOVE JANSSON TOOK A TRIP TO ITALY WITH VIVICA Bandler. From Italy, they went on to North Africa.

POSITANO [*Postmark 3.4.51*]

Dearest Atos!

We had to fight our way through a real tangle of difficulties to get down to this peaceful place, a narrow strip of sand looking out onto the sea, enclosed by a dramatic massif, with the town climbing upwards above our heads. At night the fishing fleet lies out there like a pearl necklace of light and we fall asleep to the sound of lazy surf.

It took us a long time to catch up with the spring. In Stockholm I had to wade through the snow between my various relations, freezing in optimistic summer clothes. In Denmark the ground was bare of snow but brown, and it was only in Germany we saw the first flashes of yellow broom and a few anxious crocuses. Switzerland welcomed us with snowstorms. It was only at the Italian border that the streams in their spring spate were starting to tidy up and the first cherry blossom made us throw our woolly knickers out of the window. We travelled through Italy overnight, this time without a sleeping berth, and arrived in Rome pretty cold, tired and out of sorts to devote ourselves to hotel – money – and passport troubles, plus racing around a confusion of monumentality.

Italy and the realisation that I was finally on a Journey didn't really sink in until I went up behind the Forum Romanum on my own and sat there quietly, watching and feeling for a long time. White architectural fragments against static, dark-green foliage, warm ochre tones in the heat, attractive children shouting, skinny dogs, priests flapping by like bats.

I walked slowly home through the dusk, ordered a white vermouth and bought some red flowers, stood on the Spanish Steps and thought of nothing. Simply existed. Other than that, the days and nights in Rome passed in one hectic whirl. This is the first time I've really tried the nightclub life – it's entertaining, but I can't keep up. When we next meet I shall tell you about my most potent experience in Rome, a human one, of course, Vera. Her tragedy still haunts me.

Quick dash through Naples, where we only just caught the boat to Capri. On board we got talking to four charming youths, hominids from America on scholarships, making for the hominid paradise of Capri. They then came with us on daytime and nighttime outings, and Uca was the boss of us all. I must tell you more about all this. Capri is a strange place of beauty and indolence, of decay and primitive simplicity, of superficiality and intensity. Parting from the youths on friendly terms, we looked over our finances, and discovered to our horror that our funds were very much depleted. But we were in luck. While the Positano bus was waiting at the piazza, we met a real local character who for the price of a night at the hotel let us rent two ramshackle rooms down by the beach for a week. The walls are caving in, the door won't shut, dirt everywhere – but thoroughly homely. On the outside of our green door someone has scrawled in big letters "Votate per la monarchia!" (vote for the monarchy!) and in each bedhead there is a special little compartment for one's prayer book.

To atone for our offences hitherto, we've been buying food and wine to consume at home. For me, the Positano hovel is the best place we've stayed. No front doorstep, you just walk straight out into the street.

Today I shall walk up into the mountains and find a primitive little village. I yearn for scenery, Uca for people. But I'm not very bothered about them at the moment. I sense that there won't be any mymble on this trip, neither one kind nor the other. All I want is warmth and colour and peace.

You would like being here. And could do with it. I'm hugging you in my thoughts, wishing you all the best!

From here our trip takes us to Tunis, then Paris. We'll be there from the 17th onwards, until the 30th. Take care of yourself and don't forget your

Tofsla

7.7.70 [*Helsingfors*]

Dear Irja and Atos,

A sad letter to you both. Ham is dead.

They let me stay in her room at the hospital for the final forty-eight hours.

The end came quickly and without dread, another blood clot. She was able to go as she wished, without paralysis or a long wait and without losing a scrap of her intellect. Lasse and Prolle came to her every day. And Ham sank into extreme exhaustion.

We will bury her on 14th July. I am going around in a great sense of unreality, calm but so alien.

I send you lots of love.

All the very best.

Tove.

Signe Hammarsten Jansson died on 6 July 1970.

1.7.71 [*Klovharun*]

Dearest Atos,

The fact is that your aphorisms do not need illustrations. I reread them yesterday, as soon as they arrived, with great reflection and joy. Both the earlier ones and the new batch. It will make a fine book but should not have pictures, not even abstract ones. I'm convinced now that it would seem forced, and irritate rather than stimulate.

You write to me so beautifully that I want to take you in my arms. I think it quite wonderful that we both have such a cheerful sense of gratitude to one another – not a debt of gratitude! – it's very important for me, too. You had already given me "Framtida", so I am sending back your copy, as the book is so hard to get hold of.

I'm so glad you were able to find the right English translator.

We shall come back into town sometime at the start of September. Atos, remarkable things are afoot! Tooti and I are off on a Round the World Trip! It's an old dream we've been saving up for, and we're all prepared and won't be back until next spring. Our destination – Japan – was decided by a job I have to do in Tokyo, the Japanese are paying for that lap. Then Hawaii, and San Pedro, you know, where Taube loaded gasoline – and where Tooti's aunt lives, and Mexico and then by multifarious ways and means (including paddle steamer!) up through the States to New York.

I still can't really believe it's true. Tooti's studying English 4–5 hours a day and we keep the Map of the World permanently opened out.

Give my best regards to Irja and tell her about our plans. We must all meet up this autumn. Until then, a big hug and

enjoy your summer!

Tove.

Tooti: Tuulikki Pietilä. See Letters to Tuulikki Pietilä.
where Taube loaded gasoline: A reference to "The Ballad of Gustaf Blom from Borås" by the Swedish singer and composer Evert Taube.

*"Under the names of
Tofslan and Vifslan"*

LETTERS TO VIVICA BANDLER
1946–1976

Photograph of Vivica Bandler, signed "To Tofslan from Vifslan"

VIVICA BANDLER IS THE FIRST WOMAN WITH WHOM TOVE JANSSON truly falls in love. They meet at a party in November 1946. But their time together is short, a mere three weeks. When Vivica Bandler goes to Paris at the end of December (via Stockholm, Copenhagen, Geneva), their relationship is kept alive in frequent letters and occasional telephone calls. The plan is for Tove Jansson to follow her to Paris, but this remains a dream. The letters written in spring 1947 speak of passion and yearning, expectation and disappointment. This is a new and rapturous happiness, but it must be hidden from the outside world. Homosexuality remains illegal in Finland until 1971. Vivica's letters to Tove Jansson are shorter and more restrained, urging caution. Both of them have commitments to other people: Vivica Bandler had married Kurt Bandler in 1943 – she went to Paris with him – and Tove Jansson had been in a relationship with Atos Wirtanen for three years.

Vivica Bandler (1917–2004) was the daughter of Erik von Frenckell, Chairman of Helsinki City Council, and his wife Ester-Margaret von Frenckell. The family had an estate called Saaris in Tavastland, and she trained as an agronomist, completing her studies in 1943. She also became involved in student theatre, and during the war was active in the Women's Voluntary Defence Service. She made her debut as a director in 1948 with Jean-Paul Sartre's *La Putain respectueuse* (*The Respectful Prostitute*) at the Swedish Theatre in Helsinki. The following year she staged Tove Jansson's first Moomin play, *The Moomintroll and the Comet*, at the same theatre, and this marked the beginning of a long-term collaboration between the author and the director. Vivica Bandler went on to direct many productions of Tove Jansson's Moomin plays in Finland, Sweden and Norway. In 1955 she assumed charge of the Little Theatre in Helsinki, and in 1967 took over at Oslo New Theatre. From 1969 to 1980, she was the head of Stockholm City Theatre.

In the world of the Moomins, the love between Tove and Vivica is coded in the symbiosis of Tofslan and Vifslan [known to English-language readers as Thingumy and Bob], identical in appearance except for Tofslan's pointy cap, and the two of them speak a language of their own. Their suitcase conceals the sparkling King's Ruby which, when it is shown to the world, radiates its light far out into the universe (*Trollkarlens hatt/Finn Family Moomintroll,* 1948). In

1947, the two characters also make an appearance on one of the *Garm* covers and in an advertisement for a fizzy drink. From the very start, Tove Jansson writes in terms of a close relationship between two people, interweaving her loved one's landscape and her own – the island of Kummelskär, which she coveted so much, and Saaris, the von Frenckells' estate: "Sometimes I think about the journey we will embark on together, writing and drawing. Under the names of Tofslan and Vifslan. On Kummelskär and at Saaris." (21.12.1946) In her own notes of about the same time, she sums up what this is all about: "All that's most important will be there, work, love and play. All year, every year." When she is not painting she finds herself torn between, say, finishing off the fourth Tofslan and Vifslan chapter, or drawing a map of the house-to-be on Kummelskär. She devises trips for them to go on together, but none of these ever progress beyond plans and dreams. In a letter to Eva Konikoff before Christmas 1946, Tove Jansson describes the woman she loves:

> Vivica is Erica v. Frenkell's sister, three years younger than me. It was actually Lasse and Erica who had been saying for ages that Vi and I might get on well together, and one day they brought her to the studio. I saw a tall dark aristocratic girl with a prominent nose, thick straight eyebrows and a defiantly Jewish mouth. She is blind in one eye, but the other is clear, dark, penetrating. A mop of short hair and the loveliest hands I've seen. She's such a gorgeously feminine creature, and one day I shall paint her as she is, chiefly as a profusion of fruit and blossom in full bloom.

Tove Jansson's love for Vivica Bandler finds many forms of expression, in words and pictures, the grandest among them the pair of frescoes for the restaurant at Helsinki City Hall, to which Tove Jansson devotes the spring of 1947. "What a painting I could do of you," Tove Jansson writes as she waits to hear whether she has secured the commission (which comes from the Chairman of the City Council, namely Vivica Bandler's father). But by the time Vivica Bandler returns to Helsinki in March 1947, their relationship has altered and Tove Jansson writes repeatedly of breaking with her for good. In the fresco, the artist turns her back on the dancing woman who has borrowed Vivica's facial features. Their respective positions have been rearranged. One of them is in motion, one sitting still. Work on the frescoes is described in some detail in letters to Vivica Bandler, and is also mentioned in letters to Eva Konikoff. But pictures are not enough when the relationship falls apart; Tove Jansson writes poems. One collection, held in the Helsinki archives of the Society of Swedish Literature in Finland, is called "Songs for a Lady", but there are several versions. In the letters, Tove Jansson refers to "Songs to my Beloved".

Once their love affair's roller coaster of emotions and sorrows has subsided (which takes time), Vivica Bandler gradually becomes a close friend and work colleague. Her influence is certainly discernible in Tove Jansson's dramatic works, but Bandler also has an impact on her friend's artistic development. One example of this is found in the letter in which Tove Jansson describes her work on the altarpiece in Östermark (1953), a project that she intersperses with reading the Bible and writing *Farlig midsommar* (published in 1954, and in English as *Moominsummer Madness*). The story is largely set in a floating theatre and is dedicated to "Vivica". It is an idiosyncratic take on the nature of theatre, and Moominpappa is even seen composing (with some difficulty) a drama in hexameters, which he calls "The Lion's Brides or Blood Will Out". Tove Jansson's own, not dissimilar, agonies are revealed in a subsequent letter. Vivica Bandler is clearly of great importance for Tove Jansson's dramatic work, not only her Moomin plays but also other texts for the theatre. Later, they collaborate on a TV project, the traditional advent calendar programme for Swedish television. Vivica Bandler is also (like other addressees in this volume) entrusted with reading drafts of the Moomin books. As with her other friends, Tove Jansson calls Vivica by a variety of names, including Vi, Vifs and later Uca.

Vivica Bandler's memoirs *Adressaten okänd* (1992, Not Known at This Address) include a short chapter, "Tove", about their friendship and how they met, but she says nothing about the all-engulfing passion that runs through Tove Jansson's letters of the 1940s. Her rapture is expressed in other, more universal ways: "When Tove is near, every stone, every blade of grass, every hue and tint has meaning, and also therefore every word." In her own, often lyrically couched, letters to Vivica Bandler, Tove Jansson, too, draws on nature for her many images of love. Here we find carpets of seashore flowers, uninterrupted horizons, but also angry breakers, rocks and seaweed.

Translator's note.

This translation retains the original Swedish names Tofslan and Vifslan, which Tove Jansson uses for herself and Vivica in the letters, as well as for the two characters she invents in their image for the Moomin books. The literal meanings of the names approximate to 'Tuftsy' (i.e. the one with the pointed hat) and "Viftsy" (the one who's out and about), and their initial letters match the names Tove and Vivica. English-language readers of the Moomin books know these characters as Thingumy and Bob, names coined for *Finn Family Moomintroll* by the translator Elizabeth Portch, possibly in consultation with Margaret Washbourn and Lars and Tove Jansson. These names are much further from Tove and Vivica's own than the originals and the name Bob would generally be considered masculine, whereas the names Tofslan and Vifslan have the typical form of feminine diminutives in Swedish.

* * *

THE FIRST EVENING YOU ARE IN STOCKHOLM.
[*December 1946, Helsingfors*]

My darling,

This evening I'm clearly and patently jealous, I who was so proud of my noble incapacity to experience jalousie. I have been standing here all day, pasting gold flowers on to pale blue Christmas wrapping paper – and thinking as you once did: make them black! It's already late. I'm sitting in a corner at Arbetarbladet while Gudrun Mörne makes up the paper and Atos writes the leader. Gudrun is telling us about her father, and the last poem he wrote. The opening poem in this year's posthumous collection, his request for one more spring. The book was already at proof stage, but Arvid Mörne's room was not at rest, he was there and wanted something. Then they found the poem, and included it – and the room calmed down. I've heard people claim that what you do with your hands and brain is worth nothing to you after your death. But if it was the most important thing in your visible life, it must be the same afterwards, too. I mean, the art in which you try to bring alive the best in you is, more than anything else – your self. You know that.

I know you don't believe there is an afterwards. How surprised you will be, Vi, when I come floating along on a little cloud one day and say, Hello! Do you still want me?

Tomorrow I shall buy a tree, set up Bethlehem at Lallukka, do some baking. All of that. Gentle things. In actual fact, these last days I've been doing everything as absently as I would fasten a necklace round my neck.

Now I'm out at Grankulla. Atos is writing a speech, it's late at night. I was intending to go home, but I leapt up when the train started moving. I didn't want to be alone tonight.

You will get wittier letters from me later on, Vi. Letters that are full of action and Moomintrolls. But I can't do it yet.

In words, any old words – I am desperately trying to make contact with you, now you have chosen to leave ... Ick. What else can happen but that my love for you goes on expanding, growing ever warmer and more honest.

Take care of yourself. Bye.

Tove.

Ick: One of the many pet forms of Vivica's name used by TJ in the letters.

21.12.46 [*Helsingfors*]

My darling –

It's as if I can't really be properly happy until you are here again. As if I have retreated deep into myself and am waiting there, leaving my umbrella-fixated, friend-meeting, Christmas-rushing self to perform for the outside world. She performs well: laughs, takes an interest and is genuinely involved – and yet she is not entirely present.

When I was very young and very much in love, it was different. An unconscious dance, confusion, stimulation – and I let myself be carried away by it, unaware of what it was doing to me. After that came the safety margins, those little skills for attracting and keeping someone, the doubt and anxiety, the observing and weighing up.

Now it's as if I have circled back to being the bewitched devotee who asks no questions – but bringing all that awareness with me. It hurts! I am filled with happiness – that is true, but feeling so lonely is tearing me apart.

There is no possibility of my coming after you. Time is shuffling past at a horribly slow pace. It's only four days since you left – and there are four months still to go. Something might happen to you over there, and I won't be with you.

I went out to the Vannis' so I could talk about you, but Maya's disagreement with Svenska had nothing to do with us. I felt so disappointed and tired – I'd been planning to defend us and tell them how wonderful you are. Ham says nothing these days. After Christmas I shall look up Illo or Ulla. They know. I was tremendously pleased about one thing: a card from your parents. I think it was Ester's handwriting. Going through the wrought-iron gate with the flowers, I suddenly had this overwhelming sense of excitement. It would have been so natural to see you coming towards me.

Would our lovemaking be different some other time when we weren't under such strain from exhaustion and time running out and our first discovery of one another? Will events and people come between us and change things? Time? Distance? I don't believe so.

My trust in you is unbounded And for my own part, I have experienced something of a miracle, which nothing can diminish or corrupt. If I could only see you for one moment! The bold cloak of cheerful self-belief you gave me can slip off sometimes.

If only we'd had a little more time. Why didn't I ask you to come to the studio then – when you first wanted to! Why didn't you go to the automobile club party so we could have met earlier. A year ago, two years ago. You were here all the time and I knew it.

But we have a boundless length of time ahead of us. And surely we must be able to keep part of it for ourselves without hurting anyone else.

Sometimes I think about the journey we will embark on together, writing and drawing. Under the names of Tofslan and Vifslan. On Kummelskär and at Saaris.

I think about the way we will be part of one another's other's work. There is so much to wait for, so much to be happy about, I know it.

But sometimes longing for you too much drives me frantic.

We must try to cope without each other for a while. It would be wretched if we couldn't.

I wish you a truly auspicious trip. Not remotely overshadowed by missing home. Or perhaps just now and then – by missing me. When you're by yourself and not working.

Tove.

P.S. After a long break I have started a new chapter of Moomin 3. It's all about Tofslan and Vifslan. And the Groke. This year's Moomin 2 has gone down very well.

Svenska: The artist Sven Grönvall.
Illo: Illo von Walzel, a good friend of Kurt Bandler's.
Ester: Ester-Margaret von Frenckell.
Moomin 3: *Trollkarlens hatt* (*Finn Family Moomintroll*).
Moomin 2: *Kometjakten* (*Comet in Moominland*).

29.12.46 [*Helsingfors*]

Vifslan, my sweet!

Some days I feel as strong and happy, as slender and vigorous as a tree.

On those days I laugh at being sensible and couldn't give a fig about the interior design of City Hall. And then this, oh you tulip flower, you crowning glory of my heart: I shall get my press pass from le cocu to write about the gloire of Communism and take passage on a cargo boat as soon as the snow starts to melt to conquer you and the big city with Moomintrolls and the sound of cymbals.

Do you think I make a passable model? I'm a bit skinny perhaps, but my anatomy is nice and visible for beginners, and realism is modern. And I'm good at posing.

Last night I dreamt we lost each other at the flea market, and woke up to find I was shouting out for you. Then I had all the trouble of explaining who Vifslan was. A character in my new book! Who goes round holding hands with Tofslan and can't speak a word of sense!

You know what, I've got toothache today, but it doesn't bother me in the slightest. I stacked all the wood for the winter, and thought:

good job it will be out of the way by the spring when they do the alterations to the attic and I'm not here ...

Every object is only of significance as an article to be packed, every individual is considered as an opportunity to get away. Never before have the desires of my heart won out over my work, never before have promises been swept aside. It isn't Paris I'm yearning for. It's you.

Can you work out when you'll get to France? How many months? As long as I can provide guarantees of a monthly press allowance, they'll let me go. We'll keep your invitation as a last resort. Think if I were to have an exhibition over there?

Vi, I miss you so dreadfully. Hold me in your arms – and don't let me go!

Tove.

le cocu: The cuckold; a reference to Atos Wirtanen.

30.12.46 [*Helsingfors*]

Darling,

Your express letter came zipping in just now – and I feel as if you have been here talking to me. You often take me in your arms, my sweet. Those wings that fly me to infinity exist nowhere else, and I no longer care about any other embrace.

So yes, I have been indiscreet, still am and will continue to be. You'll have to be in charge of the common sense for a while. I do promise, though, to stop being dithyrambic on the telephone, but only so you won't be hanged for your "perverse inclinations". Next time you talk about them, just remember that I'm equally afflicted, and might feel deeply offended! Never in the world have I felt as natural and genuine as I do now! I don't want to hear anything about collars, either. I loved the person wearing them – and when I love, everything becomes clean and pure – shirts included.

You're wondering what he said. Well, not all that much. "There's no need to use so many Words". And a slightly surprised "But you're my wife, aren't you?" Perhaps he was slightly troubled, but it's possible he's forgotten the whole thing already. I mean, he's so often seen me crying because he didn't love me and then cheering up again, so for me to be crying now because I don't love him isn't all that different.

Just feelings, women's feelings. Happiness and Loving and Heart and other Words!

At any event, he's still turning up as usual. Affection, and feeling comfortable together, have a lot to recommend them, and I'm as much in love with his intellect as before. It's just that my heart isn't involved any more; it yearns, like my whole being, only for you.

And the reason Ham isn't saying anything? It's nothing to be concerned about, Vif. She's preoccupied with worrying about Lars and being cross with Peo for "wasting his artistic talent". His family book is out now, written (as she sees it) to impress his wife and the public (quite apart from being a great source of delight to everyone who knows us.)

Faffan, thank goodness, is so indignant about the erotic details that he's barely noticed how much it gives away about him.

It may have made Ham a little uneasy to see events moving me and Atos apart, but I've calmed her down again now.

Today I wrote a long, careful letter to Lasse, trying very hard not to trip over his personality or force mine on him too closely. But it was an honest letter. I only hope I've been able to help him a bit – or at least to relieve his sense of isolation for a moment. Maybe he already knew about us. It sometimes surprises me that everyone can't see it *"written all over the place"* – that I love you (is the Gestapo watching the post, too?) and do so more with every passing day, more joyously and exaltedly, and less fearfully.

And the Muse be praised for those fatal Words that only exist for telling Vifslan that Tofslan loves her! You go ahead, "sit down in an armchair and feel superior", I shall just sit down in another and laugh at you. If you wrote to me that some Vera had swept you helplessly off your feet, I would draw you a misabel in reply and write Zut! underneath, not believe you for a moment and laugh even more.

And now you must answer me the following: Who is c/o Robin? Some character in whose house I can't be seen, no doubt. And where else should I stay if I came to Paris but with you? You're there for February and half of March? That's still a month away. Have I got time?

Will your progenitors have a nervous breakdown if I say I'm turning down the City Hall interior for a trip to Paris, to be made just when their daughter is there? Later in the spring I have an invitation to Stockholm with Ham. But will I be able to see you at all then – is there anywhere we can meet – or does it all have to be underhand and nerve-racking?

There, see, all manner of common sense raising its head and saying "in that case" and "but".

Yesterday I wrote to you in all the reckless delight of my heart – one single thought: to come to you as soon as possible. Now I'm starting to wonder whether we are ruining our future happiness by rushing ahead. If we were able to marry, I would accept the proposal that I presume you would make. Just now, I feel I shall love you for as long as I exist – and I must start right away to construct the defences for the years we might perhaps be able to spend together. Do we risk tearing anything down if I come to you now? Think about it, Vif, think carefully! I'm not afraid of anyone, but I am afraid of any harm coming to us. This is the most beautiful relationship I have ever encountered and I'm busy building it up and securing it.

I can wait, I know that now. For as long as I have to, if only you take me in your arms when that time is up.

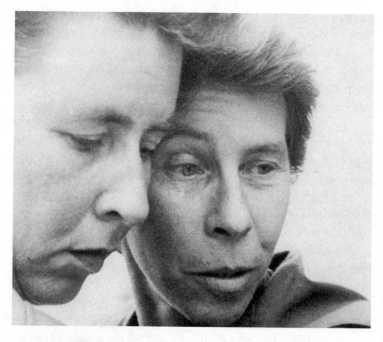

Vivica Bandler with Tove Jansson on Bredskär, early-1960s.

Eva Wichman was here just now. She could see it! "You're different through and through, your manner, your face, the way you move – maybe your thoughts?"

I certainly am different. Or perhaps it's only now I am truly myself. Because I love you, Vivica.

Tonight you are here with me.

Tove.

P.S. I got my hairdresser to write the brown envelope so you won't have to start the year with a dreadful scene. I can be sensical! Next time I'll get the caretaker and after that the grocer. My sweet one!

His family book: Per-Olov Jansson's *Ung man vandrar allena* (Young Man Walks Alone).

[*Undated, but the content shows it was written 1–4.1.1947*]
FROM TOVE JANSSON. ULRIKABORGSG. I H:FORS

Darling!

It's the first day of the New Year, the year I already think of as "ours". I've been partying for twenty-four hours at the Vannis' with Atos, the Bäcks and Kutter and am utterly exhuasted – but I can't get to sleep until I've chatted to you for a while. I can't send off the letter for a few days, to make sure you don't receive too much post in Denmark. – That's why I'm writing a little at a time, and perhaps we'll meet tomorrow as well.

I know how hard it is for you to get the time – and the quiet – to write to me. A letter prompted by duty can feel excruciating when it's like that – but a letter prompted by yearning even worse. Don't you think I understand what it takes for you to find the space to talk to me every couple of days amid the whirl of people, impressions and travel engulfing you at present! Every letter brings me affection and strength. In a new, strange way you are with me everywhere, sometimes so close that I give a start and look up.

That night things were hard for you I lay here longing for you, repeating your name – and really did hold you in my arms. On the stroke of twelve on New Year's Eve I strode out into the snow and called out for you. But time and distance no longer frighten me. It's as certain as my painting that we will come to one another this spring. I'm waiting calmly now to see how things go with the commission. If I get it, I suppose I'll do it. Atos's press pass would have been a cynical way out, after all. Good night, my sweet.

Good morning! We were just talking to each other! Your voice still lingers with me, your slow, soft voice. And I dance around and bless Blomberg and believe you'll be home when the snow thaws! I ought to be absolutely terrified and think of Kurt with remorse – but I simply can't do it. In the past I was always a bit of a deceiver and sinner because I dragged so much around with me: ideals, principles, consideration, guilt and duty and demands for fairness. Perhaps it's only now I am the deceiver, but greater than all that sorry fandangle is my love for you, Vif who is the sweetest of all! Happiness is what I feel – and today I am not so much a tree as a bouquet. A bouquet with colours and bees and honey (and thorns and spiky grass) bound with little bandlers, and I present it to you!

What a painting I could do of you.

3 Jan.

And tomorrow you move on to Denmark. Somehow that is a little nearer to me, because you have already reached the second stage of your trip. Today the sun is out, the stove is roaring away, there's dripping on the windowsill. The whole room is filled with dancing spots of sunlight and I have Lenten roses and white cyclamen on the table in front of me. This very instant, in the middle of the day, I feel like having a party in your honour. It's unthinkable to spend a day like this on sensible pursuits. Perhaps I'll finish off Tofslan and Vifslan's Moomin chapter, or draw up a plan of the house-to-be on Kummelskär.

The biggest window facing the sea, wouldn't you say. But should the other one face west or east? What would you like best, waking up in the sunlight with me, or for us to have the whole room suffused in glorious red in the evenings? We'll put the door on the north side, where there's only the mainland.

But I'm seriously considering a skylight; it's so nice to look at the stars before you go to sleep.

I'm starting to wonder if we should give up on the Call of the Wild approach. The sauna I bought fell to bits when they took it down, five generations of ants having gobbled up the beams from the inside. It has to be new timber, and we have a completely free hand. The idea of the ascetic's solitary eyrie appeals to me sometimes. But just as often I feel the urge to build something barbaric and comfortable with lots of colour and let my *horror vacui* run riot. What does Vifslan think of that? No garden plants. No ghastly seats for admiring the view. Just little winding paths through the heather and the bog bilberry. As for the boat I ordered in the summer, we'll have to haul it up with some kind of winch mechanism, because there's no safe harbour on the island. And the hollows in the rock are the only source of water, so we'll have to bring Vichy with us. And wine. But there is a clump of osiers, birches and bird cherries growing in the middle – it's possible we could get a well going. Naturally you'll also have to learn how to operate the two lighthouses. I've been to the Maritime Pilot Administration to discuss the matter. They had no objections to a lighthouse keeper. Their last tenancy payment for upkeep of lighthouse, path and landing place was made in 1889 to a person unknown. Not to the state, that is.

Now I'm frantically hunting for the owner of my island. I dragged a lawyer off to the Land Registry and went through piles of old papers from pre-land-reform times, before the Great Partition. After a day's search we found a meeting at which all the farmers were arguing over Kombelskär with a crown bailiff named Hindrikson. None of the later meetings say whether the island fell to the village or the crown, so maybe they all went out for a drink on the question and forgot the whole thing. In that case we shall lay claim to it by custom and prior ownership. We can call the building work renovation of an ant-eaten sauna, otherwise we'll be sent to jail.

But we must be sure to get ahead of some other smug contender who had blatantly been through all the documents not long ago, making notes. Just imagine, Vif, what a superior air it would give us to be able to drop into conversation in company: Oh yes, our land rent from the Maritime Pilot Administration is due tomorrow!

But darling – I was forgetting that you already <u>are</u> a landowner! Even so, you <u>must</u> find Kummelskär exciting.

Night.

The clear weather brought the cold with it, and in my room it's only 8°. The studio's below zero. Moonlight reflecting onto the ceiling now. I got home from the Social Democrats' New Year review, which the philosopher was keen to take me along to. His round and kindly mother looked so sweet in her black headscarf, as solemn as in church. – The thing is – I always find their Community Centre dreadfully depressing. It's all so worthy and cheerless.

Vifslan, you know what, I've started getting a strange new sense of "coming home" when I go into the studio. Home to you. Of course there _could_ be a letter waiting, and your chain is hanging on my bedhead. I look at it before I go to sleep and when I wake up, and hold it in my hand when I'm unhappy. But it isn't only that. Sometimes your thoughts are here, I can sense it. And sometimes it's as if you are folding me in your arms. Vi, I long for you so much this evening. I'm lonely without you, Vi.

Hold me, my darling.

4 Jan.

My sweet, I got the City Hall wall, 10 x 3 ½ . So that's that – I won't be able to see you until the spring. Time seemed to drag on so, for a while. I really had hoped, in spite of everything. I suppose it was wrong of me to wish you home in March; your work down there is certainly more important than what you can get from Blomberg in Finland. I shall have to start being a bit more of a painter now – not just go around yearning and dreaming. Do some sketches – but not of Kummelskär, not yet.

I think I can risk sending this letter now. But surely the cat is out of the bag now, Kurt knows about me. And if he comprehends the slightest thing, he must loathe me. I would. Austrian humanity _must_ have its limits!

This has never happened to me before, a big, engaging work project being less important than my love. It feels odd. But maybe I can combine the two. That ought to give your father a beautiful wall to look at!

Tove.

Kutter: Hans Kutter, theatre and film critic.
Blomberg: Film director Erik Blomberg, with whom Vivica Bandler was planning a Franco-Finnish film project.

16.1.47 [*Helsingfors*]

My darling Vifs,

now, you see, I have put all my sketches up round the walls, and I know what composition I want. "Breakfast" has turned into simply "Joy of Living". The girl in the tree is leaning down to kiss the boy, who I've made younger and more bashful. He's no longer a *"he man"* strong enough to have hoisted her up there; his raised arms express tenderness, not power. But the fiddle player is bolder, and the tiresome breakfast table has had to give way to a well-endowed woman with armfuls of garlands, her much foreshortened arm extending towards the centre, and a child in the background who is running to her. Through the branches and blossoms there are glimpses of water and the bodies of bathers. It so happens there are eleven figures in each of the two compositions. My "Party" has been in progress for so long now that the participants have lost their formality, are kissing one another on the cheek rather than the hand, look freer in the way they move, and are dancing a polka at the very least. I'm now working on two details, cartoons of 1 m x 75.

I'm intending to keep all the sketches I've done, from the first chaotic sheet of writing paper – to amuse you when you come home. Whatever flaws or merits the compositions may have, it could be fun for you to follow their development, understand why I altered an arm movement, muted a tone, changed the dominant.

My own insights into art are something I'd very much like to share with you. You will get infinitely more pleasure out of paintings if you're aware of what you are seeing. And having once learnt the steps of the dance, one can forget them and simply – dance.

Today you are in Geneva. Soon you will be travelling north again – and I'm pretending this is the start of your journey home. You are a little closer to me in Paris. Vifs, sometimes such an intense feeling of joy comes over me that I have to put down whatever I'm doing and just stand there smiling to myself.

It is some sort of miracle that we have found each other and will be able to experience the spring together. Won't we always be in each other's lives, whatever happens? My confidence in you and my affection for you are growing by the day. It feels to me as if I have suddenly become a happier, more serene person. My work has grown richer and my ambition no longer drives me so furiously.

Even my bitterness towards Faffan has been completely erased and my nervously obsessive conviction that "everyone's persecuting me" is starting to wear off. It's as if you have created me anew. My love for Atos, you took that – but other things have happened, things I'm just starting to notice and be surprised by. I'm not scared of him any more. My respect for him is the natural, self-evident kind I have always had for an intellect brighter than my own, but my self-esteem has calmly expanded. After all, it's only right that anyone who is an artist thinks differently, in pictures perhaps. He expresses himself in colours, not in the Word.

I have started to express myself without that persistent fear of committing some faux pas, and am no longer trying so hard to be witty but am just being myself. And all at once we have much more to talk about than before, much more to laugh at and reflect on. Maybe that is friendship in its best form. The erotic side has such a small part to play at present. It is as if I were asleep. I feel nothing and don't even have any desire to do so. It's true that this is what I often find when I am in the middle of a major piece of work, but there's also something more. My heart is with you, and I have never been capable of loving without that.

I am happy for you to do with it as you will; I have never given it away with a greater sense of trust.

Tomorrow I shall see my lawyer and draw up a letter to the farmers of Stor-Pellinge. By all means raise an aperitif glass for the success of our plans. Kummelskär has to be ours, even if only for me to sail you there for a single day, climb onto the rocks with you and say: our island!

Vifs, will you do me a favour. I so much want to know whether Herbert Rosenfeld died in the concentration camps during the war. He was a Jew, an author and writer of film scripts. I am aware of only one person who would know anything about him, and that is Clelia Assayas, and her husband who is Armenian. In 1939 they were living at 11 rue de Magdebourg Paris XVIe. Look them up in the telephone diectory and see if they are still there, that's all. I assume they are in some completely different part of the globe. And Hebi must be dead – otherwise he would have written to me. We were very good friends. My ring in the shape of a coat of arms with a helmet was a present from him. He lived in a studio that Faffan once had, 7 rue Belloni. Suffren 3445.

If I could just dash down to you for a single evening and stroll along the boulevards again. The boats are hooting in the harbour again, making me uneasy. But we've got time. We will walk together there some day. Take me in your arms, my dearest. Write and tell me about your work there!

May this be a happy and fruitful time. I kiss you.

Your darling Tove.

Herbert Rosenfeld: He is referred to as "Hebi" in TJ's letters to the family from Paris in 1938.

31 JAN 47 [*Helsingfors*]

Darling,

Your letter from all over the place arrived by express and took me in its arms!

The model has gone, the walls are lined with endless sketches in every scale. It's at that gruelling stage when one keeps recomposing and does battle with foreshortenings and objectivity and can't find the right faces among the models and feels it's either all high-minded motifs and anxious naturalism or too uneducated and loose. But I've sworn on my linseed oil not to start adding the colour until all my nice ladies are positioned where I want them and I've got hold of some prodigy in possession of a tail coat.

On the subject of tail coats (and to avoid a single word more about the wretched frescoes), I'm planning to celebrate your birthday by going to the big Runeberg party at the Artists' Guild. I shall go on my own, and intend to make myself as beautiful as I can and drink a toast with you.

And in the morning I shall take your present to Villagatan, so you'll find it there when you get home.

If I could see you for a single minute. If I could just look at you, and you smiled at me for a few moments, it would fill me with serene joy and nothing in the world would seem difficult any longer.

The distance has suddenly become real distance; I've lost the feeling that you could come running up the stairs at any moment, I don't turn round when I hear a car stop. You no longer come to me at night as easily and naturally as before. You are far away in your own world of despondency and I can't help you. If you could only find someone to help you relocate your happiness – find it more quickly – because it will come, I know it. Perhaps we are just a little tired just now, it will pass.

My own darling, I have so little idea what to write this evening, except that I love you, more than before you left, maybe more than I have ever loved anyone. I have been given the greatest gift of all, and carry it with me as carefully as I can.

Yours.

My loveliest, most reckless, extremely earnest day-after Vifs,

Your letter came today and made me happy again. I never thought you would be able to write again so soon! It's wonderful, Vi, that your work is going so well!

And oh, you must believe I am longing for us to go to France together as well. You must believe I am "trying" too! But I can't push my work beyond a certain point; I would lose my nerve and the results would be poor.

The very <u>prospect</u> of a trip in September, too – you don't know how much lighter it made my heart, and my hand. These frescoes are possibly the most important project I have ever had, I simply must pull it off. The story has come out, people are indignant that I got the commission without a competition, but they aren't openly kicking up a fuss yet. I have to show them that I <u>can</u> do a fresco. And for that I need time, and peace of mind. Today I crawled out of bed and am going around on shaky legs, the very picture of misery.

Thank goodness you can't see how repulsive I look. Every now and then I make a brushstroke and ponder the result with a sigh. I can't even write a proper love letter any longer – but you'll have to believe me, even so …

It's hard to take in that you'll be coming home so soon. I needn't count months any more, I can count weeks … Darling mine, I would write odes and dithyrambs, I would fashion my words into garlands and love wreaths to hang on your door – but fatigue is to blame for my sending only a vase of withered flowers.

Just think if you could make the trip in the autumn instead. Would your work suffer – answer honestly. <u>Can</u> you wait for me? Because then I will come, oh yes indeed, even if it has to be over the authorities' dead bodies.

Cuddles me tonight – you likes me, doesn't you, even though I look like something the cat brought in and fail to send you the poems I ought to be writing in your honour every morning and evening, if I was remotely worth my salt.

Tofslan al Fresco

PS Faffan got the statue commission for Åland after all. Isn't that good news!

the statue commission: Viktor Jansson's statue of Julius Sundblom, who was speaker of the Åland parliament.

15 FEB. –47 [*Helsingfors*]

My darling,

Good morning! Beethoven's fifth is marching through the studio, solemn and rapturous. Atos brought it back from Stockholm with him. I'm not working today, not even bothering to heat the place or cook anything. I finished the colour cartoons last night, and now I can't bring myself to care about Art for a whole day. I want to think about you, listen to music and be outside time.

Rejoicing and triumph, my lovely is coming home! Only two weeks to go, because the third one doesn't really count as "time without Vifs". Everything I do (even cleaning out the coalbox) will be like a welcome to you, a caress of you, like dancing alone at one's party just before the guests arrive.

The guest! It will be the happiest spring – I'm not even afraid any longer of tempting happiness by saying it, and I'm waiting for it without a shred of doubt. We will be working, both of us. But the time we spend on that will not separate or harass us, our professions will be new gardens where we can show one another the way around,

Facsimile of a picture letter to Vivica (3 February 1947), comprising a series of Moomin drawings, with captions, charting Tove Jansson's recent activities and feelings.

and if we close them to each other occasionally it will only be so we can later reveal all the new growth there.

You'll be the model for the woman with blue hair who is dancing in the middle of the balcony ball. You'll meet my friends. You'll come out to Kummelskär in the new sailing boat with me and show me Saaris without mist and grey skies. You'll win over your mother Polly at last. And we won't be hounded by the knowledge that you will soon be leaving, but will have a trip together to look forward to.

All my life I have dreamt, planned, waited and hoped for a variety of different things, but seldom been able to appreciate them when they came to me. The joy of the moment is one of your gifts to me, I think. And being braver.

My dearest, take me in your arms! The best elements of me are yours, because you created them yourself.

Tove.

UNDATED [*spring 1947, Helsingfors*]

Darling,

It is utterly impossible to let you wake up and remember everything has gone wrong and maybe go off feeling dismal and wretched. I find it hard to talk to you on the telephone because I can't see you – and even when we meet I'm no less tongue-tied. Perhaps it's best for me to write down what I want to tell you.

It isn't so terribly much, really. Only that I'm so grateful to you and proud of you and my trust in you is boundless.

Of course I don't imagine I shall ever be able to keep you for myself.

But I know that you will always exist and be fond of me and that we will follow one another's work.

If you could believe in your work as much as I do! What you do is so genuine and has such great potential for the future – it is like you.

Vivica, you mustn't forget how much richer and more concentrated my life has grown so since you came into it. What does not being happy matter, as long as one sees and feels and thinks more intensely. I know I am living more full-bloodedly than ever and perhaps this last fresco will be the best thing I have done, in spite of – or thanks to – how it weighs on me. And if I don't rise to the ambitions I have for it, then that will come later.

I know that my whole way of painting is changing at the moment, growing stronger and more alive, and I have you to thank for it. Beautiful lines and colours are not enough unless they are backed up by expression and real pith and intensity, albeit the intensity of despair. If I don't instantly find the form for what I want to paint, it doesn't matter. It will come.

So there is no need for you to feel distressed about the frescoes, my dearest. Both of them are you – and one can by no means assume that the best you have given me is in the first.

Vivica, I long for you very much, but it is a new kind of longing that isn't sad and fruitless. It makes me feel surprised and a little in awe to realise that my love for you is perpetually growing, and I am altogether too proud of it to be able to hide anything from you.

Tonight I feel almost happy – and could barely be more so if you were here. I am writing poems to you that may be a little strange, and drawing you – though the likeness isn't always terribly good! and if I knew anything about musical notes I'm sure I would optimistically be trying to write a song in yourses honour! Everything you touch begins to live and grow – that's what I am so grateful for.

You mustn't be sad, Vivica, because I know this trying period will not only end, but bring something exquisite with it.

Are you so sure that the most crucial thing is to make me happy? Delete that from your conscience, Vifs, otherwise I shan't dare love you as much as I could.

We will never find our way back, Vivica – if we don't free ourselves from the weight of one another. Remember you have <u>no more</u> responsibility for me than whatever feels like proud delight, and there's no limit to the walls my yearning can paint if it only liberates itself from wounded vanity and exaggeration.

Darling, let us try to be patient with one another a little longer.

And do you know what we will do then – that terrific picture of you in the red shoes. I think I know how I want it now.

Tove.

Translator's note: "Yourses honour", as with other words such as "sickses" and "goeses" in the letters below, refers to the play on words used between Tofslan and Vifslan in *Trollkarlens hatt* (Thingumy and Bob in *Finn Family Moomintroll*).

30.6.47. [*Helsingfors*]

Yesterday I got it into my head that I didn't love you any longer and I went up to Villagatan to test out whether it was true. But it wasn't, unfortunately.

I suggest we stop seeing each other, and definitively this time. It's miserable having to concede defeat after so much work, but it can't be helped.

If you plunge back into feeling guilty, that's stupid of you. (But I don't think you are stupid.)

The fact of the matter is that I can't cope with feeling unhappy any longer, and fighting for you with a joy I don't possess.

I'm sending you some poems: "Songs to My Beloved." Please don't ring me; I feel so calm now.

Tove.

TOVE JANSSON WRITES FROM FRANCE, AFTER HER TRIP TO Italy with Sam and Maya Vanni, previously described in letters to Atos Wirtanen.

13.6.48. [*Brittany*]

Dearest Vifslan –

I am utterly enchanted by your daring Moomin idea. Why not indeed, just as well that as Sleeping Beauty or The Pearl of Truth?! Of course The Loveliest of Them All will have to feature ... not just my peculiar little creatures. It would be fun to build a fantastical fairyland in the wildest of dream colours: trees full of fruits, jewels, sweets, flowers, birds – one act incredibly lush, one a landscape of ghastliness. If the comet is included, the sky can grow redder with every act – and at the end it will be bright blue with a Van Gogh sun in the middle ... Am I interested ... <u>You bet</u> I am! It will have to be rewritten into something completely new – you could do that.

Sometime when we are in the right, light-hearted mood, we can set to work. I take it for granted that we will work together again one day, and perhaps on less limited projects than old Kålle Syra. Maybe with our stomachs pressed to warm rock on Bredskär, planning Moomin plays or "The Lady in the Pocket" who became the crows' cook. (Yes of course, I and my younger and wiser will live in the Chateau – the idea was for Tofslans and Vifslans and their ilk to be put up in the annexe!)

You can't send me any letter more "real" than one about work. I am glad and wish you all the success you <u>certainly</u> deserve.

We didn't end up at rue de la Gaité after all – it was too irresistible to stay at the same hotel as Willy ... So are you wondering what she said? Well, that Vifslan hadn't written at all. And she was polite. Kut! Unbelievable! French, cool, courteous, amiable but reserved. Oui? Vraiment? Tant mieux! We danced a little. I can well understand a certain Uca being unfaithful in Paris. I went there again the next evening, without Maya, but that time Willy only sent me a correct smile and asked about choice of subjects in Helsingfors (she only meant for painting, unfortunately). How deep inside is she hidden, that person who sent those vivacious letters? I suppose one has to be a Vifslan to find her.

And after that I lived the provincial life in Chevreuse beside a miniature triangle of market square with the five streets of the town clustered around it, enclosed by green hills and a brown river. A jumble of roofs, fences, bridges, delightful dusty greenery and silence after eight, with a clock thoughtfully striking the hours. (but Paris far too close!!!) I calculated that those hours would be all too few if I didn't hurry straight off to Bretagne and live cheaply. Now I have broken the "family circle" and am here in a fishing village with a nice tangy smell of rotting seaweed, and the beam of the lighthouse sweeping across my whitewashed wall each evening. Colour and stiff wind and another kind of peace, a mobile one. You can consider Tofslan a happy person and imagine her clinging on here as long as she can. Spread greetings around you and reserve a seat of honour in the stalls for your opening night, and may the muse free you from Grokes, infidelity and every kind of depression, so thinks

Tofslan!

your daring Moomin idea: The first Moomin play, *Mumintrollet och kometen* (Moomintroll and the Comet) premiered in 1949 at the Svenska Teatern, Helsinki.

The Pearl of Truth: a play by Zacharas Topelius, based on a Finnish folk tale.

Kålle Syra: A reference to drawings and advertising slogans for Kålle-Syra fizzy drinks, which featured Tofslan and Vifslan.

my younger and wiser: TJ's playful name for her brother Lars.

Willy: One of Vivica Bandler's French loves, also referred to in Bandler's autobiographical *Adressaten okänd* (Not Known at This Address).

Kut!: possibly intended to be Zut!

UNKNOWN DATE IN A SNOWSTORM. 1950
[*Saaris Manor*]

Dearest Vivica and Kurt!

Ham and I have only been here for a couple of days, but it feels as if we have always lived here and will go on doing so. We really are sleeping in "the spotted room" with Kurt's flowers in the middle of the table, which incidentally is a pyramid of work tools.

Anni is full of moans about our (sporadic) energies, but the fact is that we discovered a whole new urge to draw beautiful lines as soon as we arrived. Some places seem to take the effort and anxiety out of work, lend it fresh impetus and leave all the relish intact. Ham is drawing muscular postage-stamp lions and I am illustrating "My stormy youth" and finding it just as enjoyable as building houses. So now you understand!

Other than that, we are doing absolutely nothing – and it's really good to see Ham's face sort of smoothing out with every day that passes; she feels at ease here and fits in so well. Sometimes we go to look at Oskar [*written in above the line:* horribly ugly!] who (according to the genealogical table) begat almost all the cows, and are astonished. Once we walked to the foot of the hill with the lookout point but then decided we could be let off climbing it because everything this week is meant to be completely and self-indulgently optional. So we went back home for some coffee. And today I took a sauna and now I am delightful and scented with anti-hemulen water. A terribly fat cat is in the habit of fishing for bits of crispbread in our lavoire. Oh, and we're waiting for a slight thaw because Ham says she wants to make snow lanterns. She brought two candles with her for the purpose. She says they always did that at the vicarage in Sweden. There seems to be quite a lot here that reminds her of it. So it must have been a rather grand place.

As for me, I intend to make the most of any thaw by building a giant Moomin on a pedestal at the front entrance and letting him turn to ice.

Uca, it's your birthday any day now! You always thought the Runeberg candles were being lit in your honour, didn't you? How stupid of me; I should have remembered that was why the two of you couldn't be here for Sunday. We'll have to have lots of special hugses and think of something nice to do when we meet again!

We weren't particularly sickses on the bus, but we almost died of heatstroke after we got here. Once we had stuffed ourselves with food, you see, we decided to sleep, so with that aim in view we piled on all our wool jumpers and snuggled under those violet eiderdowns. When we woke up the temperature in the room must have risen to 40° and we had to stagger over to the window and hang out of it for half an hour.

We've got used to living without woolly drawers now and are sleeping with just one thin blanket. I wonder if there's anything I enjoy more than being able to go round in a thin dress even though it's winter and get up to a warm room. Ham is sleeping much better here. At nine o'clock, Anni brings in the coffee and puts up the blinds. She really is a terrific woman – combining enormous goodwill with such capacities. I swear on my linseed oil that you will find me a somewhat Junoesque figure! (One of these days I shall jettison all the padding in my clothes, she said gaily.) And so far I haven't noticed anything asymmetrical about Anni's serving.

It's so lovely here, and so nice to be with Ham but away from the frenzy of Lallukka and from all possibility of going to my studio – such peace descends on one, a kind of natural resignation.

I also wanted to convey something of that to Polly and Eric, whom I hope to see soon after we return home. Give them a hug in advance – and an embrace to both of you, too, from your happy and tranquil friend

Tofslan,
and with a special x to Eca!

5th.

Birthday kisses to Uca! The weather is milder and we are going to make a statue in your honour. I telephoned yesterday and am so glad Polly is better and no longer in pain. But tell me, what's this I hear? My younger and wiser has been surly with Eca and wouldn't even go and look at the Runegren statue with her? I wonder what everybody's up to over there. The only bad part about living in your house is that I can't pop in to see you night and day to chat madly away and cuddle up and get cross with people. What if you were to send them out here, any friends you need a little rest from?! How was the Runeberg party? Did Moomin go really badly and will Nicken cancel its run because we've been such short-sighted dramaturges. Who's doing what and with whom? An awful lot must have happened. What terrible things are they saying about us, and who <u>adores</u> us?

I know I adore Anni, anyway. She clucked with delight just now when we finished the snow lantern and she saw a new ornamental entrance going up at Saaris. So we've been working our socks off for you all and are dead beat, can't do anything but sleep, and in a minute we're having whipped cream. From what Eca says, you'll get this letter in a couple of weeks.

Hugs to one and all! Bye!

"My stormy youth": TJ is illustrating *Muminpappans bravader* (*The Memoirs of Moominpappa*).
Polly: Ester-Margaret von Frenckell is often called Polly in the letters.
Eca: Erica von Frenckell.

THE CHURCH AT TEUVA (SWEDISH NAME: ÖSTERMARK) BURNT down in 1950 and a new church, designed by the architect Elsi Borg, was built in 1953. Tove Jansson began work on the altarpiece in May and returned to the project in the late summer and autumn.

28 AUG [*1953, Teuva*]

Dearest Uca,

You sounded happy on the phone, so presumably she is more gorgeous than ever? How goeses her disc selling? I imagine you'll build up a fine record collection. Pass on my regards and have a lovely time. She made a very cute impression on that recent visit to the studio.

Today I painted a cobalt blue dress and a carmine black cloak on Edla. All the girls have names, you see. She's called Edla because she looks a bit stuck up, and to get my own back on Luoma, who wants his daughter's pin-up-pretty face there. Thank goodness the altarpiece doesn't look too small, I'd been worrying about that. It fits beautifully into Elsi Borg's proportions, and if I keep the planes big and simple and make the most of the outlines, as in fresco, it can certainly be appreciated from further back. The church is airy and light, with clean lines. Airy, above all, because there's a gale blowing through the gaps where the sanctuary windows are to go. In felt boots and with Jussi's winter scarf round my head, I'm chasing sheets of gold leaf to and fro along the scaffolding while they hammer sheet metal below. The sheets are meant to be transferred to the wax on the walls with cotton, while one holds one's breath, but with things as they are I can only flick them up into the air and slap them on where they happen to land, if I can catch them. The sanctuary windows can't be put in "because there's no workman who'd dare cut such big panes of glass to size". I've made such a fuss about those windows that every time they catch sight of me they say all right, all right and go and hide. One day the whole tabernacle they'd erected to block up one window blew in, and wood and chipboard came crashing down on me and my painting. My tracings had paint splashed all over them. I was so livid that they promised to ring a more intrepid glazier in the next town. Or so they said. You know I need light for deciding my colours so I don't get unpleasant surprises when it's all done.

I feel terribly clever when I'm applying gold. It instantly looks so shiny and beautiful and can't fool you. Not like paint can! Of course it may be that all the sheets of gold leaf will peel off eventually, because the wall is still very damp despite being hard, and good for painting on. But as long as they stay in place for the consecration, I can always pop some more up later. By all the rules of secco, the wall ought to have been in a fit state to work on ages ago, but today I found out they used soaking wet bricks for the outer walls and it's been raining here since the end of June.

When I came back I got such a fright because my whole niche was covered in big uneven patches of damp, with one wide, dark band running horizontally right across. I thought it would all have to be pulled down, but then I found that the fungus, or whatever it was, could be scraped off with a knife. So I scratched away at the whole wall between the outlines of the tracings and scrubbed it with a bath brush. Now I'm praying to heaven that the patches don't break out again. The whole of Teuva is a sea of mud and the stooks of rye are standing in lakes. In the middle of the day I have to leg it to a restaurant several kilometres away, because they've closed the catering huts. Sometime between 6 and 7 I walk through the wet, horizontal landscape in the other direction, where the vicarage is.

There's a cooking stove in my gatekeeper's lodge where I can prepare meals. The dean himself is away with his family and I'm very happy on my own. Even the workmen have stopped watching me when I'm chasing after my gold or painting cloaks, so I'm left in complete peace and quiet. In the evenings I'm revising the Moomin book, following your directions (they are even better than I thought), thinking about the sketch for the Cooperative Bank and reading the psalms of David, which are actually rather dull. He spends most of his time moaning about his enemies and asking God to destroy them.

There are two of the workers that I particularly like. One of them gilded the cross on the steeple, and we talk about work and offer each other cigarettes and sweets, the other is a skinny middle-aged woman who is the most cheerful person I've ever seen. She positively radiates happiness. [...]

Can you imagine, I swear my room was full of bats last night. Maybe they live in the chimney. Or they could be little devils, out to tempt me just when I'm producing something as solemn as an altarpiece. Joking aside, I'm very taken with this job and will be more upset than usual if it proves a *flop*.

I started with the strongest colour, the fiery red cloth Magdalena is kneeling on in the foreground. I made it as red as I could, with a layer of white paint underneath. You see, it lifts the whole colour range, which is brightened and lightened by the perpetual <u>obligation</u> to match all the colours to the cadmium red.

Now Jussi wants something on the organ loft as well. It's divided into panels. But first they'll have to find another Luoma (hopefully childless). Presumably they'd have to use me for it, having started with me.

The Vasa plane is just going over.

You know what, Ham was so pleased with her trip. I delayed leaving so I could see her for one day, at least. What a storyteller she is! She gave me an absolutely brilliant picture of the family *meeting* at Ängsmarn, funny, touching, ridiculous, sublime, full of pathos. They're totally barmy, the whole lot of them, but nice, and very intense. Do you know why cousin Karin didn't come to the island "to finally let myself be lazy and happy, talk about <u>everything</u>, not have to be so terribly <u>moral</u>", as she wrote? She's joined a sect that's even stricter than her parents and is waving her arms about and going into ecstasies. And Kerstin has become very good friends with Karin's sister, and Elsa's husband has converted Torsten. And everyone's still squabbling about the privy and who eats the most. As far as I could gather from Ham, she was cheerfully "dafratty", vaguely shocked and very jolly with them, and refused to be pathetic and this-is-the-last-time-we'll-ever-meet.

So now, loads of hugses from me and awfully good wishes to everyone. Kisses

Tove.

Edla: A play on words because the name sounds like *ädel*, the Swedish word for "noble".

Luoma: A local sponsor of the church-building project.

Jussi: Jussi Annala, the dean of Teuva.

the Moomin book: *Farlig midsommar* (*Moominsummer Madness*).

sketch for the Cooperative bank: Design for a mural TJ painted in the staff dining room at Nordiska föreningsbanken in 1954.

"dafratty": Swedish *dafratig*. Derived from "dafrat", meaning "so what", "who cares", a Viennese slang expression introduced by Kurt Bandler and adopted with alacrity by Vivica and Kurt's friends.

TOVE JANSSON REPORTS FROM HER TWO "WORKING WEEKS" IN London in March. Her later trip, in April–May, is described in the letter to Eva Konikoff dated 7 May 1954.

TUESDAY 9.3.54. LONDON

Dearest friends,

First let me introduce sister Mutton's poem, which he sang and danced for me one evening:

> Moomins, naked Moomins,
> they were flown to England
> from the Finnish dark
> straight into Hyde Park
> all their navels petrified
> now they're buried side by side!

Maybe he composed it in sheer relief at handing over all comic strip duties to Mr Phipps. Phipps is 2 m tall, very English and a typical practitioner of their *"understatement"*, which I've only started to value and feel comfortable with since I came here. To take one example, the solemn gentleman with the pipe and foxy moustache by the pond in Kensington Garden, trying to get a boat going. It was slightly over 1 m long and its name was Smoky. I and fifty others stood there watching for a long time, getting very cold. He finally carried his work of art out into the water and with much smoke and hooting, Smoky set off among the swans (who seemed used to it). No one showed any emotion as they witnessed this Event, but there was so much interest and goodwill among those frozen onlookers that you could sense the appreciation in the air.

There's definitely only one thing in England prone to *overstatement*, and that's comic strips. Any action in them has to be reacted to with *"sobs"*, *"oomph"*, speed lines, sweat and tears. I'm achieving all this with an insight into Fleet Street that grows by the day. I don't really object to queuing for the bus in the morning, going to work like everyone else, grabbing a standing lunch at the reporters' bar round the corner and spending my tired and not remotely touristy evenings out in town.

After discussions with Phipps I am cutting up my strips and sticking them back together again, anglicising the captions, adding some things and taking others out, all the while with a strong and reassuring sense that it's <u>my</u> *stories* they want, and that they like the Moomin family as it is. I work in Forkes' office, he's one of their great comic strip idols. He's away for a month, possibly at a nerve clinic. His creature, which is hairy except for a bare face with a trunk, is staring at me from all directions – in plaster, fabric, papier mâché, wood ... There's a dog-eared sheet of paper on the wall: *Ideas for "Flook"*, *"Couldn't he go to Hollywood ... Something with winter ... Flook has flu ..."*

I'm seeing Liz tomorrow, and Francis in a few days' time. A rep from Benn's publisher's took me out and made a fuss of me one evening. Tired cartoonists sometimes come into my office to take a look. They all say "be sure to have *stock-material* so you don't get behind, otherwise you'll go crazy ..."

I find time for a bit of art, a bit of theatre, mostly I like just to drift aimlessly along the glittering streets at night. Everything's bigger and more frenzied than in Paris, it feels like drowning in a whirlpool of speed and a few million people's unconcern.

I'm captivated by that sensation of indifferent metropolis and anonymity – but perhaps I wouldn't be if I didn't have my work and a few interested people in the background to hold me steady.

Kensington, where I live, is a quiet place that seems to be populated mainly by ancient little old ladies whose clothes are as individual as their dogs. Doesn't it strike you that a considerable percentage of the women look as fresh as daisies while an equally large proportion are soberly dressed ghosts, bags of bones with stick-like legs? And that the men, regardless of age, have a comically young and boyish appearance?

It's expensive here, dreadfully. But in spite of that I've indulged in a Delightful Act of Folly, a Skirt Suit that's apparently "mole grey *in a flappy style*". What they mean is that the peplum waist of the jacket sticks straight out, the collar is feminine and the skirt a straight line. And, even more irresponsibly, I allow myself whisky.

And, by the way, I miss everybody very much. I've been away so long – anything at all could have happened to you! I send all manner of wishes, for opening nights and success and every kind of peace and quiet, and that you won't forget me, and will pass my greetings to Erica and Ester and Eric and all the other friends who might appreciate them. A big hug,

yours trolly Tove!

sister Mutton: Mister Sutton, i.e. Charles Sutton.

Mr Phipps: Julian Phipps, head of the comic strip department at Associated Newspapers.

Forkes': Wally Fawkes, who from 1949 onwards drew a popular series of strip cartoons featuring a boy, Rufus, and a small creature named Flook.

Liz: Elizabeth Portch, who translated *Trollkarlens hatt* (*Finn Family Moomintroll*) and *Kometjakten* (*Comet in Moominland*) into English.

Francis: Francis Crowdy, an English actor friend of Vivica Bandler.

THE ISLAND 7.7.56.

Darling Uca –

<u>Thank you</u> for your nice, loving letter! I read it in the greatest confusion you can imagine: Harald's birthday with wife and daughter and in the middle of it all the Peos for breakfast and pouring rain and someone fell into the sea with all the comic strips and thunder and alarming English letters and a tent that almost blew away.

And it made me giggle and cheered me up awfully to read about other pretty kettles of fish and to sense in the pages of the letter your understanding of it all – and at once everything went much more easily and it seemed terribly good fun to have all these people trying to combine themselves out here.

It's such mayhem here now that I can hardly impose any order on this letter – but there's <u>one</u> thing I want to get straight and clear:

that you and Nita are heartily welcome on the 21st and that it would be really lovely if you could come a bit earlier – whenever suits you.

And I'm assuming you'll ring Abbe yourself. Stor-Pellinge 12. You see, I think everything will be all right, whoever happens to be here then. It could even be empty, who knows – and the two of you can finally have some time to yourselves for a while.

You see, nothing seems so bad now I'm calm and happy and not so nervous and have at last learnt to be honest.

I shall do whatever work I need to for certain hours of the day, remorselessly setting my friends to work as well – and take the rest of the time off with a clear conscience, to enjoy your company. Happy in the knowledge that you've thought it worth the effort and cost of coming out to this primitive jumble of mine!

Darling, you needn't worry, I'm thoroughly rested and content with everything and I will find time for what has to be done. I've completed pencil sketches of all 10 of Landström's advertisements – and been able to fit in some peaceful summer hours with Ham and Faffan as well.

These days have been perfect. Ham has finished off Moune's frigate – it is a masterpiece, and has been terrific fun for her.

"Moune – Borgå" it says on the stern. She swims every day, slowly and sensually with her cigarette in her mouth, out at the red rock, reads wickedly bad books and simply exists. In the evenings she and Faffan set out a little net so his favourite seagull will have something to eat. The filleted (and sometimes cooked) seagull bait is laid out on the rocks, a bit closer to the cottage every day – and it is Faffan's hope that the seagulls will eventually come strutting in through the door.

He's taken over the guest room, wakes at 5 every morning and goes out to wait for his coffee and study the wind direction – no games of patience, no politics, no anxiety. An awful lot of messing about with sinkers and sculling seats and snells, he's even started playing the accordion. And if I bring out the kiljun (which turned out well, and <u>strong</u>) he only takes a glass or two – never fancies more than that.

Ham sleeps and looks as fresh as a daisy – (die Boschena und die Marjanka – God knows how you spell it) like that time Kurt was here.

You'll understand how glad I am to see them having such a good time. As for me, I'm finally at deep peace with my world – waiting patiently for Tuulikki, and my previous guilty consciences are, I fear, being rocked to sleep by the south-wester. Because I know full well that I don't really deserve it, having my existence made as easy for me as this.

The children, Peo's and the rest, are just putting in at Viken, but Peo will be back again this evening for the "blow-out dinner". And the kids, the whole lot of them, will be coming later to camp out. That's a long-standing promise. I just hope the weather will be good.

Goodness, Vivica, I've so much to say – even though we had those two whole days together. And weren't <u>they</u> wonderful?

You know what, I suppose Bitti will just have to turn up whenever she happens to. Her trust, which evidently hasn't been remotely shaken, is so precious to me that I don't want to impose any restrictions. Her letter came at the same time as yours, and she writes that she might already be on the island by the time I get it. And she definitely wants to meet Tuulikki and be here at the same time as her. I'm not at all apprehensive. I'm sure everything will be fine.

It would be jolly nice if people told me as clearly as you when they are arriving and how long they plan to stay – but you know how hard it can be to ask sometimes. They think they're not welcome. That's why I can't give you the plain answer I would like to: who else will be with us when you get here.

But don't worry, it know it will all work out and everyone will have just as much freedom and privacy as they want. And on the same subject: things have gone very wrong for Maya in that business I told you about. You know what, in nine years she's only ever been here the once – and now she writes, despite her usual reserve, and begs me to let her come here with him for a few days to "sort things out". I haven't the foggiest notion when that will be, whether he wants to, or if it would be a good idea at all.

But of course she's got to try, and of course we'll do our best to help. It's rare for Maya to ask for help. I told her in my letter that you – in accordance with her wishes – knew all about it, and that she ought to call you to confer on dates. Both of you would prefer to come separately, I'm well aware of that.

It <u>is</u> a pretty kettle of fish. But for me the main thing is that you visitors are comfortable here and feel that in spite of my moods and clutter, it's a place you can come for some rest. If all my friends suddenly shunned Bredskär I would throw in the towel, because it would mean the best thing I tried to build had been in vain.

– Now the whole lot are asleep, some of them on the floor. There are wet clothes drying on the stove and the mist is right outside the window. [...] Uca, do give my warmest regards to Kurt. I hope his germs aren't dangerous. Kisses to you and Nita, and I really look forward to having you here!

Tove.

Landström: Björn Landström, artist and writer. He was artistic director at the Taucher advertising agency at the time.
Tuulikki: Tuulikki Pietilä (Tooti). See Letters to Tuulikki Pietilä.
Moune: The *chanteuse* Moune de Rivel.
kiljun: Home-made wine.

2.6.64 [*Bredskär*]

Darling Vivica,

Tomorrow Tooti's going to town and I want her to bring you a report from the island – so you and Kirsten will know everything here is going better than I could ever have expected!

Right from the start, a cordial, natural atmosphere, perhaps partly because I've made friends with Bredskär again – not sure how that happened. I presume largely because I've worked off a lot of my feelings in this book, which I fervently hope you'll be able to read sometime over the summer.

Or later, there's no hurry. I shall be sitting on it for quite some time, until I'm convinced it holds together. It's called "Pappan och havet" [*Mooominpappa at Sea*] and in retrospect it seems to me to be largely about Faffan. If it weren't for the fact that it's a touch pathetic and revealing, I'd dedicate it to him.

It's turned out rather melancholy, of course, despite my best efforts and despite the positive ending in which Pappa, Mamma and Moomintroll each find a way out of their individual loneliness and become a family again, and the lighthouse is finally lit on the beautiful hostile island to which Pappa has dragged them to assert his manliness and restore his self-esteem. Little My is with them to provide some much-needed contrast in les brumes nordique and the Groke has come to the forefront. Apart from them, just one slightly maladjusted fisherman who sculls about in the background and wants to be left alone.

Anyway, you know how grateful I am to finally have a long, concerted stretch of time for working with true zest and a real sense of need – a rare phenomenon these days.

I'm sure it was the Spanish trip that unknotted things for me, one of the nicest presents I've ever had from my friends.

Today it's sunny, with a sou'-wester blowing, "the darlings" and Nita are down on the sand, Lasse's preparing clay for a bust of Sophia and Tooti is rummaging about in the attic for suitcases.

I'm sad that she'll be gone for such a long time – of course, but it feels like just the right time for a pause. There are the lithographic materials, a whole printing press of stones, which she bought for an amazing bargain price just before we came here and is going to install in the library and bring into use. And the possibility of going to Venice to superintend an exhibition in June.

After a long break in her work it's hard to get going again on an island like this, I think she needs her own surroundings and the stimulation that a new working technique can provide.

What's more, the old Ham friction is bound to set in again sooner or later, and I want to spare us the dreadful gloom of last summer.

Yes, I'm sure it's all for the best. And something happened yesterday that is going to resolve all our island problems, I got my permission to build on Klovharun!

I certainly never thought I would pull it off when I went to Borgå to charm the Building Board with that rather antiquated map in my bag, I was convinced their wall would be adorned with the new one, with "Property of the State" stamped in red all over the archipelago.

O how I've had to battle, and how many setbacks there have been – and I don't suppose things will get any easier from now on, either, with lots more "irrelevant" obstacles to overcome – but I got my island, Vivica!

It's sure to be a long time before anything gets built there, but I <u>know</u> it's mine, I can go there and root about in the soil, plant stuff, maybe make a jetty or a place for chopping wood. And Tooti won't be so wound up.

Yesterday evening, Lasse and Nita planted lots of bushes they'd brought with them from town and chopped down the little fir tree in front of the cottage. It's going to look very good and, you see –

it's such a positive sign that they're starting to feel part of Bredskär, taking pleasure in the ownership of it. Ham delightedly pitched in to help.

Her birthday was a cheerful and festive occasion. Our first triangle week, warm and windless, was just heavenly. Ham herself suggested that she should sleep in the guest room and I accepted. Got up at 3 and lit the stove for her when the morning chill crept in. We tidied, repaired, got everything in order, Tooti made a handrail up the stairs to Ham's room and helped her with lots of other little things.

There, see, my island report is excellent this year! I'm so glad you and Kirsten are coming here, hopefully for more than just a few days.

It must feel awfully desolate for you, now she's gone off to her seminar.

Lasse and Nita were full of praise for the premiere and eminent critics agreed with them. How wonderful that it was such a success! A special congratulatory hug to Kirsten!

That must have been quite some theatre party you had. Lasse and Nita were glad you were all able to meet up so much. Isn't Sophia even more delightful now you can have a bit of a conversation with her? She blends into the landscape like a flower and bawls every time she sees a boat, imagining it's coming to take her away from here.

Later: Tooti got her travel grant of 2000, so now she can go to Venice!
A huge hug and warmest wishes!
Your Tosla.

Kirsten: Kirsten Sørlie, a Norwegian director who for many years worked in collaboration with Vivica Bandler and was one of her lovers.
"Pappan och havet": The book was published with the dedication "To a pappa". It was published in English as *Moominpappa at Sea*.
the Spanish trip: TJ and Tuulikki Pietilä went to Portugal and Spain in the winter of 1963–64.

VIVICA BANDLER IS IN JAPAN WITH HER FATHER ERIK VON Frenckell on the occasion of the Olympic Games in Tokyo. Tove Jansson is in the initial hectic and exciting stage of building on Klovharun.

VIKEN 24.10.64

Darling Vivica,

Your letter felt like you taking me in your arms and it conveyed an instant and total image of what you're experiencing over there. Of Japan, much more intensely than anything I've read about the country – maybe because your account of it was so powerfully spare and on the specific wavelength that we share. [...]

I find it utterly absurd that you're so far away, a strange sensation of being abandoned. Of course I know we don't meet up that often. But we exist, near each other, all the time – One can ring on a whim, or in despair, or for something very matter-of-fact. Anything at all.

We didn't have time to see each other those last evenings before you left. If we had, I would doubtless have poured out my latest fright: a pilot from Pellinge (representing the Fishermen's Guild) has submitted a petition to the County Administrative Board requesting that my building permit be revoked because Klovharun belongs to the state and I could scare the birds and fish.

The Building Board eventually ruled in my favour (after Gylling had drowned them in all sorts of documents) but the County Administrative Board is still considering the case.

Before anything could happen I set to work out there, having found out that cellars and blasting don't count as building, but as upright timbering – and that uprights (the construction) are allowed to remain standing for the winter if roofed over. I rejected my first desperate idea of a dummy cottage, prefabricated Puutalo Oy style (for many different reasons), tried to hire some local builders but Pellinge was like a brick wall and I didn't want to land Abbe in the soup of spiteful village politics that my island problems have evidently stirred up.

Then Brunström, a fisherman from Kråkö (near Borgå), promised to help, despite the difficulties of working late in the season. He's the one who once got a drift net tangled round his propeller and spent the night on Bredskär.

So Brunström enlisted a blaster, a sailor and a boat builder plus the skipper of the Sophia and we set about it as if our tails were on fire, to get ahead of the authorities (Brunström doesn't like them – nor does he the Pellinge folk, who claim he pinches the laveret from their nets. Which he almost certainly does)

It's been blowing a gale almost non-stop. The Sophia tried to come out with her cargo three days in a row, but had to turn back. A man fell down into the hold with the wheelbarrow but was miraculously unharmed. (I insured the lot of them after that) And a small boat sank. And Sophia ran aground, but not seriously.

On the third day we got everything ashore, (it turns out I'm very good at shovelling sand. 35 m^3) timber, sections of railway track, drainage pipes, metal, sand, cement and they threw a huge bridge from one rock to another over the spit, for transport of materials.

At first I camped on Klovharun and the men stayed on Bredskär, but after one night of gale force 8 and pouring rain (apart from the practical inconvenience, it was glorious), I moved over with them and am sleeping in the attic. On Fridays I go back to town and to Ham, and on Mondays I return to Harun. We go out there before sunrise every morning and come back at dusk, and I'm their assistant and cook.

All back and other aches have vanished along with all melancholy, my happiness is complete as I carry stone and sand and planks and make terrible cabbage soups in high wind.

Tooti has returned from a trip with Lasse & co. that went well in every way, but she's thrown herself into her printmaking and has only (today) come out to see the building work. I understand her – she's got to be able to get on with her prints now, there's been too much of a break for other things and her lithographic nerves are stretched taut. We're staying at Abbe's.

That's basically what has been happening here at home – or at any rate, the only parts I care about at the moment. I intend to fight for that island, you see, and I intend to keep it. Though I know they <u>can</u> pull down finished houses, I discovered that yesterday.

There are lots of details from my own personal building site that I'm sure would amuse, interest and even enchant you – tiny things, little incidents and comments people made. Or images. But that will have to wait until we're sitting in the studio or kitchen one evening. I've sort of been living aside from everything, differently, or it almost feels as if I've only now come alive. (terrible suspicion: because I don't have to paint) Things are growing, taking shape, they come into existence if one only has the stamina, and fears and worries are about tangible things which can be overcome, a boat in a storm, cement threatened by rain, tents blowing away, food running out.

Like you I'm forgetting to write about "The Olympics". But I expect we'll get round to it. And yes, Lasse has submitted two good instalments of the TV project. Much better than before. – I miss you, Vivica. But you'll soon be home now.

Tove.

Puutalo Oy: Wooden House Co. Ltd.

OCT. 69. [*Helsingfors*]

Darling Vivica,

I have your little brush that I'd intended taking with me to Sthlm – but then the TV show was postponed and I, useless person that I am, hadn't the wit to post you the brush.

So nice that you're coming over, the seventh, isn't it? By then I shall be back from the picture hanging and exhibition opening in Jyväskylä – and a few days later I have to dash back there so Tooti and I can take the whole lot down again.

Here's a cutting I meant to put in last time: examples of middle-aged absent-mindedness; Tooti cut it out the day it came but then took it down to the yard, realised what she'd done and dashed to Reima to buy a new one, gave it to me but I put it in such a safe place that I couldn't find it again afterwards – and I expect you've read it long since!

That's <u>just</u> what it's like – so how will we be by the time we're 80? I'm functioning awfully well at the moment and producing a good deal, to my own amazement. Lasse and I have set up a COMPANY – Moomin Characters, registered and everything. Do you remember the Moomin craze ten years ago, with the promotion at Stockmann's and Bitti trinkets and marzipan and candles and Batujewa's puppet theatre? And My on sanitary towels? It's all started up again thanks to our TV effort and the star of Moominry is shooting up to undreamt-of commercial heights.

All of a sudden we're stinking rich and stressed! It's simply massive, the whole thing, they're calling from the foreign ministry and telegraphing from Australia and Lasse's taking at least five calls from abroad every day. He's dealing with all the business correspondence, thank goodness, and doing it well. What's more he's designing *commercial articles* at the same pace as me and has gone and bought himself paints and brushes (!) and got such a shock when he saw how expensive sable brushes are!

Bulls Press Service is sharpening its claws, talented housemaids have started making Moomintroll-shaped potholders again, the journalists are swarming like grey cats and Lasse Pöysti is singing Moomin songs on the radio, so by this point he must be pretty much a social misfit. Kuuskoskis had manufactured several thousand Sniffs before the customer in Sweden realised Sniff wasn't in the TV programme and cancelled the order, then Fauni's tried putting a saucepan on Sniff and he looked like a Catholic priest (not a Muddler). Lasse and I were chauffeured out to Järvenpää in Kuuskoskis' big car for new contracts and new Muddlers and ancestors with luminous eyes. They gave us Peikko-juoma in one of their cafés.

Oh, and Film-Takahashi in Japan has sent a case of a soft drink made by the gentleman who is financing the film, which apparently had its premiere in October. Unfortunately Takahashi didn't send the samples of the film as promised, but he did send Lasse some cufflinks, composed to look like the badge of his clan (or whatever they have there) two thousand years ago, and I got some Japanese stories that were older still, and not a soul can read them. He and his family are coming in person at the end of November, to study the Finnish fjords.

We're drawing the line at Moomins on food. "Mmm, Moomin!" (Slogan) But we've done such a lot, including sheets of pictures for scrapbooks, paper dolls, greetings cards, Pop posters, books of sheet music, Moomin houses, blankets, curtains, dress fabrics, wallpaper, albums of poetry and photographs, diaries, nursery pictures – I won't make you read through all the rest but there are new products all the time and it seems as if – well, I hadn't realised just <u>how</u> important TV is to people. It's <u>incredible</u>. Everyone is fixated on the magical date of 5th December.

As you can tell, life has assumed new dimensions and without Lasse I'd never keep up. However, with the growing insight of age I've gone into this relatively calmly (none of the hysteria of ten years ago), picking and choosing in quite a matter-of-fact way and thinking that this is all positive, after all, and it's happening right now, and it's a gift and an opportunity and money means peace of mind later on, a buffer against more frivolous ideas while one tries to shape what seems more important and less lucrative.

Naturally I feel a bit proud as well, not just worn out and petrified of what the next post brings. And sailing above it all is the cheering and reassuring awareness that our TV work is <u>good</u>, and you – mainly you – have made it so good. We've nothing to be ashamed of, we haven't cheated the least little scrapbook-picture manufacturer or child when our work is released. Isn't that actually rather nice?

That book I tried to write last summer wasn't any good and the publisher didn't want it, *inside information* – and what a brilliantly honest and non-commercial publishing house! The summer was too messy, too many people, but that's an excuse really, one can write in spite of such things if one really has something to say. But I still believe in the idea behind this book, and in some sections of it. The setting is the forest in Nov.–Dec. and I want to go now – not to the island but to Pellinge, to immerse myself in the dismal decay of autumn before the snow arrives. (I'm so afraid it might start snowing!). God knows if I shall get that week, I do hope I shall be ruthless enough to simply <u>take</u> it. Otherwise another year will pass, won't it, and I'll lose the whole book, it'll become a matter of conscience and duty, not a pleasure. You know. A hug for you now, Vivica. Welcome home. It was good that I was able to explain in writing – when I do it in spoken words, it sounds so foolish. This is just a quick cross-section – as a starting point for the seventh.

Warmest wishes –

Tove.
<u>Thank you</u> for the little Ulla poster!

the picture hanging and exhibition opening in Jyväskylä: An exhibition mounted jointly with Tuulikki Pietilä at the Alvar Aalto Museum.
Lasse Pöysti: An actor.
Fauni's: The company Atelier Fauni made so-called Fauni trolls from the early 1950s. In the mid-1950s, its owners Helena and Martti Kuuskoski were licenced by TJ to manufacture Moomintrolls. Fauni's Moomintrolls, eleven figures in all, proved extremely popular and were even exported abroad.
Peikko-juoma: A fizzy drink.

Film-Takahashi: Refers to the first Japanese animation of the
Moomin cartoons, which was shown on Japanese TV 1969–70 but
never approved by TJ for broadcast outside Japan.
the magical date: 5 December 1969 was the date the *The Moomins* TV
series was first shown in Sweden.
That book I tried to write last summer: The first version of *Sent i
November* (*Moominvalley in November*).
God knows if I shall get that week: TJ did get her week at Pellinge in
November; it is mentioned in Greta Gustafsson's contribution to
Resa med Tove in 2002.

PARIS FEB. 75

Darling Vivica,

[...] When we first came here, I was pretty scared – I knew I was
"a blank", washed out by the past year's scenes, some of them cleared
up, some of them such classic faux pas, too much, too different, too
many people, and I thought a whole spring in the Cité and I shan't
be able to work at all, and that will take its toll on Tooti of course and
she's never been in greater need of a *refuge* [in English or French]
so she can find her way back to her lithographs.

It was terribly difficult at first. I pretended to work, writing, but
nothing came. Then I remembered Lars Löfgren's request, which
I'd long since turned down, and it was something to latch on to, an
assignment (rather like an essay at school), and the fact that I wiped
out the whole world in my haste may possibly have had something
to do with that initial anguished spell in the Cité.

Just think. One of Tooti's best working periods happened precisely
here, 6–7 years ago, – and when she was young, another, lasting
five years. Fixation with a particular place, entirely natural. You
can imagine how happy she was to get started on her printmaking
after a break of several years, not a thought of going out with her
cine camera, she hid herself from everything and just worked. She's
produced <u>ten</u> exquisite lithographs, something entirely new. And
not abstract, but with a <u>warmth</u> to them.

The building is ghastly, like an oversized Lallukka, bare, narrow
corridors with black doors, the furniture black plastic, the rest a dirty
yellow, and down below the typewriters squat among interminable
glass walls and the whole place is heated by hot air, hissing up day

and night through rigid grilles so your eyes run and your head is bursting every morning, the sound – a torrent, like endless lashing rain, has driven lots of people away. We try to block the damn thing off with scrunched-up paper but it doesn't help, so we feel seriously tempted to get ourselves a tent to sleep in. What an indescribably stupid situation.

Apart from that we honestly are happy and on very amicable terms with one another. When I couldn't write (and it truly is awkward, pretending to be creative with someone always watching), I started to paint out of sheer desperation. And I'm persevering doggedly. Tooti's relief is touching. And before I knew it, I found myself interested. Something might just be starting to stir. I certainly <u>can</u> do it, I know that after a life as long as mine, I can even <u>see</u> sometimes, but the element beyond price, and scarcely within reach any more, is the <u>urge</u>. That's what I'm waiting for, the only thing that really matters.

Sometimes I think I catch the scent of it, just a little.

The exhibition in Hvitträsk has gone to Gothenburg. (minus comic strips, posters and *commercials*, just the illustrations) They wired and asked me to come, but I shan't, I know you understand that if I lose my grip on painting at this point I shall never try to paint again, this is my last chance. I don't know whether it's really all that crucial and I'm not going to think too hard about it. The exciting thing is that right now I don't care about my future <u>audience</u>. It's <u>me</u> trying to <u>see</u> and to reclaim the urge, and I'm not doing it for Tooti's sake any more.

She's cheerful. I haven't seen her as cheerful in years. She works regularly and brings home books and music. This trip was exactly the right step. We'll gradually start seeing people of our own accord, once we feel <u>confident</u>.

Moune is singing at a club and our plan is to make contact by going there to listen to her. I shall write to Hilde in the next day or two.

I had a letter from Gunnel who was very enthusiastic about the performance of Kirsten's Troll-in-the-wings.

We've had a few invasions here, compatriots, folk from London (publishing types) and those romantic materialists from Japan. But it's still starting to feel like freedom; all those gaffes back home are fading, I'm getting used to this horrible building and feeling my way towards the aforementioned rekindled urge, I know Tooti is happy, what more can one ask?

Tooti and I embrace you both –

Bye,

Tove

Lars Löfgren: Director, head of TV theatre at Swedish Television.
Hilde: Kirsten Sørlie's daughter.
Gunnel: Gunnel Malmström, TJ's Norwegian translator.

WORK AND OTHER PROJECTS CONTINUED TO BE TOFSLAN and Vifslan's common concern over the years. *Sommarboken* (*The Summer Book*) was eventually filmed for TV under the title "Sommarön" (The Summer Island), directed by Britt Olofsson, and shown on Swedish TV in spring 1979. The radio plays, meanwhile, were turned into short stories: "The Woman Who Borrowed Memories" and "The P.E. Teacher's Death" are among the stories in the 1987 collection *Resa med lätt baggage* (*Travelling Light*) and "The Daughter" was published in the 1998 collection *Meddelande* (*Messages*).

APRIL –76

Hugs to you, Vivica, and it was so nice to see you!

The only thing we didn't talk about was forthcoming jobs – and that felt good – but now I want to fill you in on some facts.

I called Gunilla, who's been very noncommittal about the film potential of The Summer Book, partly because of its lack of continuity. I was ready to pull out of Britt Olofsson's project, but she now seems to have written a synopsis that Gunilla thinks is very good. That's a relief.

Both of them are now coming over at the start of May for discussions.

"The Woman Who Borrowed Memories" seems to have hit some snag even though they've agreed to take it in principle. I know it didn't "appeal" to you. I shall try again over the summer, though I'm rather tired of the whole "Woman" now.

But I hope you might be interested instead in "The P.E. Teacher's Death", which I think I will offer to Finnish Radio. And you know I won't have a breakdown if you don't want to work on him.

Lars Löfgren wrote one of his charming letters and gave me his critical opinion of "The Woman", which largely coincided with my own.

He was interested in the P.E. Teacher – I'd talked about it at the Stockholm lunch.

So although those are radio plays rather than TV, and in this case I'm thinking of Finnish and not Swedish Radio, I've asked Gunilla to pass on her copy to him *for the fun of it*.

I didn't tell you that the Finnish Telephone Service is holding a competition for its jubilee and I wrote two short radio plays for it, on the subject specified: Telephone Call. I enjoyed doing those.

We'll have to see if anything comes of it. You should hear the daughter with the guilty conscience who rings her lonely mother every day! Ugh!

So there you have it, my business report. I can save the rest for next time. Bye!

Tove.

Gunilla: Gunilla Jensen, dramaturge at Swedish Television.
Britt Olofsson: Director, producer and actress.

"Do we really appreciate how lucky we are ...?"

LETTERS TO TUULIKKI PIETILÄ
1956–1968

Tuulikki Pietilä in her studio.

MEETING ENGRAVER AND ARTIST TUULIKKI PIETILÄ PROVED A turning point in Tove Jansson's life. They found one another at the Artists' Guild Christmas party in Helsinki in 1955, at the gramophone where the two of them were looking after the music, and their relationship gradually developed in the course of the following spring. "At last I've found my way to the one I want to be with", Tove Jansson wrote in one of her first letters to Tuulikki Pietilä in the summer of 1956. They had spent a few days on Bredskär and their love was deepening. I feel like a garden that's finally been watered, so my flowers can bloom, Tove Jansson confided to her beloved, who had gone to teach at an "artists' colony" in Korpilahti for a few weeks. Tove Jansson was left alone on the island, but she felt calm and full of confidence.

The letters to Tuulikki Pietilä contain a succession of love metaphors about blossoming and abundance, imagery that also recurs later on, in a poem to "Tooti" in 1985. Here she is likened to an orange tree.

> I would compare you to this sturdy tree
> lovely to live with in all its finery
> and all the fruits that its branches do adorn
> are your desires for projects yet unborn!

In the summer of 1956, Tove Jansson drew a picture of "a new little creature" in one of her letters and Tuulikki was transformed in the name of love to "My Too-tikki". In the sixth Moomin book *Trollvinter* (1957, *Moominland Midwinter*), the name took on its Moominesque form of Too-ticki. Large parts of the book were written during the winter she spent with Tuulikki Pietilä at the latter's studio on Nordenskiöldsgatan in Helsinki. Privately and within their close circle of friends, Tuulikki Pietilä was known as Tooti. She and Tove Jansson lived together for forty-five years.

They had already encountered one another a few times in their earlier lives. Both were studying at the Finnish Academy of Fine Arts (Ateneum) in 1938, and in 1951 their paths crossed at the famous Monocle nightclub in Paris. Tuulikki Pietilä had been living in the city for a few years and Tove Jansson was on her way home from travels in Italy and North Africa. Paris assumed a special significance for the couple; it was the city they loved above all others.

Tuulikki Pietilä (1917–2009) was born in Seattle but moved back to Finland (Åbo) at the age of four. She was the daughter of Frans and Ida Pietilä (née Lehtinen). Her brother Reima Pietilä (1923–93) became one of Finland's best-known architects. Tuulikki Pietilä herself attended the Åbo Academy of Fine Arts (1933–36) and then went to Helsinki to study at the Ateneum (1936–40). In the war years she was in East Karelia and later worked in Sweden, looking after child evacuees from Finland (1944). After the war she lived in Stockholm while she trained in etching at the Royal Academy of Fine Arts (1945–49). On moving to Paris she took tuition at various establishments including Académie Fernand Léger and studied with the eminent engraver Louis Calevaert-Brun. She also taught for a time. She did not return to Helsinki until 1954, after almost a decade abroad. She went on to teach engraving at the Academy of Arts (1945–60), and wrote a textbook on metal engraving. Her exhibitions can be numbered in the hundreds. Tuulikki Pietilä was awarded a professorship in 1982.

In Tuulikki Pietilä, Tove Jansson found a traveller, seeker and freedom-lover just like herself. This was something new. In her youth she had travelled alone, later with Ham (and with Faffan a few times), and occasionally with friends. But now she had a travelling companion on equal terms. "Tooti is fantastic, of course, she always is – but a Travelling Tooti is something exceptional", Tove Jansson wrote to Maya Vanni from Vienna (23.4.1982). The short-story collection she published five years later, *Resa med lätt baggage* (*Travelling Light*) was dedicated "To Tooti" (1987). Interviewed at some length by Helen Svensson for the book *Resa med Tove* (2002, Travels with Tove), Tuulikki Pietilä talked about life on their many trips. They journeyed as the fancy took them, never booking hotels in advance.

On their first trip together, in 1959, they visited Greece and Paris (see Letters to Signe Hammarsten Jansson). Accounts of their subsequent journeys can be found in letters to various recipients in this volume. They also travelled separately, and Tove Jansson would write to Tuulikki Pietilä. Sometimes she would be on the island while Tuulikki Pietilä was in the city and sometimes the other way round. In later years there was no need for them to write to one another. As they grew older, they increasingly both lived in Tuulikki Pietilä's studio flat at Kaserngatan 26 C.

The letters to Tuulikki Pietilä are all about love and work, recent and present, but a shared future is in their sights from the outset: "I love you as if bewitched, yet at the same time with profound calm, and I'm not afraid of anything life has in store for us" (26.6.1956). As the years passed, the narrative of their lives seen unfolding in the letters changed and evolved, but its basic premise remained the same. On the island they lived together (often in a tent), but in town they lived their own separate lives, albeit under the same roof. In the early 1960s, Tuulikki Pietilä moved to a flat in the same building as Tove Jansson's studio – the building was on a corner – and they simply walked across the attic to see one another. The letters reveal their life on Bredskär, increasingly preoccupied with family and friends as time passes, and subsequently on Klovharun – *their* island – once Bredskär grows overcrowded and starts to feel claustrophobic. They quite literally built their life, piecing it together with work and love, but the process was not painless. Anyone who lived with Tove Jansson also had to live with her family. After Viktor Jansson's death, Signe Hammarsten moved to Lars Jansson's, but she spent the weekends with Tove Jansson. Relations were distinctly strained at times and, in a letter to Vivica Bandler in the summer of 1964, Tove Jansson wrote of the need for a break. Tuulikki Pietilä would install her new lithography equipment at Kaserngatan and then go to Venice to supervise an exhibition; "she needs her own surroundings and the stimulation that a new working technique can provide", wrote Tove Jansson, citing "the old Ham friction" that was bound to set in again before long.

It is another Tove Jansson we encounter in the letters to Tuulikki Pietilä, open and sharp yet also trusting. She writes about her parents in a way she never does in any of the other sets of letters in this volume. Tuulikki Pietilä also receives some unusually frank comments from Tove Jansson about her Moomin work – everything from merchandise to texts and illustrations – sometimes including hilarious accounts of her growing fame and everything that goes with it, book tours, public appearances, trips and huge numbers of encounters with people of many different kinds.

"All things are so very uncertain, and that's exactly what makes me feel reassured", says Too-ticki in *Trollvinter* (*Moominland Midwinter*). Life with Tove Jansson brought changes for Tuulikki Pietilä as an artist, too. The letters clearly show that collaborating on projects played an important role in their lives. They worked on the world of the Moomins, constructing Moominhouses and tableaux with their friend Pentti Eistola; they mounted a joint exhibition (Jyväskylä, 1969); and they published a book in words and pictures about their life on Klovharun, *Anteckningar från en ö* (*Notes from an Island*) in 1996.

Quite a number of Tove Jansson's literary works can be traced back to her life with Tuulikki Pietilä, from *Trollvinter* (*Moominland Midwinter*) to the novella *Rent spel* (1989, *Fair Play*), a portrayal of two women's life together. One is an artist, the other an artist and writer. In the final chapter, "The Letter", the artist has been awarded a scholarship to go to Paris, yet is hesitant about leaving her partner and making the trip alone. But, for someone who is "blessed with love", as the final words of the story have it, solitude presents its own opportunities.

* * *

26.6.56. [*Bredskär*]

Beloved,

I miss you so dreadfully. Not in a desperate or melancholy way, because I know we shall soon be with each other again, but I feel at such a loss and just can't get it into my head that you're not around any more. This morning, half awake, I put a hand out to feel for you, then remembered you weren't there, so I got up very quickly to escape the emptiness. And worked all day.

The science fiction synopsis is done now, it took about 15 more strips.

This morning I roused the social conscience of the whole of Viken and wrote an application to the county sheriff on behalf of seven penitents without fishing licences. Then I was at Odden and admired all Anna-Lisa's planting and concreting and other curious arrangements, and was given a whole basket of little plants that I've popped into the ground, dotted around the Island.

The Island looked very solemn without you when I arrived here at sunset. It had turned in on itself and I felt like a virtual stranger.

It was only when I got up to the house that it looked friendly and alive again. The wagtails were yelling in great agitation, complaining volubly because the copper jug we had our midsummer leaves in had fallen down and clearly frightened their babies out of their wits. They probably got a dousing as well. Now the idyll has been restored and the mother is so tame she stays perched on the top of the flagpole even as I go in and out of the house. I brought some mud for the swallows from Anna-Lisa's bay – but they continue with their furtive visits and seem reluctant to commit to family life.

Late one night I started off some kilju in the "best water bucket" and supplemented the recipe with all our raisins.

It was a fine night, calm and quiet, and I still couldn't take it in that you weren't here, kept half turning round to see what you were doing or to say something to you.

Today there's a strong south-westerly blowing and we would have found it hard to get over to Viken.

So I assume you've now plunged deep into the all-engulfing life of the city and are dashing about getting hot and resentful so everything's ready for your departure.

That first day in town is always such a horrible contrast to life out here on the island. Everything that's been lying in wait for you comes tumbling in like one big shock and at nights you miss the sound of the sea and feel totally lost.

Wherever I go on the island, you're with me as my security and stimulation, your happiness and vitality are still here, everywhere. And if I left here, you would go with me. You see, I love you as if bewitched, yet at the same time with profound calm, and I'm not afraid of anything life has in store for us. This evening I filled the tub with water from the big rock hollow and tried to pick out the dreadful Sea Eagle Waltz on the accordion. I'll play it for you! Now I'm going to read Karin Boye and then go to sleep – good night beloved.

27th.

Today I brushed and cleaned the hollow after I'd emptied it and then sprinkled sand into it like you told me to.

And I wrote that awful article for Svenska Dagbladet, "What it's like to write for children", which I've felt uncomfortable about for so long. I tried to spice it up with the kids' own healthy taste for the macabre, the obvious and the reckless, in the healthiest sense, and to write as little as possible about myself and my blessed old troll.

Then I hauled stones to make a fine terrace in that place where the grass is yellow and started thinking about the next synopsis, the one where Pappa is a lighthouse keeper. A story about the sea and different sorts of solitude, and everything that can happen to you along beaches. But I've no clear idea of how I want it yet.

The wine is bubbling away madly and the place smells like a moonshine factory. It's spitting with rain on and off and the sea is grey and austere.

28th. Suddenly there's lots going on again. I'd hardly had time to make the bed before Björn Landström came over the hill, with Vivica after him – they'd both arrived by water taxi.

The first thing Uca did was to ferret out your letter, and after an enormous amount of coffee drinking and going through the Moomin advertisements for the Co-op Bank and seeing Landström off, I was finally able to read the letter.

You're right that it always tends to be easier to go than to stay – even if you're happy being with the one you are leaving. I know. But this time it would have been more right and natural for us to stay with each other.

I can't help feeling terribly smug that you long to be back here. I'm waiting for you already.

Everything I do, everything new that I see – there's a parallel reflection: I shall show this to Tuulikki. Waiting is a sheer pleasure when it's for you – and the calm awareness that all I have to do is add together a number of days, and we'll see each other again. I haven't dared try the mosquito song. That would make me sad and I'd miss your embrace so much.

It's wonderful that your brother got the Brussels Prize! That's a really great accolade. And it's excellent that you simply took a taxi and went straight round to celebrate with him, not worrying about the whole sensitive family situation!

I'm sure the two of you forged a new kind of contact that evening, perhaps found you could be natural with each other like before. Uca told me about the prize, too, and everything you both said when you met, and you more or less insisting she came directly here, which made her incredibly glad and proud. She's sound asleep beside me, exhausted. The Paris séjour went well, but it was all a lot of trouble, and the reaction afterwards, and now she has a long, overwhelmng year of theatre ahead. She's tired but composed, and pleased with the results of her work, and we've let the day go by just talking to each other.

Thank you for the fly swatter my darling, it seems extremely effective. To think of you remembering it amidst all the rushing about, "dark love" and picture hanging and exhibition planning and *what not*!

I appreciate that you haven't had time to go to a doctor, but it worries me a lot that you couldn't.

How is your knee? Does it feel any worse? I can understand your insides being in tumult. They don't like having to move from place to place, and demonstrate it by rearranging the days all wrong. Can't we wait a few more days for each other in August so you've time to go and get the wretched thing looked at? Beloved, I understand your lack of relish at the prospect of Korpilahti. But just think, this is the last time ever! Then we can do whatever we want with our summers.

And our winters, the whole lot! I'm so unused to being happy that I haven't really come to terms with what it involves. Suddenly my arms are heaped full of new opportunities, new harmony, new expectations. I feel like a garden that's finally been watered, so my flowers can bloom.

10221!

The last evening with Uca – tomorrow she goes home and Ham and Faffan will probably come out. We still haven't done anything but talk; it's so rare for us to be on our own together, and so much has happened since the last time. But the strange thing is that, whatever I talk about, it always seems to come back to you, and I sing your praises in uncontrollable dithyrambs. She doesn't contradict me.

Goodnight darling. Look after yourself.

Tove.

science fiction synopsis: The comic strip "Moomin and the Martians".
kilju: Homemade wine.
that awful article for Svenska Dagbladet: "Apropos rita och berätta" (On Drawing and Storytelling), *Svenska Dagbladet* 1.12.1956.
10221!: This figure and those in the following letters refer to the number of comic-strip frames TJ has completed.

5.7.56. [*Bredskär*]

Beloved,

10,227!

At least today I got in first.

I wonder how the sunny Finnish weather here on the island looks at Korpilahti – maybe it's just heat there. Maybe you're working indoors and longing for an overcast day to make your task easier.

You can't leave your sheets of paper for a while as I can, go down to the red rock and slide into the sea, or let off steam splitting chunks of firewood.

I'm working on the Landström job now. And talking of chunks of wood, I've accumulated a pile of them for you, the ones I couldn't get through. The trick of hammering the axe in with another axe mostly results in my having to saw them both out. (Already used as a comic strip idea, unfortunately ...)

Ham and Faffan actually did come out the day Uca left, looking tired, a bit grey and, you know, awfully pleased to be here.

Since then, every day has been perfect. Faffan isn't playing patience but has thrown himself into fishing and catches so many that we have to share them with the seagulls. Faffan's favourite seagull is called Pelle, it screeches with joy whenever it sees him and sits in the same spot all day long, waiting. And Ham feeds the wagtails at the verandah table, where I can see the whole family hopping around while I draw.

In the mornings the nylon net is hung up to dry on your knotty wooden hooks and every day Faffan goes paddling off to Måsskär with his rods and sinkers and all the other paraphernalia. He's grown tanned and cheerful and if I offer round the kilju he only has a glass or two.

Even though this batch turned out delicious, and <u>strong</u>! And Ham is tinkering with a bark boat, a frigate, which is going to be completely incredible – with Moune-Borgå on the stern. (A commission from Vivica, for Moune!)

I'm so pleased to see them enjoying themselves and looking healthier with every passing day. One day we went out to Tunnis and I dashed straight to "our" camp. But someone else had used it since we were last there, the cooking place, the stock of fuel, everything – even the tins – and nothing was where it should be and there was paper littered everywhere. I was just as cross as when they made such a mess in the guest room. Next time we'll camp at a new site of our own. I dug up loads of lily-of-the-valley and planted them behind the woodshed where the birch stump is, and I also collected some shore plants with violet flowers, which will look lovely at the beach where we pull up the boat.

And the terrace behind the house is finished, completely round, 1.90 in diameter. The wild strawberries have appeared, and all the blue and red beach flowers. And the wasps have simmered down, but now there are flies everywhere instead. Summer is moving on through its stages and sometimes I feel so melancholy that you aren't here. But perhaps it's good to have a bit of distance between us. I know now that I couldn't possibly be more attached to you, in a harmonious and happy way that can only grow stronger and more tender.

But I've known that all along.

Now it's evening, with a restless nighttime wind, and Ham is lighting the paraffin lamp.

Guess what, she'd run into Eva, who exploded on the spot at the news that you'd been on the island. I realise you were obliged to mention it. Good grief. But perhaps it's just as well for them to start gradually getting used to us.

The evening Ham and Pappan came out there was pouring rain, and a storm blowing in from the north. We sat chatting to Abbe late into the night, drinking rum.

At five in the morning we were woken by two young fellows, half frozen to death, whose monster of a motorboat had ran aground. It broke down in the storm and was hurled onto Lilla Båtskär (where we picked the ox-eye daisies). Once the weather calmed down in the morning, the boys managed to get over here, using their one oar. The boat had a huge gash in its hull.

We poured coffee and rum into them and dressed them in Lasse's trousers. Then we took them home to Kungshamn in the rowing boat. We'd barely had time to get back to sleep when some agitated relation of theirs turned up to tow the motorboat home. They'd waited up all night and called out the coastguard and were as angry as you'd expect with their kids (who'd been well on their way to drifting across to Estonia), the way one is when relief has followed hard on anxiety.

The swallows are flitting in and out of their nest, but sometimes they're out partying orwhatevertheydo for half a day. So I hope their babies shuffle well down inside while they're waiting. I read in the bird book that they do that as soon as the food stops coming.

It's night now and a big thunderstorm is veering in from the south.

But where's the excitement in that when you're not here to protect me. Ham's lying in bed in her fine Bredskär nightgown giggling over "Funny things people say" and Faffan has withdrawn to the guest room with a flame-grilled roach.

I shall immerse myself in Putkinotkon. When Vivica saw it she shrieked with delight to see what it was and said it was a book she adored.

Käkriäinen has just left home in a fury. Incidentally, I'm also reading the Bible – or simply falling asleep, worn out by all those things I find so hard to explain when people ask: But what do you do all day on that island!? Don't you get bored?

No, not at all. But I do miss you. Lots!

P.S. your letter just arrived – no time to read it right away because Cay's going straight back. Ham's brother from Sweden, and his family, have come to visit.

Eva: Probably Eva Wichmann.
Putkinotkon: *Putinotko* is the name of a novel by Finnish author Joel Lehtonen.
Käkriäinen: Juutas Käkriäinen, one of the characters in *Putkinotko*.
Cay: Abbe and Greta Gustafsson's son.

10.7.56 [*Bredskär*]

Beloved,

Now my adored relations have finally gone to sleep, strewn about in the most unlikely sleeping places, the chatter has died down, the storm too, and I can talk to you.

Thank you for your letter, which felt like a happy hug. Oh yes, my Tuulikki, you have never given me anything but warmth, love and good cheer.

Isn't it remarkable, and seriously wonderful, that there's still not a single shadow between us? And you know what, the best thing of all is that I'm not afraid of the shadows. When they come (as I suppose they must, for all those who care for one another), I think we can manoeuvre our way through them.

I'm glad you have the advantage of a room to yourself at Korpilahti, so you can just get on with your work and not be disturbed by the cares and intrigues of the colony.

If you write in Finnish, please could you be a dear and use the typewriter; your handwriting's a bit tricky sometimes. I very much wonder if you could read <u>my</u> last letter at all, Uncle Harald having fallen in the sea with it, along with a consignment of comic strips and a bag of whisky.

It's all been intense family living here since they arrived on their sailing boat from Sweden. I ruthlessly go off and draw when I have to, but between times I'm available for household tasks, Bacchanals, childminding and conversation, whatever turns up. Part of me enjoys it, the other part takes out its frustrations chopping wood. Harald arrived just in time for his birthday, which has traditionally always been a big bash, celebrated at sea.

This year it was magnificently framed by a storm and ended in the traditional joyous whirl of dancing on the rocks, tumbling into pools and climbing trees. Gentle mother Saga looked after their children for the evening, but in return, all the youngsters from Viken will be coming over to sleep out in tents sometime soon.

The invasions of our beaches are intensifying. Bitti's in town and will be coming out any time now. After the 20th Uca and Nita. Maybe Kurt. Maybe Maya Vanni. I'm going to try to try to keep my work very separate and leave the cooking to them as much as I can – which is hard, because it's easier and more natural to do what's necessary myself.

But I expect it will sort itself out. Presumably there are going to be various strange collisions, but I'm not worried. As regards you and Bitti, it might be much better for you to meet here than in town. The island stays just as beautiful and relaxing, whatever the context in which folk come gadding over the rocks.

One day the whole of Viken came out, Peo as well, bathing was soon in full swing and I had to cook like crazy. It's good to have the strip cartoons to work on sometimes, I can cope with those however lively my surroundings. I've put up the nesting box for the starlings – other than that I've been busy with work or socialising. I miss those quiet June days when you were piecing together your mosaic or whittling away at some knotty bit of wood and it was possible to listen, contemplate and explore how we felt.

On the subject of mosaics, Ham and I gave your "Fishermen" to Harald for his birthday. It was for sale, after all. You said eight, didn't you?

He was very pleased with it, and it will have a fine place in a home that actually has good taste when it comes to beautiful objects.

Tuulikki, I long to read more in the book of you. I long for you in every way, and I'm more alone with all these people around me than when I was wandering about on my own, thinking of you.

And here is a new little creature that isn't <u>quite</u> sure if it's allowed to come in!

Your Tove.

IN THE SUMMER OF 1956 THERE WAS A GREAT DEAL OF WORK to be done, but also a succession of visitors to Bredskär. Tove Jansson completed some advertising illustrations, wrote an article and a short story, worked on the Moomin cartoons (which she referred to as "strips") and designed a number of products for the forthcoming Moomin window display at Stockmann's department store in Helsinki. "I need these jobs and still can't say no to anything," she writes.

Beloved,

Now all the phantoms have gone to bed after a great deal of talking, dancing to Nita's radio, partying, a little Misunderstanding and general enjoyment, very much as usual.

The whole house has suddenly grown amazingly feminine with loads of little pots and jars, and clothes discarded here and there, and I'm going round like the captain of a cargo boat, making sure the load is evenly distributed. Outside it's women's week as well, with sun and rain all mixed up together and near-gales that force us indoors. I continue calmly with my strips and notice a tangibly friendly atmosphere starting to pervade the place, the island is gradually smoothing away urban fatigue and old complications, and everyone is changing down to a lower, quieter tone. Despite their defiant high spirits at finally having the freedom to be natural and talk about ghost matters without lowering their voices.

Uca and Bitti seem to be getting on better and better, and Bitti has finally started to understand Nita. And working gives me such joy and pleasure. I've sent off all 10 of Tauchers' advertisements, and the map they wanted – so now it's only the colour covers for the brochure. They changed their minds and don't want the advertisements in colour any more – which saves loads of work that I wouldn't have enjoyed.

And I've illustrated the Sv. Dagbladet article and sent it in, and finally overcome my terrible aversion and written their Christmas story. They're using two-colour printing for the illustrations.

The Mars synopsis has been approved. To my amazement they seem to like it better than anything they've had from me before – and I was afraid they'd turn it down; I thought it was too flippant and *crazy*. And lacking that knowing sense of intimacy I try to inject into the comic strips.

Today I'm up to 10,246 and there's a new batch on the petrol shelf, ready to go off. Bitti has been baking, the foul weather continues, the radio is on, the kilju is running out and the wood as well. Moreover the baby swallows have flown the nest and the finches aren't getting caught in the nylon net any more. And we're completely cut off by a strong northerly wind – so I can't receive any letters from you to explain that you got entirely the wrong end of the stick and are happy again, believe in me and will come out here as soon as you possibly can.

I'm starting to get really fed up with being without you now. It's utter idiocy, in fact, to be apart just as we've found one another and are engaged in the tricky process of sniffing out precisely <u>what</u> it is we've found.

I miss you quite dreadfully.

10252.

I've had a letter now and know you are happy – but sick and tired of Korpilahti and all the barmy people there – and that your stomach misery is over and I shall soon have you here on the island.

Tomorrow Uca and Nita are going into town and they'll try to track you down in order to send you out here as soon as is humanly possible. If there's no suitable boat, you can take a bus to Borgå and another one from there to Tirmo. And make sure Abbe knows you're coming. I'm sending you the bus times – bring them with you when you come.

Since 10,246 I've been working non-stop and have produced the illustrations for the Christmas story and some squiggles for Stock-manns' Moomin window display this autumn, namely some wrapping paper, paper dolls, transfers and decor for a square candle; each as idiotic as the rest. But it's the sort of thing I can't say no to. Not yet!

In the meantime it's been raining and blowing a gale the entire time and my poor womenfolk have started to droop, tucked up in their sofa

corners, and resorted to reading art history in desperation. On the only sunny day they swarmed out onto the rocks, all of a twitter – and just then a big water taxi carrying part of the Stockmann management turned up to spoil the whole thing and shower me with extra work.

But they had their uses, even so, because while I was organising an early lunch on the beach for them and talking business, Uca borrowed the taxi and popped over to Viken.

She fetched water and post and rang Kurt to get some wigs for Abbe's play in the village and half a dozen other things. Once the management had taken itself off home the foul weather set in again – and it's taken until today to turn fine and blue. So I gave myself the day off and washed all the rugs in the surf, and we had lunch up on the rocks with a couple of bottles of wine that Uca had been hiding as a surprise. Then, when we were all sufficiently merry and seized by a vague need for activity, we put out to sea with five boxes of rubbish to sink in the sea. The boat had been pulled up on land for a couple of weeks and had sprung several leaks, so we almost got sunk ourselves. Tin cans and empty bottles went flying in all directions and there was much squealing and lifesaving, and in the end Nita fell in.

Now they've all nodded off in their various corners, and I'm drinking buckets of coffee so I can carry on working.

Kurt was here for two days, muted and mild and not much jallu at all. He's going for an examination at the hospital now – he gets worse in the evenings and is terribly thin. We hope it isn't his lungs but some kind of malaria-carrying mosquito the Russians allegedly left behind them in Porkala.

And now you, poor thing, shall have the traditional list of commissions that's generally only sent once couples have been mymbling for a few years.

As far as I recall, you already had vegetables, bread, cheese, butter and potatoes on your list.

To this should now be added:

A blade for the wood saw.

Fazer's long spaghetti.

1 box standard candles.

Sugar of each kind.

Possibly a can or two of meat.

And Bitti's longing for:

10 30-mark stamps, 2 bottles of rum at around 900 mk plus chocolates at 500 mk. You know, the big ones in shiny paper. Here's 5,000 mk to be going on with.

It's not a disaster if you can't get hold of all this, or if any of it is too heavy and awkward to bring. The only vital thing is for you to come yourself, and quickly, otherwise I shall come and carry you off!

Hugs!

Tove

women's week: the name traditionally given to 18–25 July, seven days when all the names in Finland's name-day calendar are female. Also refers to the week when TJ invites all her female friends to the island.

their Christmas story: the story "The Fir Tree" was published in *Svenska Dagbladet*'s 1956 Christmas supplement. A slightly revised version appeared in *Det osynliga barnet och andra berättelser*, 1962 (published in English as *Tales from Moominvalley*).

the Mars synopsis: "Moomin and the Martians".

jallu: Full name *jaloviina*, a brandy with a certain percentage of cognac, indicated by a star rating.

Tove Jansson was awarded, and received in Stockholm, a diploma from the International Board on Books for Young People (IBBY). She was also nominated for IBBY's prestigious children's literature prize, the Hans Christian Andersen Award, for *Farlig midsommar* (*Moominsummer Madness*). The prize was awarded for the first time in 1956, and went to the British writer Eleanor Farjeon. Tove Jansson received the medal ten years later; see Letters to Signe Hammarsten Jansson.

UNDATED [*Postmark 16.9.1956. Stockholm*]

My Tootikki!

It's a peaceful rainy Sunday, the phone is silent and at last I have a breathing space for appreciating that I've had a good time and been thoroughly spoilt. Ham and I have the whole approach to the Old Town laid out beneath our balcony, but it's only now we have time to admire our expensive view.

The most momentous part of all is that I've taken the hand of a real princess and curtseyed to her. She looked shy, incidentally. The diploma was on ordinary paper without very much gold, but at least I'm taking home a prize to Finland as one of the best storytellers for children.

The best was a 75-year-old Englishwoman, but her medal wasn't the kind you can hang round your neck. For women in particular, they really ought to award honours that can be worn as decoration!

Even on the flight over I was already missing you and the feeling has persisted regardless of what I was doing.

What I was mainly doing was talking on the phone. For the first few hours the businessmen were queuing up to call, all with the blatant intention of duping one another, and probably me as well. One publisher swept me off to a slap-up lunch after softening me up with red roses – but I duped them! I insisted on having milk and an anchovy sandwich at the Skansen self-service cafeteria and looking at the Poppolinos. The surroundings threw them off their stride and made them incapable of talking percentages.

Then there was a big banquet with Gebers and the ice cream was lit up inside as usual and eaten in darkness. I can't remember what food I ate but, whatever it was, my stomach didn't seem to like it.

The remarkable thing is that Ham copes with the eating, drinking and rushing around as much as she likes – all at once she's fit as a fiddle and almost as strong as I am. It's terrific that I can treat her to this trip, the best part of this whole business. Her favourite brother Einar came to the banquet and the party in Bromma afterwards, and saved me by delivering one of his famous speeches of thanks. Today he's going to drive us round the multitude of family members until he has to get back to full-time duties – not his isotope research but making apple sauce, which he seems to consider even more important.

And I spent half a day wearing a petrified smile as I wrote little Christina and little Peter in people's books at the NK store. To one side of me I had a ludicrously enlarged picture of myself in profile, to the other a Mrs Fillyjonk with a wilting gladiolus. Little kids came filing up with plasticine Sniffs and wonderful drawings on graph paper – as did a succession of people who claimed to have known me but never said when or where.

I only dared look at the front person in the queue, nervous every time of seeing some face I didn't want to meet. After all, it was there in the newspaper that I would be available for inspection between the hours of such and such.

Then there were more meetings, I climbed in and out of cars with various shady destinations, and once I had made my trembling curtsey to the princess and the day was over we were taken out to Drottningholm to see an Opera buffa.

It was called something like Fitti Diritti and was very much of its time with people bending at stiff angles and singing about something impenetrable for three hours. By the time we got back to the hotel after an equally impenetrable taxi conversation with an irate Japanese congress visitor, we were feeling done for – and it was only today we realised what fun we'd had.

I'm going out in search of some new environs now. I shall take the letter with me so you'll hear that I love you as quickly as possible.

My arms are firmly around you – and best wishes to all our friends at home from your dazed and tired and terribly happy Tove.

Skansen: the open-air museum and zoo in Stockholm.
the Poppolinos: Green monkeys (*Chlorocebus sabaeus*). The Jansson family once had a green monkey, which they called Poppolino.

IN MARCH 1957, TOVE JANSSON WAS IN STOCKHOLM FOR A variety of launches and meetings. The trip was a present to her parents, or a "bouquet" as she puts it one of her letters. It was the only time they went on a trip together, just the three of them. In terms of work commitments there was an intensive programme of events and appearances at various venues including the NK (Nordiska Kompaniet) department store. Tove Jansson also had to make a speech at the centenary of the birth of the founder of the Scout movement, Robert Baden-Powell, at Stockhom City Hall. Signe Hammarsten Jansson was spontaneously acclaimed at the event, she and two teacher colleagues having started scout groups for girls in Sweden before the Girl Scout movement was established in 1911.

22.3.57. [*Stockholm*]

From 1 April my address is: Howard Hotel, Norfolkstreet. It's close to the Thames and the Strand. A quiet sort of "Family Hotel". London W.C.2.H.

Beloved mine,

It's evening now and so far everything has gone well – only I'm a bit concerned about Ham who is getting pains in her heart.

Faffan beamed his way through the flight and declared he would always take the aeroplane in future. Every detail fascinated him and he suddenly seemed so much younger.

We had fine, clear weather all the way to the Sea of Åland, and from there it was wet snow. We got to the hotel in a flash and the family settled in. Faffan, impressed but appalled, watched me retrieve our travel funds from my bosom, and then went straight out for a beer.

Then he blithely headed for the off-licence and bought a whole cellar of wine, which is out on the balcony, along with some camembert and prawns and sausage. We got caught up in the Slussen intersection when Faffan came to a definitive halt to watch the ducks at Strömmen, and after that we thought we'd never get across the flow of traffic, but we finally made it to the Old Town where Faffan, enchanted, poked his nose down every narrow street and alley.

So I had to gallop off alone to Nk. where the old men were conferring about their events. Then I found the family at the soda fountain, wilting rather after all that wandering around.

It feels strange, being here en famille, great fun but with a slight sense of responsibility. But simultaneously, I'm with you all the time. And how am I to get through the coming night in such a lonely and unwelcoming bed.

Saturday.

I kept waking up, not in gentle warmth but in sticky heat – it really is too unnatural and unnecessary to sleep alone. And the hotel's elegant breakfast tray paled in comparison with our week-old loaf and sludgy coffee in the last two yellow cups! But I did like coming into the parental sitting room to find them smiling broadly in the sunlight from the balcony doors, with Ham now restored to vigour again. I was afraid last night's underwater film might be too much for her *on top of* a strenuous day – but they were so keen.

It's late evening now, I'm writing with my new memoir pen which has had to draw so many shaky My figures in little children's books at Nk. My tiny room is full of flowers and I'm drinking airline cognac to celebrate yet another small step in the tricky evolution of my self-confidence. May the Gentle Muse be thanked that no one told me how big the Blue Hall in Stockholm City Hall is! I had a fit when I entered that tabernacle, it's simply vast! There were millions of little scouts milling around, and not even the consoling fact that most of the scout leaders looked like ghosts was enough to calm me down. Ham was reticent and a bit tired after lunching with the Nk. directors, going to see the huge hole behind Hötorget with Faffan, and having dinner at her brother Einar's.

The programme dragged on, my mouth felt dry and my hands were damp as I tried to convince myself that my wishy-washy comments really <u>would be</u> forgotten a hundred years from now. Faffan had escaped to the hotel for a nice quiet time over beer and newspapers. (Incidentally, all his bottles froze to the balcony, so we had to pour warm water over them very carefully, drop by drop.)

At the start nobody could hear a peep of what I said, but then they set up a microphone right in front of my face, so my voice sounded like an agitated elephant. After I'd almost died a couple of times, the audience (hopefully) realised I was trying to say something about a hemulen and settled into a rather surprised sense of goodwill.

I gradually started to sound more natural, and now, looking back, I'm trying to believe I didn't dishonour my family.

Then they hauled poor Ham up on stage and announced that one of the three founders of the girl scouts in Sweden had come to Powell's centenary celebrations. They didn't insist on any contribution from her, thank goodness, she just stood there looking sweet, beaming as she handed out raffle prizes (for the Centre for the Handicapped). Then they gave her a huge bunch of red carnations, and all of a sudden the jamboree seemed wonderful.

There were massed standards and torchlit processions everywhere in the darkness, and even up at roof level there were little scouts with flaming torches, boys' choirs sang patriotic songs and I was terribly moved and thought I really ought to have become a scout leader. Once I'd simmered down and the lights were back on, I sneaked behind a pillar for a cigarette, but Ham didn't dare.

When we got home Faffan was asleep, already worn out by the wild Stockholm life, but we sawed some beer and sausage out of the snow on the balcony and had a nice gossip in my room.

Tomorrow I have to work, then we're having dinner at Ham's brother Harald's. On Monday it's Gebers and Bulls, and the drawing on the wall at Nk. which is the thing I'm dreading most. But I'll cope. I intend to get through it and, what's more, to stay cheerful and calm <u>and</u> enjoy myself. I'd cut a pitiful figure otherwise, wouldn't I. Tonight my Too-tikki is out partying. I hope you're having a good time! And that sometimes when you raise your glass you do as I do, toast your beloved friend and embrace her in your thoughts.

Nk.: The NK department store.
the huge hole behind Hötorget: A district of older buildings had been demolished to make way for new, high-rise blocks.

25.3.57. [*Stockholm*]

Darling,

Now the horrible day is over, and it went much better than I expected. Of course my drawing was all shaky to start with, but then it got steadier – and a bevy of children and balloons around one does lighten the mood.

Some kindly person came and gave me some Bellergal pills instead of the cognac I'd brought with me in desperation – and they really did have a soothing effect. So I drew with one hand while holding a microphone in the other. Quite a show.

Tomorrow I shall do it all over again. *Couldn't care less*. It does no one any harm to perform circus tricks for once in their life if it helps them be more confident. And confidence when faced with people you know nothing about is a defensive bastion that in other, more important contexts can save a lot of time and energy for more essential things.

So I realise now that this is a study visit. Not in painting but in the art of protecting my privacy. The art of shrugging my shoulders, giving them their doodles, discreetly turning my back and sinking into myself. Into my painting.

But this trip is also a bouquet for my parents. We went out to dinner at Bulls this evening, all three of us. Luxury, liquor, words and sudden flashes of authenticity if you could be bothered to listen.

Even the most hard-boiled, self-assured individuals can turn out to be pathetically insecure sometimes, you discover with astonishment that the hard-scaled director has weak and fearful chinks in his armour. And you aren't scared or impressed any more – and like him more and work better with him. Faffan was terribly sweet tonight. I was a bit apprehensive, because he'd been tippling all day – and he <u>was</u> pretty drunk at Bulls. But he restrained himself splendidly and even made a delightful speech of thanks for the meal. I told him afterwards how proud I was of him – and he was pleased. As for me, I behaved myself tolerably well.

Tomorrow I'd like to go and look at dresses before I have to draw "freehand" again. Need to let off steam. But I fear it will be Vällingby and the Historical Museum instead! [...]

I also went to Gebers to deliver the book and the calendar. I practised "freehand" drawing at Nk.'s decoration workshop for a few hours. Business meeting in Bulls' office. More books to sign. Family, intensive.

But the spring sun is shining over it all at last, there's dripping and melting and I've put my woollen drawers in a cupboard. At nights I dream uneasily and longingly of you. It's strange to have such an awful number of unfamiliar people around me but to yearn only for a single one. I behave as I should, do what is expected of me – yet at the same time live an inner life of recollection and longing that no one but you can understand.

The remarkable thing is that whatever I do, even the facial contortions of this commercial farce, it's with a sense of not wanting to disgrace myself – in your eyes. The same with my efforts to be cheerful and self-composed, and not to lose face in an alien world. I want to emerge from this trip with credit, to do what I have to and then come home at last and make the journey to the island, to you, to my desire, to all that's natural. I'm very tired and slipping into your arms, goodnight.

Tove.

P.S. How lovely to get your letter! I carry it with me everywhere. Yes, I'd like to sit on the hill at Brunsan and get a cold backside and a red nose and eat an awkward orange that makes a mess of my gloves and step in a deep puddle and then go home to our balls of fluff and tumble into your arms and fall asleep with my whole head full of spring!

I love you!

to deliver the book: *Trollvinter* (later published in English as *Moominland Midwinter*) came out in the autumn of 1957.
Brunsan: Brunnsparken in Helsinki.

TOVE JANSSON WAS ACCUSED BY A SWEDISH ART PROFESSOR of stealing the idea for Moomintroll from the artist Verner Molin's 'Dark Sow' illustrations. This was pure invention, but in an article in *Expressen* on 31 March 1957 the professor claimed that Tove Jansson should pay Molin financial compensation. Tove Jansson's response was published the next day and that was the end of the matter. From Stockholm, Tove Jansson and her mother travelled on to England to meet Charles Sutton and discuss contracts for the Moomin comic strip.

UNDATED [*1957, Stockholm. The second part of the letter is dated "2nd April", London*]

Darling Tootikki,

Friday night, just back from the big family party. Twenty-one Hammarstens had been scraped together at an inn on Lidingö on a hill in a deserted valley that looked like one of Arosenius's melancholy spring landscapes. An old farmhouse with low ceilings and an open fire and Gustavian antique furniture.

We were left to our own devices and had the run of the place, and never in my life have I seen my reserved and well-bred relations so merry and relaxed!

But then I had made an impressive number of purchases at the off-licence! And raided the indoor markets by the bag load, bought flowers, and some roast beef that was kindly prepared by one family member, we spent the whole day organising everything and I feel a great sense of relief that it's all over and went well. And I did so enjoy playing hostess for once to all those who were so kind to me when I was "a grubby little thing and scared of trains".

Tomorrow it's a newspaper lunch and a Bull conference and yesterday we had the publishers' party at Berns with die Leander. Faffan was delighted to revisit the scene of his youthful sins, and Ham contemplated with amusement the dangerous restaurant which her clerical family forbade her from visiting. And one evening I went to Konows, a proper, quiet evening in which I was able to make better contact with them than ever before. And I had a chance to talk about you, at last!

Sunday evening. We leave tomorrow. I've got Monday's cartoon strips done in pencil and for once I think I'll have an early night. Faffan is out on his final beer stroll in the sparkling light of the night, Ham is packing. We were at Stallmästargården yesterday with her favourite brother Einar, but I was so washed out that I didn't feel like eating or drinking – just tried to radiate goodwill.

You poor thing, feeling so awful after the party again. It really is too unfair, having to pay so dearly even when one has behaved with such moderation!

I wonder how Uca's mix-up over the key resolved itself. As I go about here, longing for you, and lose myself in my hopelessly big bed – I find myself thinking of those who have to snatch every minute. We've the whole summer waiting for us and it isn't far off!

I just had an interruption: Jörgen rang, furious about a whole-page article in Expressen claiming the idea for Moomintroll was stolen from Verner Molin's Dark Sow and I ought to pay Molin compensation. The entire tabloid page of it was crammed with pictures and photographs. So I galloped down to Slussen to get a copy of the drivel and rang the editor to make sure my rebuttal will go in tomorrow. The piece said that Molin first exhibited his Dark Sow publicly in 1942, and that I was studying in Stockholm at the time. I studied there in 32, by 42 there was a bit of a war going on in Finland, unfortunately, so I couldn't possibly have been influenced by Mr Molin, who is adamant that I stole his idea! Actually it's quite bracing to get such a cold shower at the end of this whole week of marzipan, but I'm still angry. Jörgen was terribly kind and helpful – he's a true friend.

I'm saying nothing to Faffan about all this.

Now – where was I. I'd planned to tell you about entirely different things – but never mind. For better or worse (but mostly better), Stockholm is over for this time and we are moving on. I love you awfully awfully much, Tooticki. Good night.

2nd April. London, a big room, heavy furniture, traffic noise, beautifully harmonising colours in the haze over the city, and colder. The hotel is in a narrow little street between the Strand and the Thames, very close to Fleet Street.

Sutton was there to meet us in the lobby but we were too tired to go out and merely collapsed into bed. Today we had a nice peaceful wander, ate at a little Chinese place in Soho, I found a good hairdresser – and tonight there's a cocktail party for us with all the old boys of Fleet Street. Tomorrow, *business* with Sutton, ho ho.

The grass is green here and the fruit trees were in blossom in the suburbs. I'm absolutely determined to meet as few people as possible and say no to more or less everything, leaving myself the space to feel I'm alive and not a time and motion machine.

Hugs!

Your Tove

die Leander: Zarah Leander, Swedish singer and film actress who had enjoyed success in Nazi Germany in earlier decades.

SATURDAY NIGHT [*undated, early April 1957, Sussex, England.*]

Too-ticki, darling mine,

I'm looking out in the moonlight over the long hills of Sussex, near Kent. A black cat is asleep on my stomach and there isn't a sound outside. Beside Ham's bed stands a bunch of spring flowers, primula and violets, wood anemones and wild hyacinths. You would have liked to caper about with me in all this freshly unfurled greenery. All the fruit trees are white, the sunshine is punctuated by blustery showers, and endless serene and puffy pillows go scudding by.

You should be here, rather than getting snarled up in Guild intrigue and being dragged from pillar to post for the benefit of art. But we'll do it again sometime, together. I always keep your most recent letter with me, read it over and over again, feel that you love me and that I can see you going about your business in Nordenskiöldsgatan, at the Ateneum, the Konsthalle, everywhere I can imagine you being.

There's so much happening here, so fast and furious, a kaleidoscope of different surroundings, people and situations.

For instance there was the fancy cocktail party in our honour with a crowd of formally dressed Fleet Street types, every one of them sporting a Moomin tie – and long contract discussions with Sutton, and the gentlemen from Bulls who came over for a meeting on the sly to get me to influence Sutton in a way that would serve their interests ... But just now it's hard to summon my thoughts for an account of my complicated *business*, because today I'm more interested in the asparagus patch I dug over and fertilised, and Kipling's grey stone house and endless grassy slopes of green velvet.

And then there was the nightclub where I was able to dance as much as I wanted and was made an enchanting fuss of and drank an awful lot of whisky, and was hungover for a while, and yet more conferences, a bit of shaky drawing, a strange negro club where all the ladies had silver eyebrows and a lunch at the Zoo that ended in the most surprising way.

They wanted to photograph me for the Evening News, so I had to climb onto an elephant. It was like scrambling up a hairy mountain, without a ladder unfortunately. I still smell of elephant. The picture with the zebra must have turned out quite oddly, because it got hysterics and tried to push me over.

But I was in raptures when they let me hold a *bushbaby*, a strange, fluffy little creature with little hands and enormous eyes. It was terribly cute and reminded me slightly of you!

And then they let me into the hippo pen while they stuffed him with cauliflower, presumably so he wouldn't gobble me up instead. What's more I was introduced to the only hairless dog in the world. A glum photographer recorded the whole thing with the comment: *Oh well it's all the same to me, animals or criminals* – but they insist on their pictures ...

Out here the animals are less exotic, gentle cows and goats and pigs and <u>28</u> cats in, on and around the house. Illingworth, the cartoonist who owns the place, can never bring himself to get rid of the kittens, so they'll soon fill the whole of Sussex! He lives here with two old *ladies* who are involved in the village amateur dramatic society and make costumes for the cast. It was the opening performance tonight, so we traipsed off to the school and did our bit for local ambitions. The cat wants to sleep now, it keeps clambering over the letter – so I shall kiss you goodnight and vanish into an enormous, lonely feather bed ...

Tove.

IN THE AUTUMN OF 1957, TOVE JANSSON WENT ON AN AUTHOR tour of Sweden. Her new book *Trollvinter* (*Moominland Midwinter*) was a success and the prizes came flooding in. The initial print run was 25,000 copies, far more than had been the case for the previous books in the series.

20 NOV. 57. [Malmö]

Darling Tooti,

Last night I pretended I was falling asleep on your arm, I imagined the pillow was you, and that made it much easier and less troublesome to sleep.

I was in Småland then, but now I'm in Skåne again – I'm starting to have a better understanding of travelling salesmen ... Sthlm, Lund, Tranås, Wärnamo, Malmö – tomorrow Hälsingborg, my last reading. Though of course travelling salesmen don't get remotely spoilt, unlike me ... But even so, all this travelling is dreary, through towns one is never able to visit properly – a perpetual string of new faces that never have time to be more than politely impersonal – sometimes a glimpse of somebody I'd like to chat to for longer – but then I'm on the move again.

The best part was the long journey down to Lund with Göran Schildt – I forged better contact with him than ever before and we spent all those hours talking about real, substantial things. And the author Maria Wine who was my companion in two towns was engaging and personal. Apart from them it's been largely a kaleidoscopic sort of jumble – or in fact the surprising repetition of a particular "formula" – this is roughly how it goes: early morning wake-up call at the hotel, sometimes at ½ past 6, I throw together my things, grope my slightly (perhaps) hungover way through the morning darkness down to a train. Reading passes the time as I'm carried to the next town where yet another polite bookseller waits on the platform to accompany me to the town's main hotel where my room has neon lighting, three walls in an understated creamy grey and the other in lilac or black. I eat a quick, solitary, overpriced meal in the hotel dining room and go to the shop to sign books. Half the kids in Sweden are called Christina or Agneta, the other half Jan or Michael. Then I return to the hotel and am interviewed about how Moomintroll came about, have a bath and a rest, get changed. Then I'm escorted to the party venue, parish hall or library, read about the squirrel's funeral and listen to speeches of welcome, and Bach.

Then there's more signing, and another interview about how Moomintroll came about. Sometimes the audience is younger and I opt for the winter bonfire and Sorry-oo's wolves. Then I treat the bookseller to supper and later that night pay the hotel bill and request a morning call. In some ways it's a lazy existence – in others quite a strenuous one: in that I never get any real privacy, can never take off my smile, have no space for thoughts other than of what is imminently expected of me.

The old gents here in Malmö didn't invite me to supper, so instead I was able to spend it talking to you – and I'm grateful for that! And it's satisfying, isn't it, to eat a posh dinner in total privacy and propose toasts to whatever one feels like?

I'm toasting our coming Tootikki winter, when I can be with you, work with you and fall asleep with your arm around me. I don't want to go on any more trips now before we start planning for the island, nor to meet any faces but those you and I are fond of. And I have the secret excitement of knowing that now I will be trying to describe my experiences, and you and your surroundings, in Finnish. It's the biggest present you've given me for a long time, perhaps you don't realise. Darling, I miss you so much and am utterly calm in the awareness that you need me just as much.

Tove

MIDSUMMER DAY. –58 [*Helsingfors*]

Darling,

I know you've already heard from Abbe what has happened.

I'm just writing now to let you know Faffan didn't have any pain or anxiety. He didn't know who we were, but he could see pictures on his wall, beautiful sculptures of young men and women.

It all happened terribly quickly, and I'm clinging to the thought that it wasn't too hard for him.

Peo didn't get there in time. I tried to ring him out there, there was no reply, but I finally got through to the pilot station.

It was me who told Peo he could definitely wait until Sunday evening to come. But Faffan recognised Lasse, I could see that.

Ham is calm and intensely controlled. I shall be with her until after Faffan's funeral.

And my request to you now, my darling, is to stay calmly on our island – that's the most important thing you can do and the one that will help me most. I shall come to you, as long as you don't mind a little wait.

Let me hug you close

Tove.

WED. 25 JUNE. [*Helsingfors*]

Darling Tooti,

It's reassuring to know you're holding onto the summer for me out there. Next week – maybe even early next week – I'll be coming back with Ham. It feels the rightest thing we can do.

We've talked quite a lot about control in general, and about Ham's self-control. Right now, it's the most dignified thing I've ever seen – and not gloomy, but glad.

She is finding it terribly hard. They must have loved each other more than I properly understood. That was underlined again when we opened Faffan's boxes yesterday evening. Such moments aren't easy, as you know. But Ham made it into something positive – not horribly emotional. Touching, one might say. He had kept such an incredible amount. And most of it was to do with the rest of us –

Viktor Jansson, Tove's father, died on 22 June 1958.

and then restaurant bills from occasions he'd enjoyed – plus other stuff, you know, the kind of things boys have in their pockets. No Secrets. He had none. His outer life was as transparent and simple as his inner one was complicated. Maybe I told you that after Faffan was on the island last summer, the two of us exchanged letters more personal and warmer than any we'd written before.

You can imagine how happy it made me to see that both of us had been carrying those letters in our wallets all year.

The whole studio is full of flowers that people have sent. They've been awfully kind. Kurt came dashing in from Kalvholmen to see us for an hour and was the picture of dejection. Enroth barged in. too, and said bloody hell, what can I say, but he liked Faffan and did we fancy a trip round town in the car to cheer us up. Then he went off with a canvas he'd given us and brought it back a few minutes later, signed and varnished. Everybody here at Lallukka has dropped in for a while, one by one.

But most people are away, of course, and Uca's in Rostock. I only managed a quick word with her on the phone. She thought we were right to have a quiet funeral and avoid a big family get-together afterwards.

Tomorrow is Friday 27th, and the urn is to be interred on Monday.

Lasse has been wonderful and helped me with all the arrangements. It may sound stupid, but it's actually the first time I've felt the support of having a brother. There's such a horrendous amount to do and think about when a person makes their exit.

We put the notice in 2 Swedish and 2 Finnish newspapers, and in the latter we added Impi's name to our own. All the papers have written about Faffan and the Association of Sculptors sent us some huge, bright white carnations. And a wonderful bouquet from the Artists' Guild, through Koroma. And just think, Maija Karma and Aune Mikkonen sent flowers too!

Then we had to write letters to all the relations. Uncle Harald is on a driving holiday in Monaco, Einar is in Karolinska hospital with some sort of injected poisoning but likely to recover, it seems Torsten's wife might have lung cancer.

We haven't been able to get hold of Toini and Meri. And Misan has pneumonia, but is going to be all right.

We decided to ask Paul v. Martens, Lasse's vicar friend, to take the funeral service, and I wrote something for him about Faffan, to help him be more personal and not have to resort to clichés.

We managed, with great difficulty, to persuade Impi to stay at her boarding house. She rang when she got my letter and was completely beside herself. I suppose it will now be a case of making arrangements for her to retire, without hurting her feelings. After all, Ham will have to move from here now, but not for six months, thank goodness. So there's time to arrange everything for an orderly departure.

I asked Lasse if he'd had any thoughts about how he might organise his life in the future. He answered that he would still want some form of joint living arrangement with Ham – which I was delighted to hear.

Hamsie is an unconventional artist's widow – she isn't trying to cling on to everything that reminds her of him; she wants to dispose of as much as possible, and for Faffan's sake she doesn't want to keep any of his substandard work. She's taking a positive and healthy attitude and is able to be very objective.

We went together to look at flowers for the coffin, which is in a very light oak. We chose lily-of-the-valley and violets. We're not having any hymns, just Bach's Toccata and Fugue.

And in the midst of all the bustle, there's a sudden vacuum in which all these arrangements seem so baroque and far removed, so irrelevant – and everything just feels awful and desolate. I really must have loved Faffan terribly dearly, despite his being so difficult.

We've just come home after seeing him for the last time. Tooti, he was shockingly small. He looked very much at peace.

The flowers are continuing to multiply here. Ham is on a constant round of clearing and sorting in the studio, and I'm helping her. She's found a lovely clay head under some rags that haven't been unwound for a long time and now she's trying to rescue it, rework the surface and model it so it can dry without cracking. There are various unfinished things lying around that he hadn't exhibited, they could have been very beautiful.

Abba can have Faffan's gold family watch, we were thinking. I'm sure we'll find a keepsake for you. And I'll get some flowers from you in time for Friday.

You know what, Faffan's watch stopped at the very time he died. Isn't that a strange thing about watches – it often happens, apparently.

Darling, I wanted to write about all this in confirmation of the connection I always feel between us. I shall see you before long, and start working again. And we'll put the roof on and do lots of things together.

I love you so much and you are always my great joy.

Take care of yourself. Ham sends a hug.

Tove.

Enroth: The artist Erik Enroth, presumably also a resident of Lallukka.
Koroma: The artist Kaarlo Koroma.
Maija Karma: Illustrator and lithographic artist.
Aune Mikkonen: Lithographic artist.
Misan: Per Olov and Saga Jansson's adopted daughter.

FRIDAY, BEFORE CHRISTMAS
[*1958, Stockholm*]

Mrs Tossavainen!!

Here we're having a long lazy morning, padding about and talking quietly, the sleeping arrangements are a bit haphazard with people on the floor, and we're trying to be considerate and not rush anyone.

I get up at ½ past 9 in a sleeping house and make coffee, sweep up the most obvious balls of fluff, add a few indecisive lines to my strip cartoons and make a little porridge for breakfast.

Outside there's a vaguely suburban landscape with a mixture of shabby old mansions, elegant Coop stores and bumpy hillocks, mist and melting snow. Inside it's hot, with a mood of fatigue and goodwill.

Ham collapsed as soon as we got over here, a reaction I'd been expecting. She did nothing but sleep and retch, and had a sore throat. She's rather better now.

Einar is much the same. A week before we came he'd had the results of seven years' work, decomposition of nucleic acids (if I've got that right ...) and in the relief of it all he fell ill. So we're taking things nice and quietly.

Lasse is tapping away at his book, Ulla is pottering amiably around and sometimes they play canasta. The time-honoured visits to all parts of the family. And a few Christmas presents from Nk.

Einar insists on cooking dinner, and does so with scientific speed and intensity. The most complicated dishes, in a sort of casual excess and with a sublime nonchalance that would make a frugal housewife blanch. Ulla does the washing up, in similar fashion.

They are living together in a new and very charming way and seem to have solved their family problems.

This whole atmosphere ought to be a complete rest cure, just what one needs after all the complications of the autumn. Yet oddly enough I find I can't slip into it but feel restless and troubled in some indefinable way.

I'd very much like to be at home and working, dug into my usual old rut. It's a reaction that makes me feel ungrateful, and I'm doing all I can to help it pass.

I expect it's more or less how Uca felt when she'd gone to such efforts to gather all the family for a peaceful and enjoyable Christmas and then the whole of Christmas Eve was as black as night. I'm not as black as night, of course. But feeling tense and anxious all the time – as if on the wrong train.

Now, though, I'm off into town to buy Christmas tree decorations, so perhaps it will pass.

The others want to go to Ängsmarn, the first stretch by car and then by horse-drawn sledge across the ice, but I'm worried it will be too much for Einar and Ham. They, however, insist on showing how hale and hearty they are, so my cautious attempts to deflect them from the rigours of settler life have gone unheeded.

By now you'll have told everything to Mamu Pietilä in her rocking chair, she'll have noted your successes with satisfaction but also observed that you're as thin as a rake and cooked you lots of Christmas fare.

Did you get there all right with all your things? Were the last days very hard going? You know what, Anu's pills were marvellous. There was a brisk wind, but we were fine – though they did make us feel a bit odd.

I shall write again and let you know how our touring production is progressing.

Look after yourself. A big hug from

Your Tooosla.

... yes, yes!

– and I was rooting through my bag when what should I find but something exclusive, filled with the sweet scent of violet – and I sent such grateful thoughts to Tooti who is so fond of me, she said presumptuously! Thank you!!

"Troll in the Wings", directed by Vivica Bandler, had its premiere in 1958 at Lilla Teatern (Little Theatre) in Helsinki. In the spring of 1959 the production went on tour, first to Åbo (Turku) – where it proved a hit – and then to Stockholm, where it was staged at the Casino Theatre. The dress rehearsal failed to come alive and the opening night was initially chaotic, but the play had brilliant reviews, except in *Dagens Nyheter*.

TUESDAY MORNING
[*Postmark 12.5.1959. Stockholm*]

Darling Tooti,

If you knew how many letters I've written to you in my head – and only now, at eight in the morning on our opening night, am I starting a real one.

What's more, I'm currently in such a total state of terror that this won't be remotely like the letter I would have sent on any of those other days.

I think about you all the time.

Alas and alack, Tooti, they don't seem to have understood our play here in Stockholm. Åbo was a clear and emphatic success, you see, a long and exhausting merry-go-round, but enchanting – whereas here I'm starting to wonder if everything hinges on the different mentalities on the two sides of the Gulf of Bothnia. We had the dress rehearsal last night with the management of the Casino and various actors in the audience – and everything just sort of froze. I don't know what went wrong: the acting was perfect, the scenery didn't collapse, the special effects worked and nobody had hysterics – but there was this wave of polite incomprehension from the auditorium. And the actors' mood sank into their boots, of course – they'd got used to sailing on the wave of success in Åbo and had been so cheerful and confident. We'll have to see how it goes this evening.

I shall go over there again shortly with a drop of cognac and a couple of tranquillisers in my stomach, and then we'll spend the whole day trying to make some kind of mainland-Swedish connection.

If I'm suddenly summoned by phone and have to dash straight there, you'll get the letter as it is – but I shall go on writing for as long as they leave me in peace.

The trip to Åbo was a delight – Packis entertained us the whole way, so safe and secure in his ingenuity, though I did succumb to the H:fors tummy bug at one point and felt terribly queasy. It had eased a bit by the time we'd installed ourselves and charged straight off to the theatre.

They hadn't done a <u>single</u> thing there and the scene shifters were hanging about in that nonchalant way only scene shifters (and sometimes waitresses) can. I rang Wolle and got some good advice: lots of coffee and buns and jallu.

I wasted no time getting hold of some three-star and two full baskets of refreshments from Aschan. After that, work was soon underway – and an hour later we realised we wouldn't have to ring Uca with a tale of disaster – but that things would sort themselves out eventually.

I was soon so popular behind the scenes that all I had to do was dart a look of concern in some direction and the lads would come rushing over to ask what they could shift for me. They really were terribly sweet, and by the time Uca turned up the next morning most things were in place.

I only managed to see Wolle for an hour at a café. But we spent quite a long time with Mamu and Papu – and I could tell it was a <u>really</u> successful visit. Ham found your parents absolutely delightful – and the feeling seemed to be mutual. You've no idea how exquisitely they'd arranged it all, with herring and soured milk and fish salad, fruit and mead and coffee with loads of cakes and stuff. We spoke a funny mixture of three languages – but with pace and conviction, and the contact was always there. Your parents really are quite lovely, you know! And this time I got a much more rounded picture of Papu Pietilä – he has such irresistible charm!

The next day the scenery rigmarole continued. Thanks to the vast space where the stage could lose itself in magical shadows against the curved backcloth, we were able to put together wonderful sets for Acts 1 and 2. The theatre was chock-full, and what an audience!!!

The ensemble acted better than ever, it all flowed along with a sweeping rhythm that was irresistible – especially in the later performance.

And they seemed almost happy to be working.

Afterwards there was a little party at the Swedish Club, all in the same easy-going spirit, though they wouldn't let us meet the theatre folk themselves, only the management and bigwigs.

The morning after, Uca, Packis, Ham and I flew back to Sweden with the scenery. The Helsingfors bug made its presence felt again and I was in such a wretched state I could hardly walk straight when I got off the plane and couldn't even carry my flowers! (+ being on my period didn't help of course).

At the Aero terminal, three enthusiastic women rushed up and launched themselves at us. It was Lisbeth, Sewe and Edna, who'd come down to meet us. The whole party went to our hotel (and it <u>was</u> the Örnsköld in Nybrogatan) where I treated us all to cognac. (To Uca's mild disapproval). Then we went gadding off to the Casino where we had to wait three hours for anyone to turn up and set the whole thing in motion. (the result of a misunderstanding – that crucial theatre word!) Packis had a terrible asthma attack because they'd mixed the paint with casein or ammonia or some other infernal additive. I wasn't feeling well, and we had none of what we needed – the theatre, by the way, is utterly charming in its colour, proportions and atmosphere. It was only when we found a wonderful curtain – a silken "patchwork quilt" in glorious colours (unused for the past ten years) that we started feeling hopeful again.

We toiled all day to get the set and the technical side sorted out, and in the evening it was finally time to eat. Uca, Ham, Packis,

Lisbeth and I walked to Catteline – where we had several hours of complete peace and hopeful relaxation.

The next morning the actors came thronging in, and all day we had the same sort of muddle as I try to describe in the play. And then, as I told you, came the disastrous dress rehearsal ...

Now I'm going to walk over there again with God and the muse in my thoughts – and you, too!

If I come home covered in shame, I hope you'll still like me just as much, nonetheless.

Take me in your arms – and look after yourself, darling. I'll write as soon as I've seen how things are going. Ham sends her regards! Let me have a few short words on how things are going on <u>your</u> merry-go-round.

Mrs! Tooslan

Packis: Harry Packalén, Lilla Teatern's expert in technical matters.
jallu: Full name *jaloviina*, a brandy with a certain percentage of cognac, indicated by a star rating.
Aschan: A large café and cake shop in Åbo.
Lisbeth: The actress Lisbeth Bodin, from Sweden.
Catteline: Restaurant Cattelin in the Old Town.

13.5.59. [Stockholm]

Darling Tooti –

We did it! Excellent reviews across the board – except in Dagens Nyheter where that waspish Ebbe Linde was full of complaints.

The last twenty-four hours, after the dress rehearsal, were spent in deep dejection on all sides, spats and more rehearsals and, actually, most of what I attempt to depict in the play.

Uca and Lisbeth had some miserable spats, I had stomach cramps and my usual curtain of silence, you know, Packis had his asthma and the head of lighting was in fits of despair. We entirely rebuilt the set and even the cleaning lady was in tears.

So everything was just as it should be! We barely had time to get to the hotel to wash off the worst of the grime we'd accumulated since 8 in the morning and get changed.

When the audience flooded in, almost my entire extended family turned out to have bought tickets – even Torsten came hobbling along on his stick!

To begin with, absolutely everything went wrong and I felt the queasiness rising in my throat. The train record that Emma was supposed to try out behind the curtain just wouldn't play. It was Bisse who saved the situation with a clever improvisation – the play started, but right away a scenery flat painted with roses fell over with a crash. Soon after that, Lasse tripped over a bucket and almost fell down into the auditorium. He took quite a knock and found it really hard to recover his concentration.

Or so he said later – I thought he was as brilliant as usual. But after that they got underway, thank goodness – and I assume the audience thought all the mishaps were part of the play.

I prowled around aimlessly as usual, feeling churned up – but gradually realised the audience was really enjoying the performance, which calmed me down a bit. After the final curtain there was lots of hugging and kissing on stage and the whole lot of us went off to the bar at the Royal Dramatic Theatre for the customary steak with schnapps and wine. And in due course back to the theatre to read the reviews. Between 4 and 5 we all went our separate ways and the Pöystis, Ham and I walked home to the hotel. En route we bumped into a couple of young hooligans who wanted to make trouble, ruining Lasse's flowers and waving knives around. It was pretty unpleasant and they stayed hot on our heels all the way back, jeering that if Lasse's "white-haired ma" hadn't been at his side there wouldn't have been much left of him. Lasse said afterwards, slightly apologetically: I'm sure you understand I couldn't get into a fight because I hadn't got a knife ...

And today, there were various odd types milling about in search of interviews and all those other things people suddenly want, or can make money from ... you know, the inevitable chaff that blows in from all directions after an event. Uca is helping me deal with the many things that reduce me to panic, so I think we'll acquit ourselves decently. There are so many details to tell you – but very little opportunity to do it. But we'll have time, soon, to talk about everything that has happened to us while we've been apart.

At any rate, Mrs Tossavainen won't be returning home covered in shame, which is very nice indeed!

A big, big cuddle from your Toooosla!

Bisse: The actress Birgitta Ulfsson.
Lasse: The actor Lasse Pöysti.

STOCKHOLM, 20.5.59.

Darling Tooti,

Thank you for your latest letter, letting me know about the new turn of events.

It really is uncanny that every time you have to make important decisions and are finding it hard – I'm away on a trip.

Perhaps it was meant that way, and the part of your life that affects you most closely – your work – is something you have to make your own decisions about, not be influenced by anyone else. But I feel sad not to be with you when you're finding things so tough.

I've read your letters very carefully – and can detect that you stuck to the same strict line throughout. And a sensible one. If today, in spite of everything they've done to you, you decide not to abandon your students yet – I still think you can claim to have stayed on the path of self-respect. My own darling, you know I follow you in everything that happens as closely as if it applied to my own life, for you are a part of me.

We'll soon be with each other again and can go and celebrate at Salme's in the old familiar setting. I'm not feeling as homesick as I did last time, because this is a work trip.

Most of the people I have to meet, I'm seeing because of the theatre. Thanks to my play, which has proved a real success (can it really be possible ...) with almost full houses and a captivated audience, both Vivica and the ensemble have been able to make important new contacts here in Sweden. (But – "my play" depends at least as much, if not more, on brilliant directing, good music and actors who are getting better with every day that passes)

Anyway, I'm sharing the responsibility by willingly having meetings with everyone of potential use to the theatre. So I won't be coming home until the end of this week – on a Monday flight at the latest. I don't quite know yet.

Bredskär – you and Bredskär are within reach and the thought makes me happy – if the manager of the Casino, Järrel, and Marianne Höök had arranged their *parties* for the start of the week I'd be leaving right away. Ham is dealing with the relations and generally taking care of herself, glad to be with Einar and walking her own streets.

Nita was here for a few days, so Lisbeth had to move from Uca's room to Huddinge. We had major ghost dramatics that I'll tell you about sometime when we're lying on a sunny rock looking out over glittering blue water. Ah Tooti, do we really appreciate how lucky we are ...?

Then Uca's mother came over – and today it's Irja. They <u>can't</u> leave Vivica in peace. But she receives them all with a brusque kind of affection that Lisbeth can't comprehend.

There was a ghost party at Huddinge – I'll tell you about that later, too.

Inger, who is still sick in bed, sent flowers for the opening night. I sent a letter of thanks, and will try to make time to visit her. I don't stay up all night any more, I can't cope with as much partying as the rest of them.

Opportunities are crowding in on all sides, it's too much, and in the end one just stops, and sits in the hotel thinking, not calling anybody at all. I met up with Börje, and rang Jürgen who hasn't found time to see me yet. Bought spark plugs. Publishing house breakfast and journalists. The play has been shown on TV. Haven't bought any presents for myself except the bluest necklace you've ever seen. I'm being made a great fuss of, and it's fun, but not important. I often think about packing for Bredskär and wonder how the lettuce is coming on. And I'm longing to chop some wood.

A huge embrace from your Tove.

Salme: Salme Sevelius, a good friend of TJ and Tuulikki Pietilä.

Järrel: Theatre manager and actor Sven Järrel.

Jürgen: Jürgen von Konow was an artist, a friend of TJ's, and they had attended the Technical School together in the early 1930s.

Tove Jansson and Tuulikki Pietilä, 1960.

IST MAY 62. THE ISLAND.

Dear Doj!

Here I am now in my supreme springtime solitude – it is rather lovely, but a bit odd without you!

There are great white icebergs bobbing out at the points, looking strange, and I threw snowballs at Psipsu and my aim was really good. She took possession of the island with natural delight, clearly recognised every part of it and headed straight for the chopping block to sharpen her claws. It's very hard to get her to come in and her tail is constantly in a quiver. But at nights she snuggles up close as usual. And there's much rolling on the blue rock ...

At present we're drinking rum toddy and have sawed up a dry fir that blew over E. of the path to the sandy beach. I've excelled myself with the wood chopping and started amassing a pile of knotty Tooti blocks that need attention, and I've gathered twigs from the forest to fill the basket, of course.

The oil spill has avoided the red rocks but edged all the bays around our island in black. The worst things are the clumps of oil-clogged reeds and all the bits of wreckage from the Colaroo. I'm gathering them into piles as best I can and burning them. The sandy beach has been left untouched and has shifted west in the most remarkable way, while the potato patch has vanished into thin air. I suppose I'll have to make a new one.

The boys left the place very neat and tidy (or Kiki?). Abbe, Greta and Max brought me out and had a snifter while the fire got going. We had the little boat in tow but its boards had dried right out and it came close to sinking before we got here. I spent the first night in my sleeping bag because the bedclothes just wouldn't get warm. I kept the stove alight all night.

Now the temperature is normal in here, all the windows are steamed up, and there's a nasty northerly blowing outside. I wonder whether you've been up to anything special – or managed to avoid the awkward Walpurgis Night celebrations and 1st of May entirely. Have the wild Norwegians been letting their hair down? And <u>what</u> is happening at 26 Kaserngatan? I'm so pleased about it that I have to break into a little dance sometimes – just think, your studio! On the same block as mine! I'm finding it hard to believe it's really true.

It's going to be twice as much fun moving in and getting my Serena Castle in order now I know you've got a decent amount of space, too, and are putting up Shelves and feeling happy! Darling Tooti – isn't it great.

And the Awful Numbers will sort themselves out somehow, won't they.

Guess what, a swallow just came sweeping by to take a look at us. [...]

I'm reading Atos's Strindberg book at the moment and it confirms what I already knew, namely that he's brilliant and that I don't like biographies.

I've raked and tidied all round the house outside, the roses have shoots like tiny red dots, but nothing green has dared come up yet. Just a few hepatica leaves ...

The island is sodden, with patches of snow here and there. And I can't get to the supplies of jam until the hatch cover warms up and the wood shrinks.

2.5. See below for a little oil-spill greeting from Psipsina ... I'm dreading the paw prints this summer ...

Last night there was a ferocious wind from the north and I had to go down about 4 in my pyjamas and wellies to rescue the boat. As usual! Sleety snow.

Now it's greyer – but it doesn't matter!

Regards to everybody!

From your cheery Tooooosla

4th May.

And here it just keeps raining and blowing a gale, so I've started painting. As soon as it brightens up even slightly we're out like a shot, Psipsu and I, burning stuff from the wreck and other rubbish caught in clefts in the rock, salvaging seaweed, chopping wood ... and then the Weather sweeps in again from some angry direction and drives us indoors. It's at its most vicious now, from the north, and the whole island is a palette of wet, earthy colours, with splashes of white snow and black oil.

At the northern point of Tunnis, the oil has formed huge pools, and the driftwood is the kind not even our friend from Glosholm

would bother himself with. I made a few minimal heaps and thanked
God for the stocks we've laid in.

But I found pussy willow and alder catkins and the birds were
singing like crazy in the branches. We miss our third Doj. And
neither of us likes *Corned Beef*.

Doj: This was the nickname TJ and Tuulikki Pietilä took to using for
one another – and also their cat – at around this time. There is no
evidence that the word had meaning or special reference beyond its
affectionate sound.

Psipsu: Tuulikki Pietilä's and TJ's cat. Her full name is Psipsina
(Greek for "cat") but she is also sometimes called by other names,
such as Pipsu.

Colaroo: A misspelling on TJ's part. The Swedish cargo vessel the
Coolaroo sank in the Gulf of Finland in October 1961.

Kiki: Kiki Hielm.

Max: Abbe and Greta Gustafsson's son.

26 Kaserngatan: Tuulikki Pietilä moved into this building on the
same block as TJ.

IN 1963, TOVE JANSSON RECEIVED THE FINLAND-SWEDISH
cultural prize awarded by the newspaper *Stockholms-Tidningen* for her 1962 story collection *Det osynliga barnet och andra
berättelser* (published in English as *Tales from Moominvalley*).
Eminent Swedish author Per-Olof Sundman wrote a long
article in the paper under the title "The anger and beauty of life"
(5.2.1963). For the award ceremony, held at the Grand Hotel,
Tove Jansson travelled to Stockholm with Signe Hammarsten.
They also paid a visit to Sankt Jakobs kyrka (St James's church)
in Kungsträdgården Park, where Fredrik Hammarsten had
been the rector.

6.2.63 [*Stockholm*]

Darling Doj,

The official world has finally turned its polite back on me to
concentrate on other topical events – I think.

It feels that way. And it's such an incredible relief that if you didn't know your Toosla inside out you'd think I was ungrateful.

I'm not, not at all.

But has it occurred to you how dangerous it is to constantly be obliged to repeat what one knows – it gets so threadbare! Inevitably the spontaneity goes – and in the end one is nothing but a repetition, a reproduction, a representation.

How sorry I feel for those folk whose job is representation, official limelight people who've deliberately chosen exhibitionist professions. In parenthesis: One repetition that only grows deeper and more intense: I love you. I love you ...

Well, anyway. Just back from an embassy breakfast. Prawns in pears with advocaat. Loads of people, and a hat was the right choice. The hostess wasn't well, but put a brave face on it, insubstantial conversations, keeping things vaguely in the air on all sides, very consciously (except when gentlemen take refuge in, say, fishing and hide in a corner) and a single honest and anxious dorga, an under-secretary something-or-another, who insisted on talking about his divorce.

Then we were rapidly transferred to the Stockholms-Tidningen where I continued expressing my thanks and was rushed through dozens of basements and up and down stairs, where the newspaper presses were spitting out the latest news with a great thunder and crash.

Ham is lying down, a contented wreck. The whole week is fully booked, a worse prospect than the flight in a snowstorm. We waited and hung about in Helsingfors, onto a bus to Åbo, off again, more waiting, sent home, another flight in the evening, rang you, Ham turned grey with travel nerves, we found some tinned food, off again, felt a bit queasy, were welcomed with flowers and a photographer, and taken straight to Dr Näsström's supper party in our snow boots and without our luggage, reached the hotel in the middle of the night.

The next day more radio, but the press conference had been dissolved by the snowstorm, thank goodness.

We padded round Kungsträdgården freezing our socks off and went into Sankt Jakob's where the organ was playing. I don't know what Ham made of it all, she stomped along pluckily with her stick, staggered around the streets of her youth and said very little. We changed into our best and answered the telephone to a string of interviews with the same questions and, God help me, the same answers and then we were shovelled off to the Grand, where a TV crew was lying in wait with its cameras and neon and unprepared questions, and there was a great deal of filming for what I fear were pretty meagre results. It went on until the rest of the party were having their dessert and was brought to a halt by various socially engaged busybodies wanting this that and the other for the Sweden–Finland town-twinning movement, Save the Children, Pro-Peace, the scouts, the library association, collectors of ex libris and every old Tom, Dick and Harry.

Before that I delivered my speech, slowly and impeccably but scared stiff, from the big lectern in the hall with the golden curlicues.

There was a heck of a pause after they handed over the prize, while several hundred ancients, the great and the good of the arts establishment, sat there waiting, and then I finally twigged that the moment was <u>now</u> and not at the dinner (as I'd been instructed), so I didn't even remember to take my crib sheet up with me.

Afterwards it was rather nice for a while. I danced with loads of white-haired barons and commodores and drank loads of whisky and everybody thought I was wonderful, even me – almost.

Then the exhaustion hit Hamsie and I remembered the polite thing is to leave early, so we went.

Early the next morning I was woken by another TV crew wanting a comment on the cultural situation and panicked and blurted out, I regret to say, but I'm flying home any minute now …

I'm not, of course – I've still got masses to sort out with family and cousins and children's culture reps and translators and art galleries and old mymbles.

This is certainly one way to live one's life … and I'm sure there are people who do. I'm feeling pretty cocky but also trying to maintain my image: gentle, cultivated, enraptured child of nature …

They didn't have any of those long-sleeved white nightshirts left, but I've bought a new, earth-shattering shade of eye shadow that makes me look sophistical. And by the way, I dream of islands every night.

You know what, it's exactly like in the Zonta Club, one feels one is occupying a place that could be taken by someone who would do it better and enjoy it more.

What a long and unbroken silence it would take, actually, to be able to seize pictures, and words, by the tail. And you, how many days have you had "to yourself"?

Spring will soon be here, and things will calm down, you'll see. They're tying to lure me back over again for A Thousand Important Tasks – but the only important thing just now is a shoe-and-studio life at a nice slow pace. *Let's do it*.

Regards to everyone. All the best –

Tove.

dorga: This word occurs from time to time in TJ's letters, sometimes with the spelling *dårga*. She uses it in a general, non-pejorative sense for a person of the male gender, young or old.

Stockholms-Tidningen: One of the main Stockholm daily papers.

Zonta Club: An international organisation for professional women.

12.5.63 [*Bredskär*]

Darling Tooti!

It feels all wrong to be here without you. And to know you're feeling lousy (and will have to see the dentist). The fact is that this island needs three shoes. Or any island, for that matter ...

But as it happens, I do feel quite at ease on Bredskär this year, calm and benign. I think it's because all at once I find myself taking the island without ambitions, envy or an owner's sense of responsibility – waiting and not demanding too much, not getting upset about oil spills, broken branches or scuffed up moss, you know.

Just padding about and feeling fine, using my ears, nose and eyes, with comfortably crumpled clothes and my hair a mess. I do what needs doing with a certain leisurely satisfaction.

It's a love affair that has turned into friendship, if you like – after all the violent disappointments and aversions. Funny. Have you read "The Man Who Loved Islands"? How about "The Woman Who Fell in Love with an Island"?

The journey out went well. Psipsu said her goodbyes in all the food shops. At Jungfrustigen an indulgent Peo, paying a Mother's Day visit (oh the darling traditional dårga), was on hand to carry our cases down! Then we were whisked to Borgå at 90 km an hour, at least intermittently, and as usual we honoured Café Succes with our presence. By that point Psipsu was so worked up (she sang her lament on the journey) that she wriggled out of her harness, but instead of running away she climbed onto a chair and sat at the table just like at home, to the Café's delight.

Then we got out the map and compass (Pakarinen sniggered) and were whizzed off to Tirmo. On the way the car ran right over a big adder. And wasn't it just like Pakarinen to stop the car and walk the long way back to see if the snake was dead (it wasn't) and make sure it didn't go on suffering?

Then I had a bright idea and asked whether he felt like coming out to the island with us and going back with Holmberg. Pakarinen leapt at the chance – "haven't seen the sea for ages, and it's Friday today, all day!" [...]

Everything as usual at Viken with coffee, presents, lots of people. Pakarinen most impressed with Abbe's boat which is almost finished now, peering into every corner and wanting to know all about everything.

Out on the island we plied him with cognac, and the luggage (including yours) came up in a trice, carried by three strapping fellows. I hardly had a chance to lend a hand. We shut Psipsu in the guest room and only saw her reaction after the others had gone. She came out, as stiff as a board, stared around her for a long time and then went over to her old sharpening stump and got busy on her claws. She did a circuit of the house, sniffing at everything, eating grass, and after that she was a vanished cat. And happy!

We'd barely got all our kit indoors and taken the little boat round to the sandy beach when the rain started, with great crashes of thunder. Very gratifying.

The wood was soaking wet, the snow must have drifted into the woodshed – and there was so little of it that by the time I'd filled under the stove, the shed was empty. I must have been <u>so</u> angry with my poor island last year – didn't even chop wood! Now I've set to work, and am enjoying it. Again. (thankyougod). For now we'll have to make our fires with the dryish sticks I've found on the beaches round the island.

In a wild burst of energy, Ham has cleaned the stove and the little frigate on the ceiling. She coped well with the journey, blissfully happy, but now she's flagging and spends most of her time dozing. (but still happy)

We fell asleep at 8 the first evening – I was up at ½ 6 this morning. It's so warm here that I haven't even had to get out the oil stove.

Very little seaweed this year, only enough for the potato patch. The big pine on the sandy beach has lost about ten of its thickest branches and looks bald. So that's going to make a good bonfire for you. No more oil has washed ashore, but the old stuff is just as sticky as last year.

The hepaticas are in flower and the willow's got catkins, but nothing else has come up. The "sacred rose" looks a bit peaky.

Today May and Max came out with a pike for us and some roach for Psipsu. I've sunk them in the sound, temporarily.

We couldn't face putting out the proper boat rollers but winched it up on planks and duckboards. I had to lever the hatch cover open with an iron bar. Ah, that was Psipsu "ringing" at the door to come in. It's strange, she seems to remember everything. She slept in my bed, and kicked around in her sand tray last night and woke us up. The strapping fellows had trouble prising your built-in cardboard box from under the bed, but it stayed in one piece, anyway.

The old beds have gone to Viken now. The new ones are first-rate, and your box fits. If you'd like to be able to roll it out when you need to get to your papers, then bring 6 little castors with you. There's room for them.

Bumblebees and butterflies are here already, and the ants formed a caravan to the sweet tin (I've put a tragic stop to it now). All is as usual, only we're missing a Tooti.

How I hope your trip to Sweden is enjoyable – and flu-free – and that moving Mamu goes splendidly!

Goodness only knows when this letter will get on its way – I couldn't believe the youngsters would come out the very first morning! But at least I've been able to talk to you for a while, and tell you how we're getting on.

A big hug and all the very best!

Your Tosla.

P.S. Ham sends you many good wishes. She says it's empty here without you.

[...] 17th.

I'm sending this letter to Mamu's address. Give her my warmest regards! You leave the day after tomorrow, and I'm agog to know how it will all go, with over-organised speeches, discussions and socialising grand-house style or with friends. Merde!

It's utterly silent here and entirely still, unbelievable. No horizon, dead calm.

That rackety outboard motor wouldn't start, though I even studied its instruction book. So I took to the oars and set off on my own to Klovharun.

It took me ½ an hour to row there. The island is larger than I remember it, and the plateau for the house is wider than I recalled. If the shack's going there we won't need to touch the big stone in its decorative black hollow, there'll be room anyway.

Imagine one of the house "legs" on a concrete stilt. That would create a nice cellar space. The pool is nearly always milky white and opaque later in the summer, of course, but at present the water's clear and to my disappointment revealed neither skeletons nor smugglers' liquor, only very ordinary stones! It wasn't even deep.

On the other hand there seem to be a deep hollow or two that could be set up for drinking-water collection and the meadow where we could plant things is a decent size. A big cleft right up on the island would make a lovely plage if one filled it with sand.

And the rock at the harbour inlet is so low and flat that one could easily pull up a boat on duckboards. If we cleared some of the stones we could even get the boat into the pool. At present the water's extremely low and it shows on the beaches ... the vegetation is at its puniest. But in spite of that, it all seemed very hopeful. – There were already gulls' eggs.

A hug and all the very best! Write and tell me about your trip and long for me now and then.

Tove.

May and Max: Abbe and Greta Gustafsson's children.

that rackety outboard motor: TJ's term for it is "baksmälla", a pun on the word normally used for a hangover, which literally means "the crash at the back".

POSSIBLY 10.6.64 [*TJ's approximation of date.*
Bredskär]

Darling Tooti,

As you know, Abbe's telephone has now collapsed for good, so I'm sending this greeting with Lasse and Nita who are off to town to lay in supplies and have a good time.

I miss you constantly and was so glad to get the message that you might come out for midsummer with the ghostses.

It could be a lively séjour, with the overcrowding made up for by the excitement!

What sort of numbskulls are these people who've promised someone else the house Reima and Raili were to have? I'd already slotted them into the archipelago and was looking forward to an impromptu visit now and then – here or at their place. And on Klovharun.

 I haven't been there yet – it's been either gales or fog the whole time. But the building permission and blueprints came out with Abbe & co. one evening and I'm collecting more seaweed for our future plantings and packing the year-old seaweed in boxes, ready to go.

So you're off to Venice in the autumn instead. I assume it would have been too much of a rush at the moment? I wonder if you've got your lithography equipment set up, and how the library looks now. And whether you've already started nosing into the new technique.

Lasse read my book and liked it, changed a few words. He plans to go through it again and mull over whether there are whole sections I could improve. Decent of him.

I've done sketches for the illustrations and will gradually make a start on the more detailed versions. It's a bit tricky because I haven't done any drawing for so long. Have you still got any of that thin paper for use with a radiograpf [sic] pen? It would be great to have some. And more typewriter paper? And a rapidograph pen no. 2 – the broad one.

We celebrated Nita's birthday because she's in Sweden on the actual day – it was a great success with a party in the evening, the accordion and the radio, quite a riot. She liked my yellow *sweater*.

The level in the gallon of whisky is sinking steadily and there aren't that many vodkas left – in confidence, of course. And the house is overflowing as usual and Sophia's energy is all-consuming.

But all is going well – things feel friendly and relaxed all the time and naturally I'm tremendously grateful that there are no atmospheres brewing in any corners. I'm not getting cross about anything – just letting it all trundle on. Long may it last.

And sometimes I cast a lonely glance towards the horizon in the east. Thank goodness they didn't take our dream away from us.

Today I turfed everything out of the tent, it was pretty damp. All the mist – and then a night's rain with a force-sixer from the east. It was like on Klovharun – that time! But it didn't rain in, even though the base of the tent was wet under the mattress.

Psipsu sometimes comes in and sleeps in her chair – especially when Sofia's out. I boiled some fish for Psipsu – and east of Tunnis we got a 3-kilo pike! Lasse has finished the bust of Sophia and I think it's terribly good And really not idealised!

Now he's hard at work on the strips. We do them mostly in the middle of the day when everyone else is asleep.

They've made a new salad patch and are busy sowing and watering. It's looking good. I'm sticking to the potatoes, they're already coming up. I've been collecting sticks in the forest and generally rooting about, glad that it feels good to have "things to do" on the island again, albeit not with the old intensity. After early-morning coffee I quickly get the washing up done and bring in wood and water, then I'm off, leaving the rest of them in peace. A good system. After that I take the day as it comes.

I wrote to Maya that you're in town – have you two met up? Have you run into Pentti? I assume you've seen Vivica. Strange how part of me is always geared towards town whenever you're there.

Right ho – I don't think there's much more to tell you from here. It's all going well – but I do long for you.

I long to be a new settler again, and there's a capsule of yearning for solitude deep inside me, but I can be patient.

And you? How have things been for you in town? I really hope you got into studio life somewhat, through your lithography – being at a loose end around town just now is too hellish, otherwise.

Well – I suppose we'll have to make the best of the situation. Sometimes I think that if we get through this we'll be able to get through anything the future has in store.

You're in my arms and I'm waiting happily to celebrate midsummer with you. Can you ring Pentti, give him my best wishes and let him know that we got permission to build? And my regards to Mamu and Reimas and everybody else!

Kisses,

Tove

PS Make a note of what things cost if you bring anything with you, I'd really like to pay for them. Loads more money has come in.

Raili: The architect Raili Pietilä, Reima Pietilä's wife.
Lasse read my book: TJ was working on *Pappan och Havet* (*Moominpappa at Sea*).
Pentti: Pentti Eistola, a doctor and a good friend. He helped TJ and Tuulikki Pietilä build the big model of the Moomin house.

4.9.65 [*Klovharun*]

Darling Tooti,

A PS to the letter I sent with Sven; he took the Penta with him to sort out and promised to empty it, and he also took the red petrol can but didn't want the tool bag, leaflet or funnel, and we might need those ourselves anyway.

Then I gave him the big milk can and asked him to empty the petrol drum into it, but he wouldn't, even though I explained it was the right mixture. He had a gentleman called Gideon with him, they'd been on Bredskär several hours before it emerged that Nita and Gideon were childhood friends. They came over here at dusk and we had coffee and the vodka they'd brought – and I was able to get some milk for Ham – and then they went off to Kummelskär. The next morning we had Baltic herring, which I'd grilled, on the rocks, and some porridge – and no being sickses.

Ham is properly up and about today, wearing her dress for the first time, but sleeping a lot. I think she'll be able to travel the day after tomorrow. Lasse said yesterday over the Talky Walky that Pentti

Tove and Tooti's cabin on Klovharun.

thought she ought to go back to town, so we've got an authority on our side there.

It was a wonderful day today, so smooth – the whole sea – and sunshine. Yet even so, I'm working, trying to get earnestly into Alice. Practically all the black and white pictures are done, not in their finished form, that is, I want to redo several of them. Next week I shall try to start on the coloured pictures. I wrote to Runnquist to reassure Bonniers and said I wouldn't be sending anything for now. Not until I'm back in town.

Brunström read a piece in Borgåbladet about *Pappan och havet* [*Moominpappa at Sea*] which is evidently out now. All he could tell me was that whoever wrote it "seemed" to like the book and thought adults could read it too.

Lasse & co. dropped in at Viken but there wasn't a soul at home, so they picked mushrooms instead. They're still working away on their windows.

Peo's hardly likely to come out this weekend, I expect they're busy acclimatising to town. We haven't heard anything from the Abbes – it's autumnally empty everywhere, like shutting the door on a party. There's a half-moon, very yellow, and every evening it's as if the island has floated another ten kilometres out to sea. The evening it was still, I lit candles on the verandah.

Did you know Brunström's planning to spend a week here at the start of October and shoot long-tailed duck. Presumably that would be ok? After all, we won't be coming until later. I've already started stowing stuff down in the cellar. It might be a good idea to have our first solo guest as an experiment. And I'm getting everything ready for winter out here.

Sun. Thank you darling Tooti for the fabulous parcel! It made me so happy. I offered Peo a glass of Cap straight away, he turned up with Peter last night. They brought milk and butter too, and lots of post from Bredskär where Abbes had just paid a farewell visit.

Now the damned wind can blow (and it is, by the way) and the rain lash as they will, I'm battened down. And I can get on with my work. Thank you, my darling – for everything, and I've never possessed <u>so</u> many nuts all in one go in my whole life!

They also brought the Gyllings' present, that wonderful clock, and a delightful letter to you and me, which I enclose. I shall write to thank Kaj and Ulla today. I'll send the clock to town with Lasse & co. If you want to take a look at it in the studio (and perhaps have it at yours?), it's in its cardboard case in the box of books. I'm sending a box and a suitcase with Lasse. While you're at it, could you take the two dresses out of the case and hang them up?

The Peos have heard nothing from our cousin's son and Peter reckons the young man is sleeping at his girlfriend's and far from keen to meet up with family. It would be good if he could sleep at Ham's instead, she needs somebody there at nights at the moment.

Oh, and I got the Pappa reviews from Borgåbladet and V. Nyland, benevolently positive and naive, mostly summarising the book "which is suitable for children and adults alike". They hadn't noticed any difference, thought the Moomins were as cosy as ever. Well, that's reassuring in a way.

Peo took the "big boat" in tow when he went, which was good because the water's very low and the inlet is cut off.

I've leafed through all the Finnish crime novels twice but not found Raili's hundred note. So soothing to think that others do silly things with their money, too! And congratulations on finding yours! See, it <u>was</u> in the studio.

To be on the safe side I'm sending a copy of my songs, <u>if</u> Erna hasn't received them there won't be time to send the lyrics later and that would be a pity. Could you ring her one day and ask. It's important, you see, a promise because I never wrote to her on the subject. They were talking about this competition on the radio the other day, it seems to be quite an extensive thing.

I suppose I thought you might find a children's nursery in your studio – thank goodness it was only stuff you could move aside so you could get going on your work. *Good luck* with your "ugly pictures".

Kruskopf asked me to do a Lucifer cover before October but I can't fit it in – so I just wrote and thanked him for the offer. *Moominsummer Madness* is into its third edition in London. And Virkkunen's sent a book of poems called "Älä välitä" with an extremely kind inscription in it.

Right ho – that's about it from here.

Today it's blowing like the devil and I wonder how getting to the mainland tomorrow will go. I feel more and more nervous about having Ham here.

Mon. The wind has died down a bit but the water's still ruffled, and choppy in the sound. Ah, these departures. But once I'm on my own I hope there's a Big Storm – that would be splendid!

Kisses and hugs and say hello to everybody!

Tove.

Sven: Sven Brunström

Talky Walky: TJ's name for the walkie-talkie the family uses to communicate between the islands.

Alice: TJ had been commissioned by Swedish publisher Bonniers to illustrate *Alice in Wonderland*, see Letters to Åke Runnquist.

the Gyllings: TJ's lawyer Kaj Gylling and his wife Ulla.

A copy of my songs: the letter contains three songs, "Gökvisa", "Höstvisa" and "Kärleksvisa" ("Cuckoo Song", "Autumn Song" and "Love Song").

Erna: Erna Tauro, pianist, composer and long-time collaborator with TJ.

Kruskopf: Erik Kruskopf, art critic.

IN AUGUST, TOVE JANSSON IS TOLD SHE IS TO RECEIVE THE Hans Christian Andersen Award, and she plans a trip to Ljubljana with Tuulikki Pietilä to receive it. See Letters to Signe Hammarsten Jansson 29.9.1966.

See Letters to Signe Hammarsten Jansson 29.9.1966.

HARUN 26.8.66

FINE WEATHER AND LIGHT SSW WIND

Darling Tooti,

So I <u>have</u> been decorated, finally, after all those Tomtebo prizes with their china plaques. Please let this be the kind that I can wear! I was really, genuinely pleased, especially once I'd talked to you and realised it wasn't some petite fantasie the Yugoslavians had invented, which would barely amount to more than wretched speeches and interviews to drive me out from Harun.

Of course we shall go to Ljubljana and then on to the Biennale, Makkonen is busy applying for travel grants from some kind of ministry – by plane, she said – and then we've got my foreign currency account, of course. And our summertime golden handshake from Gylling. I told Ham the minute I hung up. The whole house was awfully interested.

How to combine it with the forty-year-olds is not something I'm taking terribly seriously, this trip certainly has to be considered Important. And naturally one ought to stay a week or 10 days when one has travelled so far, eh? What had you been thinking of – longer? [...]

It made me feel sad, leaving you in town – very unnatural to come to the island without you.

When we got to Viken they were having the engagement dinner, with a giant pike almost ready, so Cay brought me over at high speed to be back in time for it.

Ham was sitting there all ready with her luggage of course but they'd given up waiting for me and had just let out the cat, which had been shut in the loft all day. Pipsu's been wildly jealous of Pelle so they've had to take it in turns for an airing, and every time your cat had to stay inside it spat and fought like a tiger. And Sophia was going through a phase of severe Mayavanni phobia so I'm sure they were glad when I turned up. Dashed into the forest and shouted and my cat came like a shot.

Then I yelled that I had crayfish with me, Sophia shouted party! and Mother, cat and rotten roach put to sea and headed at great speed to Harun, where we were tossed ashore any old how.

I'd scarcely cleared up a bit and got the table laid (the lanterns were under my bed!) before the Bredskär crew arrived, all dressed up and pleased with themselves, with roses in silver paper. I gave them a quick account of the consecration of the church and other adventures before the crayfish were served, the schnapps was poured and the lanterns lit – and then we spotted a boat with an outboard motor heading towards us. In a sort of gloomy panic we guessed it might be Nybondas, Assendelft, even Olsoni – but in fact it was Abbe, Greta and Max with a bunch of sweet peas and a lot of confused blather about the Yugoslavian Nobel Prize for children. Very surreal. As was the party that followed.

Miraculously there seemed to be enough crayfish for everybody – and watermelon, and the vodka circulated and a half bottle of cognac and I think they went on until 1 o'clock.

Nita was extremely lively and chatty, but calm. She told us about her more dubious relatives and acquaintances and Viken's eyes were on stalks.

Among other things she gave them a detailed description of the party and delivery when Sophia came into the world with champagne and a Caesarean, amniotic fluid and all the rest. Sophia trumpeted merrily throughout, and spent most of her time enquiring about the sex of the crayfish, absorbing Ham's quiet disapproval of the females.

And it was hardly surprising that Ham was a bit quiet. I found out the next day that she's had some gastrointestinal bleeding and a letter from Harald saying Einar had to be taken from Ängsmarn to hospital by emergency ambulance and things were looking very bad. And even worse the way Harald's described it, his language is as black as night.

Torsten has sent his net and in my thank-you letter I asked him to write and tell us how Einar is doing and what's wrong with him.

Well, the night was as dark as pitch and there was a stiff wind so we put the family to bed wherever there was space, I recited my protest song of course and everyone went to sleep except Nita, who sat there with the last candle, her hat hanging down the back of her neck, frowning as she recited protests to herself.

The next day it was a complete muddle, but very good-natured. Lasse toyed with the idea of going over to fetch his comic strips, but in the end they all embarked before breakfast in a heavy sea.

It's been blowy ever since, to varying degrees, angry gales from the NW – and it's only today that we've suddenly got fine weather. Ham and I took up the cat net without difficulty, around 30 roach and they were much needed. Even the saithe was starting to smell. That fish cage is rusting to pieces by the way, you barely have to touch it and a whole row of mesh breaks. I spent an hour mending it with twine and heaven knows how it will fare if the wind gets up again. Maybe I'll make a new cage – somehow.

Ham's bleeding has stopped, thank goodness.

The day we had to go over to Viken for the telephone she came with us in Lasse's boat, there was a very strong swell and it was rather a wet crossing – especially on the way home. We had to climb ashore on the SW side of Harun where it was quite tricky putting in through all the shallows.

Lasse, Sophia and I went on a grand mushroom hunt in the forest next to the village, all the way over to the big boggy area, and the child coped very well and was cheery and agreeable. Over two hours of trackless forest, mainly to Faffan's mushrooming places. We found lots, it was just like it used to be and I really enjoyed myself. Lasse's wonderfully patient with his daughter and they seem to get on tremendously well together. Well, you know that.

Meanwhile Ham made her way to the Laxvarpet forest with the dog and investigated her own mushrooming places with good results, but a bit unsteadily, toppled over and lay there in the moss for a while to get her balance, and Sessan went hysterical with worry and the urge to help, licking her and barking and carrying on.

So there's been lots of mushroom cooking and out here we've dried a big batch of ceps. [...]

In between I'm trying to write a presentation for Yugoslavia with the help of bits out of that speech I'd luckily copied into the Fact Book. That speech you came up with. It's hard going and not altogether agreeable, as is the couplet that Monica Nielsen insists on having partout after I refused to budge over Bisse. Hah hah. Oh well.

I've done the washing, Ferrexed the ring bolts on the signal mast, mended the tent. Ham stitched all the verandah mats together into one, and now it stays more or less in place in the wind, cut up a few cartoon strips and sprayed the greenfly on the flowers with DDT. It's more peaceful round the islands now, hardly any boats any longer.

Tomorrow it's Saturday, so maybe someone will turn up and I can send this leter back with them. I do wonder what Pentti decided.

The cat has just turned up and is yowling for food. Warm wishes to our friends and a big hug. I miss you, everything's a bit wrong without you. Apart from that we're fine, things are companionable and serene.

I wish you well!

Tove.

Tomtebo prizes with their china plaques: TJ had won the Nils Holgersson Plaque in 1953 and the Elsa Beskow Plaque in 1958. The children of Tomtebo were characters in Beskow's picture books.

Mayavanni phobia: TJ's friend Maya Vanni –see Lettters to Maya Vanni, p.423..

Monica Nielsen: An actress and singer from Sweden.

9 AUG 67 [*Klovharun*]

Darling Tooti,

Thank you for your lovely presents – sea and psychology – very us! It's fine, calm birthday weather, Ham is deadheading the old velvet roses that were fatally battered by Sjöberg, Nita's washing her hair and Lasse's down in the inlet with his daughter tied to a mooring rope, teaching her to swim. It's as if there never was a storm. […]

As soon as you had vanished in a strange direction we heaved all the boats into mummun maha, moored the little boat fore and aft with its nose into the wind in the inlet and pulled everything up from the shore. Then we tidied the cottage after all that partying, I threw a glass of water over the pelargonium but Nita shrieked oh no! and it turned out to be her discreet morning vodka, but the pelargonium's been flowering hysterically ever since.

The storm came in fast and of course the family got all worked up and took delight in disaster as usual. Lasse and I rushed round looking at the breakers, the usual waterfalls started up and the inlet turned into a torrent. Before we knew it the water was up to the sauna and there was the usual boat business, ropes tangling in all directions until the whole ravine looked like a spider's web. By the time it was over, the waterfalls over the eastern rocks were so violent that we couldn't get out to the little boat. Nita was determined to jump in and rescue it and went on about it all day, and it was very hard to stop her without losing one's temper.

Nita is strong, willing and brave but has no sense of judgement. As long as the storm was just a normal August storm, the boat just bobbed around nicely, but when we got up to force eight such huge waves were breaking over it that it filled with water and capsized.

We ran down to the inlet with a boathook but oars, duckboards and bailers were heading out on the midstream current in a dead straight line. We had already tried to haul in the fish cage but the cable had got twisted round the shackle – so off that went, too, and with it hundreds of seasick roach. I soaked the herring we had from Brunström and boiled them up, and once Pipsu had worn herself out yowling she chewed off a few tails and got some chatka as a reward. Absolutely no reward for that animal today, though, because it ate some of the yellow buntings who arrived in a big flock for a family reunion on the verandah. But the cat net is in the sea at last.

I've never seen such a sea on Harun before. It rose as high as the chopping block and came halfway up the sauna stove. The floor started floating away. The outer cellar was full of frantic frogs and the waves brought the full chaos of Sjöberg breaking over us, right up to the bare rock outside the cottage. The spray beat against the panes like whiplashes and ran down the windows like it used to in butcher's shops in the old days.

We felt so sorry for you, missing out on the ghastly majesty of it all, but you wait and see, we're bound to get even bigger and better storms on this island, you wait and see! The first day we just gave ourselves over to the experience – and then came the radio reports of all those missing at sea.

Thank goodness Reima's family weren't caught up in the wretched business, we heard from Abbe's lot that they were out in their boat. But by Sunday the only remaining shadow for us was the little boat flipping over and over in the inlet, first its sides and then its keel in the air. Nita continued her slow and muddled deliberations on swimming out to get it. Ham told the story of Jonah in the belly of the whale and other Old Testament tales. The house was full of wet clothes. I sat for a while on the bench in the sauna, writing Pappa's memoirs with the waves splashing around me, trying to brace the roof every now and then and moving the soaps higher up. But then I just sat and looked at the little boat, which had pulled free of its aft moorings and was bashing against the rocks. The whole building was vibrating.

Sophia kept on counting to fifty and Nita persisted in weighing up her swimming prospects. Just before it got completely dark, the wind veered round to the north and Lasse said right, I'm going to bring the boat in now. Poor Nita wasn't allowed to go with him so she crept under a blanket and stayed there. Ham sat at the window with Sophia who was screaming and crying my wonderful daddy, and he picked his way carefully between pools and inlets, fished the rope out with the boathook and started to tow the boat round. It was dead heavy of course, and I had to get into the water down under the rock and receive the great pudding when it arrived. We took it across the broken rocks into the maha and on up under the jetty behind the tent. So then there were more wet clothes on the breadpole.

When we got inside, something new had happened. Sophia's tooth had come out, to general delight, and been put under Ham's bolster so a Spanish rat could come for it in the night and give her some coins in exchange. (rats are a bit dangerous so she didn't dare have it under her own pillow) We lay in a row across the floor and stoked up the fire. All the firewood was wet of course, but that tarry timber burnt well, anyway.

Around 2 o'clock I went out and shone a light on the boats. There was still a storm raging in the cleft and the little boat was trying to get into the sauna. The only rope I could find was the one fastened round the woodshed roof. By the time I'd fixed the problem there were even more wet clothes in the cottage. A section of the gunwale got smashed in the inlet, it was all rotten, but otherwise the boat is unharmed and more dear to us than ever.

The next day we had a normal storm, and it was the day after before we could get over to Bredskär to see what damage Sjöberg had done. We had already seen through the binoculars that the boathouse was gone. Ham stayed on Harun, voluntarily. (!?) We found the metal boat skewed across the beach (a new and perfect sandy beach) and entirely full of sand and seaweed. The door of Sophia's playhouse had been smashed in by the wind and the boathouse was non-existent, just a few broken ends of metal piping left in the water. What a shame ... Lasse worked so hard on his boathouse! Yet Sjöberg hadn't laid a finger on a deckchair and an inflatable rubber mattress, they were still lying on the sand. Walked round the island, unmentionable debris but nothing interesting. Suddenly a helicopter came flying in low and circled the island, then rapidly came in to land on the smooth rock in front of the house, a chap leapt with the engine still roaring and the propeller shaking the rose bushes, wrote the island's name and ours on his list and then took off again. The Abbes came in to land at the same time, alarmed because they'd seen the helicopter put down on Harun too and feared disaster. We had coffee indoors and chatted away about the storm to get it out of our systems before we parted again, and we islanders did a quick sprint round Tunnis to scout for all the gear from the little boat. But the only thing we found was the sculling seat. Perhaps the rest was hidden under the enormous banks of seaweed.

When we got back (with one blue boot, a strange machine and a broom, the rest was nothing but firewood for the next five years, but we left that) Nita had thrown out her most putrid food, found her beer and neatened up the old roses. So we pushed off to Harun, back to a dreadfully agitated Ham and a yowling cat.

Today I've had to keep restarting my writing on account of the great clear-up of all the chaos before the Viken lot arrive, and Sophia's arithmetic exercises. Lasse's working on his book, oblivious to it all. He's fantastic. Ham was retching a bit – she'd aired out all the rugs while we were on Tunnis and cleaned the stove and all the copper. Just now I made 2½ litres of coffee for all the guests – and found I'd used seawater, which some kind relative had fetched in.

So it's all a glorious muddle here, as you can tell, but a genial one. Tomorrow we'll all have been living here together for a week, and we've coped well.

But I am longing to get down to work. Not play about any longer – but work.

Longing for you a little as well. Maybe you'll turn up with Reima & co, that would be nice. Greetings to everybody who matters and lots of love to you

from Tove.

Sjöberg, Sjöberg's chaos: Gales and storms were known by the name of Sjöberg, meaning literally "sea mountain", but the word also sounds like a surname.

mummun maha: Finnish for "Grandmother's belly", i.e. a sheltered place.

The storm came in fast: A violent storm raged during the weekend of 6–8 August 1967. People caught unawares out at sea were still missing on the Monday evening.

chatka: Tinned crab.

writing Pappa's memoirs: TJ is working on *Muminpappans bravader* (*The Memoirs of Moominpappa*).

breadpole: A pole traditionally running along under a cottage ceiling for the storage of crispbread, baked in rounds with a hole in the middle.

View from Tove Jansson's studio in Helsinki by Tuulikki Pietilä, 1958.

18.1.68 [*Helsingfors*]

Hello there, Doj –

Shall I give up on this awful writing paper? Ola rang today and has read my book in its final form. He thinks it's good and is going to send it for typesetting before long. Isn't that great! But they're not printing it until the summer, for publication sometime in September. Prolle's doing the cover and will get a proper fee for it. The format won't be standard paperback but a few mm. bigger than *Pappan och havet* [*Mooominpappa at Sea*], no pictures.

The post office returned the letter – it was lying in your hall – with the rec. for the picture of the president.

I was pleased to hear that you are working and feel comfortable and that the lilies of peace are fluttering over Cité des Arts. Maybe your etching table has arrived by now? I know how excited you must have been at the prospect of the flood and how disappointed when the water started going down again!

Of course we'll go and buy curiosities in the Chinese shop and scoot off to the Musée de Cinema, I shall go down and buy provisions in your local quarter, and wine – oh Tooti, guess what I've gone and done: embarked on a teetotal spell! A <u>complete</u> strike. I was so fed up with myself after the Aili session that went on until 3 in the morning and was followed by such a mournful and unproductive day that I decided to give up all my sundowners and shots of schnapps while I work and dinner vodkas and see whether I felt less tired and a bit brighter in the bonce. After five days' abstinence I honestly can't feel a thing, except for a slight headache that wasn't there before. Oh well, alcohol dilates the veins and nicotine contracts them. Maybe one's vices cancel each other out, in the end. But I shall carry on now, for the sake of my self-esteem if nothing else. And who knows, it might make me more beautiful. I lugged the juicing machine over here and I gulp down a jug of the stuff daily, my throat must be crawling with vitamins.

Oh yes, I managed to get your mattress across the attic and up onto the sleeping platform, fear of Christmas lent me terrifying powers. As soon as I received the Odd Door and the new mattress I'd ordered, I took yours back (with help). I borrowed it so I'd have room for Harald and family.

I'm painting constantly now, and spend the evenings groaning over my tax return, a vast number of letters, a trademark for the Haarla company and Toffle television. All the yellows and pinks in the book have got to be repainted to make them stand out better, and they want extra pictures and text.

Today Reima turned up with a new builder and I took them to the attic to ponder the party wall, using my own keys that I'd cunningly obtained. The irate caretaker refused to give me the key to his side of the attic even though we've held half a dozen conferences up there, for which I had to borrow it from his wife while he was out and run like lightning to get a copy made at Högbergsgatan. This magistrate business seems pretty all encompassing. If that doesn't work, it'll have to be referred to the Court of Appeal. Voi maailman kaikkisuus. It worries me that Reima won't hear of a reasonable fee. It feels wrong! Can't you talk some sense into him next time you happen to be writing? The phasing out of Moomin products in Finland is going to plan. You can bet Kuukoskis have no objection to that! Production of figures at Oy Muumineitis has also ended, and without any awkwardness. Their trolls were silly – and of course the name of the shop made people think they originated from me.

It's still abnormally chilly here. That Jungfrustigen cold germ is on its way back. Lasse takes Sofia to playschool in Fabriksgatan every morning before 9 and goes to fetch her at 1. She comes home with a big smile and lots of terrible little paper cut-outs and things covered in glue. An excellent establishment. They're spending this weekend with Börje and family so Ham will come to me if she's up to it.

21st. Ham, Lasse and family, and Penttina came round to the studio for some meat soup. They've all gone now. I served them schnapps, wine and whisky without drinking anything myself, it certainly feels ridiculous.

I shall eventually try a drink, it's getting harder. Or perhaps not? What do you think? The worst of it is that without my vodkas I can't find anything I particularly feel like orating on or telling stories about. Perhaps that's a good thing?

Uca was here for a few days again, a dejected couple of hours together. Nice and cheerful to begin with, but then the whole bundle of regrets comes out, Kirsten and middle age and Villagatan and the lack of interest here at home – no offers. At least she likes the theatre job in Oslo, that's hugely important. Then I went and put my foot in it, of course. There were the usual lamentations about how cruel Kerstin was – and then I expressed my fervent hope that Uca might get away from "that horrible Kirsten" at last! It was really awful. First an interminable black silence – and then! But I stuck to my argument that since Kirsten obviously says and does horrible things all the time, one is allowed to call her horrible, and that a touch more brutal honesty can only do us both good.

Then the roof fell in and Vivica said accusingly that in that case I hadn't been honest but untruthful up to now. Well, you can imagine. She was never going to mention Kirsten again. Which would be jolly nice, of course. I felt very tired and downcast on the way home.

I really don't know if it would be any fun ending our trip in Oslo. What's more it doesn't seem at all definite that Vivica will be there in May. Sometimes I wonder whether I should make the Uca visit sometime in February to get the wretched thing out of the way. And a couple of days with Bitti on the way back. They've been asking for so long. One could of course start the Paris expedition with them – but then I wouldn't get my boat trip!!!???

There's been a great rumpus about the art commission, cuttings enclosed. But it's very obvious, thank goodness, that you had no appetite whatsoever for the whole thing and are away anyway. An invitation from Oittinen, the Minister of Education, was lying in your hall today but doesn't need an answer. No other post of any importance.

Valovirta, the dentist on your staircase, has bought 2 pictures from me, one big and one little. And one night the temperature shot up from −17° to 0. Peculiar climate.

Did I tell you Ham has given me a new Little Boat, which is standing ready in Abbe's shed? A birthday present. Shall we let Sophia have the old one so she can learn to row?

Now I'm going to bed with Pipsu round my neck. All the very best, my darling. And guess what, I've _finally_ found the bill of sale for my studio. What a _relief_.

Tove.

Ola: Ola Zweygbergk, head of the publishing house Holger Schildts Förlags.

my book: *Bildhuggarens dotter* (*The Sculptor's Daughter*).
the Haarla company: A papermill that had commissioned a logo from TJ.
Toffle television: In 1968, TJ was doing illustrations for a new TV version of *Vem ska trösta knyttet?* (*Who Will Comfort Toffle?*).
Voi maailman kaikkisuus: These Finnish words rather poetically express the sentiment "Oh what a world". TJ was perhaps quoting an expression favoured by Tuulikki Pietilä.

TOVE JANSSON HAD PLANNED TO VISIT VIVICA BANDLER IN Oslo and Bitti Fock in Stockholm before she went to see Tuulikki Pietilä in Paris. Then she found she had a further reason to make the journey: her uncle Einar Hammarsten's funeral. As the letter reveals, it proved a trip full of contrasts.

ILMATAR 23.2.68

Darling Tooti,

Your letter came just before I had to catch the train to Åbo and I only just had time to find your French CV and send it off (how I love proper instructions and matter-of-fact women!)

Your letter cheered me up, and was a comfort. No one's <u>said</u> as much about Einar as you. Us Finnish mussels and Janssons, you know how it is. Ten years together shows – at moments like this, when one can step off the edge of everyday *understatement, you know.*

By the way, I'm completely French these days. Nothing but Simenon, and the language is slowly coming back to me. There are Les abimes abominables, though, which you'll have to help me fill in Paris. In London I'm *the boss*! It's a great idea, going home by direct boat from London – and then to the island!!

I'm glad you could understand my urge to undertake "le voyage féminine" tout seule. Before I left I had the usual panic, the fear of setting off that has been making itself felt these last 15 years, intense enough to make me feel physically sick – but on the train all was peace and quiet and Simenon, who came with me to dinner on the boat and stayed with me through the whole affair with its prawns and schnapps and all the other delicacies. I took childish pleasure in having a single cabin, in the luxury on board, in the rarity of having money and spending it, in working some magic to get a vodka as a cocktail in the bar (it was touch and go, even with Vivica eyebrows) and in sitting in the café with a cognac (as you can see, my abstinence didn't last) right beside the dance floor as they play for me, and writing to you. I took the smallest table to be in peace but was joined by another middle-aged solitary who has arrayed herself in all the finery she owns and clearly feels a burning desire for something to "happen". I can tell by the bobbing tip of her toe, eager to dance, by a green chartreuse and by her hands.

I wonder what would happen if I was allowed to ask people to dance? Would I opt for the most beautiful and brazen or for those who never get to dance and who yearn the most? I wonder.

Later: She's a saloon stewardness but this trip and all the trimmings were a <u>present</u>, you see, and the café is full of men not inviting her to dance! So I bought her a cognac instead and after she got a bit tipsy we decided that in Heaven we would dance from morning to night!

When I get to Stockholm, Bitti will meet me off the boat on her way to work and bring the manuscript of The Sculptor's Daughter with her. I shall take it to Oslo and give it to Uca. Over the winter it emerged that she was very well aware of having hung onto *Pappan och havet* (*Moominpappa at Sea*) for six months without reading it, and was clearly even more upset about it than me. So I thought this would be OK. What sensitive prima donnas authors are! Suddenly her verdict isn't important to me any more – isn't that awful. Ça passe, J'espere. But this Oslo trip is important, at any rate; I'm anxious about our friendship. The bridge has had to bear too much weight, I need to shore it up.

I shall also meet up with Gunnel – I told Uca and she looked as if she'd bitten into something sour. But it can't be helped, I want to see Gunnel as well and shall make sure it's a pleasant and natural encounter.

Tomorrow I'm spending half a day with Ulla and as you can imagine I haven't the faintest idea how that will go. I'll take it as it comes, if she wants to keep conventionally silent and talk about horses, that's fine – if she wants to explode then tant mieux. The funeral is on 28th Feb. at 5 o'clock. So I can be there, I'll be staying at Bitti's. Ham was so glad I'd be able to represent us. So was I. Well not exactly glad. I'd been planning to go and see him but I arrived a week too late. You're right – he was important to me. One of the most important people in my life.

If you knew how it torments me now that I wrote to all those others, the ones who demanded and nagged – whether they were family, friends or fans, all the people <u>pushing</u> for letters, and not to him. Well, one can only bite that bullet and accept it for what it is, clear it aside. But I wanted to say it, <u>once</u>, and to a shoe for example.

(What–a–relief, someone asked her to dance. I shall have another cognac.)

Dialectically enough, I've also been invited to a hippie party in Oslo. On se deguise (is that right?). With the Wild West very much to the fore in my mind (they still have their bar, can't bear to part with it) and an unshakeable determination to have a good time in spite of Everything, I went to Tempo and bought lots of plastic daisies and made a wreath for my hair, a big wild one with flowers sticking out in all directions, and fixed two of the daisies on my shoes. And I put in a dance record when I was packing, feeling rather sheepish. You know! I'm sure they're no more straight-laced in Oslo than here. And my urge to dance will persist until my dying day. I often do it on my own in the studio, with or without Pipsu. And have such fun. But my exhibitionist streak shouldn't be denied or scorned, should it? As you can hear – my trip and the motivation for it are as varied as everything else, simply everything.

And you must write and tell me, <u>where</u> is your notebook with the list of ghost places in Paris?!?! <u>I want to dance with you!</u>

Yesterday Lasse came by and said the Evening News doesn't want his Moomin comic strip any more. Its distribution is now to be worldwide and the fee considerably lower. What a terrible shame. The same job – and payment per panel. Naturally we responded by making light of it in our typically Janssonian way (do I?!? Still? I hope not) and Lasse wrote to reassure Fleet Street, which was feeling bad about breaking the *bad news*. You may recall that Lasse was planning a trip to London to ask for a <u>higher</u> fee?

The elementary-school teachers' magazine Julstjärna had approached him to ask for a Christmas short story (50 marks!) with illustrations (25 marks!) which made him groan but I could tell he was very interested. Today he showed me the results – a Moomin story! I was taken aback, laughed – accepted it, the tale was good. What confidence! He was awfully embarrassed when he realised his Moomin short story came as something of a surprise to me! [...]

– I shall now retire to my luxury cabin and wish you a – good night's sleep!

Tove.

Les abimes abominables: Terrible gaps.
"le voyage f'minine" tout seule: TJ's visit to Bitti Fock and Vivica Bandler, which she describes in more detail in the letters.
Gunnel: Gunnel Malmström, TJ's Norwegian translator.
Ulla: TJ's cousin Ulla Hammarsten, Einar's daughter.

5.9.68 [Klovharun]

Darling Tooti,

All is well on Harun, neither thunderstorm nor stomach cramps nor anti-Semites. Strangely empty. I'm pottering and thinking. I tried writing for a while but it wasn't any good, went in the wrong direction. Have to wait until I find an obvious opening gambit and get some pictures done instead.

It's been very windy since you left and the weather was foul for a while, I got busy in the cellar where the bastions are growing. I used beach sand, it was excellent, the concreting went like a dream. Now the cement is practically all gone, which I'm glad of, it would be all too easy to go a bit mad like at Odden otherwise. Joining on the vertical sections will have to wait for next year but all the top surfaces are done. And I've sawed the barrel in two and put it on the verandah. I saved the best bits from the middle, maybe they can be used to mend the rotten parts.

I weeded all the grass from Lasse's patch and evacuated all the plants to a rock hollow, and am shoving things into the cellar for the winter, uhh, what a lot of <u>stuff</u> we have. The Honda's been behaving like an angel and has lapped up all the canisters of petrol, but yesterday it suddenly wouldn't go. I got it started again and it went for a while, then stopped. I can manage these final hours with candles, though. The gas ran out but I connected the new tube with

Tove Jansson in the cabin on Klovharun, 1960s.

a single twist, she said very proudly. You are a good – and oh so patient – teacher! [...]

I found the cooking oil in the chest under the water buckets. The first days I lived on sandwishes with tea and coffee, then fried tomatoes and onions. Now I'm cautiously embarking on tins, the small, easygoing ones. I haven't washed any dishes at all. My stomach is finally back to normal and I feel as strong as anything.

Saturday. Thanks for the nice letter and bottles from you and Lis! Warm wishes to her.

How horribly dusty and hectic it must have been for you in town, my poor darling. But it was unavoidable really, not least for the sake of the passe-partouts. And even if you'd stayed, you would only have gone about here feeling anxious about meetings to come, the town had already wrapped its tentacles around you.

You know, right at the start it's impossible to work, I mean "properly". One gets things organised, and is all set. That leeway is always

Tooti and Tove in Italy.

crucial, and you've got a head start by going back so early. So you mustn't worry about the fact that you went. Now you've got a free run at your studio, your place of work, and all the social side out of the way, you know what I mean. One *week end* here wouldn't disturb the even ripple of those circles – and what fun that would be.

Guess who's sitting there eating my last nuts in front of the verandah – a squirrel! It appeared on the island this morning. When Lasse came with Kiki and the kids it had just discovered all the bread for the birds – and fled in panic. Now it's back again.

They only stayed a few minutes because they were off to pick mushrooms and cowberries. Between us we unloaded lots of peat that I'm going to put in front of the house for next year's Show Garden. I think it could be magnificent! There was only nice post, some good reviews, the new paperbacks are out, a draft contract from WYSOY for "Daughter", an enthusiastic letter from Elin Svedlin who likes the book, letters and apples from Ham.

She's anxious about that unlucky splinter I got, woe is me – Abbes will fill you in on the details. Some of it came out with a pin, to many an ouch and yelp, while the rest, along with all the ointment and sulphur powder, has closed up and is slowly growing out. It doesn't hurt at all any more. Do let her know, if you feel like ringing. My letter to her has already gone off with Lasse (and, at last, the difficult letters – to Nita and Tia) but he's popping back to the island after the mushroom hunt to pick up this letter to you.

And anyway, he wants to offload some more peat he'd been storing over at Viken. Lasse's taking this Garden very seriously, decent of him, isn't it.

Yesterday I wandered round in the nude all day and took a dip in the inlet now and then – ugh, how hot it must have been for you all in town. I sank some stones and household rubbish and rowed to Hästhällarna while I was at it for the last of the shelf stones for the cellar (which is finished now). I found another barrel while I was there, and a Mysterious Chair.

Apart from my perpetual and natural worries about how hard it is to make art and above all how hard it is to get started, I'm feeling shamelessly and undeservedly good. As I have been for several superb months in a row. You wrote that I need this peace after a tough summer – and I was surprised and started to think. It wasn't tough, was it? The film week was terrible – but after all it was only a week and the wretched thing should probably be a source of pride, rather than anything? And anyway, I've put it out of my mind. All the rest has been smooth, first-rate, a rest cure – I was horror-struck by sudden invasions I suppose, but there weren't many of them and afterwards one just feels grateful the thing was pleasant and went well. I have a general sense of it being a very fine summer, warm in terms of both weather and company – and I'm very grateful for that feeling. Thank you Tooticki!

If only I could convert it into pictures or words it could turn into something very good. Perhaps it will, one has to be patient.

My regards to all Pietiläs and other friends. A big

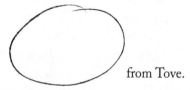 from Tove.

anti-Semites: Refers to some kind of insect life, possibly ants.

Lis: Lis Hooge-Hansen, Danish sculptor and engraver.

the film week: Margareta Strömstedt was filming "Moomin and the Sea", which was shown on Swedish Television at Christmas 1968.

Elin Svedlin: Widow of Thure Svedlin, who was head of the publishing house Holger Schildts Förlags.

"Dearest Ham"

LETTERS TO SIGNE HAMMARSTEN JANSSON 1959–1967

Signe Hammarsten Jansson.

FOLLOWING VIKTOR JANSSON'S DEATH IN 1958, SIGNE HAMMARSTEN Jansson had to leave the Lallukka artists' home. She moved in with Lars Jansson and spent the summers with Tove and/or Lars on Bredskär. From 1964 onwards, she took it in turns between Lars Jansson and family on Bredskär, and Klovharun, where Tove Jansson and Tuulikki Pietilä lived.

The visit to Greece in the autumn of 1959 was the first trip Tove Jansson and Tuulikki Pietilä made together. It began and ended in Athens, and in between they led an island-hopping life, including some time spent on Mykonos, and a stay in the Peloponnese. After that, a month in Paris lay ahead. Tove Jansson's decision to leave her mother behind was not an easy one – previously they had travelled together – and a drama of jealousy, distress, guilt and depression ensued. But Tove Jansson did not forgo the trip. In her many letters the closeness between mother and daughter is a recurring subject, interwoven with descriptions of places and experiences.

In her short story "Den Stora resan" ("The Great Journey") Tove Jansson presents a similar situation. Two women plan a trip, and one of them is anxious about leaving her mother. But in the story, the woman travels with her mother rather than her loved one.

* * *

4.II.59. ATHENS.

Dearest Ham,

Thank you for your first letter, which was here to meet me in Athens! At first they told me there was nothing for me, and I was scared stiff. But by the time we got up to our room (which is relatively small but as tall as my studio, with enormous beds), they came scampering in with the letter.

I knew you'd find the first night miserable, darling. Even as a young, healthy individual, I felt rotten for the entire first part of the trip – and I know it's because I was going so far away from you. We're so close to one another that we can't really cope with being separated for any stretch of time. But think how wonderful it will be when we meet again, and how soothing to know that we've no particular farewells ahead of us.

I know you're glad I got away on a real trip after all the wretched cartoon strip business, so I can bury it properly and start afresh. And I sense that this very different world around me is going to smooth out the old and build something new.

I threw away the Artists' Guild Yearbook card. But the other news was good, about Lasse's synopsis, Aschehoug and Sutton. I suppose he'll just have to keep the drawings, then – the main thing is that we know where they are. But he is a bit silly – and presumably doesn't know much about publishing.

Couldn't care less about Carroll – it was just an experiment. (5th. The letters from England came today.)

I think your stamps are lovely, now I've seen the finished articles on a letter. What do you think of the Greek stamp? The postcards here are quite grand – but I still prefer writing you letters as usual. You're the only one I feel the need to tell all about this trip. Little cards will do for the others. Well – the letters are partly for Lasse too – it's true.

Today we went up to the Acropolis and it was so striking and beautiful that one felt a great air of solemnity. Even in me, a rudimentary sense of the historical connections is starting to stir, and I'm eagerly reading up on Athens. All we've done so far, by the way, is wander round. Regard things in wonder – we'll only take in the museums once we've got some kind of overall impression of the city, the ruins, people's mentality. The street where we're staying is wide and bustling, and just opposite they're building a house with much crashing and shouting, every single vehicle makes as much of a racket as it can and the street vendors supply the rest. The houses are mainly white with bold splashes of colour – the people we've had contact with are friendly and, with a few shameless exceptions, mostly minded to guide and help us.

I had fried octopus (again) with white Greek schnapps (one glass!) and olives sprinkled with salt, which made me retch half the night and today I went over to candied pears and fermented raw cabbage. Perhaps that will be better!

It's a relief to find that Tooti seems as tired as I am by all this walking around. She's not at all as over-energetic as I thought. In

Switzerland, for instance, she guiltily avoided the museums, saying she wanted to "look" instead. There, incidentally, I bought a pair of high-heeled plastic rain shoes, cheap ones – they look as if they're made of white glass. Our basic see-through rain macs, you know the ones, cause a great stir here, people come up to us to touch and feel them.

Clothes are terribly dear, but the wonderful hand-woven skirts and shawls they make on the islands are ludicrously cheap. We've been past that sort of shop several times, and next time I'm afraid we shall go in!

The pastries are like the Turkish ones, sweet and sticky, the pitch-black coffee thick and explosive in tiny cups. Cats everywhere, of every colour.

From time to time a raging wind blows, then there's a rain shower – and the next moment it's as hot as summer. Between ½ past 1 and ½ past 5 the whole town sleeps, (literally) the shops and restaurants are closed. Then everything opens again and continues long into the night. Tooti quickly adopts these habits – she can sleep just like that – but I find them a bit harder to adjust to.

On the whole this country has exceeded my expectations – and I'm very pleased we were able to make the trip. Though I notice I haven't quite as much energy as before and have completely given up the night walks, for example.

That flight you wrote about sounded horrible. Now we've decided not to fly to Crete but to catch a boat to Santorini on a calm day – we won't be taking a single flight for the whole trip. I've bought a boat ticket to come back via Åbo because Tooti wants to see her parents. And incidentally, I might possibly come home a bit earlier than her, if she decides to extend her trip with a week or two in Paris.

I chose those hairnets for you, and then Lisbeth insisted I let her give them to you. I couldn't refuse without making a scene – she wanted to you to have a present from her at last. I've been wondering about one of those pretty shawls, by the way – but I'm not sure if you like that kind of thing. I shall wait and see, maybe I'll come across something better.

I'm always sending you my love in your direction and profoundly hoping you won't be melancholy. Write to me sometimes, so I know how you are – while we're in Santorini, the hotel here will take in our post. (We'll probably go there in about 10 days' time and then come back to the Apollo.) Warm wishes to Lasse and give him a hug. And a huge embrace from your own

Tove

Aschehoug: TJ's publisher in Norway.
Carroll: see Letters to Åke Runnquist.

Tove Jansson and Tooti changed their travel plans once they realised the crossing to Santorini would take nineteen hours. They decided to go to Mykonos instead, arriving in the middle of the night and walking along the beach until they found a small hotel. Tove Jansson wrote to Ham: "it feels safe, being on an island, a bit like at home."

MYKONOS 15.11.59.

Dearest Ham,

The Mykonos tub has changed to her winter timetable so she didn't put in at the island with the post after all.

For two days the Greek autumn (they call it winter) has put in a guest appearance here, with torrential rain and gales. The few tourists blow down to the harbour and sit in the cafés drinking hot chocolate with cognac or ouzo, a kind of white Pernod. And they've all caught colds. Including me.

The local gossip gets an airing. There's the American group with existentially long-haired girls and men in shaggy sweaters, and the English one, pleasant, strict and inaccessible. Then the Swedes, still more decimated (each group only comprises 4–5 people) with a charming and boastful star photographer, among other things, and a sidelined Kerstin (that really is her name) who is in love with a Greek, has terrible problems with her parents and is considered an amateur by "the others". She's always offering to buy people coffee, has no money and reads out her letters from home.

And now all the palms are being blown out of shape and the town's pelicans are sheltering at the restaurant and everything is wet. We are wrapped up warm and tuck ourselves into walled corners to sketch, and our paper flaps about and the whole Aegean is green and angry.

Somehow I can believe in it all much better now the picture-postcard weather's over (perhaps only for the time being?), everything seems more genuine and one has a sense of actually living here.

One day we climbed up onto the much higher ground of the island and looked inland. The ground is barren and eroded into huge, grim indentations, with a network of primitive walls, a few cactuses, and here and there a tiny white church or a house huddled between the boulders. There are only a few thousand people here at most (1600, I think) but 360 churches. When sailors narrowly escaped shipwreck they often promised God a church if he saved them. He clearly did that quite often!

The police, a few lonely fellows who always stick together, are not liked. They go in wherever they fancy and eat and drink for free – and anyone who objects is made to regret it bitterly.

Women are never seen at the café, but later in the evening the men dance to the bouzouki, which is a big, banjo-like sort of instrument, skilfully taking up the rhythm on two spoons, which they wield like castanets. The song is a monotonous whine, and as the mood gets more excitable the dance is performed by two men, one of them very obviously taking the woman's role with belly gyrations and deliberate coquetry.

The best weaver is called Viennola, a very proud and self-assured woman who holds a coffee salon in her workshop among the narrow alleyways. The fact that she can speak English means the tourists gather there to buy and gossip. Her beautiful daughter fell in love with a Dane a few weeks ago and is going to marry him and move north. So she's questioning all the Scandinavians and trying to get a picture of her new country.

The days pass in a peaceful, humdrum way, with work, an ouzo, a bit of chat with some colleague over dinner, and an early bedtime. We sleep in woolly tops and long johns. They are more tolerant here than in Athens, so everyone goes around in jeans and looks however they want to. The shops are few and the souvenir sellers zero now the summer is over.

It's brightening up outside. Big hugs to you my darling. All good wishes to Lasse. And Impi. And be [*the end is missing*]

MYKENES [MYCENAE], PELOPONNESOS 25.11.59.

Happy "Little Christmas"! Just imagine, artificial Little Christmas trees are on sale in Athens. They are slimmer than cypresses and have snow on them, and they come in all sizes, wrapped in cellophane!

Dearest Ham,

This evening I'm sitting in a rather dreary café (the only one in the village) in Mykenes, writing by the light of a carbide lamp. Sheep and chickens and turkeys and donkeys are making are making a hell of a racket and the last tourist bus has just come round the corner in a cloud of dust. (Tooti is trying to draw a donkey and getting its legs the wrong way round)

We came here by train from Athens, had to get up at six in the morning – and arrived some time after 10 in a large and peaceful valley surrounded by vast mountains. Nobody else got off the train. No buildings, just a long road to a village (smaller than Söderby) with one small hotel. Then another long road in among the mountains and there, after an enormous climb, the ruins of the fortifications and palace where the Mycenaean kings lived and were buried, and created the oldest and most important epoch in Greek history.

There wasn't much left of the splendour of 1660 years BC – except the lion gate, you know, and pieces of wall composed of gigantic blocks. Agamemnon's huge grave was inside a hill, with little excavation shafts here and there. It's strange to think that this was once the capital of Greece and that this deserted valley was the centre of artistic life. Even I could feel History tingling up and down my spine.

All around there were sombre grey-brown mountains, line after line of them, and the ground was grey dust and splinters of rock. This is where they found the biggest and most beautiful gold treasures in Greece.

We were due to leave yesterday morning, but the day before I got a message about a telephone call from Stockholm. They hadn't been able to reach me, and asked me to take the call at 10 the next morning. So I had to cancel the tickets and waited anxiously to find out what the call was about, while we made all sorts of guesses. It turned out to be Moomintroll of course.

Nyman & Schultz rang to ask if they could use him on a brochure. Can you believe it? I gave them your address and hope you and Lasse will be so good as to pick a passable troll from one of my drawings and let them use that. Maybe a Moomin in a boat – from the lighthouse synopsis? The one where he's starting the motor, or something like that.

Otherwise they'll have to wait until I get home. And I reckon they could pay, say, 10,0000, or what do you two think?

Uca is the only one who has my address apart from you. If anyone asks you for it, please could you tell them while you are at it that they are to <u>write</u>, not ring or telegraph.

Talking of Nyman & Schultz, perhaps they ought to ask permission from Bulls. If they write to me as they promised, I shall ask them to do that.

Today we did a serious dash through the Athenian museums, sorted out our finances (the Basel money is fixed at last) and paid for the three nights in wagons lits to Paris. After the rain the city was sunny and warm again but as soon as it clouds over it's freezing cold. One never knows what to wear. But it was even colder on the islands. I forgot to tell you that I saw the first real cockroach invasion of my life in the cabin on the boat from Mykonos. They came in all sizes, and my goodness they could run fast!

<u>If</u> I send a package from here before we go to Paris, that means it's a Christmas parcel (or at least part of one) so you people mustn't open it until I've had time to send instructions!

Hugs and kisses and a thousand greetings!

Your own Tove – who misses you.

P.S. Tomorrow we're moving on to Olympos and Delphi.

Söderby: A village in Pellinge.
Nyman & Schultz: A travel agency in Sweden.
the lighthouse synopsis: The strip cartoon "Moomin and the Sea".

WEDNESDAY. [*Undated, September 1965, Klovharun*]

Dearest Ham,

Abbe & co. might come out today; the weather has suddenly turned fine – so I'll be able to get a few words off to you. Maybe they've even heard something by telephone.

I'm naturally wondering how your trip back to town went. The stairs must have felt like a trial after you'd been been horizontal for so long – I'm sure you're still terribly tired after the whole move and might be staying in bed.

Has the young man turned up and settled in? That blanket of autumn melancholy came down over the archipelago once you'd left. At nine that evening I was close to getting up and looking out towards abandoned Bredskär, but I didn't. Because just think if I'd seen a light, out at the point.

I've been working exclusively on Alice and have moved over to the colour pictures. I've done three. It's more fun than I expected but awfully hard, perhaps I'll gradually accumulate enough insight to redo the whole lot once all 14 are finished.

The palette is restrained, almost sober, with a single bright colour as the dominant. But perhaps that's too cautious a technique.

The first evening I really was a bit scared of the dark although I sat there reading for ages and didn't set up any kind of curtain arrangement the way I usually do on Bredskär. But the next night it had passed and I even went out in the storm with a torch to see if the water had risen in the ravine.

It was quite some gale and it blew up suddenly as darkness fell. Remarkable how a storm can flush away all melancholies and fears, it was so nice lying there and hearing the crashes on the copper roof.

For a moment I felt a prickling in my hands and feet, when the ship's bell started ringing outside the door. But then I realised it was only Sjöberg testing out the wind gauge and left it to clang while I carried on reading my murder mystery.

Today I spread out all the mats to air and saw that he, Sjöberg that is, had snatched away the smallest verandah mat.

I switched on the radio last night and all of a sudden there was somebody talking about my book. It was the arts programme "Kulturspegeln", some kind of résumé of Pappan with a few chunks of the text, summed up at the end with the view that I'd lost the Groke as (a useable and expressive) manifestation of evil but gained a new dimension by taking the family down from their pedestal of niceness and bringing them closer to the reader. And that I would very probably never get them back into that position again – or into the valley, I forget exactly which. I missed the beginning. But they seemed to be taking the book very seriously, so I was pleased about that.

We've reached Friday and I've still had no company but Alice. There's a row of curious little pictures propped on the bureau and I wish you were here to give me your verdict.

Today I polished copper jugs and cleaned the cooker and the floor around it and brought in fresh flowers – apart from that I've just been pressing on with my work for as long as it keeps stumbling forward. The house and island will have to take a break.

I've eaten my way through Bredskär's three packs of bacon with my own new potatoes and will soon have to come up with something new.

I suppose this weekend will bring some kind of news from town, anyway. I think about you all the time and wonder how you are. And whether you really will let me know if you start feeling worse. I shall come like a shot, if so, Alice can very well continue in town and this mournful autumnal archipelago isn't too hard to leave. We've had the summer, we're grateful for it, and pretty much ready for winter life.

Saturday. Brunström came past, going out fishing, so I'll give this letter to him. Bye and hugs!

Best wishes to Tooti!

Tove.

résumé of Pappan: *Pappan och havet*, 1965 (*Moominpappa at Sea*).

IN 1966, TOVE JANSSON RECEIVED THE PRESTIGIOUS CHILDREN'S literature award, the Andersen Medal, awarded by the International Board on Books for Young People (IBBY). The award was presented at a congress in Ljubljana.

29.9.66 [LJUBLJANA]

Dearest Ham,

The congress is in full swing now and we spend our days sitting in a curlicued town hall with a patio and a fountain in the middle, listening to talks in lots of different languages. If we can't understand them we put on a sort of Talky Walky that can tune in to 8 different translations. All done on the spot. (and they sound like the cacophony of announcements at a railway station) Sometimes they say I can skip a *meeting*, and then I dash happily out into town, or sleep, or read through my speech. Tooti mooches around museums while I'm busy congressing. We are in very smart accommodation in a skyscraper called The Lion, which even has its own hairdresser and nightclub.

Naturally all the Scandinavians wanted to go to the nightclub – the others were too jaded or had been warned in advance. The line-up was pathetically bad – except for an acrobat and a *sexbomb* who did a high-speed *strip-tease*, galloping round with her curves swinging, and the act culminated in her standing on her head to the accompaniment of a police siren. It was great fun. (Inger, a female Swedish colleague, said they were post-natal exercises)

My head gets in a complete whirl from trying to speak so many languages at once, and sometimes a blank curtain comes down. On one of the most chaotic days they suddenly dragged me in front of the TV cameras completely unprepared, for a discussion with my translator here (who is a surgeon). I was so petrified – as was she – that we asked for a slivovitz on the spot, and things went relatively smoothly after that.

1.10 And now I've got the medal which is very lovely but unfortunately also very big (!) and when I, completely shattered and happy and terrified and worn out, got home after the whole affair, there was your card which was as good as a whole letter. Thank you dearest – how nice that it came at just that moment! So Lasse & co. have gone now, assuming they got away all right – especially Nita ... there must have been so much upheaval lately but I really hope most of the mess has been in my studio.

No, we didn't get ill after all and I suspect it was the flying that made us feel like that, plus the flumidin. And although I seemed to shed all manner of my possessions as time went by, I did somehow hang on to my speech and my glasses.

My presentation went really well and I spoke (thanks to it being in English) very slowly. People were actually moved – though I can't fathom which parts had that effect. After me came a white-haired Swiss who'd won the big illustration prize they've set up this year, a whole series of authors got their diplomas, the choir sang a triumphal madrigal and small children handed out carnations with silk ribbons in national colours. Before all that there was a long speech about the main prizewinners and much to my surprise I found myself listening to accounts of Harun and Bredskär, your and Faffan's work, Ängsmarn, Peo and Lasse, Lotsgatan and above all the hurricanes in the Gulf of Finland. It was extremely odd.

After the triumphal madrigal everyone raced round congratulating everyone else and talking rapidly in nineteen languages, publishers and journalists asked for details and addresses, all at the same time, I even had a caricature drawn of me and camera flashes in my face from all directions. Then in a trice the whole lot vanished and Tooti and I were left standing there in a mass of carnations and asparagus fern with no recollection (that is, I had no recollection) of where we would be eating the official meal.

We went back to the hotel where they eventually tracked us down – the supper was formal and a bit weary – nothing but super-bigwigs who, moreover, were distracted by Internal Congress Intrigues à la Artists' Guild – all the younger, merrier and less Important types were having a knees-up at some cheaper venue. That's the way it goes!

But *so what*, not a single soul could have had such an exciting and glorious time as I have done, and I'm very grateful and happy about the whole thing, though now flagging.

The most splendid thing of all (apart from the medal of course) was the Caves. The country invited the congress to a three-hour coach trip to some stalactite caves, formed in the course of 6,000 years – they are utterly indescribable. For nearly two hours we walked through a Dante landscape of tremendous, surreal formations in strange subterranean hues – some of the caverns were as tall as cathedrals and had been adorned with chandeliers by nineteenth-century romantics. Lots of the leading lights of the congress got panicky and claustrophobic and wanted to escape, and most of the group felt some unpleasant effects, but I could have lived there for <u>weeks</u>! In the company of little red salamanders, bats and – well – rats, but even with them! The outside world felt totally banal afterwards – despite the beautiful rolling landscape.

One evening there was a cocktail party hosted by a minister, very formal, but the Scandinavian breakfast the first day, by contrast, was really good fun and full of Nordic temperament. I've tried my best to be amiable and say the right things in the right language to the right people – and now that we're sitting in a peaceful, everyday fashion on the train to Venice I can feel that it's been quite a strain. I mean to say, we were thrust into the midst of this almost straight from Harun! Nobody wore long dresses here in Ljubljana, the Swiss woman was wearing a kind of Marimekko with red embroidery.

It's been raining most of the time, but perhaps the scenery here looks even better in the mist, it's so earnest. Houses, roads, gardens are so well-tended, everything looks freshly painted and genteel – not at all like when we once travelled through here to Greece.

People we asked for advice in the streets of Ljubljana were helpful, one of them even came with us to hunt out Yugoslavian records in a shop. It's nice to feel the kindliness following us as we leave.

When we see each other I'll give you more details and show you all the conference papers and the little curios we've bought. I hope you've got the two cards we sent. Perhaps your greetings will be waiting for me in Vienna. Warmest wishes to everybody. And a hug from Tooti!

I think we're getting near the border, where I will be able to post this. Look after yourself, my dear one.

A big 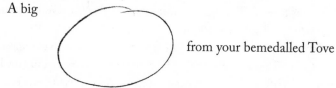 from your bemedalled Tove

SUNDAY [*Postmark 10.5.1967. Klovharun*]

Dearest Ham,

It may be that Abbe comes out to visit and can take a letter with him – despite the terrible weather. It's a typical Finnish spring, with angry gales from the north or east, squally rain and hellish cold. There was one nice day in town, so we heard on the radio. But you know how it is, at the start there's always so much to do in the house, and it really makes no difference what Sjöberg is up to. At least he was feeling benign when we came out here, and we had a fine, sunny evening.

Tooti discovered with outraged delight that some winter guest has shot a round hole (a real one this time) through the window-pane on the north side and also indulged in target practice on her crispbreads hanging up by the ceiling. They also used up every last bit of firewood, burning the lot. So we had to lug loads of wood into the house to dry and at first the weather was so vicious that I had to saw the wood indoors. All of this actually added to our relish of the new-settler feeling, though we cursed, of course.

One day it was calm – with a mist, so I planted all seven rose bushes (what was left of them) in peat. One by the potato patch, one by the big hollow in the rock, one above the inlet and the other four round the house, one on each side. We'll see how it goes, they looked a bit droopy after their stay in town.

Pipsu is now very clearly "my" cat, follows me everywhere and sleeps on my pillow every night. We haven't had time to put a cat net out, but the fish we brought with us is keeping well in the cellar, which is ice-cold. That's still in a state of chaos (except the food shelves) but we've got the house tidied up.

Various bits of romantica nautica have been discreetly stowed away so the place doesn't look quite so much like a maritime museum any longer.

Tooti is in the middle of making a tool cupboard to go in the corner where her carpentry bench is, it's going to be perfect and she's totally and happily absorbed in her woodwork. The curtain in front of the wardrobe, a drab architect fabric design, has given way to the patchwork quilt (the Pietilä relic, you remember) that she tearfully persuaded Raili to let her have and now the place looks much more like a fisherman's cottage. It's made of lots of small-patterned fabrics in pale colours. The studio rug fitted well under the table and its top is now exactly the right size.

First thing in the morning it's only 10° in the house, even though we keep the fire burning like crazy all day (20° by evening) and later in the night, around 4, I have to put on a woolly hat. The first mornings we got up at 5, but now we've calmed down to 6 o'clock. The pennant is mended and has been hoisted up the signal mast.

I'm still trying to knock Kometjakten [Comet in Moominland] into shape in the same naïve style. Assuming it can be patched up.

A terribly bad book but with some oddly authentic sections. Too few of them, unfortunately.

Oh, and guess what else Sjöberg has been up to – carrying off the morass of rock blastings again and depositing it in the channel where the boat has to be pulled up into the grass! It looks pretty hopeless this time.

And he's also cleared nearly all the red rock (where we go down from the house to the inlet) of stones. I can see how beautiful the bare rock is, so I shall let him have things his own way in that department. Now there's only a narrow edging of stones to keep in the earth up top, unfortunately. He swung the green barrel round as well and ripped out the wire it was fastened with, and stripped off all the seaweed I'd laid out on the steep rocks to make a kind of rock garden. But the woodshed is unscathed.

A few scraps of green are starting to poke through here and there, but very cautiously. There's no wood or oil spill on the beaches.

Everything looked fine on Bredskär as we came past, including Sophia's house. What a wonderful time we shall have when you come out with them! Just to think that we've this family archipelago to enjoy spending the summer in.

Now I'm going to dive into the ice cellar for a while and carry on with my rooting. Kisses! Bye!

Monday.

Abbe and Greta are here on an evening visit – with greetings from you!! We've finally had a still, sunny day and done loads of nice outdoor things – sauna, driftwood stash, putting out nets – without having to freeze. Forgot to tell you Pel left the whole potato box behind, 15 kg! Maybe Lasse could bring a few cooking potatoes out to us when you all come? For now we've got some that Abbes have given us, and are eating macaroni and rice, so it isn't that crucial.

Tooti wonders if you would kindly give Reima a ring, just to let him know she's OK.

A big hug, my dear one. Look after yourself. I expect we'll go over to Viken before too long and give you a call. My very best wishes to Impi and our friends.

Your Tove.

"A letter that you burn – please! – is better than talking"

LETTERS TO MAYA VANNI
1957–1983

Maya Vanni, 1940s.

MAYA VANNI AND TOVE JANSSON BEGAN THEIR CORRESPONDENCE in 1957. Maya Vanni, who had been to visit Bredskär, wrote a letter of thanks, and in her reply Tove Jansson observed how readily her friend had slipped into island life: "we simply <u>lived</u> together as if we always had".

They had already known one another for a long time, but their friendship deepened. Maya Vanni, née London, was married in 1941 to the artist Sam Vanni, one of the men with whom Tove Jansson had affairs in the 1930s. The couple was part of her close circle of friends over a long period. "We meet at events now and then", wrote Tove Jansson to Eva Konikoff in autumn 1944, describing Maya as "a dear, wise person when you get to know her a bit better". During the harsh war years, she and the Vannis dreamt of "constructing a happy society and a peaceful world," as she put it in her diary in March 1944. When Sam and Maya Vanni, their marriage by then creaking at the seams, went to Italy and France in the spring of 1948, they asked Tove Jansson to go with them. But after a couple of months Tove Jansson abandoned her "mediating role" as she wrote to Eva Konikoff (18.6.1948) and went off to Brittany to get on with her own work. Sam and Maya Vanni later divorced, although not until 1958.

Maya Vanni (1916–2010) lived in Paris at the end of the 1930s and later studied Romance philology at the university of Helsinki. She worked as a translator and was employed for many years at the Post and Telegraph Authority and at the Prime Minister's Office in Helsinki. Her various jobs are sometimes commented on in the letters. After retirement she studied philosophy and wrote a master's thesis on Martin Buber.

In Maya Vanni, Tove Jansson found someone else to talk to through letters, a successor to Eva Konikoff, although on a smaller scale and in a different way. She wrote about her work on the illustrations for Lewis Carroll's *Alice in Wonderland* and Tolkien's *The Hobbit*, about short stories, plays and exhibitions. The letters revealed the energy she put into the honing of artistic expression: there is no mistaking that they are the work of a practising artist and author. There were Tolkien pictures that had been redrawn 60–80 times, Tove Jansson confided to her correspondent in the summer of 1961. Maya Vanni was also one of the select few allowed to read and offer opinions on the author's books before they were published, and the letters teem with references to texts and illustrations in progress, including the picture book *Vem ska trösta knyttet?* (1960, *Who Will Comfort Toffle?*) and *Pappan och havet* (1965, *Moominpappa at Sea*). The laborious nature of the Moomin strip-cartoon work is vividly evoked, as is the sense of liberation when it finally ends: "I'm living island life with such relish, especially since I finished with the cartoon strips once and for all a few days ago – and I've suddenly started taking an interest in planting and fishing and hammering in nails and other natural activities I only tackled out of duty or guilt all these years" (11.7.1959).

Most of Tove Jansson's letters to Maya Vanni were written in summertime. They take the form of reports from an island, where the seismograph-like correspondent recounts tales of life and work, joys and problems, hard times and happy times in various circles of family and friends. Hamm and Faffan (in the earlier letters) occupy a lot of space, as does Tuulikki Pietilä. Her importance as a life partner and artist is expressed in vivid and concrete terms. But Tove Jansson also writes of trying to strike a balance within the triangle of herself, Tuulikki Pietilä and Signe Hammarsten Jansson, depicting in close-up the interactions of the three protagonists: daughter, mother and life partner. The process of leaving Bredskär for Klovharun proves a testing time for the mother-daughter relationship and Tove Jansson writes somewhat dejectedly about the black wave of "guilt–melancholy" she experiences (14.7.1963) as plans for the new island start to be realised. Correspondence with Maya Vanni also allowed for an airing of the recurrent dilemma of duty versus love. Tove Jansson writes of her need for solitude, but also of friendship and love, and of inviting "ghost invasions" from her various circles of friends to come swarming across the rocks. But the most important element of all is the changing landscape of the island and the sea.

Maya Vanni moved to Israel in 1992, at which point she returned the letters to their author. "I'm so pleased that you are going to look after them," she wrote in an accompanying note. Tove Jansson asked her in several of the letters to burn them after reading, but this clearly did not happen. There is no way of knowing whether any other letters were in fact destroyed by either Maya Vanni or Tove Jansson.

* * *

20.7.1957 [*Bredskär*]

Dear Maya,

thank you for your warm and news-packed letter which really did make me happy.

It gave me the urge to write a letter of my own, right away – and I certainly haven't felt anything like that for many years.

I'm so glad you felt as much at home with us as we did with you. It's rare for anyone to slip into island life as easily as you did, we simply <u>lived</u> together as if we always had.

When you left I thought a lot about how the town would receive you with all its tangles and complications. The tangles are still there, apparently – but <u>you</u> were able to put up your defences and stick your nose in the air!

We relished your account of the conversation with Sigrid! What you said was so unruffled and factually correct – and should for that very reason have taught that woman not to be so impertinent or to offer her opinion on personal matters that she can't judge. I imagine August, when he comes back, isn't going to be an easy month for you.

But your attitude is clear: you know what you want and can maintain your composure.

I especially admired your presence of mind when our friend rang. That was definitely the only right and <u>fair</u> thing for you to do. To think that you actually managed to pull it off – and that you weren't plagued with doubt and anxiety again afterwards. I think that little by little, despite all your regret and disappointment, you've grown stronger than him.

That can only bode well – whether the outcome is definitive liberation or a new kind of contact in which he finally brings himself to be honest.

I was terribly pleased to hear about all your commissions. So you're now the no. 1 translator from French and translating for Uca and a mechanical engineer! Isn't it funny how everything comes tumbling in at the same time, once it actually starts! I just knew <u>Svedlin</u> wouldn't take long to discover what you were made of. Nice that <u>he</u> was the one to say it, and was grateful – clients don't often do that, just take delivery and pay.

In a few days I shall be sending him 34 illustrations, when Ham goes back, and I despatched 30 into town with Peo a while back. I've only five left to do now, on scraping paper. That feels good!!!

Oh Maya, I'd have loved to see you at the Embassy party in all your glory! It really is a very special sensation, knowing yourself to be as right as you possibly can be and then floating around at a large social gathering, feeling utterly at ease and comfortable with your-self. I struggled for half a lifetime before that happened to me for the first time. It was like when you learn to swim and find yourself buoyant for the first time.

So Willie is coming over. In that case we must confront her with Tooti's Andree who is already here in Helsingfors. A telegram that had been lying around in Söderby belatedly got through, completely deflating Tuulikki. Now we've arranged for Ham to take keys and a letter to Andree's hotel, so then she can stay at Tooti's flat and some-time around the 10th Tooti will go in and make sure she's all right.

Faffan and Ham came out for a few days after you'd left. Faffan instantly found his seagull Pelle, laid claim to the guest room and settled in for an intensive three weeks of fishing. So we were in no danger of getting scurvy from lack of phosphorus!

I think he had a good time until he started missing city life. The day he went, Kurt arrived for a weekend with some lovely steaks, and wine. We picked him up from Tirmo and the machine ran like an angel. He had good weather and everything was rosy. A couple of days after him, yesterday, Uca arrived – tired but happy, and bringing the play with her. If only she could have a little rest in this week she's here!

Since you left we've had various knottywood projects on the go – mainly Tooti of course.

We emptied and scoured one of the big water-collecting hollows and Tooti built a greenhouse near the mergansers' nestbox. Just behind it I found an uprooted bit of tree that had brought a clump of earth up into the air with it. I broke it open, freed the roots with the saw and scraped out lots of soil from between them to plant salad crops in. Good going, eh? Then we ran down every couple of hours to check whether any of them had come up.

The most interesting thing we made was definitely the beaded curtain for the door. One of those real bordello-style affairs, multi-coloured. We soon ran out of wooden beads so we complemented those with velvet grass, bamboo and reeds. It rattles nicely in the south-westerly, scares the flies (we hope) and catches round everything as we try to get through it. We also collected round stones all over the islands and Tooti made some of them into abstract sculpture! And we deepened the western harbour with Hamsie's help.

One little serpenticle has sneaked into our paradise – a sort of rivalry between the two former scout leaders, which I've found quite hard to handle and am seriously worried about.

Maybe I'm exaggerating – or it will pass. I shall talk to you about it sometime.

This evening the thunder is rumbling along the horizon again, but not bringing any rain. The danger lamp is lit and suddenly the late-summer darkness is outside, with frogs and flashes of lightning.

Uca's translating, Tooti is tapping tacks into silkscreen printing frames, Ham's making a plasticine Fillyjonk and I've been groaning over an idiotic scrapbook sheet for Bull's. Then I shall get started on Save the Children. Ham leaves tomorrow and Nita will be here in a few days' time.

Then, on the 30th, Lasse will have the island for his friends and Tooti and I are heading for even greater solitude on Kummelskär. I'm hoping it will be splendid. Everyone sends you their warmest wishes!

Thanks for the lovely time we had while you were here. And look after yourself.

All good wishes, your friend Tove.

Svedlin: Thure Svedlin, head of the Holger Schildts Förlags publishing house.

Willie: See Letter to Vivica Bandler 13.6.1948.

Andrée (sometimes spelled "Andrée"): An old friend of Tuulikki Pietilä from her student days in Paris in the early 1950s.

34 illustrations: TJ is working on the illustrations for *Trollvinter* (*Moominland Midwinter*).

knottywood projects: Swedish *knaggbestyr*. The invented verb *att. knagga* (derived from the word *knagge*, used in the letters for a hook fashioned from driftwood, or other handcrafted object) came to be applied to any kind of practical project. The phrase was probably coined by deft handywoman Tuulikki Pietilä.

former scout leaders: Ham and Vivica Bandler.

BREDSKÄR, 18 AUG. 58.

Dearest Maya,

Thank you for your long, entertaining letter. Your glimpses of the Post and Telegraph Authority tally well with Ham's accounts of that institution. Rather long-winded, idyllic in a benevolent and dignified way, not to be rushed and awful sticklers for etiquette.

On the whole I think your job outline sounds pleasant enough – I assume it will be entirely up to you to develop the work and organise the time-sheme, as Uca would pronounce it!

Ham would very much like to know the names of those fellows – she knows them all from when she was designing stamps.

Island life is going better than ever for the three of us, and suddenly there's not the slightest doubt that Ham and Tooti are friends – and our days together pass peacefully and harmoniously.

The island has worked wonders – Ham is much better and feels like pursuing all sorts of activities again – the worst shock of Faffan's death is behind her. But as soon as anything disrupts the uniform tranquillity of the island she can't cope and is ill again and starts to brood. That's why I was grateful you didn't bring Andrée here. A Frenchman and complete stranger to converse with in gales and torrential rain wouldn't have been particularly good for her. This summer just needs to be calm.

As for me, I find the prospect of new people very unappealing. You know Uca and Nita have been here for a few days – the only fine weather we've had, as luck would have it – and that went well and was very pleasant. Then Mary turned up for twenty-four hours to talk plays with Uca – she blew in unannounced and full of charm to scatter anxiety and rash indiscretions among us – and then blew out again. I can't help being bewitched by her, liking her – even though she always seems to cause trouble.

Uca liked the play – that was nice. Mine has now been rewritten three times, getting better each time, but that doesn't mean it's good, of course. I've another new version to show Uca. And I'd like to show you, too, I think you'd be interested and I know you've a critical eye; it's important not to release anything mediocre.

And I've been illustrating "The Hunting of the Snark" for Bonniers. Lewis Carroll's – and as far as I know, never illustrated before.

I normally make damn sure not to venture into the classics. It was tricky, but interesting – very much like a modern nonsense poem. [...]

In fact I'm in a sort of vacuum at the moment. The only thing I care about is having peace and quiet around me, nothing happening, just a long succession of placid working days in which the only excitement is the variation in the weather. It's mainly varied between

Illustration for the Swedish edition of Lewis Carroll's *Snarkjakten* (*The Hunting of the Snark*), translated by Lars Forssell (1959).

rain and gales lately. The hot clifftops you're dreaming of are some way west of here, I reckon.

I feel sorry for people who've only had a week or two's holiday, but it doesn't matter much as far as I'm concerned.

Tooti and Ham are coming back into town on 1st September – I don't know yet if I shall steal a week on my own or come with them. There's going to be lots to do. We have to find a new home for Ham somewhere and Faffan's sculptures will need to be placed or housed. Furniture and other possessions will have to be sold or given away. There'll be masses to throw out. Impi's getting a new flat. She was out here for a week and wonderfully enough was quite amenable to our suggestion that we go our separate ways. If Ham will be living in a small flat, the idea of Impi's tyranny and depression is just impossible. Impi doesn't want to take on a position with another family, she can't face it, poor old thing – but she still wants to carry on doing her job. So we'll arrange for her to come in and clean for Ham and me by turns – and that will also be a natural way of maintaining contact.

Out here, Impi either couldn't stop talking, or sat there with a mournful stare, assuring us so often she didn't want to be in the way that she actually was. Her humility was so all-consuming that we found it very painful and pretentious, and she said she planned to put her future in God's hands.

We shall just have to get started and see what provision we can make. I, stupid ass, have gone and tied up nearly all my money in index funds, but I'm sure they'll give me a loan. That'll certainly keep us fully occupied this autumn.

We're busy catching small perch from the sea and setting out a roach net for Faffan's gull. We've relaid the roof with slates of a cool green so it looks almost like a company director's house. And we've repainted the inside in a lighter shade of blue.

This has been a blessed interlude of calm and I'm anticipating the autumn without any worries or cares.

It will be so nice to see you again!

Until then a big hug – and lots of good wishes from Ham and Tooti!

Tove.

P.S. I've decided to come back into town on 1st Sept for the estate inventory etc.

Mary: Mary Mandelin-Dixon, journalist and author.
Mine has now been rewritten: Refers to TJ's play *Troll i kulisserna* (*Moomintroll in the Wings*).

IN THE SUMMER OF 1959, TOVE JANSSON DRAWS HER LAST Moomin cartoon strip and is freed from her seven-year contract as a cartoonist. Her brother Lars Jansson takes over the role. In the course of the summer she starts work on the picture book *Vem ska trösta knyttet?* (*Who Will Comfort Toffle?*).

11.7.59 [*Bredskär*]

Dearest Maya,

Thank you for your nice letter! I've thought about you a lot, wondered how things have been for you, working through all the heat, and whether you can cope with an unbroken city summer before you can finally get away to "your own town". [...]

I'm living island life with such relish, especially since I finished with the cartoon strips, once and for all, a few days ago – and I've suddenly started taking an interest in planting and fishing and hammering in nails and other natural activities I only tackled out of duty or guilt all these years.

Suddenly I even enjoy letter writing. It's as if a great weight has rolled off me, and I can see everything differently. Everybody's going round worrying about my "problem filling all that free time", fearing that I'm going to be unbearable.

Perhaps I shall be a bit <u>less</u> unbearable now, but what do I know.

The main thing is that it's over and I can now calmly devote myself to just being – until something, some urge to be active, starts to flow again – not as a duty but as a need.

And I won't get frantic if it doesn't happen ...

Ham (furtively) brought 2 Dopff with her in anticipation of the big day, and I couldn't work out why they all kept asking me how many of the last batch of drawings I had left to do. What a stroke of luck that I finished on the very evening they all dressed in their best and produced the surprise from the cellar.

Now Uca and Lisbeth are here for a week, along with Lasse, who in great spurts of Indian ink is drawing comic strips for all he's worth, poor brother. Ham and Tooti have been here the whole time (apart from one week when Ham was in town, arranging for the removal of the tiled stove from Jungfrustigen.)

You know what, the record player and the icebox sound tremendous! To think that he found such splendid presents for you, and that you accepted them so gracefully.

You're right, of course, he really did need to make some sort of gesture like that. He probably feels more at ease with his conscience now and will find it easier to have a gentler and more natural relationship with you. How nice that he got the prize. And oh what fun it will be to be able to play records at your place!

Out here we're getting on fine. Tooti's been working a lot, with good results, and has also been knottywooding quite intensely. This year it's chests and boxes, pigeonholes and storage jars in such numbers that I'm sure the therapist in my last synopsis (Dr Hatter) would have had his suspicions.

She's cheerful and blessedly even-tempered, easy to live with. Sometimes she and Ham squabble in a disrespectfully-gruff-but-friendly sort of way. Tooti and I have been staying in the guest room, Ham and Lasse (who's been here more than he was in the years we were building the place) in the main house. Now that we've got the ghosts in the guest room, we're in a tent on the little sandy beach, which is lumpy and romantic. (Nocturnal sounds and the lap of waves)

Ham's been working on her maps for Hornborg's big historical work. She's bright and contented enough, but sometimes loses momentum – and instantly feels a lot worse. The angina makes her dizzy and gives her leg cramps at night or pains in the heart. It was worst at midsummer – she was intensively reliving everything that happened a year ago.

We had a little midsummer bonfire and some fireworks and schnapps – and I sang to the base accordion to lighten the mood, but oh dear me how melancholy it was. Then she was really ill for several days.

Now things are all right again. I think it livens her up to take such an angry interest in the ghost invasion. And in the midst of it all, Nita turned up unexpectedly for a weekend.

She was bubbly and on top form, with vodka and a radio, trim and self-assured. Uca was delighted and dismayed, and ran anxiously to and fro across the island, dividing her charms between her ladies, because Lisbeth refused to sunbathe in the same cleft as Nita. The sleeping problem was discussed for hours behind the rocks before they decided all three of them would sleep inside with Ham so nobody would feel left out. It was an exciting twenty-four hours, but everything resolved itself very elegantly. After Nita left there were fallings-out and tears and earnest explanations at different ends of the island, and I had to race like a sheepdog among the womenfolk. Ye gods, what havoc.

Tooti was grim and disapproving and Ham went about snorting at things in general. Then it all calmed down again.

We had a journalist here, turning up so inopportunely that he had to stay over, and now I'm sleeping on his sheets.

Börje and co. were here for five days with Lasse, and Ham went over to Viken for the duration while Tooti and I took the tent to Kummelskär. We had one gloriously sunny day of knottywooding together – since then it's just been rain and gales. I sat in the tent drawing comic strips in big dark glasses (magnifying, admittedly) because I'd gone and left my proper ones on the island. I drew like mad so as to be free as soon as possible: 2 months' worth completed since I came to Bredskär.

We've put in gutters and new window frames, and a bookshelf running along under the rafters, the full length of the house.

Lasse's planted digitalis in various spots and Ham's carved some peculiar creatures out of roots and given them owls' eyes from Schröders. And the swallows are back.

Abbe's lot came out to visit us a couple of times – he's got a very grand boatbuilding commission from Sweden, for a 10-m yacht with a WC, fresh-water tank and all sorts of extra features. The Peos have gone to Åland for a little holiday. Leaving Misan with some woman while they're away. Saga isn't feeling particularly well and is quite down, so she's got to go into hospital for observation when they get back. I fervently hope there's nothing seriously wrong with her.

It's been a great year for wood, with lots washed up along the beaches, so I've been able to let off steam at the woodblock.

What a shame Bredskär is so far away from you that you can't pop over for a weekend. Everyone sends their warmest wishes, the whole heap of them. Do write to me again sometime. And take care of yourself.

A thousand greetings from your friend Tove.

Dopff: An Alsace wine.
How nice that he got the prize: Sam Vanni won first prize in a mural-painting competition at the Helsinki Finnish Workers' Institute.

29 AUG. 59 [*Bredskär*]

Dearest Maya,

Thanks for your letter and birthday wishes! I often thought of you and wondered how on earth you were coping with the heat. It must have been unbelievable in town. Even here we would stagger down into the sea after five minutes at the stove and find the hot weather altogether too much of a good thing. [...]

Are you still holding together after your draining summer of work? Won't you be utterly exhausted by the time you can finally get away? And when are you going? Tooti and I won't be leaving until 1st November.

She's in the middle of packing her stuff to go into town on Tuesday, the 1st. She'll be in Åbo for a week, spend the following week "organising", and then term starts at the Ateneum.

Ham and I are planning to stay on here for the time being, we're not suffering any violent craving for the town and we both have work to do, the historic maps in Ham's case and a coloured picture book in mine.

It's to be in the same format as "Hur gick det sen?" [*The Book about Moomin, Mymble and Little My*] but without any holes or other original touches and will be called something like The Romantic Story of the Lonely Toffle. No Moomintrolls. A verse epic. I've finished the words (14 verses with 12 lines in each) and now I'm doing the pictures, some of which will be in Indian ink, the others double-page spreads in colour. I shall enjoy showing them to you and hearing your verdict when we meet. When will <u>that</u> be? October? I hope you'll still be around to get my letter, which Tooti will post in town, but otherwise I assume they will forward your post?

As for the cartoon strips, I never spare them a thought now it's over. I've completely drawn a line under all that. Just as you wouldn't want to think back on a time you had toothache.

Lasse left a week ago and went first to Saaris to see Erica who is over here on a visit – then to London to arrange his contract. He's probably somewhere in the North Sea at the moment, experiencing the storm at sea that he's always dreamt of. (I think a bit less than gale force nine would have done fine, but I've decided not to worry)

Lasse has now decided he's going to use a pseudonym, it's finally sunk in that if he has thoughts of becoming a sculptor and having artist friends in the Guild, he can't put his name on a cartoon series. I know. And I'm not exaggerating.

Other than that he's happy about the job – so far. I advised him against long contracts – and know that once he's accumulated enough money to be able to work freelance, he'll give it up. It's been so nice having him here all summer. He's been hard at work on the cartoon strips nearly all the time and I've offered constructive criticism and taught him a few "tricks of the trade". Hah. I managed it without any sense of discomfort, as if the whole thing is a joke that has nothing to do with me.

And oh my lord, what a gaggle of folk we've had here. Ragni Cawén with Matti and wife, Gebhard and family, Peo Barck and The Earth-Brown One, Kurt and Salme for a weekend, Uca and Nita for a week, also Uncle Harald and Rut with daughter and boat, and then Börje & co. again and Kiki's sister with her French husband, and then we went to Ragni's and met the so-called "merry Troil girls" and then we had the consecration of Pellinge church and assorted birthday bashes – those are the things I can remember, anyway …

But now they've all blown away in the big storm. It was the most spectacular thing I've ever seen. The whole house shook and it took two of us to open the door. The pilots say a tornado (column of water) 10-m high passed close by the island. What a shame we didn't see it. The boat, which was pulled up on the shore, was carried quite some distance across the sand by the wind and a bracing atmosphere of imminent disaster hung over the whole island. It was cold, we suddenly had to keep the fires going day and night (the sudden transition from the heat happened overnight) and hang blankets over the doors and windows.

Now there's a solid bank of seaweed round the beaches and everything's been sluiced and cleansed after the long dry spell.

Ham and Tooti send warm wishes. It's a shame we won't see each other before you go. Perhaps you'll drop me a line from Paris. If you feel like it. A big hug and all good wishes!

Tove.

TOVE JANSSON AND TUULIKKI PIETILÄ RETURNED FROM THEIR trip to Greece in November 1959 via Paris, where they stayed for a month, from early December until early January 1960.

PARIS 10.12.59

Dearest Maya,

Love from both of us! Now it's Tooti's turn for a sore throat, so today we're looking out over our grey roofs and eating out of little bags and drinking wine, and Tooti is applying some bright blue French medical product to her throat and reading books about the secret signs of the Sibyl that she found on the bookstalls along the Seine.

This is still such an enjoyable trip – I'd never thought, you know, that we could be so serene and happy, such friends, day after day, week after week. Ham told me in one of her letters that you two had met up, how nice. And that Ham "read out some parts" of my letters. So you've heard a bit about teeming Greece and the trips we went on down there. When we see each other I'll give you a more detailed picture of the whole thing, some evening when we're all in the right mood and have the time, wine and inclination.

Everything's stayed with me, intensely, all those vivid impressions; the unfamiliarity, colour, vitality and unsettling aspects of Greece – both the people and the landscapes. Yet at the same time, Paris infused everything with its own very personal atmosphere within a couple of hours. You know.

One was, quite simply and as if it were the most natural thing in the world, in Paris again, slipping into it all with no great surprise.

But there's something entirely different about being here with Tooti, who seems to have settled in here even better than at home, if that's possible. She's always happy and even-tempered, never irritable, regardless of any mishaps that befall us on our travels. A couple of times she completely lost her temper for two minutes, but not at me – and how she laughs afterwards at her own infuriation.

We always want to do the same things, we both get tired at the same time, and we're never bored – not even in those slacker moments of anticlimax that always find their way into a continuous chain of intense experiences and ever-changing scenes.

It seems a bit childish, in fact, to try to describe what we "saw and did" in Paris. To you, I mean! But a few words – to remind you of your own eyes and all the details you've ever absorbed in the same way …

Mostly we've just walked and walked. Shown each other "the old places", which the other one obligingly tries to appreciate – and then, with cheerful impatience, found new places, together. To remember. Flea markets with savage winter winds, and moules. Tooti ferrets about in boxes while I admire fluffy animals on the same quai.

We wonder whether to go to the Musée du Louvre or the Magasin du Louvre, cast enquiring glances at each other and head without comment for the Magasin.

Zigzag walks through the arty streets down towards the Seine, the first time I've ever been drowned by a squat toilet not in working order. The sheepish lighting of a candle in some church, an act that one doesn't care to investigate further.

We go through our addresses and decide not to look up so-and-so yet. We eat a bird's nest each and then want ordinary food for a while – and go to a Greek restaurant just so we can say Kalimera sass <u>and</u> parakalo – and the waiter stares at us because he's French!

And then one goes to Jacqueline (where Everyone remembers you) to get one's hair cut and comes out with one's whole face repainted and some vastly overpriced beauty products under one's arm, not knowing quite how it happened.

And after "Les enfants du paradis", which goes on for four hours and leaves one utterly bowled over, we emerge into the rain – and the strange thing is that people are <u>still</u> talking French all around us, and we're not at Skillnaden after seeing a first-rate French film!

Then Rue de la Gaitée with its cheap snail eateries that were different last time, and Rotonde has completely disappeared, and the Madame who used to dote on me has forgotten what I look like.

And Monocle, which isn't at all as exciting as I remembered – but one can dance there and put on a Vivica-style show, and the flower girl unhesitatingly sold her rose to Tooti, not me. Anyway, the whole nightclub was full of men fooling about drunkenly and disrupting the show, and they were the ones dancing. Perhaps through Moune we can find some quiet ghost venue that hasn't turned into an ordinary nightclub. Gaby was there, and she recognised Tooti (the first one to do so at any of Tooti's "places") and was enchanted and drank a fair bit of champagne with us.

You were right – everything is insanely expensive (except the hotel) and our money just goes sailing off in all directions.

We <u>have</u> been rather spendthrift in these first days, but so be it – after Moomintrolls and academies, among other things. Black dollars will no doubt see us through to the end of the month. M.me Marabella came padding out of her lair in ecstasy at our arrival. She was pleased that we wanted to stay with her, told us about her life, embraced Tooti, and only once we'd brought in all our things by mutual agreement did it emerge that she hadn't got a room – she'd given it away. After some hullabaloo and conferring with the local concierges we got a poky little room on the 6th floor at 6 rue Blainville just next door, in a ramshackle hotel with the proud name of Hot. De la Paix. Furnished mostly with mirrors and plush rugs and very, very French. So if you feel like dropping a line to let me know how you are ...? We often think of you, and fondly. We send you our very best wishes – and a big x from your friends

Tove and Tooti

Kalimera sass and *parakalo*: Good morning and please.
Skillnaden: (Finnish *Erottaja*), a public square in central Helsinki.

7 JUNE 61. [*Bredskär*]

Dearest Maya,

A hug for you from the island, where our all-female household is running as usual, tranquilly and amiably. We've been living in the house, all three of us + cat – and it was only today Tooti moved into the self-contained guest room.

We were in a rather sorry state here for a week. Ham mostly stayed in bed and ate barely anything – the growth obstructing her diaphragm was very troublesome. And Tooti went and lifted a log that was too heavy, something gave way in her back and we were barely able to get her up to the house. I was really scared – slipped discs and so on – but evidently it was only a badly pulled muscle. She had to lie flat for a week.

They're a bit livelier again now. Tooti's started a silkscreen print but she's not allowed to lift anything – Ham is up and pottering around, but still hasn't the energy for her maps. I'm illustrating Tolkien at top speed, all the vignettes and thumbnails are done and now I'm onto the whole-page illustrations. I drew some of the smaller pictures 60–80 times before they started to "flow". It's damned depressing how one can get so stuck on something one is "expert" at.

One day we drove the boat out to Klovharun and found a dead seal at the harbour entrance. It was on the bottom, looking very beautiful in the clear water – a little way off there was some torn drift net. Clearly the poor thing had been choked to death – and very recently. We rolled it up the sloping beach a little way with the oar, and before it could fall into the deep water I went in and grabbed hold of its tail. It was awfully hard getting it into the boat, which was also full of driftwood from the beaches.

So Abbe can have the jawbone, which is worth 2000, and Tooti the skin because she "saw it first". Ah, such Christian tomfoolery. Incidentally, after a long time with no catches at all we've been blessed with lots of pike. Things had got so bad that we even borrowed roach from the cat net when we got too sick of tinned food.

Tooti's made a new oak table for the verandah and a little bench, and done plenty of other general knottywooding. Abbes paid a couple of visits – and a huge Sutton disagreement erupted, with

Map of Storpellinge drawn by Signe Hammarsten Jansson.

hysterical, 100-word telegrams – I had to go back and forth with 8 years' business correspondence in a big macaroni tin, and call London and wade through contracts and lose my temper. The story is too long and dull to repeat, but I <u>found</u> the letter that proved I was neither the big baddie nor the little idiot.

Finance companies, television and *what not*.

Lasse is currently in London and will be on his way home soon. They had a nice honeymoon "with no sightseeing at all" and the car was fine. Two little postcards, brief and happy.

I expect before we know it he'll be here with his strip cartoons – and Nita's coming in August. Uca and Kirsten after midsummer and then Uncle Harald and family from Sweden.

I couldn't get hold of you the day before we came out, felt like a chat and some nice bits of gossip. Wasn't it a remarkable wedding! The next day we waved them off at Bore and Lasse had taken every single flowerbud to decorate their cabin.

Off Villagatan in the roadstead the ship stopped for some reason, and Uca was seized with a terrible premonition of disaster – Margit might have fallen overboard and Lasse jumped in after her, or something – and she called the harbourmaster's office, the steamship company, the pilots, and finally the ship itself.

We got hold of Lasse who was mildly surprised and hadn't noticed a thing – but thought maybe they'd run aground. They were drinking beer and were absolutely fine.

And how are you?

The heat in town must have been awful. The island is as dry as hay and everything's wilting, we sleep under just a sheet and keep all the windows open. Send me a few words so I know how you are! The others send their best regards!

Kisses and hugs –

Tove.

Tolkien: TJ was illustrating *Bilbo. En hobbits äventyr*, the Swedish edition of *The Hobbit*, published in 1962 by Rabén & Sjögren in Stockholm.

TOVE JANSSON AND TUULIKKI PIETILÄ SPENT THE SUMMER OF
1963 on Bredskär with Signe Hammarsten and Lars Jansson,
his wife Nita and daughter Sophia. It was a summer full of
friction, tensions and "guilt–melancholy". The following year,
work started on their house on the other island, Klovharun.

14.7.63 [*Bredskär*]

Dearest Maya,

I feel I have some kind of summary of our archipelagic situation
clear in my mind now – and want to write that letter I've been
thinking of for a long time. That is, thinking of you and the contact
I owe you, especially after the fragmented and slightly overwrought
insights into island life that you had from me at Lehtovaara.

Which I'd now like to supplement.

Well, over the first ten days with Tooti on Bredskär, something
resolved itself for me, something important, and I don't really know
how – but I felt I was on the right lines with it all. I calmly started
"doing things" on the island again, almost enjoying it, seemed to have
got over my resignation and lack of initiative and instead of (with
some effort) "being nice" I had a nice time myself.

You know how seismographic it gets on an island when you live
close together; every tiny change in atmosphere is registered and
has an effect. I think I only realised things were on the up for me
when everyone suddenly seemed happy rather than amicable. And
then I directed my anxiety solely towards Tooti and her reaction to
the Change.

Initially everything seemed fine, she rootled happily among her
bits and pieces from last year, organised, had a good shout about dirty
nappies in the toolbox but was cheerful again a minute later – you
know – mended Sophia's shoes and hung a swing from the ceiling,
applied mustard plasters to the child's cough morning and night, got
cross with Ham in the card game as usual, mended the steps and
everything appeared to be going well.

Nita was scared of her for the first few days and tidied away the
messiest baby pants and had the coffee ready (!!) when we came in
from the tent in the mornings, had made the bed, was dressed (!!!) –

then those worrying symptoms abated and everything went back to normal. Lasse sat there doing his cartoon strips, silent and charming and a bit distant, Ham let herself be ordered around by Sophia and occasionally hid in the guest room, worn out.

Then Tooti turned very subdued and just spent all her time reading in a deckchair, day after day, and I knew something was seriously wrong; there wasn't a hope of her being able to start her work in the benign but unbelievable muddle all around us. So when ten days had passed I quietly asked Tooti if she felt like five days on Klovharun. She said nothing for a couple of hours but then she leapt on the idea and we were both seized by a kind of pre-move panic (God knows how that happened) and dashed round throwing things in baskets (forgetting loads of stuff, of course) to everybody's mild astonishment. Then off we went with tent, pots and pans, wood and pickaxes and the whole caboodle.

And it was only once Tooti was out on Klovharun that the infectious Enthusiasm which periodically grips her (God bless her) blazed up and she went scurrying round, delighted with absolutely everything on that fierce little skerry, and it wasn't until then I felt myself transferring my love to that rock and believing in it – and Bredskär turned into a friendly place without yearning or rancour.

We had a rather wonderful time out there, and I'm afraid we indulged in orgies of scouting, constructing hearths and primitive furniture and height gauges and incredible arrangements for securing the tent and organising our hastily assembled provisions.

All at once I felt the sort of eagerness for activity that I thought middle age had definitively taken from me, and hacked up reed roots, emptied hundreds of buckets out of the deep rock hollow that we're going to build our house on top of and use as a huge cellar, lugged stones around at the harbour entrance, wrote some couplets for Lasse and <u>swam</u> in the ice-cold water.

The paradise weather lasted for two days, then this summer's first area of low pressure came crashing over us with pelting rain, thunder and a force-six gale.

Oh my, it was a very different matter from what we're used to on the "inner island"! The surf boomed like cannon fire, the water rose and the little "lagoon", the lake, was a boiling whirlpool with no inlet or spit to be seen. We saved the boat nipin napin and bits of the tent blew apart. The poor baby seabirds who had peacefully come into the world and grown up around us tumbled head over heels like peas and blew out to sea when they tried to get across the lagoon.

The storm taught us a lot about our harbour, the location and design of our house and the possibilities for the little meadow and the ravine. We've now decided to have the giant rock that the ice age left in the hollow "under our house" blasted apart this summer and not wait.

And start building (getting the builders in) next summer. We've simply got to, even if it only amounts to a week on Klovharun now and then.

When the wind dropped they came out from Bredskär after us, Lasse, Ham and Uca who had already been on the inner island for three days – that was a surprise. And the day after she went to Kalvholmen for a fortnight, taking Lasse and family with her.

Tooti threw herself straight into her work right away and she's still hard at it, happily carving woodcuts. I was so pleased about everything that I rashly started making models of the house on Klovharun and collecting seaweed so I'd eventually be able to grow flowers in the reedy ravine.

And then it was Ham's turn to have all the life go out of her. "We ought to leave, Bredskär was done for, she was alone, she was in the way", the whole saga.

That was yesterday, a difficult conversation, back to front, with a greater sense of distance than ever and a black wave of the guilt–melancholy I've been struggling with for so long.

Today we're doing our best again, but I've put away the model of the house. Peo and co. have started their month's holiday and the youngsters came canoeing over from Viken with bilberries, post and milk. They brought a parcel from Impi, which turned out to contain vodka for me and the dearest little jar of caviar for Ham. Impi's trip to Leningrad was a great success; she described it in the happiest and most touching terms in lots of letters. So here we sit with a vodka each (the house had run completely dry), while outside there's pouring rain and loud claps of thunder but our own atmospheric pressure is easing.

So there you have the essentials of my island report.

[...] I'd so much like to hear a few words from you about how you are. Hot – and very busy, I fear? Ham and Tooti send their very best regards. The thunder has stopped now, and the rain, which filled our empty barrel in half an hour. The fishing boats that were waiting out the storm in the lee of the island are on their way to sea again.

Fondest wishes – a big hug from your Tove.

Lehtovaara: Restaurant in Helsinki.
nipin napin: (Finnish) by the skin of our teeth.
Kalvholmen: The Frenckells' summer place at Pernå.

17.8.63 [*Bredskär*]

Darling Maya,

Thank you so much for a long and affectionate letter, so considerate in the midst of your own dull summer – a letter that made me happy and concerned at the same time. And for the clever little birthday card, which arrived on the exact day, just think, with doves and gold, and – thank goodness – news that your teeth are going to be all right.

Teeth problems are, I "somehows" think (to quote Tooti) worse than anything else one can suffer, physical or mental. Of course one's friends have been visited by all manner of afflictions in the lifetime one has known them – but nothing else seems as ghastly as your tooth troubles. So it feels just like a birthday present that you are better.

Thank you for your wise words about our island triangle. I'm sure you are right. But still – it seems insoluble. Maya, believe me, even if I hoisted every sail in my (rather pitiful) rigging, I wouldn't be able to steer this one safely to shore. It goes its own way, regardless of what I do. And of course I've tried – and keep trying.

It's dark outside, Tooti's gone down to the tent on the beach and Ham has retired to the "guest room" with Psipsina, who she likes to have with her.

Lasse went into town this afternoon to see Staffan (who was here for a few days) and meet Nita who is coming home from Sweden with Sophia after the special family occasion.

Just after Tooti's and my camping trip to Klovharun, Lasse & co. went to Kalvholmen with Vivica and stayed for three weeks. Tooti got straight down to her work and has been steadily at it ever since.

Woodcuts, and then some silkscreen prints. I'm pleased she's been able to work – if my gaggle of relations had sabotaged her working routine it would have been ten times worse than them making her feel personally uncomfortable on the island.

In due course Lasse came back, on his own, and sat there quietly and obligingly in the house, drawing his cartoons, writing his musical for Uca, dealing with his Aero photo correspondence. That didn't disturb Tooti – they're used to each other.

He's off again now, so I've moved into the house in his stead, so Ham won't feel lonely in the August darkness. I know how it makes her feel, mortally melancholy, like being totally shut off, a harbinger of ultimate isolation from everything.

I haven't felt like letter writing for so long (though I've had to write plenty) but tonight, now I'm suddenly alone, I had the urge to write to you. (And you are someone I like far too much to think of writing to simply out of duty)

First of all, congratulations on passing the technical part of your driving test, which must have been pretty difficult? What colour car will you have? Just imagine, Maya, never having to freeze on your way to work, never having to wait for a bus! When you actually get the car isn't so important – it will definitely come, now you can drive. It's just a question of time.

Tooti's talked of nothing but cars since she heard about your plans. I'm sure you're right that she could do with a more active existence than this stagnant island life. Some of our troubles may well arise from that. Now she's pinning her hopes on Portugal this winter.

Ham has been invited to Ibiza – meanwhile, we're flying our separate ways – I shall meet Ham there for the journey home, and spend a few happy weeks with her in Paris. That sounds splendid, doesn't it? Not that Ham seemed particularly pleased when we unveiled our excellent plans. Perhaps she thinks the whole thing has been devised not for her sake but for ours. I expect one grows distrustful with age and illness. [...]

It's really dark outside now – and it still feels just as fascinating to be utterly alone.

No, I didn't do any work at all this summer, apart from six paintings of dubious appearance and a dozen couplets I painstakingly welded together for Lasse's musical "Crash".

He took them into town with him to show Uca, I hope they pass muster. I do hope his play will be a success.

I also did a bit of charity crap, of course, Save the Children and the Red Cross and letter-from-Father Christmas-to-Children-of-the-World, but I don't count that as work. It's as if I've lost all my drive and things are just closing in all around me – I don't know what to do.

You see I've finally accepted Bredskär again, the way you take back an unfaithful friend. I potter and prettify and arrange and keep house as usual and feel at ease – (though I'd rather be in town of course) but it's as if there's no point to it any more.

It's the same with work, with everything I do, as if I'm desperately trying to play a role I'm unsuitable for, and haven't even learnt my lines properly. And Klovharun, my refuge, is now like a guilty conscience – we haven't been there once since those five happy days with Tooti.

You realise, I'm sure, that if Ham views Klovharun as an enemy and just hopes she'll die before I move there, then it puts quite a dampener on the spontaneous sense of pleasure one would associate with a dream finally coming true. I've started feeling scared of the whole lump of rock, and I'm having to develop and refine our plans for the house there, to encourage Tooti.

It's awful that everything I touch turns into a matter of conscience – and it explains why nothing feels like a pleasure any more.

You can see that if everything I've tried and sacrificed and battled with, and given with all my heart, has only resulted in Ham feeling she's in the way, feeling lonely and sidelined, being unhappy and wishing she could die, then it's all been totally in vain. Everything is just one big disaster, not helped by the fact that Tooti is also uncomfortable and as nervous as a kitten, and feels I've chosen Ham over her. One relief, naturally, is that Tooti is adamant she won't spend another summer here.

There are only two weeks to go now, which I'm glad of. Around 1st September we'll be heading to town with cat and child and the whole crowd, and then at least it will be a different kind of emotion.

Maya, nothing on earth (not even toothache!) can be worse than being old and ill and awaiting your demise. Believe me, I'm trying to understand, putting myself in her shoes to the point where I think of precious little but death. But one can't keep laying that ace of spades, that trump which grinds down everything else, too often. It isn't *fair play*. I'm writing all this now so we don't have to talk about it when we meet.

You need to know, in any case, you and I are too close for me not to tell you. And a letter that you burn – *please!* – is better than talking, I think.

Maya, it's so awful, these two women I love, one of whom wants to die and the other to live at any price – and I can't help either without making things worse for the other. Sometimes I think I hate them both and it makes me feel ill.

And I can't bear the bloody sight of islands any more, big or small.

Things will be better when Nita gets here with her amiably nonchalant sloppiness and the whole house is full of nursery and clutter and nappies – then there's no time to think, only to get on with it.

And it will be better still when we're back in town. Then we'll go to Lehtovaara and eat crayfish, won't we?

I so look forward to seeing you again. I'll ring as soon as I'm back.

Bye,

Tove.

P.S. And for heaven's sake, you surely won't go off to Egypt until I've had time to see you!?

Later. All three of us went out to Klovharun on Tooti's initiative and marked out crosses for metal mooring rings. It defused the situation a bit. Now I'm transporting seaweed for the flowers on Bredskär and Ham will put it out next year.

They send warm wishes.

DURING THE SUMMER OF 1964, TOVE JANSSON WORKED ON *Pappan och havet* (*Moominpappa at Sea*), a book in which she "let off steam", as she expressed it in a letter to Maya Vanni. Maya Vanni read the manuscript and Tove Jansson was grateful for her comments. She reached her fiftieth birthday on 9 August.

JULY –64 [*Bredskär*]

Darling Maya,

Thank you for your nice long letter, which I've read many times. I'm as glad as you are about the trip to the Mediterranean! The boat seems good. And I'm sure it's very sensible not to make any detours that are too exotic this time – you'll be able to concentrate more cool-headedly, with a sense of having plenty of time. And North Africa certainly is exciting enough. Algiers and Morocco are supposed to be much more colourful than Tunis, where I went. And that was pretty exciting in itself. Then you'll fly home from some suitable city. I know no one else with your capacity for delighting in preparations and plans. And you certainly need it when you're being frazzled in town.

We're wickedly well off out here – and the easy, affable atmosphere is holding. At the moment we're sitting on the sandy beach. Tooti's pulling nails out of a navigation mark, (it's illegal to salvage them, but they're so handy for pulling boats up) Ham is reading detective novels. She's a bit sorry for herself after having some pains in her heart. The first time this summer.

With the patience of an angel and two fingers, Tooti has typed out my book, and I'm now busy illustrating it.

I'm terribly glad you feel the book is up to scratch, thinking back over it afterwards. I've done quite a lot more work on it and lightened the parts that are too grown-up and dull, refined the language and tried to distil it down.

[...] The first ten days of our free working month were entirely taken up by unexpected guests – Salme and Harry – Assendelft – Uca – Gylling, my lawyer, plus wife – a gifted young fellow from Gothenburg who came to complain that the girl's parents had refused to him let him into the house in Borgå (Moomin fans) and another lad who is going to write his dissertation on Moomintroll. And a few Abbe invitations with the Pellinge folk.

So things have been pretty topsy-turvy, as you can imagine. I'll fill you in on the details when I see you.

Though quite how much news one can fit into a fiftieth birthday I'm not sure. Maybe the event itself will be quite good fun. Lots of people and booze and feelings and fruit cordial for the children. It's very nice that you actually want to come and join the throng. Don't forget sheets. And the occasion will be cat-free!

We're expecting Reima and family for a week, before long. It's going to be a veritable island of aunties. As you can see, Tooti can hardly gear herself up for a spell of work with all this social life in full swing; the gaps between interruptions are too short.

I can fit in some illustrating – that's different (though it can be a struggle at times). But she takes it in her stride, gets on with some knottywooding and is placid and agreeable.

The Uca sojourn was a great success. – I can just imagine how it was with her invitations and plaintive telephone calls about feeling abandoned – you describe them to a tee. Thank goodness you can take it as you do.

But unfortunately – the gloss inevitably wears off a friendship over time if there are too many repetitions of that sort of behaviour.

Ah, so you didn't write. I'm sure that was a good decision. And the most important thing was for you to regain your composure afterwards. I've been waiting eagerly to hear – not what you did, exactly – but how you reacted.

As I haven't heard from you since then, I realise nothing can have happened on that score – perhaps a note scribbled while travelling. How I hate getting those!!!

You know what, sometimes – at long intervals – I also experience that sense of gloom – at times even anguish– that something has been irretrievably lost, has slipped by. One tells oneself with a degree of amused indulgence that it's all part of the ageing process and will pass. But it's horrible. Ah well.

Now it's another day, towards evening, with gentle, long-overdue rain. The island is tinder-dry and with much cursing I dutifully water the Spaniards' pathetic little salad patches with seawater, their snowball trees, delicate chromosome blueberry plants, myrtle and other touching idiocies. Dill growing in seaweed!

Good grief, it's like going back to the first years we lived here and tried to establish tender plants from the inner archipelago. I realise now that I must have been too dominant and snatched the initiative away from Lasse. Now he can start settling in here in his own way at last. Nasturtiums! So I'm watering frantically and restoring the balance (or trying to, anyway) by at least not offering any good advice. – One day we saw great columns of smoke rising up, over beyond Viken, and dashed to the boat with all our buckets.

There was quite a stretch of forest burning and I set about extinguishing it with Fillyjonkian delight, the most satisfying part of all being when I found someone's axe on a tree stump in the smoke and cut down a spruce sapling to use as a beater at the fire line. Unfortunately the Pellinge hoses arrived pretty quickly.

I shouldn't say that. The people of Vik were white in the face and I've never experienced a real forest fire. I'm sure it's indescribably awful.

Ham's started some illustrations. Delicate little vignettes for a book we're publishing with Schildts (words by me) – a book for people in love, with space for them to do most of the writing. It's so nice to see her working.

We're both drawing like mad; in a week we'll have a nursery here, hopeless from a work point of view. Tooti's given up. She's knotty-wooding, as I said. And waiting for Klovharun.

We had 5 ½ days out there in our tent this year. They were perfect. I toiled away, crazily hacking out reeds and carting away sharp pieces of rock after the blasting, and was completely and blissfully happy. Perhaps there'll be a few more days in August, once Lasse gets back to look after the other island and my fiftieth is over, on the ninth.

Abbe's got his traditional birthday do on the 15th, there'll scarcely be time for Klovharun in between. Or perhaps there will. Tooti's going back to town to work after Abbe's special occasion.

Have I ever told you how much I detest birthdays and all family parties, anniversaries and High Days and Holidays generally? They've always ruined my private life and racked me with guilt, they're simply deadly. Maybe I'll get through the wretched business better with you here.

Perhaps I could go out to Klovharun on my own when it's all over and everybody's gone …? But I shan't tell a soul, they'd only worry about me not coping on my own. Who worries about me not coping in company?

Now that we haven't had anybody here for a while, island life has slipped into a peaceful, recurring rhythm that gives me a calm, blunted feeling of safe continuation with no responsibility or presentiments of disaster.

Tooti and I wake up early, always simultaneously though we sleep in separate beds. I slither over and we lie close, close for a while, and she switches on the radio.

Then I let the cat out and observe the weather and put the coffee on. Clean my teeth and throw the contents of my tooth mug at Psipsina with a yell, it's a ritual. The damn cat streaks off like a lunatic.

(we're sleeping in the house so Ham's not left alone up here at nights. While the Spaniards are away, that is) After that I take coffee and toast to Ham in the guest room, serve Tooti and myself and read crime novels while I drink mine. Later in the day I move on to "a better class of book". Then the cat comes in and howls so we go down to the beach for some fish from the cage. I'm very attached to these morning activities. Then it's time for the washing up and bringing in wood and water. We rarely clean the house and only have the occasional wash, with much brouhaha and pans of hot water on the ground outside. Then we do our own private thing until dinner, which we eat sometime in the middle of the day, our noses in our books. We get on with our work.

After dinner Ham takes a nap – in the evening we have tea and then read, set out nets or play cards. We bring the cat indoors and I go in to light Ham's lamp. Always the same. If we've any drink, we tend to have one around four. Or several, in fact. We don't talk much. And so the days pass in blessed tranquillity.

Yet I'm always longing for the Outer Island, longing to build and plan and move up into higher gear – you know what I mean.

It <u>will</u> be built now – next year at the latest – and Ham's going to live out there with us for part of each summer. I've discussed it with Tooti. My heel-dragging over the new building project has now turned into a panic to get started, but the blueprints are taking their time and I can't find anyone to shift the blast rubble.

I <u>must</u> start soon before the State gets wind of my building permit. Or Dr Vallgren reports me. You know what, he boasted to Gylling that he imposed conditions on Klovharun the way he did (on that list with his name at the top) <u>specifically</u> in the hope that those non-legal documents would wreck my building permit! You remember how he snatched Kummelskär away and set the Pellinge residents against me! Why does he hate me, can you understand it? He's got lots of islands of his own, bought at below market value, among which he spreads his multitude of relations. This Klovharun business has become a kind of secret mania for me – I've simply got to get there, all the more so when everything and everybody conspires to prevent me.

Last summer on Bredskär was hell – this year I've sort of atoned for all that and put it to bed – left things clean and tidy behind me, as it were. I finally feel I can move with a clear conscience and I've got to do it before everything gets grubby again.

It feels like when I was 17 and agonising over how to leave home without upsetting anyone. Isn't that topnotch – as they say in Sweden!

I shall so enjoy reading the new book in your "secret library".

Dusk is falling. All the best and bye for now – I shall write some more if I can't get the letter off to the post

Guess what, I went out with Abbe one day to all the lighthouses to study them for the book. It was great fun!

Your Tove.

the Spaniards: Lars, Nita and Sophia Jansson spent the winter in Ibiza.

a book for people in love: *Vi. En romantisk bok för älskande* (Us. A Romantic Book for Lovers). With words by TJ and illustrations by Signe Hammarsten Jansson, Schildts, 1965.

25.8.65 [*Klovharun*]

Darling Maya,

It's a long time since June, when I got your warm letter – we'd had our usual amicable and slightly haphazard midsummer, but it's still pleasant to recall it – you were off to Jväskylä and were finding your job dreary – and sometime in July a film script was going to be ready. By now you're probably planning your autumn trip, but I know nothing at all about how you've been because I didn't get round to writing myself. It's possible I was rather thrown by the Margareta affair attracting so much ink – as tends to be the way with me, a tiny bit of mild thoughtlessness led to a terribly involved reckoning, with sympathy the main sum on the account sheet.

You ought to come along to that "association" sometime; it's good fun and for once there's an opportunity to dance. If you also want to pay for a slap-up dinner at the Restaurant with a private violinist and a rose seller before the dance, for half a dozen scattered ghosts, that's OK – but just beware of doing any irregular dancing afterwards. I've never had to write so many soothing letters in such a short space of time before – and the matter wasn't settled until Bitti took her new friend to Lundby, where Margareta fell head over heels with the countess and was no longer friends with Bitti but intensely interested in agriculture. After that we had a succession of ghost-hypocritical cries for help until I was able to calm down the whole colony and find some peace myself, without showing how relieved I was.

The house wasn't finished until 15th July and our pirates went back to Kråkö after a strange four-man farewell party, which I'll tell you about when we meet.

So Tooti and I were no longer builders' mates and didn't have to do all that cooking any more, but instead we had half of Nyland's coastal population swarming out here to look at the remarkable house that took so long and cost so much, and to wonder how and where we actually slept when we were there with our Kråkö gang. All sorts of rumours seem to be blossoming about Harun and Schrünkel-Krünkel's original halo is well on its way to sliding over to us.

The invasion is still going on – but we've had a few days of gales when we've actually been left in peace to get on with our work. Tooti's done sketches for the triennial exhibition and will be going to town at the end of August for an intensive bout of work in the weeks she's got left and I shall stay here for the time being and try to lick the Alice in Wonderland illustrations into shape. Bonniers wants them idealised to fit in with the people's home, but I feel more and more convinced that the only appropriate illustrator for this pathological nightmare would have been Hieronymus Bosch.

Ham has been terribly ill, and still is. While the Kråkö gang was building she came to Harun for three- or four-day weekends, then for slightly longer periods. Lasse rebuilt the whole guest room, put insulation in the roof, walls and floors – but it still seems the little hut won't be warm enough. The stove was really hot, so she threw the window open in the middle of the night – the wind changed and she fell asleep with it open – and after that the pneumonia she had in the spring came back. When Ham was finally restored to health with penicillin those freezing nights set in and the whole wretched thing started all over again.

Now she's here on Harun with a violent reaction to penicillin, hives all over, rheumatic headache and vomiting everything back up. She's a little bit better than yesterday.

I rang a doctor who refused to come and said we were breaking the law and should take the patient to hospital immediately. We had Gylling's big swish car all ready to go but Ham refused point blank; she didn't want to be moved anywhere.

So now I'm trying to fix her without knowing anything about medicine or nursing and as you'll appreciate I'm even more petrified than usual. I console myself that she likes it here on Harun and that Tooti is being kind. (that is, after some earlier and unfortunately understandable eruptions which rather shook us = me and Tooti)

Oh well – it's been a positive summer and quite marvellous in parts – but not easy. The old triangle in a new way, you know. I still think all three of us have come through it pretty well, especially Ham. Tooti and I have sniped at each other a few times, but we can be forgiven that. We could have been worse.

Be that as it may, we're pleased with our beautiful house and love the island as much as we ever did Bredskär. One day I slipped off with Peo & co who were heading for my coveted Kummelskär, my isle of dashed hopes, you know – where I'd sworn never to set foot again, and it was over; I just confirmed that the island was wonderful – but that it was Harun I loved. Just like some bitter old infatuation that had faded away. (incidentally I read somewhere that ghosts have pronounced island complexes, which interest me. Some form of identification, isolation trauma, the devil only knows)

By 9 o'clock it's completely dark out here. Then one goes out onto the rocks with a completely new Gadget: a Talky Walky, and telephones Bredskär. Lasse's voice is always very clear, but mine never is. It feels very desolate, I can tell you, to stand there shouting about how Ham is and not being heard. Sometimes I hear snatches of conversations from unknown ships in unintelligible languages, sometimes I can hear Lasse talking to Peo in Viken even though they can't hear a word I'm yelling. That's the way it is with gadgets. By the way, Brunström persuaded me to swap our old 3 ½ horsepower for a 7 H.P. Penta (a mere 100,000 difference in old marks, haha) but starting this new speed monster is beyond me. And now they want a plastic boat too, flat-bottomed. And we've a gas ring in the kitchen – but that's a hangover from our November adventure of course, when I had to be builder's mate and head cook in the open air.

I threw together a few last-minute verses for Erna, who needed them for a song competition on the radio. I had a complete block, all summer, but today my conscience untied itself and I that's probably why I finally felt the urge to talk without being compelled to. I think so. [...]

The Penttis were here for a sunny, *easygoing weekend*. Reima's lot brought us a Mexican hammock for our treeless skerry and talked Ibiza building projects with Lasse & co, (can you fathom why Janssons and Pietiläs who already have a family complex would root themselves together in Spain? But Tooti seems to like the idea) – and Salme was here on two brief return visits with son and protégé, casual and disorganised, and Uca suddenly popped up after Israel, feeling positive – and a terrible short stay with Kirsten – Hilde – and niece, during which everything went wrong in spite of bottles of vodka and other generous gestures.

Since then we've had TV here and newlyweds from London, and boatloads of Kråko dwellers and locals from the village and Gyllings with champagne just when Ham was most ill, and building inspection and lots of farmers and fishermen and a few interviews and Assendelft and Börje Hielm with all the children and assorted blasters and random folk of various kinds.

Regardless of all that, which will gradually calm down, I feel a great sense of peace in knowing that we've found our island, that Ham is happy here and Tooti – in a way – accepts it – and that Lasse and family have settled into the old paradise in the right way. I think we've pulled it off.

Brunström and Sjöblom turn up quite often with their nets, carry potatoes and petrol and sleeping bags ashore like before and sleep trustingly on our floor. To me it seems quite natural.

It all feels like an extremely fortunate arrangement to me, and better at any rate than the constellations of relationships one can be exposed to in town. I don't ever want to leave, really. But will you still be in town when I get there? When are you off? You are one of the few attractions in a setting that I miss less and less. Though goodness knows this one can be awkward enough temps en temps.

Hugs! your Tove.

the people's home: A common alternative name for the Swedish welfare state (*folkhemmet* in the original Swedish).
Brunström: Sven Brunström. The "Midsummer" chapter in *The Summer Book* features the mysterious Eriksson, "who makes dreams come true".
the Penttis: Pentti Eistola and his partner.
Sjöblom: Nisse Sjöblom, the other "pirate" they had hired.

I SEPT. 67 [*Klovharun*]

Dearest Maya,

Now the heat is over and I'm sure you feel better. What a dreadful summer it must have been for you. Maybe you're at an editorial meeting in Stockholm just now, and seeing Jean – and I think the trip will be positive.

How remarkable it is that the two of you persevered and came together in spite of everything, it's quite wonderful. I don't think the form of love you two have found is pathetic, not at all. I think it's very strong, something finely honed and absolute that far exceeds the sort of affection one hasn't had to fight for. And I don't think you can hurt each other ever again – no one can damage you now, Maya, not any more.

But you certainly can be tired by your friends, grow tired of them, that small-scale weariness which your August party exemplified so well. So unnecessary, the whole thing.

I was so nervous about our women's week but for once the days on Harun went well, harmoniously – and I was tremendously grateful. You all came here out of one storm and are going back to another. Of course one hasn't exactly chosen calm-weather folk as one's friends, I know that. But will they never simmer down?

Says she, having barely started getting to grips with her own irrational whining ... I do try very hard, and I think various elements have subsided and fallen into place. I hope it's noticeable, sometimes. And I'm reading the new Karen Horney and trying to think my way through to what's right. It's very exciting and a bit lonely.

We had the big beautiful storm and I was able to see it, with Lasse. You know he's got a storm fixation even bigger than mine. We've never seen such breakers, never had to salvage so much, experience such a violently transformed landscape as ours or get so drenched through! I shall tell you our storm story sometime.

One good thing which happened this summer was that Ham and Tooti become real friends all of a sudden. Some kind of deadlock eased for all three of us and now there's such warmth and relief that it really doesn't matter how it came about. Things just happen sometimes after fighting and feeling desperate, if one just leaves well alone.

And Tooti and Nita are friends again, thank goodness. So we've been able to enjoy a serene and peaceful summer. I've reworked Kometjakten [Comet in Moominland] and Moominpappa's memoirs, completely rewriting some parts, and given the language in Trollkarlens hatt [Finn Family Moomintroll] a superficial brush-up. You know – the sort of thing one tends to do when putting together anything new proves impossible. But it's just as well – those two first books have been embarrassing me for quite a while and now that Gebers are bringing out the whole series in paperback, I've a chance to revise them; they'll have to typeset them again anyway.

And I've done new covers for everything I've produced – except for the coloured picture books of course.

Ham has started carving bark boats again, she makes little houses, potters in the garden, skims stones when she feels up to it, all sorts of playful activities that she can enjoy now she's accepted herself and her age. She's a delightful companion and friend. And I'm not so fillyjonkishly scared of catastrophes any more and don't waste so much time on unproductive thoughts. So we'll have to see where that takes us.

You've never seen the island as it looks now, tipping over into autumn. There are no bright colours out here to signal departure, they are simply erased, a withered tangle of greys and browns, the island shrinks and is somehow absorbed into the rain and sea and the evenings are dramatic with their desolate sunsets and banks of cloud. The darkness on an island such as this is like standing at the end of the world and all the night sounds are intensified, giving an impression of utter solitude – nature no longer frames one's existence, but hurls it to the periphery and imposes its sovereign domination.

Suddenly it's just the sea and vast, dramatic autumn skies. Oddly enough I feel less and less inclined to leave, the less benign my surroundings grow – the security of town is more menacing. At dusk I speak to Lasse on the Talky Walky, most days I can only hear him very faintly and indistinctly, sometimes not at all.

Then we listen to the weather forecast to find out if we dare lay our nets or if we need to pull up the boat and haul in the fish cage. I bring in the flag, feed the cat and make tea. When the sun has gone down we go to bed and light candles. Ham soon drops off but I lie here reading and listen to the sea and rain. We wake very early, coffee for me, tea for Ham, roach for the cat. I tidy the house, get water and firewood, Ham waters the plants and puts the flag out. Weather forecast, slop bucket, bail out the boat, collect rainwater from the sauna roof, washing up. Then the day can start. Always the same little things in the same order and here on the island they have meaning and bring satisfaction – they are never routine as they are in town. Another nocturnal downpour has just started. Good night – and a big

from your own Tove.

the new Karen Horney: Most likely *Our Inner Conflicts*, which was published in Swedish under the title *Våra inre konflikter* in 1967. TJ's book collection included a number of works by the American psychiatrist.

the big beautiful storm: TJ gives a vivid description of this storm in her letter of 9.8.1967 to Tuulikki Pietilä.

TOVE JANSSON AND TUULIKKI PIETILÄ'S EIGHT-MONTH-LONG round-the-world trip started in London in 1971, with business meetings and social events. TJ's British publisher Ernest Benn marked the twentieth anniversary of their collaboration with a big party and publication of the final Moomin novel, *Sent i November*, as *Moominvalley in November*. The next leg of their trip took them to Japan.

LONDON 3.11.71

Dearest Maya, hugs from me!

We've reached the end of our time in London and it all went well, even my speech thanks to Pentti's pills – I knew over half of it of by heart and Benns were very moved. A big party in my honour with loads of people, but I ask you, why must I always be so petrified of my official obligations that I only realise afterwards what fun it was?

Tooti is cheery and agreeable, and sometimes comes out with surprising things in English (in a cockney accent) and sorts out almost everything with reassuring efficiency. And plays Finnish music or Moomin music for them on her magnetic tape recorder (I think that amazes them more than anything)

We've met enough people to last us five years and I've talked enough to last me ten. After it was all over I lost my voice as usual but it came back once we'd been left in peace to wander round the streets for a few hours. I drew and gave talks in schools, and did the embassy children' party, *radio recording*, lunches and cocktail parties, and whenever we got a chance we went out into town. London is swarming with the most incredible visions, people dress however they like and the city centre always looks like one big fancy-dress ball. Fascinating.

I took Kenneth Green and consort to "Hair", which was a grand glorification of psychedelic hippiedom. It made Tooti's ears ache – but she coped well with the flight, even so. We also went to The Trials of Oscar Wilde, an incredibly powerful film that is very unlikely to come to Finland, unfortunately, and Canterbury Tales, a racy musical with fabulous stage sets.

The hotel is dead posh and impersonal, it bucked us up no end to find they've got mice in their chests of drawers, judging by the state of parcel of reindeer meat we were given for the journey. Half our luggage is taken up with presents. When left to our own devices, we've been eating on the King's Road in cheap, jolly student cafés, and we've got our very own pub. Pubs aren't at all just for the men any longer. We've stopped looking for ghost places – but you never know, we might have a try in Amsterdam. Assuming we get away at all, there are strikes at the airport, *the staff* are refusing to carry the luggage and the passengers aren't allowed to lug their own things on board. It's making us a bit anxious.

Tooti and I also wandered round various strange, outlying parts of town hunting for graphic designers so she could pick up tips to give her own graphic designer, the one she was so angry with that she was never going to offer help again. And British Mus. of course. Fine weather the whole time.

In Helsingfors the whole Reima family drove us out to catch the plane, and we arrived to be welcomed by Benns, flowers at the hotel – and at the party, all the gentlemen wore Moomin ties!

I've been practising my Japan speech off and on and trying to prepare for the TV interview. This London spell has been a kind of dress rehearsal, which is probably a good thing. And after that, just think – Maya – we'll really be <u>travelling</u>, and free!

Tooti sends her regards! All my best wishes –

Tove.

P.S. We <u>did</u> get away and now we're somewhere over the North Sea. The airport was teeming with baffled people, poor things, some of whom had been waiting there for three days! We were able to take off because we were booked on a Dutch plane but boarding was utter chaos; an hour before we were scheduled to leave, the last call for Amsterdam came bellowing through their loudspeaker horns and we pelted like crazy up and down steps and along corridors until we found the right place and scrambled onto the plane just before take-off. My worst ever. But we did get away.

4th. And just walked round the town all evening, it's beautiful here, and the people are friendly. On to Tokyo today. Tooti asks if you'd mind popping the enclosed cutting in an envelope and sending it to Raili? Laivurinrinne 1A.

Kisses!

Tove.

TOVE JANSSON AND TUULIKKI PIETILÄ SPENT THE SPRING OF 1975 in a studio in the Cité des Arts artists' house in Paris. Tove Jansson tried her hand at writing for the theatre. She painted a self-portrait and began a painting of Tuulikki Pietilä which, however, turned out looking more like Tuulikki's mother. In Paris she also did the painting of Tuulikki Pietilä entitled *The Graphic Artist*.

PARIS APRIL −75

Dearest Maya,

How lovely to get a letter from you. It's as if we are further from home here than we were on our "round the world trip", however that can be. Maybe because Paris (more a concept than a place – and obscured by memories) has acquired a touch of reality from the fact that we're only working here – a regular home life that's entirely in order … but the enormous metropolis no longer feels as if it's outside waiting to be discovered. And there's no urge to seek contact with other people, as there was when one was young.

I don't at all mean that sort of "Paris isn't like it was", I see the city as the same miracle as ever and I'm sure it's not the Parisians who have changed, but me. –

Reading back over this page, it seems muddle-headed and should be skipped – but I suppose I'll let it stand as an unfinished train of thought that we can continue later, I'd really like to talk about this.

Of course we'll see each other before Harun.

Goodness knows how moving out there will go this year, I've got to go to Stockholm first because Vivica is directing a TV play that I've put together while I've been here, a Swedish Radio commission on the subject "Vision of the Future" which will be recorded in June. I assume Tooti and I will take all the baggage out as soon as we can and get things vaguely in order before I leave and then Annukka will have to help Tooti with laying nets for the cat and we'll just hope there are no gales while I'm away. It takes two out there – and you know what, I'm starting to think even that's not enough sometimes. But that's a long way off. Or is it? You wrote that the concept of time has changed. That's another thing I'd like to talk about – but I

Tove Jansson's portrait of Tuulikki, *The Graphic Artist*, painted in the Paris studio.

haven't finished thinking it through. Perhaps it feels like that to you because of those short, intense weeks in Israel, more and more often but never for long, the quick hours on the plane, the stark contrast between happy relaxation untroubled by conscience and then Helsingfors: your job, the cold weather, the exhaustion.

I can well understand how terribly tired you are of a job where they overburden you in that inhuman way, and that you are seriously tempted to leave despite the pension. In fact the whole idea of a pension is pretty cruel, calculating, the anxiety ...

We had a letter from Salme and she was deeply depressed for the same reason. She wanted to leave, didn't dare, didn't know ... She had planned to come here for a while but suddenly decided it was too expensive.

Maya, my spontaneous reaction, off the top of my head, is that you ought to give it up and go freelance instead. Eight years, that's awful, if one's not enjoying the work any longer. There must be loads of jobs available for someone of your ability? But I can understand you agonising.

Wizo is a rather remarkable set-up. You give such a clear picture of the whole thing! I'm sure you were right to accept. And how often does one get to meet the devotees?

I'm so sad about Svenska. Backberg (some kind of distant relation) told me over the winter how dreadfully tired he was, melancholy, backache, completely done in by all the competition judging and exhibition work he took on. You're right, one loses touch with the people one was fond of, puts things off, doesn't get round to it ...

When we first came here I spent a long time trying to write, but produced nothing decent. Tooti instantly set to work on her graphic art and has been working solidly ever since – no filming except at the Flea Market and a few other incidentals. She's got almost thirty items now and they're <u>good</u>. Not a trace of abstraction ...

And then in desperation I had a go at that vision-of-the-future play for TV, which I'd resisted for so long, and you won't be surprised to hear it turned out pretty doom-laden. I exterminated virtually the whole planet and it only struck me afterwards that perhaps the future might be quite pleasant after all? Or at any rate, that they might be expecting something positive from <u>me</u>? But they don't know how much Bradbury I've read ... Then I got the block again and was left with no other option but to start painting, after a break of five years.

It made me feel so helpless. Now I've painted some innocuous leeks and apples and a landscape and a self-portrait and an interior, they don't look that great but at least I've tried – and was allowed a share in the studio so I could paint?

One canvas, a big one, is diverting me. I started with Tooti as my model but she keeps jumping up like an impatient cork all the time so I carried on without her and the woman just grew and grew and started to look more and more like Mamu, an angry Mamu.

God forbid she should ever see my "Mother-in-law". Hommage à Minkku ...

Then I was offered another TV commission – subject: "death". I wasn't keen . But I had a go anyway – we went out to the Chaplets', the French translators, and Pierre, who is a PE teacher, told us about a colleague who had hanged himself because he kept failing one part of his exam: climbing up a rope. He tried year after year but he couldn't do it ...

By the way, I've been plagued by a Frenchwoman who went and translated The Invisible Child without permission, found her own publisher and is trying to prove that Chaplets' transl. is bad. Unpleasant, but I'm staying as hard as stone. (though she is utterly beautiful)

After that an adoring Japanese girl turned up from London, where she'd been learning English so I could teach her to be a children's writer, and that was a worse saga but I did my best for three days. (she was utterly beautiful too)

Then the TV people despatched a dramaturge to help me improve the end of my Doomsday. She was awfully nice and we went to the theatre quite a lot. But Vivica now says the first version is better – though I believe in the second one ...

And then a gentleman arrived from the publisher's in London and kicked up a fuss about me writing more Moomin books, he came over just for that! And two more will be here next week, there's a terrible to-do about "children's books" and "grown-up books", Bonniers are nagging and I ought to be madly flattered but just feel uncomfortable. Every time there's a row one feels less like writing. *It's a blank!*

And then Pentti appeared! Pentti the younger has a new job, at the hotel, which he likes – a permanent position – so he couldn't come. If only that week hadn't been so icy cold. Rain and snowstorms. But even so, we rootled our way through the rows of bookstalls along the Seine and at the flea market and Ferraille. The weather's been freezing for two months, as it happens. Spring arrived in January, but then there was another blast of winter. The week with Pentti was pleasant, how could it be otherwise! We ate in the studio and then went out to brave the icy cold again.

It was just as bad for Reima & co., all three of them, of course. They were frozen numb in the gale at the Arc de Triomphe, petrified with cold up on the Eiffel Tower. They came here with two gentlemen from Tampere to study the most advanced housing estates in the banlieu (I don't think Reima and Raili liked them) and the men stuck to us doggedly because they didn't know how to make their own way to the sinful life of Montmartre, unfortunately. Then we celebrated Annukka's twelfth birthday in the studio with much festivity and lots of guests. I had quite a bad cold but it's gone now.

Tooti went and did her back in while she was using the press in the graphic art room and took three weeks to get over it, some of the time in bed. That back of hers isn't good. That's the main reason I'm reluctant to leave her on her own at Harun.

Tooti's busy with hammer and nails, making four huge boxes for sending home all our books, printing plates, cassettes and gramophone records. I reckon her intensive graphics period is over. She always goes through phases. As long as the weather clears up it'll be filming next, I bet ...

And around the 20th April we're going to the south of France for a while. We'll be coming back to Finland in the final days of May.

There's been a worse spate of work correspondence than ever, but I hear relatively little from home. [...]

Let me sum up by saying that Tooti and I are getting on fine – as we always do with each other – and that we've managed to make the studio our own in this dreadful building which is a cross between Lallukka and a hospital. We've found some friends, too, Christina Snellman and her husband Manolo, absolutely wonderful.

Best wishes to Mary. And to everybody! Tooti sends a hug –

your Tove.

Annukka: Architect Annukka Pietilä, Reima and Raili Pietilä's daughter.
Wizo: Women's International Zionist Organization
Svenska: The artist Sven Grönvall died on 20.3.1975.
that vision-of-the-future play for TV: *The Window*, a 1976 radio play.
Chaplets': Kersti and Pierre Chaplet who translated the Moomin books for the French publisher Nathan. TJ wrote a radio play called "The PE Teacher's Death" in 1976.
Ferraille: One of the Parisian markets.

TWO SAD EVENTS LEAVE THEIR MARK ON THE SHORT LETTER written in June 1981. TJ's childhood friend Abbe (Albert Gustavsson) died in the winter of that year, and there were break-ins on Klovharun. Nor was that the end of it; there were further island break-ins over the next two years.

NEAR MIDSUMMER –81 [*Klovharun*]

Hello dearest Maya,

Today it was gale force six from the east again, the worst possible direction for the boat, so we didn't go over to Viken as planned for post and provisions and to ring Reima and family to congratulate him on the State Prize. And, above all, to be with Greta. But we would have been too worried about the strengthening wind to sit calmly conversing in the right sort of way.

This spring hasn't been all that much fun. We're doing all right but something of the joy, the whole notion of archipelagic life, vanished with Abbe. We haven't talked about it, not much.

And then there was the unpleasantness of the break-in at our place after the military were out on manoeuvres again. Some soldiers broke windows – idiots, the key was hanging there on the wall – and took most of the things we were fond of – probably about 8000 marks' worth, all told. Being robbed is actually a rather interesting phenomenon – by which I mean, one feels ashamed. Not angry exactly, but there's a sense of shame. And everything rearranges itself, in the wrong way.

Still, I'm carrying on with my work. The weather's been so awful this June that we know nothing of what's happening on the other islands. We can't go there and they don't come here, either.

It's good weather for working, though, so that's okay. Tooti sends her regards!

Tove

5.6.82 [*Klovharun*]

Dearest Maya,

Here are the comments I told you about, I'm sure the protagonists' fine-tuned and irony-laden phrases will amuse you. Save the cutting!

Tooti got the tent up the other day, our great summer treat, and in fine weather for once, so now we're sleeping out there, fly-free and to the accompaniment of gulls and waves. Pellura's wife is sitting on her eggs 2 m away from us and as for Pellura, he recognized his food pot before I even had time to whistle for him and took some bread in flight when I held up the pot – how nice that sort of thing is.

Less nice is the fact that our military burglars from last year have been at it again and this time they smashed five panes in the east-facing window – no one will be able to sit in the sand on the mini-beach now. And the grass was littered with smashed bottles. They didn't get much more than Faffan's accordion, as far as we can see. But we can tell from the repeat pattern of their behaviour that it was the same characters as last spring. Isn't it tiresome.

We've now decided we'll cover the windows with shutters and get some Abloy padlocks – and how will all our shipwrecked darlings fare when they can't come in to get warm, sort out their nets, fix their motors ...?

The vandals never realised the house key was hanging beside the door! Ha. Oh, and they chucked the guest book into the sea, I found it dripping with seaweed.

Oh well. We've had an unspoilt paradise for a very long time – and are grateful. But every time we need to leave the island for a while we do it with great foreboding.

I used my time on Nyttis mostly to clear up things I'd been feeling guilty about (and the forest, to some extent), answering letters from as far back as December, and now everything's tidy.

Prolle and Saga are planning a Nyttis week at the end of June. Lasse and Sophia are out at Bredskär, we went to visit them, with a message that arrived via Viken to say Kiki Hielm's greenhouse would need ventilation and watering, plus the usual wretched business stuff, currently the fact that neither Lasse or nor I will renew any film contracts or sign new ones. Japan and Poland keep telegraphing like crazy but, you see, one reaches a certain limit and after that I'm as hard as the worst *business type*. She said boastfully.

One nice thing that happened was Tooti's suggestion that we (At last ...!) speak Finnish every other day. I'm glad. [...]

They've now refloated practically all the boats that were laid up for the winter at Viken, with the help of the boys when they're not on pilot duty, and of some friends from the village. This is their busiest time. Greta alternates between boat work and cooking for the men, never runs out of patience whatever happens and keeps the house and yard in perfect order.

It's blowing a gale again, but any day now I daresay I shall get this message off to you.

If you hear from Mary, do give her my best wishes. And Salme! Tooti sends

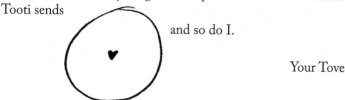

and so do I.

Your Tove

Nyttis: Abbreviation of "Nyttisholmen", a small island just off the mainland.

UNDATED [*1983, Klovharun*]

Dearest Maya,

We've been on the island for almost a week now and the news is good: the latest marauders didn't break the windows for a change, but broke in by forcing the cellar lock and floor hatch – and our teetotal life isn't causing any difficulties or negative consequences.

And the things we planted are all obligingly coming up again, not a trace of voles this year. Incidentally, I'm aware as I clamber about the rocks that my legs feel stiffer than before, I can't do quite as much as last summer and I'm being considerably more cautious. We come up with ingenious solutions; for example we lowered out luggage on a hook and line from Viken jetty (incredibly low water) and dragged it across the plank walkways on the island on a sled.

I've planted the window boxes with lots of lobelia, which will withstand gales and seawater, as well as onions, parsley, beans and peas, and indoors morning glory, to climb up to the ceiling, and we also have pelargoniums and other pot plants in the house.

In the peace out here and the quiet of spring, it's hard to comprehend the fear of break-ins that one felt in town – after all, the house is still standing even though so much of what we liked and needed has gone.

This idea of taking more of our goods and chattels to town is no longer a gesture of defiance (God knows of what or whom) but has grown almost interesting; we could turn it into a fishermen's cottage with plainer walls, uncluttered surfaces, a beautiful emptiness so Reima can't call it a maritime museum any more!

I've been reading a remarkable book by Thorkild Bjørnvig, "The Pact", about his friendship with Karen Blixen. It's complex, almost fiendish in its intensity. Like you, I generally save books of that kind for when things are quiet around me.

It's raining now, which is good, the island needs water and so do we. The same gulls have returned and they come when I whistle for them. So as you see, all is as it should be.

I can't remember when it was you were going to Paris, perhaps any day now. I'm sure it will be a splendid spring trip! I must do a bit of cooking now. Bye and hugs –

Tove

"So just conceivably another book"

LETTERS TO ÅKE RUNNQUIST
1965–1988

Åke Runnquist

A REQUEST TO ILLUSTRATE LEWIS CARROLL PROVED THE STARTING point for thirty years of collaboration and friendship between Tove Jansson and Åke Runnquist of the Bonniers publishing house in Stockholm. Åke Runnquist (1919–1991) was appointed a director at Bonniers in 1960 and edited the venerable literary magazine *BLM* (*Bonniers Litterära Magasin*) for many years. Their first contact was over pictures for a Swedish translation by Lars Forssell of Lewis Carroll's *The Hunting of the Snark*. The project went ahead and *Snarkjakten* was published in 1959. In the same year Tove Jansson contributed a short essay about Swedish children's writer and illustrator Elsa Beskow to *BLM*, another commission that came from Åke Runnquist. But what really brought them together was their collaboration over the illustrations for his new translation of Carroll's *Alice in Wonderland*. The text had an attraction for Tove Jansson that she could not resist: sheer "horror", as she termed it, using the English word. By the time *Alice i underlandet* came out in 1966, with her illustrations, the foundations of a lasting relationship between author and publisher were firmly laid. They became close friends and met periodically in Stockholm or Helsinki, along with Tuulikki Pietilä and Åke's wife Ingrid Runnquist. One of the interests they shared was writing limericks.

When Tove Jansson published her first volume of short stories *Lyssnerskan* (1971, *The Listener*), Bonniers was her choice of Swedish publisher and Åke Runnquist her editor. She left her previous publisher in Sweden, Gebers, but the Moomin books did not move with her. Runnquist did his best to gather all her titles under one roof, but was ultimately unable to do so. Bonniers, however, established itself as Tove Jansson's publisher for short-story collections and novels for adults. The letters reveal how Tove Jansson would present her current book or writing projects to her editor, examples being *Sommarboken* (1972, *The Summer Book*), *Solstaden* (1974, *Sun City*) and *Dockskåpet* (1978, published in English as *Art in Nature*). The collection was originally called "Flower Child" and the order of the stories, discussed in Tove Jansson's letter to Åke Runnquist in February 1978, was altered several times. It is also worth noting her frank declaration that the stories "Den stora resan" (The Great Journey) and "Dockskåpet" (The Doll's House) both signal a "homophile relationship", something barely registered by reviewers when the book was published. The last letters are brief, taking the form of fragmentary reports on her writing conditions. "It's good for me to be able to work slowly, without a deadline", admitted Tove Jansson in a letter dated 15.6.1988, when she was almost seventy-four. The book she was then working on was *Rent spel (Fair Play)*, which came out the following year. "There was always such a sense of calm when I met Åke; nothing seemed hurried and most things would sort themselves out eventually," wrote Tove Jansson later, in a letter to Boel Westin in 1998.

The emphasis in the letters to Åke Runnquist is on professional matters, but they also offer glimpses of Tove Jansson's life in the 1970s and 1980s: travel, writing, Moomintrolls and her longing for a new island so far away that it even lacks a channel through the sea ice in winter and she can work in peace.

* * *

8.2.65 [*Helsingfors*]

Dear Åke Runnquist,

Thank you for your letter of quite a while back, which so splendidly shored up my teetering self-esteem.

It's all decided now, of course, but think of it: illustrating *Alice in Wonderland* after Tenniel is like trying to put Fänrik Ståls Sägner into pictures when Edelfeldt has already produced the definitive version.

Now, though, I'm consoling myself with the fact that Alice's head is actually <u>far</u> too big, among other quibbles.

But shall we try to keep <u>her</u>, at least. That rather delicate face, lots of hair and skirts, utterly naturalistic and prim-looking in such a surreal context?

We <u>can't</u> make her into a modern Stockholm girl. Not even with a ponytail. (Assuming they are still modern)

These stories are terrifying. Can I draw them in horror style? The way I saw them when I was little. (I love horror stories nowadays, too)

Are they being published for children or grown-ups? Or both?

And is the translation already partly done? Thinking of the special magic of the words, the names of the creatures, wouldn't it be best to let me see the Swedish translation – or part of it – before I start? How much time can you give me? I'm working on the illustrations for a new Moomin book at present, and they're urgent. That's why I didn't write sooner.

But Alice is always in my mind, of course.

It was exciting to do The Hunting of the Snark with the translation beside me, a real tightrope adventure.

Alice is an even more serious undertaking, though. She's a kind of symbol. Shall we take the surreal approach? Not Poe, a little lighter. Keep the court of playing cards more on the margins. Dare one go for a bit of adult symbolism? The worst part is that they talk such an awful lot. Tenniel picked out all the scenes that could bear illustration – there aren't as many as one might think – anyone assuming his mantle will have to draw exactly the same thing.

What sort of completion date is Bonniers hoping for?

If you feel like it, do drop me a line and let me know what you think.

Anyway, I shall start work this summer and just draw whatever feels right, as soon as I can.

I'm trying to gather material from period prints including the horror type. I think the <u>sub</u>-terranean element of what happens should be accentuated.

Lewis Carroll was clearly completely pathological, there's no way of making anything idyllic out of it. English people must be pretty dysmorphic, don't you think, for all their cool understatement – or maybe because of it.

Can't we just do an out-and-out horror book. Because that's what it <u>is</u>.

Warm regards,

Tove Jansson

Fänrik Ståls Sägner: The Tales of Ensign Stål, a famous epic poem by the national poet of Finland Johan Ludvig Runeberg, who wrote in Swedish. One edition of the poem was illustrated by renowned Finland-Swedish artist Albert Edelfeldt.

a new Moomin book: *Pappan och havet* (*Mooominpappa at Sea*) came out in the late summer of 1965.

8.6.71 [*Klovharun*]

Dear Åke,

I'm so pleased you liked the book – particularly The Squirrel, which I worked so hard on!

Of course I know people don't like the idea of short stories and I'm not expecting miracles, far from it.

And as I said, a person can feel a chill wind blowing round her legs as she emerges from a Moomin valley.

I hope to get the cover design to you very soon. As regards the contract, I expect it will be the usual, including the guaranteed sum. Schildts usually draws up the contract.

Yes, I wrote to Gebers about a paperback series but they want to do it themselves. And they hold the rights, after all.

I won't be coming to Stockholm this autumn, Tooticki and I are going on the Big Trip we've dreamt of for so long. We're off to Japan, can you believe (I've got a job to do there) and then round America. So we won't be coming home until about the start of spring. I can still barely believe it's true.

It's a fine, cold summer. We've moved out of the house and are sleeping in a tent, a good way to work off a winter.

Remember me to Ingrid! All the best, and warm wishes –

Affectionately yours, Tove.
addr. Storpellinge
Söderby

the book: The short-story collection *Lyssnerskan* (*The Listener*) was published in the autumn of 1971.

a paperback series: A set of paperback editions of the Moomin books.

23.5.72 [*Helsingfors*]

Dear Åke,

Your letter was here to welcome me home, and I couldn't have had a nicer bouquet!

That idea of posting letters under a stone by the fence appeals to me enormously, especially after seeing what the standard postal service has amassed for me over seven months! But your missive was at the very top of the pile, what luck!

I want to answer straight away, before all my various obligations crowd in. The reviews you sent are so overwhelming that I've only read snippets of them so far – imagine the book getting such a great reception! And selling well, despite being short stories.

You're quite right that it was a relief to be leaving on our trip just as it came out, and I was pretty apprehensive about disappointing all those readers who were expecting another Moomin valley. (And maybe they <u>were</u>, when they bought the book, ghastly thought!?) I know you were uneasy as well, and I'm enormously thankful that the faith Bonniers put in me was not misplaced. I do realise how much you've all been committed to the book and its promotion.

It's nice to be able to tell you that the next book is neither short stories nor a Moomin book for Gebers. It's called *Sommarboken* [*The Summer Book*] and is about a very old woman and a very small girl on an island together. I wrote some sections of it while I was working on *Lyssnerskan* [*The Listener*], and I put them aside because

they didn't fit with the rest. I've gradually been writing more, some of it while we were away. I shall send it to you in due course for your verdict, but I want to go through the book again and try to improve it wherever I can.

Of course it would be a real pleasure to "have a quick a cup of tea" with you, or better still a vodka, here or in Sweden. Among other things, I want to tell you something of the remarkable sights I experienced on my long trip without an address – at this juncture I'm not even sure whether it's made the world bigger for me or just the opposite, much smaller than before. Or if I will ever be able to find expression in words or pictures for all the intense impressions that tumbled over me. But a lot of things must have changed now, of course, and perhaps I'll find a form for it, out on the island.

There's one thing I am sure about after all these different springtimes at different latitudes, namely that the loveliest is in Scandinavia. And the beaches, and the forest.

My very best wishes, Åke!

Many, many glad greetings,

Tove.

The reviews you sent: Reviews of *Lyssnerskan* (*The Listener*). TJ and Tuulikki Pietilä returned from their round-the-world trip in May 1972.

JUNE 73 [*Klovharun*]

Dear Åke,

Today, just as I finally finished a long, tricky job to produce a colouring book, along came a letter from you, full of warmth and good news! And some time back, your card from Peru, which I was so pleased to get. It's really good that Svalan is taking The Summer Book! What a fabulously huge readership they must have!

I recorded the whole book for Swedish Radio and they are broadcasting it as a summer programme. I also did their advent calendar this year, Moomin valley in snow with a whole host of little cutout figures, so there will be winter Moomins on TV all through December.

The colouring book is part of this campaign, 64 full pages in black and white for children to fill in. Lasse did twelve of them. I took the job without relish but found myself increasingly interested as I discovered the possibilities of a new and bolder drawing style. One thing's for sure – this has all taken a big chunk out of the book I was working on and I've got to try to find my way back into it now. It's a novel – but it's best not to talk about unfinished work – if all goes well I shall present it to Bonniers for their assessment this winter.

The island is pretty wonderful, in spite of the wretched voles eating up everything I plant. They don't like wild roses, thank goodness, so we think we'll let those take over the island from now on. With the cat so old now, we've loads of birds that are quite tame. No invasions so far, we've been left to work in peace. We do just the amount of fishing we need to, sleep in our tent as usual, untroubled by flies, and enjoy the fact that we can lie there and listen to all the nighttime sounds and see the bird's feet running across the canvas roof.

I wish you and Ingrid a good summer, in Stockholm, in Skåne and in Dublin!

Tooti sends many greetings. All the best,

Tove.

Svalan: A book club in Sweden.

their advent calendar: Daily episodes of *Moominvalley*, sometimes called *Christmas in Moominvalley*, were shown on Swedish television in December 1973.

the book I was working on: The novel *Solstaden* (*Sun City*) was published in 1974.

FEB. 78 [*Helsingfors*]

Dear Åke,

Here's the running order I've devised in an attempt to keep things varied, not putting novels with similar themes next to each other.

I'm not letting The Flower Child and the White Ladies go hand in hand, for instance: all those tippling ladies!

And then there are three stories dealing in their own ways with how people can be exploited: A Leading Role, The Parasite, Locomotive. Plus The Great Journey and The Doll's House, which both signal a homophile relationship.

And I've tried as far as possible to keep the first-person narratives separate from one another, and the same with two stories about very old people.

And naturally I've tried very hard to put the best at the beginning and end.

(I wonder if "the middle" is too weak now?)

It's an awful juggle and needless to say I'd be very grateful if you had any other suggestions.

So I suppose we're going to call the book Flower Child after all? Naturally with a cover picture that has nothing to do with the title.

Now I absolutely don't want you sit down and read the whole lot again! Just look at The Doll's House and Art in Nature, which are new, and at the cuts I've made to The Cartoonist.

I hope you'll soon be rid of the influenza!

My very best wishes –

your friend Tove.

And *please* set aside or discard all the earlier material I sent you!

here's the running order I've devised: TJ is referring to the short story collection *Dockskåpet* (later published in English as *Art in Nature*) which came out in the autumn of the same year. One of its working titles was "Blomsterbarnet" (Flower Child). The stories under discussion here were included in the published selection, "The Parasite", under the title "A Leading Role".

17.8.78 [*Klovharun*]

Dear Åke,

Thank you for your kind letter – and for your congratulations! This Austrian State Prize is very nice – and quite a surprise: initially they didn't actually want to publish "Vem ska trösta knyttet" (Who Will Comfort Toffle) because all their young-reader specialists wrote very negative reports claiming children don't like verse. The publisher produced its own prose translation, which was dire, you know: full of platitudes and lectures.

I thought it would still be better for the book to be translated into German in some form than for me to stubbornly insist on my verses, so last summer I tried to turn it into prose and they accepted. Aren't they an odd bunch, of course children like verse!

I thought your notion of the picture Tooti could do of my medal-adorned head was really hilarious. Everything would be fine and dandy if only I didn't have to give a speech, my poor brain just goes blank.

I'm very pleased about Bibliotekstjänst's opinion of *The Doll's House*! And I do hope some people will be shocked by my hard-boiled attitude. You know, I sometimes think the nursery chamber and the chamber of horrors are not as far apart as people might think.

We shall carry on working into early September so we won't see you at Manilla, but I hope later, perhaps! You're right, we'll just have to leave the weather to its own devices, it's not so very bad. But it's worse on the mainland than on an island in the sea, here we can <u>see</u> the weather coming and be overawed by its awfulness, which we can monitor from all angles.

Tooti is in town for a week to supervise the making up of her book on graphic methods, the first proper one on the subject in Finnish. And to print some etchings she did while she was on the island. First-rate pieces of work.

I'm restlessly waiting for this Storm of the Century that all the weather sibyls have promised for August, with all our boats drawn up and Tooti's film camera ready for action. *Wow*, it could really be quite something!

Other than that the island is fading, looking beautiful and melancholy. Give Ingrid a hug from me!

My very best wishes,

Tove

State Prize: TJ was awarded the Österreichische Kinder- und Jugendbuchpreis for *Wer soll den Lillan trösten?* in 1978.

Bibliotekstjänst: A book information and review service to Swedish libraries.

Manilla: TJ is referring to the annual party held at Nedre Manilla, the Bonnier family's grand villa in Stockholm.

her book: Tuulikki Pietilä published *Metalligrafiikka* in 1978.

20.9. –80 [*Helsingfors*]

Dear Åke,

Thanks for your letter!

Our summer was good and quiet: hardly any guests, so we could work uninterrupted.

Tooti has produced a lot of lovely stuff, and for the first time she was able to print on the island, with a miniature press we found at Beckers last time we were in Stockholm. And I've carried on with my book, rewriting it for the umpteenth time, but I expect it will come good in the end.

There's so much happening at the moment, too much, exhibitions and so on, we can talk about it when we meet.

Anyway, in March–April Tooti and I plan to rent a remote cottage on an island with no channel through the sea ice, that is, somewhere we can work in peace – but ski over to the bus on the mainland if necessary. We shall make sure to have a phone line and electricity.

I'm sending you "Konstberiderskan" (The Circus Rider) and am convinced Birgitta Ulfsson should be the one to sing it. It's not a bad song – I'm really glad Myggan Ericson wants to take it up. The music is super. I tried (in vain) to ring Erna Tauro, she knows more about the whole thing. Can you tell Myggan that Erna Tauro, tel. 501012, lives at Igeldammsg. 2 A III Sthlm 11249?

And we are fine.

But rushed off our feet. This Moomintroll business has grown too big.

Hugs
to you and Ingrid
a big

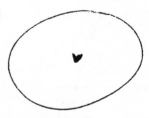

Tove

How very nice that you'll both be coming to the Friends of the Nat. Mus., which I'm sure will be much more personal than the exhibition opening.

"Konstberiderskan" (*The Circus Rider*): A poem commissioned by
Vivica Bandler for the opening of the Nya Lilla Teatern theatre in
Helsinki in 1962. It was set to music by Erna Tauro.

Friends of the Nat. Mus.: The MOOMIN exhibition at the
Nationalmuseum (national gallery) in Stockholm ran from
24.10.1980 until 6.1.1981.

30.6. –85 [*Klovharun*]

Dear Åke,

you'll both be in Skåne now, I'm sure – and if you're enjoying the
same sort of peaceful time as we are on the island, then all is as it
should be.

A whole load of "Summer Books" arrived and you know what, I'm
so pleased to see this particular book out in paperback – and that
light-coloured cover looks very nice. [...]

Oh yes, I've certainly had a go at some short stories, but so far
I've only had Tooti as a patient listener. I'm pleased that you want to
read the things I'm working on, it would be very important to me.

In the autumn we're going to get ourselves a duplicator and then
it will be easy for me to send you copies once I've tidied up the
stories a bit.

The longest story has a Spanish mountain village as its backdrop,
the one where we stayed at Lasse's casa, and its main character is
Viktoria, a former university lecturer. I wrote another story there
too, based on the ghastly experience of having my case taken, it's
only short. In Barcelona.

One of the earlier stories, "The 85th Birthday", is about dilettante
artists, and includes among other things some dawn meditations on
the quayside of Helsinki's "cholera basin", while in another I've tried
to describe some very young people at the village party in June, and
a girl who feels for the first time that she really cares, and isn't just
in love. Then there's "A Foreign City", an old man on a confused
journey. I had melancholy Warchau in mind, but kept the location
vague, a very short story.

Here on the island I wrote "The Birds", hommage à Hitchcock, a
horrific story about how the gulls drive the newlyweds out of their

minds, and then a story about the last solitary turtle on earth, told in a pub, and then The Wreck, told by a child.

Tooti, among other things, has been very busy preparing for a big retrospective in Tammerfors next year, and has done an enchanting "Tableau" of The Fir Tree, based on my story in *Det osynliga barnet* (I was allowed to play with the Christmas decorations). Now Tooti's making the balloon in "The Dangerous Journey", suspended over choppy polystyrene seas, and it's certainly going to be the most daring adventure ever, where tableaux are concerned. *Wow!*

It's been blessedly quiet and free of people here this summer. Except when Lasse and I had to go to Ähtäri zoo north of Seinäjoki to see some mechanical Moomintrolls à la Disneyland, which are going to appear in a 15-minute play I've written. It was + 35 degrees in the train, all day, and when we got there the whole thing turned out to be a misunderstanding, Bull's fault, haha.

At the end of July we'll be at the children's festival in the village as usual, where they have magicians and folk dancing and I tell some story or other at the open-air museum, this time it's "The Fir Tree" with Tooti's tableau, as long as the weather's decent and we can arrange transport.

And at the start of August we're flying to the Faroes so we can see the Biggest Wave in the World at last – assuming it isn't dead calm when we get there. [...]

Oh, and they're in the middle of filming "The True Deceiver", I saw in the newspaper, but they didn't want me on board, and I can understand that, even though I rewrote large chunks of their synopsis – assuming they took any notice, but I don't know. – And they're busy planning "The Doll's House" for TV.

Lasse's Sophia, who's been teaching English in Madrid for a year, is coming to the islands in July.

There's so much going on!

A hug to Ingrid from me. We wish you a lovely summer.

Tove.

PS. Tooti says: How could you forget to tell him The Fir Tree is electric? One morning she got the Honda going and stormed in and when I woke up all its candles were alight!

I must just tell you: we only have the one tree on the island, a rowan that we tend with great care. Last spring it seemed entirely dead – after that terrible cold winter. Now it's putting out little shoots! Isn't that great?!

Oh yes, I've certainly had a go at some short stories: Some of the story titles TJ gives here are included in the collection *Resa med lätt baggage* (*Travelling Light*), published in 1987.

the "cholera basin": the long-established popular name for a section of the harbour in front of the Market Square in Helsinki.

Det osynliga barnet: "The Invisible Child" – the opening story and Swedish title of the book *Tales from Moomin Valley*, published in 1962.

10.4.87 *[Helsingfors]*

Dear Åke –

Glad I was able to talk to you on the phone – and that you liked my idea! Or rather the stirrings of an idea … I shall send you a summary of the letter, at any rate. So just conceivably another book – sometime – What happened was that I wrote an extra short story, "Video", but I don't think I shall include it in "Travelling Light". The story features Jonna and Lena, the same characters as in the new version of "George" – the turtle – and it struck me that I could save "George" from travelling (and what's more, it might do him good to be put aside for further reflection) and make him, along with the Video-mania story, into the basis for a book about Jonna and Lena's friendship. Not short stories but a kind of novel in which each little episode is free-standing, much as in "The Summer Book". I don't quite know how it will turn out – but then I'd have something to aim for, if you know what I mean.

So can you tell that my right hand is back to writing quite decently again now?!

Hugs to you and Ingrid from

Tooti and me!

"the stirrings of an idea": This was the book of Jonna and Mari stories, eventually published in 1989 as *Rent spel* (*Fair Play*), which TJ characterises in her next letter as a "happy and bright" book.

my right hand is back to writing quite decently again: TJ broke her arm in February 1987.

15.6.88 [*Klovharun*]

Dear Åke,

I'm delighted to be sending you and Ingrid the catalogue for Faffan's commemorative exhibition, which is happening at last, thirty years almost to the day after his death.

And the best thing of all: our father's work is going to find a permanent home in Tammerfors Art Museum once they extend their domain in a few years' time. The town is a real artistic centre.

This has been a huge undertaking and there's a great sense of relief now.

The museum has also agreed to take charge of "Moomin Valley", Reima and Raili's assemblage, which is at the Main Library for now.

It feels good when things fall into place. In Tammerfors Prolle, Lasse and I got on so easily and well together, all three of us – that was important too.

Back on the island I'm trying to make some progress on my stories and I shall send you the material in the autumn.

It's good for me to be able to work slowly, without a deadline.

I gave a speech at Schildts' booksellers' event and Nalle (S.B. Nyberg) said the book ought to come out in the autumn of next year, but I imagine that would mean submission by next spring?

Please don't fix anything for now; this is a job that has to take its time if it's to be any good. But anyway, it's going to be a book that's happy and bright, I've decided.

Have a good summer, and hugs from us –

Tove and Tooti

Tove Jansson 9.8.1914–27.6.2001

SOURCES/CREDITS

LETTERS

Bonniers förlagsarkiv,
Stockholm
Letters to Åke Runnquist

In private ownership
*Letters to the Hammarsten
Jansson family*
Letters to Eva Konikoff
Letters to Tuulikki Pietilä
Letters to Maya Vanni

Svenska Litteratursällskapet
i Finland, Helsinki
Letters to Vivica Bandler
(Vivica Bandler archive)
Letters to Atos Wirtanen
(Atos Wirtanen archive)
Letters to Maja Vanni
(Maya Vanni archive)

IMAGES

Tove Janssons arkiv © Moomin CharactersTM: 12 (Per-Olov Jansson, top), 24, 32, 38, 46, 51, 61, 63, 72, 84, 93, 94, 98, 143, 145, 155, 167, 181, 205 (Per Olov Jansson), 208 (Per Olov Jansson), 229, 236 (Eva Konikoff), 253, 264 (Per Olov Jansson), 278, 328, 340, 342, 358, 380, 383 (Pentti Eistola), 393, 401 (Margareta Strömstedt), 402 (Pentti Eistola), 404, 406 (Per Olov Jansson), 418, 422, 429, 440, 459, 463, 468, 477, 482

Svenska litteratursällskapet i Finland: 256, 261, 267, 272, 298–99, 306, 418

Beata Bergström arkiv: 288

Finlands nationalgalleri: 328

Lehtikuva/Pressphoto: 6, 370

Bonniers förlagsarkiv: 472

Boel Westin: 487

INDEX